MODERN CHURCH ARCHITECTURE

A guide to the form and spirit of 20th century religious buildings

by Albert Christ-Janer and Mary Mix Foley

1962   Dodge Book Department
McGRAW-HILL BOOK COMPANY, INC.
New York   Toronto   London

Printed in Florence, Italy, by Fratelli Stianti

Library of Congress Catalog Card No. 61-8035

10796

FOREWORD

This book presents 40 Christian churches, monasteries, and seminaries; included is much of the significant religious architecture of our time. The authors have attempted considerably more, however, than to show a sampling of excellent contemporary design. As an aid to pastor, building committee, and interested layman, they have tried to explain the whys and wherefores of modern architecture. They have also attempted to interpret something of the spirit of the various faiths for the architect.

In aiming at its first goal, this book concentrates on architectural fundamentals. It shows contemporary architecture as a way of building, rather than as a superficial, applied " style. " It explains how modern structure and form developed, and how it is still developing out of the new materials of an industrial age. It describes the working philosophy of each architect represented and, consequently, the major " schools " of modern design. For the most part, these explanations do not stand apart, but are woven into descriptions of the churches, thus gaining clarity from concrete example.

In the Roman Catholic section, for example, this book traces five streams of development that are shaping that church's architecture today: structural innovation; esthetic simplicity; return to enrichment; changing liturgy; and the beginning of a renaissance of religious art. The cited churches are discussed according to these categories and thus serve to illustrate them.

The churches in the Protestant section are necessarily examined by denomination and stress is placed on the appropriate architectural expression of each faith. Examples of religious, esthetic, and structural developments are shown throughout this section as it reveals the varieties of the sectarian manifestations.

Thus both Protestant and Roman Catholic chapters, though brief and simplified, may well enlarge the technical and artistic grasp of the churchman and give him a common basis of understanding with his architect.

As a proffered aid to the architect, over and above the intrinsic interest of this collection of meritorious buildings, this book includes an unusual amount of useful historical and liturgical material.

Of particular value to the architect, for instance, may be the discussion of the Liturgical Revival, a movement that began with Pope Pius X in the opening years of the twentieth century and which profoundly affected religious architecture in Europe. Its impact is now being felt in America. For those assigned to express in building form the Christian spirit of today, the Liturgical Revival offers new opportunity to the designer.

Remarkable among Protestants are the recent trends toward reexamining the basic character of their faiths. A number of examples chosen for this book reveal a sensitive expression of actual denominational differences. Others illustrate a new unity, a return to fundamentals. A brief description of each major Protestant denomination introduces the corresponding group of churches. These explanations and examples may help architects to search out the religious emphasis of each sectarian group, which ideally should be translated into architectural form.

In addition, special introductions to the Roman Catholic and the Protestant sections have been written expressly for this book by spokesmen qualified to deal with each church and its art; the essence of Roman Catholicism and Protestantism is here summed up by theologians, experts also in evaluating modern architecture as expressive of the great Christian faiths in their constant struggle for renewal.

In the creation of the design of a modern church one more problem should be noted. This is the task of encouraging church officials, or the church membership, or both, to accept a new and unique solution presented by an informed and gifted architect. As an aid to understanding this all-too-common difficulty, we present, wherever possible, each pastor's exposition of the development of his church design and the way in which his congregation came to decide in favor of the contemporary mode. These experiences in persuasion may prove of value to clergy and architects who face similar problems.

During the next decade, congregations in the United States alone will spend an estimated $13 billion for new religious buildings. To the end that this staggering sum will be well spent this book is hopefully dedicated.

ALBERT CHRIST-JANER
MARY MIX FOLEY

ACKNOWLEDGMENT

The authors wish to express their gratitude to the Avalon Foundation and to the Guggenheim Foundation for their generous support of this work.

Grateful acknowledgment is made to the Reverend Dr. Paul Tillich, to the Reverend Edward J. Sutfin and to Dr. Maurice Lavanoux for their special contributions; to Marie C. Reilly of the School of the Arts, Pennsylvania State University, to Teresa D'Amico and Barbara C. Delany of the Art School, Pratt Institute, for their meticulous attention to detail in collecting and checking the material for this book; to Charles R. McCurdy, Art Reference Librarian, for identifying sources of photographs; to Walter Civardi and his staff of the Photography Laboratory, Pratt Institute, for photographic assistance; to Dorothy Lipes, Director of the Art and Music Department of the Syracuse Public Library, and Fern Allen, Director of the Architecture Library, Syracuse University, for research assistance; and to Paul H. Kruggel, exchange student in the School of Architecture, Syracuse University, and Mario Di Cesare of Pratt Institute, for the translation of foreign papers and letters.

The authors also wish to thank the architects whose churches appear in this book for the detailed explanations of their work, and the clergy of these churches for their thoughtful responses. We could not have done without the cooperation of all these individuals.

CONTENTS

CONTEMPORARY CATHOLIC ARCHITECTURE

CONTEMPORARY PROTESTANT ARCHITECTURE

MONASTERIES AND SEMINARIES

The most ancient traditions of the Church conceive the arrival of the people in procession from a station of assembly to the church of sacrifice. Their bishop and shepherd, who represents Christ among them, follows them in procession and vests in the rear sacristy as they take their places in a grouping about the altar. Through the midst of his people the shepherd passes to the altar, which represents the body of Christ, and then continues to his proper place at the extreme focal point of the apse, facing altar and people. Above him iconographers frequently displayed the Christ of the parousia. *Mass at the altar then becomes the joy and nourishment of Christian life in this world, and the promise of future life with Christ in eternity. The shepherd instructs his people, facing them from the throne; he then comes before the altar at the offertory and acts as their mediator with the heavenly Father during the mass of sacrifice.*

The baptistry, as seed and beginning of supernatural life, is located within every pastoral church, cathedral and parochial, as the opposite focal point, so to speak, to the altar. It is usually circular in form and descending, indicative of death to the world and resurrection into the grace of Christ. Confessionals, placed rather at the side of the nave, serve as refreshing points of grace along the way; and the chapel of the Eucharist where the reserve is retained and adored by the faithful should be emphasized as the chapel of the way, of via-ticum, just as communion in the sacrifice is the promise of the reward of eternal light and life. The liturgical service of the vigil of Easter indicates even more poignantly the function of the church building for living people of all ages.

Can art, then, be anything but an evidence of this dynamism, this life that we lead here and now? Should anyone assume that those who accept the times and try to work out their salvation *in time* are therefore contemptuous or ignorant of tradition? On the contrary, we have long been convinced that the artist or architect who is modern (that is, living) in his approach to problems of religious art is precisely the one who knows a great deal of the history of past ages. If we read medieval history aright (for example, Emile Mâle's heavily documented and illustrated tomes on religious art in France during the twelfth, thirteenth, and fourteenth centuries, and after the Council of Trent) the master builders of those days would be modern today as they were modern in their times. They accepted and controlled the dynamism of their day. Why should it be odd if architect and artist today wish to do the same?

If the veritable traditions of the liturgy are not warped by exaggerated elements of devotion nor by misunderstanding of the spirit of the norms set forth by the Church, artist and architect will once more feel the joy and liberty of being the children of God, and the Church will fulfill her mark of universality. It is at this point that considerations of architectural style and the temporalities of history are irrelevant: the architect and the artist are left totally free in their expression of the house of God according to the ma-

terials currently available, the spirit of the people, and the time in which they live. Such freedom lies within the bounds of discipline and purpose.

References

CAREY, GRAHAM. "Living Stones of Architecture," *Catholic Arts Quarterly*, Christmas supplement 1955.

"Diocesan Building Directives," *Liturgical Arts*, November 1957 and February 1958.

"Directives for the Building of a Church (by the Liturgical Commission of the Catholic Bishops of Germany)," *Liturgical Arts*, February 1950.

MARITAIN, JACQUES. *Art and Scholasticism*. Sheed and Ward, New York (1930).

THE SEARCH FOR STRUCTURE: Reinforced Concrete

The fundamental difference between modern architecture and the historic styles lies in the nature of materials. The great architecture of the past was based upon natural materials and upon handcraft methods of construction. By evolutionary stages, these were developed into remarkably different architectural forms, reflecting the unique spirit of each age.

But the even flow of style to style was interrupted in modern times. With the industrial revolution, manufactured materials were devised with characteristics quite different from the natural materials of wood, brick, and stone used so beautifuly in the great periods of the past. These new materials included structural iron and steel, plate and other structural types of glass, and eventually, reinforced concrete.

Of themselves, these new materials were inert and meaningless. Indeed, with some notable exceptions, they were used at first in unimaginative attempts to reproduce the characteristics of the traditional materials. But hidden within them were structural potentials that were to create a new architecture.

Without an understanding of these materials, and the structural systems which have evolved from them, much of the *raison d'être* of modern architecture is incomprehensible. This section, therefore, concentrates on examples of churches that illustrate the most appropriate uses of one of the most important of modern materials: reinforced concrete.*

Reinforced concrete is the unique masonry material of our contemporary era. It was developed as a result of the fortuitous discovery that steel and concrete have the same coefficient of expansion. The laying of steel rods or mesh within the concrete aggregate at the time of pouring creates a masonry of tremendous tensile as well as compressive strength. Unlike traditional stone and brick, it can be cast as columns or as one large, continuous slab, folded into thin shells, or curved into paraboloids, arches or ribs, thus opening up a whole new range of design possibilities undreamed of by past builders.

* Structural steel is discussed in the Protestant section. See especially the Stahl Kirche (No. 18).

Although reinforced concrete was invented during the nineteenth century, its potential was largely unrealized until the first quarter of the twentieth century. At that time, the French architect and builder, Auguste Perret, adopted this neglected material as his special province and began exploring its structural possibilities. Perret recognized early that the characteristics of reinforced concrete were the opposite of brick and stone, and that it should be handled in a new way to exploit its unique characteristics.

An examination of traditional masonry construction makes this clear. Because of the relative weakness of brick and stone in relation to weight, plus their lack of cohesiveness, buildings composed of these materials were of necessity massive and monolithic. Walls usually acted as both support and enclosure in order to achieve stability. In tall buildings, such masonry walls had to be of incredible thickness — sometimes as much as 20 ft. at the bottom — in order to carry not only the weight of the roof, but also the immense cumulative weight of the courses of brick or stone of which they themselves were made. The only way large windows — such as the famous Gothic stained glass — could be incorporated into such structures, was by means of interior columns and vaulting, coupled with exterior flying buttresses, which balanced each other and worked together to remove the major load from the walls. In the Romanesque style, similar problems had been encountered. Domes and vaults, built up out of separate blocks of masonry, required a tremendous thrust and counterthrust from massive interior piers and exterior walls, to support and stabilize them.

Reinforced concrete, on the other hand, combines strength and stability with comparatively light weight. Perret's stroke of genius lay in his recognition that these characteristics were more like wood than like traditional masonry. The technique he chose for most of his buildings, including the Church of Notre Dame du Raincy (No. 1), was the classic post-and-lintel system: columns (posts) supporting a horizontal member (lintel) that in turn supports a superstructure (a roof or upper story). This is the most ancient of building methods, its origin tracing back to the use of unsawn logs of wood as a frame for thatch or other materials. First employed in primitive huts, it was copied in marble by the Greek temple builders, and is still used in modified form today in wooden houses, steel-framed skyscrapers, and other buildings.

By adapting this system to reinforced concrete, Perret developed the then-revolutionary concept of the "reinforced concrete frame." He was able to build structures that had the lightness and openness of wood, but were far larger than any wooden structure could be — since wood does not possess the strength of reinforced concrete. Moreover, because loadbearing supports were kept structurally separate from non-loadbearing walls, the latter acted solely as enclosures, supporting nothing. As a result, the walls of even Perret's largest buildings could be extremely thin and glass could be inserted almost at will. With this system, Perret revealed reinforced concrete as a new material, capable of designs that heretofore had been structurally impossible. No longer was concrete a mere substitute for massive stone and brick, to be used for copying traditional styles.

As with most pioneering efforts, Perret's development of the reinforced concrete frame at first went unappreciated. In fact, his "brutal" buildings, which exposed the bare concrete, caused such controversy that scorn and ridicule were heaped upon the architect. Auguste Perret also incurred the enmity of his professional colleagues by acting, with his brother, George Perret, as building contractor for his own designs to insure that his innovations were properly executed.

Perret survived these storms to become in later years the most influential and most honored architect in France: *chef d'atelier* at the Ecole des Beaux Arts and the Ecole Spéciale d'Architecture; Grand Officer of the Legion of Honor; president of the Ordre des Architectes; Honorary Inspector General of Buildings and, after World War II, chief architect for the reconstruction of the cities of Le Havre, Amiens, and Marseilles. Before his death in 1954 he received also the Gold Medal of the Royal Institute of British Architects and the Gold Medal of the American Institute of Architects, the highest accolades that these professional societies can bestow.

The Church of Notre Dame at Le Raincy, France, was probably Auguste Perret's most significant experiment in the use of reinforced concrete. Erected between the years of 1922 and 1925, it is considered such a masterpiece that contemporary churches are still compared to it as to a touchstone. Churches around the world echo its structural system, its wall pattern, and its roof form. As critic Henry-Russell Hitchcock has written: "When Perret erected the church of Notre Dame at Le Raincy . . . concrete came of age as a building material."

It is interesting to note, however, that by the middle of the twentieth century, Perret's reputation had changed from that of a radical innovator to that of the "most conservative of moderns." This change was due to one fact. Perret limited his work, with few exceptions, to the classic post-and-lintel system described in these pages. He left to later and more radical innovators the full exploration of the plastic quality of reinforced concrete — a quality that makes it the most versatile of any known building material, and still today the newest and most challenging medium in the architectural lexicon.*

Perret was content also to retain old forms wherever these did not contradict his building system. The facade of the pioneering Notre Dame du Raincy, for example, appears today almost traditional in design. Perret would not object. In his book, *Contribution à une théorie de l'architecture*, he wrote: "He who, without betraying materials or modern progress, would produce a work which seemed to have always existed . . . I say that he could consider himself satisfied."

---

* See the Priory of St. Anselm (No. 2) and the Church of La Virgen Milagrosa (No. 3) that follow in this section; also the Abbey of St. John the Baptist (No. 36) and the Priory of St. Mary and St. Louis (No. 37).

I. CHURCH OF NOTRE DAME

Le Raincy, France; Erected 1922-1925
Auguste Perret (1874-1954), architect, engineer, builder

*"It is through the splendor of truth that a
building attains beauty."* — AUGUSTE PERRET

The combination of strength with light weight, which frees reinforced concrete from the old limitations of masonry, is shown with unrivaled clarity in Notre Dame du Raincy. Here, the entire weight of the roof is carried by rows of slender columns, spaced both outside and within the interior of the building. Walls are now simply screens, supporting nothing. They need be neither thick nor solid. Perret has formed them of thin cast concrete panels, pierced in a repetitive pattern and in-filled with stained glass. The result is a structure of incredible delicacy, whose light-filtering walls have been aptly described as "lace in concrete."

The graceful, repetitive curves of the roof vaulting of the church exploit another fundamental characteristic of the new material: tensile strength or cohesiveness, coupled with plasticity. By using reinforced concrete, it is no longer necessary to "press together" a vault or dome to keep the separate blocks from flying apart. The molded vault, one continuous sheet, can "float" upon its supports as a self-contained structure, relatively thinner than an eggshell, as at Notre Dame du Raincy.

Even the columns that support the roof are uniquely expressive of the inherent qualities of the new material. Not only are they extremely slender, they are tapered from top to bottom, a reversal of the traditional masonry requirement. As explained by Peter Collins: "... it became apparent to Perret that the stability of a concrete column was not due to gravity, as in a masonry column, but to the strength of the joint, as in a table leg. Just as he would have revolted against a table designed with each leg wider at the bottom than at the top, so he revolted against a similar error in concrete frames."

As a pioneer in the appropriate uses for a new material, Auguste Perret was less concerned with plan than he was with structure, considering the former to be the least important part of the architect's job. In Notre Dame du Raincy, he utilized the ancient basilica floor plan — essentially one great rectangular area. There are, however, significant departures from tradition.

Perret has moved the altar from its former high position down onto the floor of the chancel, thus hinting at the oneness of priest and congregation that, even as early as the 1920's, represented the beginning of a liturgical revival within the Roman Catholic Church.

The side aisles of the basilica, traditionally shielded from the nave by massive intervening piers and further defined by a lowered roof level, are here merely indicated by the placement of Perret's slender columns. This opens up the whole interior into one space and permits a direct view of the outer walls — those filigrees of concrete that provide the unique luminosity of the interior. This arrangement, too, represents a liturgical as well as a structural innovation. The elimination of side aisles and the opening up of the plan reflect an effort to keep the celebration of the Mass within direct view of each member of the congregation, thereby creating a more encompassing communion within the church.

However, no discussion of the structure and plan of the church of Notre Dame du Raincy can convey the total effect which the sum of these elements has made possible. John Ely Burchard has described this effect:

"Le Raincy was a revelation. It sits on a dull site on a drab street. You cannot really walk around it, and there is little or no important sense of the exterior. Its greatness is entirely inside, for which no photograph has prepared you. When you are in it you no longer care that it was a pioneer in the overt use of steel and concrete in a church. You are not very interested in the basilica-like, choirless plan .... Of course you feel the slenderness of the piers and how smoothly they flow into the slightly arched roof. But the overwhelming single impression is of the prismatic light which runs the gamut of the spectrum from narthex to altar. This light permeates all the walls and filters to all the floor through the consistent and orderly honeycomb of concrete. It makes our little, much admired, tries at blocks of light in church walls seem tepid and timid .... The light of Le Raincy ... [is] brilliant [yet] paradoxically ... serene."

Entrance facade of Notre Dame du Raincy, with its soaring bell tower, has an almost traditional appearance. Today it seems impossible to believe that this church once aroused a storm of angry criticism for its "radical" design. Actually, the masses of the church build up and step inward, increasing in height and decreasing in width, from the low, horizontal "narthex" or entrance lobby to the cross atop the tower. The nave of the church is the main central mass. In front of it, and at either side of the tower, two slender vertical masses indicate the choir loft, which in actuality extends through the tower on the interior. Two small, freestanding, hexagonal skylights atop the roof of the narthex illuminate an area of solid, masonry walls. The frank revelation of the function of interior areas by the form of exterior masses is known as the "articulation" of a design; it is one of the fundamental tenets of modern architecture.

Interior view of entrance shows the intricate pattern created by separation of columnar supports and pierced concrete curtain walls. The choir loft, immediately above the main entrance doors, is at once under, and a part of, the bell tower. It is reached by a graceful, spiral staircase of cast concrete — a detail of architecture that became a Perret trademark. At this rear area of the church, light enters from four sides of the bell tower, sifting down to provide a heightened luminosity above the choir. The massing of volumes here also permits side wall lighting from three directions.

At either side of the choir loft it is possible to distinguish the lowered roof of the narthex, which on the exterior is the lowest mass of the church. This device clearly distinguishes the entrance vestibule from the high-roofed nave.

Interior of the nave looking toward the altar shows the concrete lace "windows" that form the walls of the church and the glory of this design. Unfortunately, no photograph can convey a sense of this interior, which is literally aglow with light — and at the same time calm and serene.

Stained glass is used throughout, wrapping the church like a luminous curtain and rendering the whole interior alive with color. Simultaneously, its rich hues attenuate the sunlight that would have been too brilliant for visual comfort had clear glass been used. The fact that the whole wall surface is one vast window heightens the general illumination and therefore reduces the contrast between solid and void, the major cause of glare when conventional windows are set into an expanse of solid wall. In this way Notre Dame du Raincy achieves

Copyright by Bernhard Moosbrugger

G. E. Kidder Smith

the atmosphere of depth and meditation that was the architect's aim.

The colors of the stained glass range the spectrum, but certain hues predominate in each wall. The glass of the entrance facade is executed primarily in a subdued silvery gray, shifting into green and rose. At the side walls, colors deepen in hue and saturation, with blue changing to red and red shading into violet. Inset into the over-all pattern of these side walls, are stained glass panels in the same colors, depicting events in the life of Christ and other Holy mysteries. At the front of the church, enclosing the chancel, the glass gains brilliance, becoming a vivid, radiant blue. Here, only the one color is used, except for a great cross, delineated within the wall pattern in blue and clear glass, outlined in crimson. This use of color, deepening from a neutral

shade at the rear of the church to rich jewel tones at the sides, and heightening into a blue radiance at the sanctuary, focuses the whole of the interior toward the altar and upon the eucharistic rite. The result is an atmosphere of intense spiritual power and beauty.

Although these photographs cannot reproduce the effect of the stained glass, they nevertheless show the structural system that frames it. As described earlier, the slender columns supporting the roof are slightly tapered from top to bottom, though the perspective and shadows of this view give the opposite illusion. The bottom part of the wall is solid throughout the church, providing needed visual balance to the solid ceiling vaults above and a sense of privacy for the congregation. Note the repetition of the lacy wall pattern as a decorative element in the central vault of the ceiling.

Exterior view of chancel wall shows what is perhaps the most famous and most copied roofline among
modern Christian churches. The central curve, extending into horizontals on either side is encountered around
the world in modern churches erected since 1925.

In this facade, even more simply and forcefully than
in the entrance facade, Perret has revealed interior function by means of exterior form. A comparison with the
photograph of the interior shows that the vaulting of
the interior creates also the exterior line of the roof.
Then comes the lacy curtain wall. A central band of
solid wall marks the floor level of the chancel. Below it,
another solid area pierced by conventional windows reveals the working area of the church, beneath the chancel
floor. Perret could easily have made these two lower
sections into one continuous wall area, but, as always, he
chose to articulate what lay within.

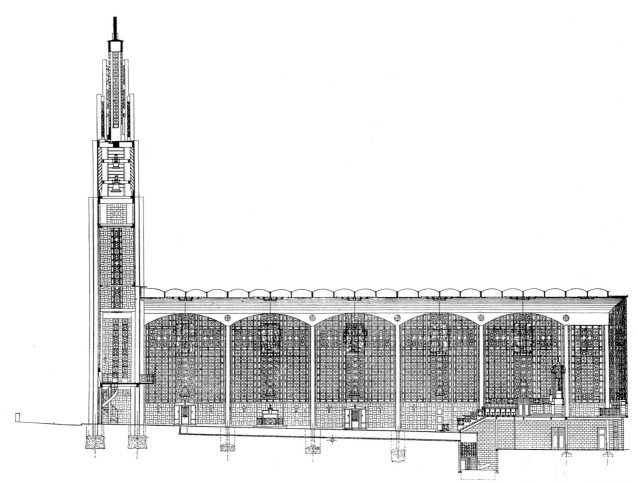

Elevation drawing of the south side of the church clearly shows the separation of the supporting columns from the lacy, lightweight enclosing wall. The slenderness of the columns is strikingly revealed when they are seen, as here, in relation to the entire body of the church.

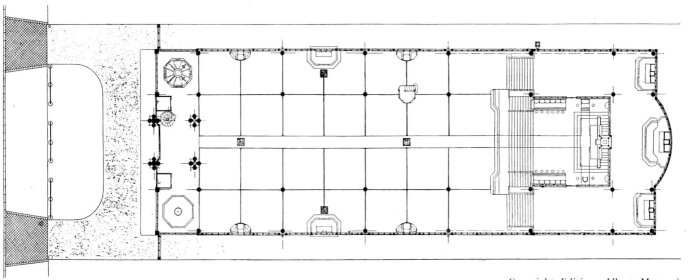

Plan is a simple rectangle except for the east end, which is curved outward into an apse. Although Notre Dame du Raincy approaches the size of a cathedral, it was built for only 600,000 francs, or approximately $ 120,000. This modest sum was due to the inexpensiveness of reinforced concrete and to the structural simplicity of the design. Today, with rising labor and material costs, the amount would be several times as much.

THE INFLUENCE OF LE RAINCY

With his masterpiece at Le Raincy, Perret created a modern system of building peculiarly appropriate to church design, and easily adaptable to different floor plans. The churches shown here bear the same family resemblance shared by Gothic cathedrals but each is a fresh solution to a particular problem.

1a. St. Thérèse de Montmagny, France, was erected in 1926. A smaller version of Notre Dame du Raincy, it was designed by Auguste Perret himself. This view is taken from the chancel, looking toward the church entrance.

1b. Women's Christian College in Tokyo, Japan, erected in 1932, and designed by architects Raymond & Rado, uses precast concrete window grilles and a stepped bell tower reminiscent of Notre Dame du Raincy. Roof, lower wall area, and rear elevation are handled quite differently, however.

1c. Church of St. Antonius, Basel, Switzerland, erected in 1927 and designed by the late Karl Moser, also echoes Notre Dame du Raincy. St. Antonius features a central roof vault and a separation of frame from enclosing walls, the latter of stained glass set in concrete mullions. Despite these structural similarities St. Antonius is an original work and in no sense a copy of Le Raincy. It was the first modern church to be built in Switzerland and to a great extent is responsible for revitalizing ecclesiastical architecture in that country. This is a view from the chancel looking toward the rear choir loft and showing the side placement of the pulpit.

Copyright by Bernhard Moosbrugger

1d. Chapelle Universitaire, Fribourg, Switzerland, by architects Dumas and Honneger, was built as recently as 1941. The wall treatment is reminiscent of both Notre Dame du Raincy (lacy, geometric patterning of concrete and glass) and St. Antonius of Basel (square columns supporting the structure). Roof vaulting is similar to that used in the two earlier churches, but here it forms a canopy only over the central portion of the nave.

References

Burchard, John Ely. "Pilgrimage: Ronchamp, Raincy, Vezelay," *Architectural Record*, March 1958.

Collins, Peter. "The Doctrine of Auguste Perret," *Architectural Review*, August 1953.

Perret, Auguste. *Contribution à une théorie de l'architecture*. Librarie des Alpes, André Wahl, Paris (1952).

2. PRIORY OF ST. ANSELM

Tokyo, Japan; Dedicated 1955
Antonin Raymond (b. 1888) & L. L. Rado (b. 1909),
architects
Noemi Raymond, liturgical furnishings

Katherine Young

"The basis of design must be function and engineering; but function and engineering only is a brutality."
— ANTONIN RAYMOND (right, above: L. L. Rado)

Although Auguste Perret chose the post-and-lintel as the most appropriate structural system for reinforced concrete, later architects began to exploit the plastic qualities of this material, thus charting new paths in architectural structure.

Antonin Raymond and L. L. Rado, designers of the Priory of St. Anselm for the Benedictine Fathers in Tokyo, Japan, shown on the following pages, can be numbered among these later innovators. A unique international firm, Raymond & Rado has maintained offices in New York City and also at the opposite side of the world in Tokyo since 1939. Although they are separated by a difference of 20 years in age and by thousands of miles in space, the background and thinking of the partners is remarkably similar. Both were born in Middle Europe, in what is now Czechoslovakia. Both studied architecture at Technical University in Prague and both later came to America, Raymond soon traveling westward, to Japan. As might be expected, their work combines the techniques of industrial construction developed in Europe and America with the respect for natural materials that is so much a part of the Japanese heritage.

When working with wood, Raymond and Rado design in the Japanese manner of utmost simplicity, revealing the basic nature of the material and creating structures that seem as one with nature. For the urban scene and with the newer materials, such as concrete, they are capable of the most advanced designs in slab or shell construction. This is no contradiction. Again they are revealing the basic nature of the material and creating buildings appropriate to their surrounding environment.

St. Anselm is typical of the latter expression. It is a bold and original experiment in the structural usage of a modern material. Here, reinforced concrete has been carried well beyond the classic limits laid down by Perret. In fact, with the same material, a similar floor plan, and what is still in essence a post-and-lintel type of construction, architects Raymond and Rado have designed a church that is structurally the opposite of Notre Dame du Raincy. The technique which they have employed is known as the "folded slab."

Although in Notre Dame du Raincy the functions of columns and curtain walls are kept entirely separate, here they are amalgamated into wall slabs, or shells, which perform the double duty of support and enclosure. This allows the interior of the church to remain a free space, unbroken by the supporting columns that were a necessary part of the structural system devised by Perret. However, since a single, thin, flat slab of reinforced concrete would be structurally unstable as a bearing wall, a number of narrow, vertical slabs have been used like columns — and each slab has been folded to increase its strength.

This ingenious design of the walls of St. Anselm, which allows slabs only 6 in. thick to support the entire roof structure, is extremely difficult to describe. Viewed from the interior of the church, the side walls appear to be a series of triangular columns of solid masonry, soaring 50 ft. from floor to ceiling, the interstices between columns being utilized as vertical window strips, inset with panes of glass. From the exterior, however, the "columns" disappear, and one sees the edges of flat slabs, running vertically from roof to ground level.

These deceptive masonry units, nine of which make up each side wall of the church, can be understood only in plan. Looking directly down upon one of them, it would become apparent that the column is hollow. It is, in actuality, a thin slab, folded to form a V and then braced with a cross piece to form a modified A, the point of the A being toward the interior of the church, its "legs" toward the exterior. Thus, in plan the entire wall of the church looks like the following: AAAAAAAAA. With this unusual construction, the reinforced concrete slab attains a tensile strength of 3,000 lb. per square inch. Furthermore, the repetition of the A-shape, with its lateral bracing, stabilizes the wall and distributes the roof load.

Since the window connections between separate wall slabs are not strong enough to tie the masonry units, together, each slab is further braced to its neighbor by a series of small lateral concrete shelves, which project between window panes at regular intervals from roof to ground level. The roof is similar in structure to the wall, a continuous folded shell of reinforced concrete, each wall slab joining a roof slab at the point of an A.

The hollow design of the slabs, the separation of masonry wall units from each other, plus the horizontal shelf bracing that ties them together again, create a web-like structure, stable, but at the same time flexible, calculated to withstand earthquakes, even of great magnitude.

Practical considerations — earthquake resistance, economy, and ease of building — dictated to a great extent the structural design of St. Anselm. But as in all outstanding buildings, the desired esthetic effect is an inseparable part of the structural solution.

In this church, the principal aim was to achieve a feeling of beautifully proportioned space, lofty and inspiring. The uninterrupted vertical lines of the slabs, sweeping up from floor to ceiling, do much to fulfill this aim, lending an effect of stateliness and grandeur to the entire enclosure. Even the dimensions of the large open nave — 50 ft. in width by 50 ft. in height by 100 ft. in length — are carefully calculated to provide a regulated order with its resultant quality of serenity. Because of the "depth" of the wall created by the repetition of A-shaped slabs, with narrow windows recessed at their outer edges, bands of light penetrate only partially into the interior, giving a mystic and brooding quality particularly suited to a church for a monastic order.

Here again, however, the blending of the esthetic and the practical is illustrated, especially if a comparison is made between Notre Dame du Raincy, and St. Anselm. In France, the major question was sunlight. Although the stained glass of Notre Dame du Raincy tempers a too brilliant sun, its perforated walls at the same time celebrate the quality of light. In St. Anselm, the problem was primarily one of climate. The depth of its wall structure forms a protective shell against an atmosphere that is oppressively hot and humid during the summer months. Thus, not only in structure, but in interior effect, these two churches are opposites. The major impression of the church at Raincy is of sparkling, prismatic light; St. Anselm is a cool retreat, in which controlled light is played against subdued general illumination — the one, a revelation; the other, a mystery.

←
View of a side wall from the interior of the church showing the triangular shape of its separate slabs, webbed together by a series of concrete "window shelves," and joined to an identically pleated roof shell at the point of each triangle. Sunshine entering the narrow strip windows, which are set at the exterior edges of slabs, must traverse a slanted wall depth of nearly 9 ft. to reach the interior of the church. The shelf-like bracing between slabs further cuts the sunlight, preventing any deep penetration of direct sun. At the same time, the surface of each slab acts as a giant refractor, diffusing the light that pours upon it. Note also the interesting planes of light and shadow created by the angles of the canted wall slabs. A balcony for the monastic choir extends across the rear wall of the church, and continues across each side wall nearly to the sanctuary, as shown above. It is reached, at the rear of the church, by a graceful spiral stairway. Like the walls, roof, and floor of this church, the balcony and its stairway are constructed of precast, reinforced concrete.

View of nave looking toward the altar shows, from a different angle, the effect of the shelf-bracing between slabs in breaking up the sunlight. As the sun traverses the sky, one wall of the church at a time is patterned with shafts of shifting sunlight, the other left in quiet monotone. Except for plaster panels behind the altar and above the balcony at the rear of the church (eventually to be decorated with frescoes) the conrete work is left exposed throughout. The aggregate of the concrete was especially selected for its color, a warm, pleasant gray. Touches of other earth colors have also been added to selected surfaces of both interior and exterior by means of a transparent, liquid plastic dye-stain, a finish that does not cover the natural texture of concrete as would paint. The floor, for instance, is stained in squares of earth red and black; parts of the ceiling are a pale blue. With pew and altar rails of natural Philippine mahogany, the effect is one of subtle, subdued coloring in the nave. This serves to focus attention on the severe black of the stone altar as it stands before the white plaster wall, over-arched by a gleaming, golden baldachino. When frescoes are added to the background panel, the concentration of richness about the altar will be even more pronounced.

View of church exterior shows the baptistry (front, center), which is on a direct axis with the altar at the opposite end of the building. This arrangement is a symbolic one, denoting the beginning of Christian life at the baptistry and its fulfillment before the altar. The entrance to the church is at the right side, and those entering encounter the baptistry before turning toward the altar. Large windows in the end wall contrast with the narrow window strips of the side walls, but are made harmonious by breaking them into similar small panes.

They are partially shielded from direct sun by the roof overhang, a kind of brim extending on all sides beyond the pleated portion of the roof shell. The shape of this overhang is reminiscent of the vaulted roof of Notre Dame du Raincy. In casting the various structural slabs that make up the church, steel, rather than wooden forms were used for the first time in Japan. This unusual technique gives concrete the sheen and smoothness of marble, adding elegance to the other qualities of this versatile building material.

View of baptistry from the nave of the church is dominated by the holy water font of concrete with a stone lining. The floor of the baptistry is mosaic tile in shades of soft blue and gray. Windows in this area are of stained glass in various symbolic designs. All church furnishings have been designed either by Raymond himself or by his wife, Noemi, a talented artist who works with him on every assignment. These furnishings include a cloisonne tabernacle and black wrought-iron altar candles, which flank it. The tabernacle consists of baked enamel inlays, outlined with silver on a black iron frame.

The spiral stairway is a form particularly suited to casting in reinforced concrete. Perret, Raymond and Rado, and many others have used it. Here, the architects have added symbolic decoration by piercing the concrete stair wall. This is a view looking down from the choir loft.

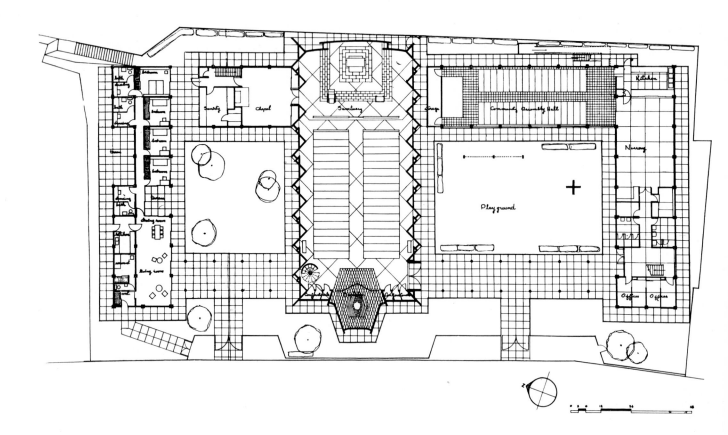

Plan of St. Anselm shows the building group admirably plotted on what was an unpromising site, facing a busy street. The group includes church, parochial school, and rectory. These buildings have all been arranged to open to inner courts within the grounds, thus achieving privacy from the street frontage. The church occupies a central location. To its right is the L-shaped, one-story school, which includes a kindergarten, assembly hall, and library, and is separated from the church by a playground. To the left of the church, space is reserved for a cloister garden and beyond it for the future rectory, a three-story building which will provide living accommodations for the Benedictine monks. Paved, covered walkways encircle each building and link them together, acting as outdoor corridors even in inclement weather. The church entrance has been placed at the right side of the building rather than the front, and is directly opposite the school entrance, providing convenient circulation between the two buildings via one of the covered walks.

The church was designed to seat 500 people with standing room for 200 more. Besides being the church of the Benedictine Order in Tokyo, it also serves as the parish church for a newly converted Japanese congregation. The cost of the church, with its floor area of 8,961 sq. ft., was just short of $110,000. The school provides 6,480 sq. ft. at a cost of approximately $59,000. The rectory, with 5,519 sq. ft. of floor area, is expected to cost between $59,000 and $60,000. This breaks down to $12.25 per square foot for the church, $9.15 for the school, and $10.80 for the rectory — unusually low figures due partly to the lower cost of Japanese labor, but mainly to the material and structural system employed.

REPORT FROM THE CLERGY
The Very Rev. D. Hildebrand Yaiser, Prior

The building of a new church and the choice of its architect are problems most parishes face only once or twice during the lifetime of a given congregation. Indeed the building through which their faith is expressed may be more permanent than the people who decreed it. Certainly the design of the church will act upon its members continually, either strengthening their vision of religion or dulling it, according to the vitality of the architecture in which this vision is clothed.

Because of the importance of choosing an architect and a type of architecture, the authors felt that an account of the pastor's experience would be enlightening wherever it was possible to obtain such remarks.

We are Benedictines. This order was founded in the sixth century in Monte Cassino in Italy. This Japanese mission is a dependency of the Abbey of St. John the Baptist in Collegeville, Minn. (No. 36). Its parish was established in 1947, after the bombardment, in an old and dilapidated factory. Our parish started at that time with only nine faithful. Today we have 1,500.

I, myself, came to Japan 29 years ago in 1931. In selecting an architect for the new church my own background was of the greatest value. Catholic liturgy and its architecture is my special field. I was Professor of Liturgy at Sacred Heart University, Tokyo. As a student of art I was always convinced that church architecture must be born of the culture of that century in which it is built. Also, I knew Mr. Antonin Raymond.

We did not attempt to educate the congregation to accept a contemporary design. Our church was set before the congregation as a *fait accompli*. It is my conviction that any other way would have led to no results.

The requirements laid down for the architect were our wishes: only one altar; opposite to it at the west end, the baptistry. These are the two poles of any Catholic church. Two pulpits near the altar, facing the people. These are the old liturgical elements of the first basilicas, here expressed in modern ways. I believe the result is just that.

Behind the altar I wanted to have a huge crucifix. Here the architect came up with his proposal of a baldachino: well solved, indeed, again in a modern way without the old columns. Personally, I wished to have the gold of the baldachino in a more subdued matte surface instead of the shiny gold leaf it now has. Yet it is quite good. The altar was prescribed by me as a simple table without any ornament, except for the tabernacle and the candlesticks that stand upon it and the lapidary inscription: *Per Ipsum et Cum Ipso et in Ipso.*

The architectural features were the architect's. I left him absolutely the necessary freedom here to create. And create he did to my full satisfaction.

When the church was finished, our faithful were spontaneously captivated by its simple greatness — some others have come to like it little by little. But there were no real objections at any time. Certainly it has increased the interest of the young people in the church. Still today many new people are coming to see the church, Christians and pagans. The greatest impression, however, they receive when attending the liturgical functions themselves. I believe that one or another was attracted by the architecture — though of course I never welcome conversions coming only from esthetic moods. They must go deeper indeed.

References
Nakamura, Katsuya, ed. *Antonin Raymond, His Work in Japan; 1920-1935* Johnan Shoin, Tokyo (1935).
Raymond, Antonin. "An Architect Comes Home from Japan," *Architectural Forum*, February 1939.

3. CHURCH OF LA VIRGEN MILAGROSA

Mexico City, Mexico; Erected 1955
Felix Candela (b. 1909), structural engineer and architect

Jane Doggett/Dorothy Jackson

"In the field of construction, we fortunately are ending a long analytical period. The ideas that nourished it are fully developed, and to continue exploiting them would be senseless. If the symptoms are to be believed, we are on the verge of a new creative epoch."

— FELIX CANDELA

During the past few years, the work of a brilliant Mexican engineer — Felix Candela — has increasingly captured the attention of his contemporaries around the world. An engineer who is a practising architect, Candela is also a mathematician and a professor at the Escuela Nacional de Arquitectura in Mexico City. In addition, with his brother, Antonio Candela, he is a building contractor, operating one of the most successful such offices in his city. With this range of operation, from academic to practical, Candela follows the same path as Auguste Perret. There is another similarity.

Like Perret 30 years before him, Felix Candela has adopted reinforced concrete as his special province. But it is here that the resemblance abruptly ends. For Candela's choice of the appropriate structural system for reinforced concrete is not the classic post-and-lintel. It is the warped slab, the antithesis of the rectilinear frame. Indeed, Candela shapes reinforced concrete into plastic forms, such as hyperbolic paraboloids and squared "umbrella vaults" (which Perret's architecture only faintly foreshadowed), seeming to bend it at will to his intuitions.

His debt, therefore, lies more to the Italian engineer Pier Luigi Nervi — characterized as "the man who let reinforced concrete out of the box" — and to the German architect Dominikus Böhm — who experimented with paraboloid forms in churches as early as the 1920's and 1930's.

But although Nervi and a few other pioneers have been working reinforced concrete as plastic for a number of years, the folding and warping of this material gained importance as an architectural trend only in the 1950's. Writes Robin Boyd:

"...the sparse contributory elements rapidly converged into a movement in a matter of months between 1953 and 1955. During this time a number of respected men made notable assaults on the rectangle... one of the major figures to emerge from the excitement [was] Felix Candela, the Spanish-Mexican engineer."

If Candela can be classified, he should therefore be placed in the category of engineer-scientists, of which Pier Luigi Nervi and Buckminster Fuller are probably the most famous.* These men are concerned with basic structural behavior and through the years they have reduced it to mathematical equations. This theoretical work — amplified by practical proof in their own buildings — has unlocked at last the hidden potential of modern materials, giving architecture a structural freedom unknown to the entire historic past.

---

* Fuller's basic investigations have been with metal and plastic rather than concrete. See his geodesic dome (No. 18a).

The Church of La Virgen Milagrosa in Mexico City, designed by Candela for the Fathers of the St. Vincent de Paul Order, and shown on the following pages, is one of the landmarks of such analytical engineering. This statement does not mean that La Virgen Milagrosa is the first building to make use of the hyperbolic paraboloid, nor that it is an architectural masterpiece standing above all other contemporary work.

In fact, from the artistic point of view, its exterior appears unpleasantly spiky and busy with detail, making the church more bizarre than beautiful. It is in the interior that the importance of this design becomes apparent. Here is revealed Candela's superb feat of engineering and his expressive *tour de force*. Just as the Gothic cathedrals pushed stone to the limit of its structural potential, this church pushes concrete to the limit of its plastic characteristic.

The great interest of the design lies in its complete unification of support and enclosure. In St. Anselm, Raymond and Rado amalgamated the usual bearing columns and wall enclosure into 6-in. thick folded slabs capable of supporting the entire weight of the roof. In La Virgen Milagrosa, Candela has visually separated columns and enclosure once more into distinct elements. But at the same time, he has structurally amalgamated everything — walls, roof, and supporting members — into a multiwarped slab, having a thickness of only $1\frac{1}{2}$ in. or less. No rivets, welds, bolts, or nails are used in the entire construction, since it is in truth a continuous shell.

Hollow columns fan out, as they sweep up, to become ceiling vaults, window frames, wall, and roof structure, flowing away from, and into each other in various combinations of Candela's hyperbolic paraboloid. The geometry of the structure is impossible to plumb by visual study. But its effect is felt at once. The interior, with its soaring vaults and triangular upward thrust, is the essence of aspiration. And the recesses created by the interplay of the paraboloids result in an atmosphere of deep mysticism. In this design, reinforced concrete comes full circle from its humiliating service as a hidden frame for Gothic imitations, to reproduce the spirit of Gothic in its own unique and completely contemporary fashion. Colin Faber has perhaps best described the effect:

"This church bears the stamp of true, authentic architecture; the squalid site and prosaic, overworked detailing are disappointing but they cannot conceal this. La Milagrosa comes close to the classic as few buildings have since Gothic times. Anyone who has entered the church will recall the strange, almost illusory effect of the interior. It is a magical space limited and defined by a complex dynamic form, and the effect is not one induced by trick or artifice but by the simple reality of a structure one can touch and feel, and in which even the layman can detect a governing mathematical order. As Einstein put it: 'The most beautiful and the most profound emotion we can experience is the sensation of the mystical. It is the power of all true science.'"

View of nave looking toward the chancel shows how hollow concrete shell columns fan out and join each other to create a vaulted ceiling, reaching an apex at the center line of the church. The two end walls — at the sanctuary and at the narthex — bear no load and are not a part of the continuous concrete shell. To emphasize this difference they have been constructed of materials other than concrete. The sanctuary wall is of handmade brick, 1 ft. thick. The narthex is infilled with stained glass above the choir loft. A decorative triangular panel behind the altar repeats and emphasizes the triangular shape of the sanctuary wall, of which it is a part, and of the ceiling vaults that frame it. It is unfortunate that the statuary adorning the sanctuary is of such feebly sentimental design, striking a false note in conjunction with the power and majesty of the church structure. Artificial illumination is provided by indirect fixtures attached to interior columns and by chandeliers in a typically Mexican design. Floors are concrete, surfaced with gray marble and terrazzo.

Jane Doggett/Dorothy Jackson

View from within the nave reveals the brooding mystical quality of this interior. Note how inner columns curve up, out and down once more, flowing into wall columns of a more distinctly triangular design. In turn, these columns sweep up and out to form triangular frames for the stained glass windows of the west wall. Confessionals are also incorporated into this nonbearing wall, one below each window. At the rear of the church is the triangular narthex window, also of stained glass.

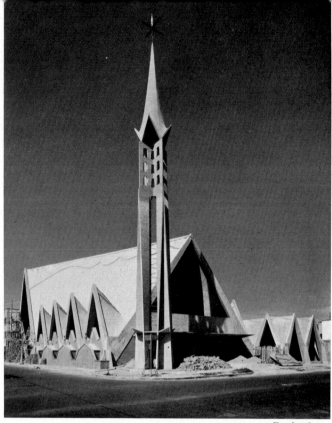

Erwin Lang

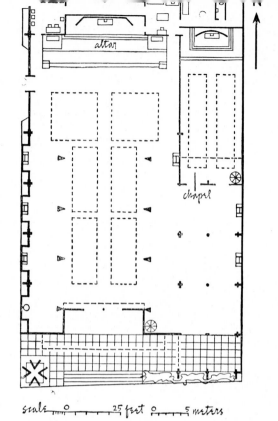

Courtesy of *Progressive Architecture*

scale ___ 0 ___ 25 feet 0 ___ 5 meters

Exterior view of church shows the triangular concrete window frames of the west wall and the way in which the concrete shell continues on once more, flowing back and down from the windows, then up again to create an unbroken, tent-like roof structure. The campanile consists of four reinforced concrete slabs, warped in the midsection, pierced above, and topped by a spire and star. On the opposite side of the church are the chapel and assembly hall, lower in height than the main nave. The structure here is similar to, but more complicated than, the window framing of the west side. Two rows of triangular vaults create wall, roof, and interior "column" structure, eventually flowing up into the main roof of the nave. Clerestory windows are inset between vaults.

Plan of La Virgen Milagrosa reveals relationship of a small, lower-roofed side chapel and meeting hall to the larger nave, which is a classic rectangle. The floor area of the church is slightly more than 15,000 sq. ft. and its cost was an almost unbelievable $43,000 — only $2.87 per square foot! However, this amount does not include a heating system (there is none in the church) nor the stained glass windows, pews, statuary, and other furnishings. Although these omissions would inevitably make a considerable difference in total cost, nevertheless the comparison with St. Anselm is dramatic. That church, itself a model of economy, cost $110,000 for slightly less than 9,000 sq. ft. — nearly three times as much for 2/5 less space. It did, of course, have a heating system — radiant coils in the floor. But furnishings were not included in its figure. And the cheapness of Mexican labor doubtless is comparable to the cost of of labor in Japan. Candela's continuous shell construction with its incredible thinness (saving material) and its rapidity of construction (saving labor) must therefore be credited with a considerable portion of the economy of La Virgen Milagrosa.

Erwin Lang

Erwin Lang

Photographs of construction reveal more truly than does the finished church the incredible fluidity of the structural system. Photograph of east elevation shows the handsome contrast between concrete vaulting and brick filler-walls. Photographs taken across nave provide still another viewpoint of the vaulted interior. Typical bays are approximately 40 by 22 ft.; the vaults spring out from their thinnest point 10 ft. above floor level; side aisles are 13 ft. wide.

REPORT FROM THE CLERGY
The Rev. Fr. Elias Alduan, C. M.

We are a Mexican mission of the Order of St. Vincent de Paul. This brotherhood was founded in France in 1625, and since that time has extended itself the world over, founding missions throughout Europe, Africa, and Asia; and in North, Central, and South America. It is dedicated to the special devotion of the Virgin Mary under the advocacy of Our Lady of the Miraculous Medal. It is both a missionary and an educational order, training men for the Roman Catholic priesthood and directing also a number of universities for general education.

Our church, La Virgen Milagrosa, serves a new suburban community in the outskirts of Mexico City. I and the other members of the Order attached to the mission made the decision to hire Felix Candela when the new church was to be built. The congregation was not consulted.

We chose a contemporary design because we believe that church architecture must evolve with the general trend in architecture in all fields. We were well acquainted with new architectural designs the world over. We feel it is our duty. As clergymen we are constantly concerned with new churches, since we are frequently called upon to erect one here or there in the places entrusted to our spiritual supervision. Professional advice is taken, of course, but always subject to the fulfillment of the spiritual aims of the Catholic Church.

We invited several architects to submit designs to us, and we finally decided to accept this one as most suitable to our spiritual aims which are the recollection and elevation of the soul to its Creator in four principal obligations: adoration, thanksgiving, expiatory acts, and petitions.

We did not wish to follow the age-old, massive, fortification style of architecture. Rather, the original idea coming from us was something lighter, with curved lines drawing up to meet in the center, reaching a maximum altitude at the rear wall. In general, the construction was to represent two hands joined in fervent prayer. The curved, elevated lines were to aid in lifting the spirit to the supernatural. We believe that these requirements were fulfilled to our satisfaction.

We believe also that the design of the church has met with general approval from our faithful, who have come to call it *"La Iglesia de las Manos Orantes"* — the Church of the Praying Hands. In the beginning some members of our congregation, especially among the older ones, were opposed to this project, being accustomed to the age-old styles of church construction and image-sculpturing. But gradually they have come to accept that times have changed a great deal and new designs and ideas are generally accepted nowadays which were not even imagined in times gone past.

Our new church has attracted undoubtedly many more members and faithful from other parishes, as can easily be seen by the increased number of couples who have preferred to join their lives in holy matrimony in our Catholic church, and the numerous Solemn Masses for the dead requested, as well as the other social-ecclesiastical functions or ceremonies. The members of our community are all entirely satisfied with the greatly increased worship in the church, and increased membership in our several associations.

THE VARIETY OF REINFORCED CONCRETE

→

3a. Chapel of Las Lomas, Cuernavaca, Mexico, by Felix Candela in collaboration with architects G. Rosell and M. Laroasa (shown here before completion), suggests the variety of form that can be produced by handling reinforced concrete as a plastic material. Because of the bold originality of its shape, this flowing "hood" is unrecognizable as a church, despite the ascendant reach of its sweeping lines. However, the great sculptural cross that towers above it proclaims the function of the chapel in powerful silhouette against the sky. Thus, the chapel itself can take full advantage of a new form potential without resorting to the recognizable "churchly" details found in the exterior of La Virgen Milagrosa.

→

3b. Olympic Sports Palace, Rome, Italy, designed by Pier Luigi Nervi, shows a plastic use of reinforced concrete strikingly different from that of the warped slab. The flowing, geometric pattern of the domed ceiling is created by a spiderweb of intersecting concrete ribs. Except as a consultant to other architects (see Abbey of St. John the Baptist, No. 36, and the Priory of St. Mary and St. Louis, No. 37), Nervi has designed no churches. Yet the technique used here could produce a religious enclosure of unparalleled beauty and grandeur — fulfilling yet another potential of this unique material described by Nervi as "a living creature that can adapt itself to any form, any need, any stress."

References

Boyd, Robin. "Engineering of Excitement," *Architectural Review*, November 1958.

Candela, Felix. "Stereo-Structures," *Progressive Architecture*, June 1954.

Faber, Colin. "Felix Candela as a Contemporary," *Arts and Architecture*, May 1956.

Nervi, Pier Luigi. "Structure in Architecture," *Architectural Record*, July 1956.

"Pier Luigi Nervi," *Architectural Forum*, November 1953.

Jane Doggett/Dorothy Jackson

Gherardi - Mascetti - Fiorelli

THE SEARCH FOR SIMPLICITY: Brick, Wood, and Stone

Pioneering efforts in the field of structure that reached their first flowering in the early part of the twentieth century, inevitably brought with them a new architectural esthetic. This esthetic was most boldly displayed in the work of several European modernists whose work has been grouped under the name of the International Style — such major figures as Le Corbusier, Walter Gropius, Ludwig Mies van der Rohe, and Marcel Breuer. Unlike the academic copyists of the day, these men consciously sought to evolve new forms appropriate to the new industrialized materials of the machine age: steel, reinforced concrete, plate glass, and glass brick. Rejecting the absurdity of historic "styles" applied on modern steel or concrete, they made the unadorned cube, the exposed frame, and the glass curtain wall the hallmarks of an emergent modern design. All decoration, except that supplied integrally by the structure itself, was ruthlessly stripped away. This movement represented a complete break with the past: with its materials, its structures, its forms, and its decoration.

As these ideas developed, the esthetic that was gaining impetus from industrialized methods and materials was applied also to the handling of such traditional materials as brick, wood, and stone. Clarity of structural expression, simplicity of detail, and the use of integral ornament rather than applied flutings, moldings, carvings, and surface finishes, became a basic tenet of modern design in all media.

The three American churches shown in this section reveal the influence of the modern esthetic on these age-old building materials — materials which are still very much a part of the contemporary scene. As with the newer materials, the search here is for simplicity, for a revelation of inherent qualities rather than a straining after grandiose effects.

Specific architects have, of course, developed personal idioms in their handling of these materials, ranging from the severe to the romantic. Many have chosen them as a means for uniting architecture with surrounding nature. Others have found them to be the logical means towards a regional expression in architecture, thus achieving continuity with the building tradition of the community: wood, for example, in New England and on the Pacific Coast; stone in Pennsylvania and other rocky regions; brick in cities and towns where it is characteristically employed.

The churches shown here are such regional expressions. They have, in fact, nothing in common with the cubistic International Style other than an uncompromising honesty of structural and decorative usage. Their importance lies not in radical innovation, but in another direction: in the ability of brick, wood, and stone to help bridge the gap between the extremes of traditional and modern design. Returned to a fundamental condition, such materials lend warmth and familiarity without compromising the honesty of contemporary expression.

4. CHURCH OF OUR LADY OF THE LAKE

Seattle, Wash.; Erected 1941
Paul Thiry (b. 1904), architect
Sigmund Avarsson, structural engineer

"My theories on design change with the times and with my increases in knowledge." — PAUL THIRY

The brick Church of Our Lady of the Lake in Seattle, Wash., represents a midpoint between modern and traditional design. It is simple and structurally honest without being stark; harmonious in its surroundings without copying existing styles; traditional in certain aspects of plan and form while at the same time serving the changed needs of a contemporary congregation. Its distinguishing characteristic is its complete lack of pretense of any sort — a fact that is immediately communicated to the viewer in a feeling of restfulness and peace.

In describing this church, architect Paul Thiry has written:

"The building was designed with due consideration for the recent consciousness of the Catholic Church regarding the early liturgy. Each material was used in its true representation, which in symbolism denotes truth in all matters... I attempted to resolve things into their simplest form commensurate with the requirements of the owner. The owner liked the form of the Romanesque and from this silhouette is derived a contemporary building with complete respect for an ancient form devoid of its arch."

This description of the Church of Our Lady of the Lake sums up not only the church itself, but much of Paul Thiry's approach to design as well. His aim is always the simple and straightforward, rather than the spectacular. And although a modern solution follows

logically from this architectural honesty, Thiry does not reject the whole of tradition where tradition remains appropriate. The client's needs and wishes take precedence always over pioneering experiments. And a highly developed sense of architectural composition gives his work a harmony and serenity sometimes lacking in the work of more radical innovators.

The Church of Our Lady of the Lake illustrates these points. Here, the structural system is the least interesting and least important feature of the church. Columns and beams of reinforced concrete act as the supporting frame for brick walls and tiled roofs. It is true, of course, that without the modern concrete frame, brick could not have been used in the contemporary "light" manner, but would have required a more massive wall structure throughout. Nevertheless, there is nothing intrinsic to this now-common system that would ensure good design.

The excellence of the church lies instead in the harmonious disposition of architectural elements; the tall block of the church proper, contrasting with one-story wings and bays. The shifting heights of these various blocks offer welcome breaks in the design, and clearly express the separate functions of areas within. Moreover, the rooflines of the lower elements, with their broad, horizontal sweeps, provide a sense of shelter and repose. A walled courtyard is an integral part of the architectural composition.

Church of Our Lady of the Lake is located in a residential neighborhood of Seattle. It has been particularly designed, both in its modest scale and in its gracious proportions, to harmonize with such a setting. The west view, shown here, reveals the entranceway, with the main doors of the church set back under the eaves of the porch. This arrangement provides a zone of quiet between the outer world and secluded worship within.

The form of the church clearly articulates the functions of interior space. The tall central block encloses only the nave. Aisles at either side of the church, plus porch, narthex, and baptistry at front, are all made lower in height than the nave and extend outward from it, revealing on the exterior the change of area and atmosphere within. One continuous roof shelters and unifies all these lower elements. The courtyard completes the composition and gives this church a measure of privacy for its own activities that is unusual in urban surroundings.

View of church from the south showing walled courtyard in foreground, and the west transept wing to the left, at rear. The beginning of the roof of the rectory is visible at right, as it joins without break the lowered roof at the front of the church proper.

Much thought has gone into planning the circulation within the inner court. Entrance porch, narthex, and baptistry are placed one beside the other across the front of the church. Each can be separately entered from the courtyard along a walkway sheltered by the overhang of the roof. The same walkway continues at right angles in front of the rectory, acting as an outdoor corridor between rectory and church.

This portico is one of the most functional elements of the design, providing as it does direct, sheltered access from the priests' dwelling to the baptistry and narthex, and serving also a number of subsidiary uses. It functions as an outdoor "waiting room" for parishioners who wish to talk with the priests; as a shelter to handle the overflow at baptisms; as a paved area for seating the congregation during outdoor services. It is here, too, that processionals are formed for special ceremonies. The courtyard as a whole offers a gathering place for churchgoers before and after Mass, and a place of quiet, individual meditation when services are not in progress.

It is this sort of thoughtful planning for day-to-day use of a church — as opposed to the copying of past forms developed to serve different uses — that is one of the most compelling arguments for modern design.

View of interior of the nave clearly shows the outward extension of side aisles under their low, sloping roofs, as seen also in the exterior photograph. This design breaks, and opens up, what might otherwise have been an unpleasantly boxy interior.

The two wall elements — high nave and low side aisle — provide the church with two quite different sources of light: rows of small, high windows that abut the ceiling for the length of the nave; larger windows set into the walls of the low side aisles. With light entering from both top and bottom, a quiet, over-all illumination is achieved, further softened by the filtering of light through amber stained glass.

The honesty with which the functions of the church are expressed in its form, extends also to structure and materials. Supporting columns and beams are of reinforced concrete, left exposed rather than hidden behind a false surfacing. Filler walls are of brick, making interior and exterior a single, continuous entity. Doors, confessionals, and the choir screen behind the altar are of wood, differentiating these subsidiary elements from the heavier masonry enclosure. Eventually the solid panels of the choir screen will be surfaced with bas reliefs of carved wood, adding richness to the simple interior and drawing attention toward the altar. Present banal statuary is temporary, and not part of the architect's design.

View of side aisle showing subsidiary seating along its exterior wall. The stained glass windows are in shades of amber, harmonizing with the tawny colors of natural brick and wood. The only brilliant color within the entire church is in the small overlay placques that accent each window. These placques, obtained from a collection of antique Belgian and English glass, are executed in vivid green, blue, red, and other vibrant colors. Their motifs, such as the star of David, the tower of ivory, the arc of the covenant, are symbolic of the Litany of the Blessed Virgin. Because the craft of intricately patterned stained glass belongs more to medieval than to modern times, the architect felt that panes of unpatterned color would be more appropriate to this simple, modern church. His statement, quoted earlier, may be relevant here: "Each material was used in its true representation, which in symbolism denotes truth in all matters." Rather than copying the past style of stained glass, Thiry used authentic pieces from the past to enrich and accent his otherwise undecorated windows.

View of baptistry from the narthex shows the arrangement of these two areas in line with each other, under the sloping entry roof. Out of sight in this view are separate entrances from the baptistry to courtyard, at right, and to the church at left. The stone baptismal font has a cover of sheet bronze in *repoussé* depicting the image of St. John the Baptist. Note the door of plain, unpainted, wood planking, tied together with strips of hammered metal.

In plan, the church is based on the cruciform of the traditional Romanesque. The west transept, which extends outward from the sanctuary, forms the left arm of the cross. When an east transept is eventually added, the cruciform will be complete.

As a neighborhood church, Our Lady of the Lake is not as large as some of those previously shown. The original seating, limited to the nave, was designed to accommodate no more than 250 persons. At that time the west transept was closed off, and used as a meeting room. This space has now been opened to the nave, providing seating for an additional 100 persons. When the east transept is constructed, it will provide seating for 100 more, giving the church a total capacity of 450 or, with side aisles, approximately 500.

The site plan shows the disposition of the church and rectory with building entrances toward the walled courtyard. Another walled court, for the private use of priests only, lies at the rear between the rectory and the future east transept. Since the plan was first developed, a parochial school has been added at the northeast corner of the property. It will abut the east transept when that wing of the church is completed.

The cost of the church — but not the rectory and school — was $32,000 in 1941. The architect estimates that today the cost would be close to $75,000. Even so, this may be considered one of the more economical churches, due to the simplicity of its solution and of the materials with which it is built.

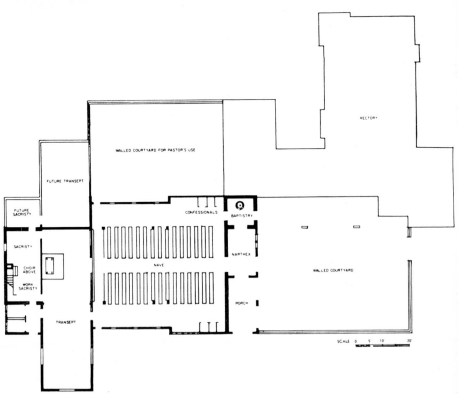

Reference

"Church of Our Lady of the Lake," *Architectural Forum*, December 1941.

5. CHURCH OF ST. THOMAS MORE

Portland, Ore.; Erected 1938
Pietro Belluschi (b. 1899), architect.

"The designer who keeps in mind the needs of those who worship is apt to avoid the shallows of contemporary irrelevancies and the cheapness of the merely startling, which is the main danger lurking in all experimentation." — PIETRO BELLUSCHI

Pietro Belluschi is one of the leading architects in America today. Although educated as an engineer, he is not one of the scientist-innovators, like Felix Candela, absorbed in a basic study of the behavior of one material — even though a thorough knowledge of materials is the basis upon which his work rests.

Instead, Belluschi is, above all, the artist-architect, the balanced designer. His structure, his plan, his detailing, his handling of materials, his esthetic effect are always parts of a single, integrated concept. Never is one element of a building exploited to the detriment of the whole. What has been described as "an intuitive sense of fitness," makes him apparently incapable of committing an architectural fault.

Born in Italy in 1899, Belluschi grew up amid the classic grandeur of Rome. This influence may be seen faintly in his work in the occasional use of loggias and open courts. The American influence has been far more important, however.

An exchange graduate scholarship to Cornell University first brought him to the United States, and here he has remained, taking his degree in civil engineering in 1924 and, after graduation, traveling west to see the country. He worked as an electrician's helper in the mines of Idaho, and then journeyed on to Portland, Ore., where he secured his first architectural job with the firm of A. E. Doyle in 1925. This northwestern region of the United States remained both his home and his most important architectural influence until 1951, when he was appointed to his present position of Dean of the School of Architecture and Planning at Massachusetts Institute of Technology.

The 26 years that Pietro Belluschi spent in Oregon indelibly stamped his work. The country is rugged. Its bracing climate and great evergreen forests have pro-

duced a typical vernacular architecture, seen at its best in stark wooden barns that rival the more famous stone barns of the Pennsylvania Dutch region. Wood is the native building material of Oregon, and Belluschi soon became a master of it, working always toward a goal of expressive simplicity. He won his first recognition for low, broad-roofed houses, so simple and so indigenous to the Oregon countryside that they have been called Belluschi's "beautiful barns."

Although he has long since expanded his palette to include the full range of modern materials and techniques of construction, Belluschi remains at his most expressive when working with natural wood, brick, or stone; in churches, these have usually been his choice.

The small, wooden Church of St. Thomas More, Portland, Ore., shown here, is typical of his early designs, having much in common with the native "barn architecture" of the Oregon region. Built in 1938, on an extremely limited budget and before the architect had reached the height of his career, it should perhaps be classed as one of Belluschi's minor works. His later churches have been both more imposing and structurally more advanced, earning a place among the significant ecclesiastical architecture of America.*

But St. Thomas More is a minor work only in its small size and structural simplicity. Within these limits it is an extraordinary achievement. Its design shows, above all, the richness and spirituality that can be created in the interior of a church with the simplest of materials and building methods in the hands of an expert.

   * See Zion Lutheran (No. 19), Central Lutheran (No. 19a), Trinity Lutheran (No. 21), The Church of the Redeemer (No. 23, Episcopal), First Presbyterian (No. 27), and the Monastery of St. Gregory the Great (No. 38, Roman Catholic).

Boychuk Studio

Interior view of St. Thomas More — a church built entirely of native Oregon wood in the traditional post-and-lintel system — demonstrates that religious character can be evoked by the simplest of materials and structure. Cross bracing, which is used to strengthen the roof, has been so placed that, in effect, it turns the church into a small cathedral.

The construction used to create this effect could hardly be simpler. Bracing pieces are merely bolted between double rafters. The material is nothing more grandiose than Douglas fir planking, stained to bring out the natural color of the wood. But, although it looks easy, the effect seen here could be produced only by a master designer, for in such a small interior, success depends upon keeping every element in perfect scale.

Like the cross bracing, the rest of the frame of the church is of fir, and framing members throughout have been left exposed to act as both definition and decoration. The color of the framing contrasts subtly with the color of the wall surfaces, the latter being of cedar, sanded and rubbed to a soft patina. Note the horizontal bands created by the exposed framing members at both bottom and top of the side walls of the nave, acting as a visual stop to the vertical siding between. It is such

thoughtful and sensitive detailing that gives the small church its air of distinction.

The spire of this church has been placed over the chancel, rather than in the traditional position over the entrance to the nave. Thus, the interior space of the chancel can extend upward beyond the limits of the lower-roofed nave, a movement that may be considered symbolic. This solution also permits the use of horizontal strip windows, placed high at three sides of the chancel in the wall structure of the spire. These three windows flood the sanctuary with light, making it appear to glow within the dimmer illumination of the rest of the church.

As in the Church of Our Lady of the Lake, directly preceding, side aisles are indicated by a lowered ceiling level, which by contrast appears to heighten the small nave. This "broken" design makes the interior seem larger than it really is. It also builds up the spatial volumes from low side aisle to higher nave, to even higher chancel, providing a rhythmic progression of space toward the focal point of the church.

Pews, altar railing, and baptismal font were all designed by the architect in keeping with the character of the church. Pews are essentially simple wooden benches,

Boychuk Studio

but their uprights are a carefully calculated part of the total design of the interior, leading the eye inevitably, by means of a receding, repetitive pattern, toward the altar. Here, their starkness meets, and is broken by, the richness of the carved altar railing.

The stone baptismal font at the rear of the church is set upon a cylinder of cedar wood, a section of a single tree trunk, which has been sanded and waxed to satiny smoothness and carved with small crosses within a larger pattern of squares.

Exterior view of St. Thomas More reveals a modesty that is entirely appropriate to this little country church, set high in the hills above the city of Portland. Walls are of knotty pine, left unstained, but protected by a thin coat of lead and oil. The roof is surfaced with untreated cedar shingles, which have weathered to a soft, silvery gray. Windows are wood casement, cross-hatched with wooden strips to form diamond-shaped panes. This touch adds a simple pattern to the clear glass.

The cost of this church in 1938 was only $17,500. Its floor area is 3,500 sq. ft. and its lot is 4½ acres. Since this photograph was taken, a parochial school and rectory have been added. It is estimated that today this church would cost approximately $45,000, because of the rise of construction prices.

References

Belluschi, Pietro. "Church Architecture," *Architectural Forum*, December 1949.
———— "The Churches Go Modern," *Saturday Evening Post*, October 4, 1958.
Stubblebine, Jo. *The Northwest Architecture of Pietro Belluschi*. F. W. Dodge Corp., New York (1953).

Eminence, Mo.; Erected 1954
Hellmuth, Obata & Kassabaum, architects
George F. Hellmuth (b. 1907)
Gyo Obata (b. 1923)
George E. Kassabaum (b. 1920)

"A reputation as a 'church architect' is of less relevance than the architect's capacity to interpret the unique qualities and requirements of the group of people desiring to build a church." — GEORGE F. HELLMUTH (Left to right, above: George F. Hellmuth, Gyo Obata, George E. Kassabaum).

This new, young, St. Louis architectural firm has come into prominence during the past ten years with prize-winning designs in reinforced concrete shell construction, ranging from the huge and technical St. Louis Airport Terminal to the flower-like Priory of St. Mary and St. Louis (No. 37). In the little stone Church of St. Sylvester, shown on the following pages, these architects prove that they can turn their hands with equal facility to the difficult art of simplicity.

Unlike Belluschi, these men cannot be considered regional architects in the accepted sense of the term at all. But St. Sylvester, set high in the Ozark Mountains near the small town of Eminence, Mo., is as fine an example of regional architecture as can be found anywhere in the United States. It is built of native fieldstone, a rugged material traditionally used in the old barns and farmhouses of this southern, mountain community. The native method of building with stone has also been employed: simply stone bearing walls supporting a pitched roof of wood. The result could hardly be more indigenous to its country setting nor better adapted to the character of its hardy congregation. When compared with the other, far more sophisticated work of this office, St. Sylvester aptly illustrates the stylistic range of which a good architectural firm is capable.

Furthermore, like Belluschi's St. Thomas More, this example proves that the problem of a very limited budget, common to most small communities, need not preclude excellence in church design. Usually in such parishes, the least costly solution is also the most appropriate. The fatal error is to try to fake grandeur on limited funds; it is equally unfortunate to settle for low-cost mediocrity. Neither mistake was committed with St. Sylvester. On a budget of only $30,000, the architects have designed an outstanding modern church that achieves its esthetic effect by using natural materials in the simplest and most direct way.

The modest budget takes on an added significance because the church was completed in 1954 — in the midst of spiralling construction costs. The architects are careful to point out, however, that the quoted cost does not include land, fees, or furnishings, and that the church was built in an area where prices and wages are still not as high as in major cities. Yet this design is not for a city church, but for a church in a small, rural parish.

For the $30,000 total, the architects have provided not only the church proper, containing nave, chancel, sacristy, and confessional, but also, on a lower level, a parish hall, a kitchen, and a bedroom and bath for visiting clergy. The bedroom doubles as study for the parish priest. A forced hot-air heating system, standard plumbing and wiring, and a paved, partially walled, outdoor terrace are also included within the budget. Although the nave is small, accommodating only 117 persons, there is a total of 3,584 sq. ft. of space within the building as a whole. This means that the church was constructed for only $8.40 per square foot. In America, in 1954, that can be considered an achievement.

Art Fillmore

View of exterior shows how perfectly this little stone church fits into its rugged setting of hill and wood and wild meadow. It is placed some distance back from a country road (barely visible at right) and is oriented to parallel this road, rather than face it. An old rail fence marking a neighboring field has been left untouched.

From this entrance view, the building appears to be only a one-story structure. But the ground slopes sharply down from front to rear, permitting a lower story which, though set into the slope at front, is above ground level at the back of the church. At either side of the church, steps lead down from the entrance terrace to provide exterior access to the rear door of the church.

The local fieldstone used in the walls is a brown and gray porphyry. Its rough texture and warm color are particularly appropriate to a country setting. With this stone, the architects have worked out a structural system of the utmost simplicity. Bearing walls are simply a series of straight slabs, 2 ft. thick, interspersed along the side walls with windows, and at front with a door. Stone walls, glass window infill, and the front entrance door all run vertically from roof rafters to ground level, thus avoiding the structural complication of small, traditional doors and windows that must bear the weight of stone above them. Another structural simplification is that no stone wall turns a corner; instead stone wall and wooden window frames always meet at these junctures. This simple solution eliminates cutting and fitting of irregular stone at the building joints.

The only surface finishes used on the exterior are composition shingles that protect the wooden roof, and white paint used on window frames, roof edges, and gutters, on the wooden portions of the entrance door, and on the wooden cross.

Art Fillmore

Interior view, facing the entrance, reveals how the natural characteristics of wood and stone are brought out, contributing to the esthetic effect of the whole design. The actual structure of both walls and roof is exposed, thus eliminating the cost of interior finishing and providing a textural interest far more handsome than applied surfacing. The ruggedness of stone walls contrasts pleasantly with the smoother surface of the wooden ceiling. In addition to the vertical glass panels set between stone wall slabs, narrow horizontal window strips have been incorporated at the top of each side wall, casting light up onto the expanse of ceiling.

The great timbers used for roof rafters do double duty as structural supports and as important design elements, providing a strong rhythmic definition to the upward sweep of the roof. The roof itself is of partic-ular interest. Seemingly an inlay of narrow strips of wood, it is actually standard oak 2 x 4's, laid on edge, so that the 2-in. dimension is the exposed surface, while the 4-in. measurement gives depth, and consequently, insulation, to the roof.

Art Fillmore

Interior view, facing the altar, shows the dramatic effect created by playing the rugged textures of natural materials against the smoothness of an artificial one. The reredos behind the altar is of plaster, painted white, the only such area in the entire church. It stands out like a symbol of purity against the rough surfaces and warm natural colors of the stone and wood.

The entire design of St. Sylvester gives evidence that the architects considered this church a challenge to their resourcefulness. The inspired simplicity of the wall and roof is typical of their ingenious solutions. The focusing of attention on the sanctuary merely by a change of texture and color is another example. The altar itself is simply a section of twisted, weathered, tree trunk, unpainted, and unstained, upon which has been placed a wooden plank decorated with a simple, white, scalloped

altar cloth. The lectern at right is also a section of tree trunk, left with natural markings as its only decoration. The altar cross is rough, unfinished wood, upon which a simple carving of the Christ has been affixed.

These furnishings, which cost little more than the idea of using them, add warmth and personal feeling to the church. But such primitive touches have been used with restraint. The atmosphere of the church, is not one of quaint rusticity, but of basic simplicity and fitness.

The respect of the architects for the native materials, and their sympathy for the religious feeling of a country parish, reveal the wholeheartedness with which they accepted the challenge of this design. Further proof lies in the fact that they did not charge the usual architect's fee. Instead they offered this as their contribution to the church building fund.

Art Fillmore

Detail of window shows the simple notched joint by which framing is held together. Interior framing members are simply standard 2 x 4's that are left rough, unplaned, and unstained, as they came from the mill. Exterior framing strips are painted, as a protection against the weather.

Plan shows the excellent circulation provided around and inside the building. Steps at either side of the entrance terrace lead down to a lower level, at which the parish hall of the church has a separate entrance. Upper and lower stories are also connected on the interior by a stairway to the side and rear of the sanctuary. Confessional and sacristy are reached through a passage at the other side of the sanctuary.

DOWN

DOWN

NAVE

ALTAR RAIL

ALTAR

DOWN

CONFESSIONAL   SACRISTY

THE SEARCH FOR ENRICHMENT:
Return of the Decorative Arts

One of the tenets of modern architecture as it began to emerge in the first quarter of the twentieth century, was a stripping of applied decoration from the new buildings then being designed. Ornament became almost a forbidden concept. It was part of the philosophy of the early modernists that the only valid "decoration" was that provided by a revelation of structure itself.

This reduction of the building to its basic essentials was doubtless a necessary step in freeing architecture from anachronism: the masquerade of structurally modern buildings behind a frosting of past styles.

Eventually, however, a reaction was bound to set in against the starkness of much early modern design. The sweep of bare concrete, the unadorned white wall, the precise rectangle of plate glass, though brilliant and arresting in effect, did not entirely satisfy. Now that the modern movement was well established as the proper architecture for our times, its severity was called into question.

Obviously, the function, structure, and esthetic of many buildings still precluded any but integral decoration. Nevertheless, where its use was appropriate, a desire for ornamental enrichment began to be felt. Tentatively at first, and then with greater assurance, architects decided that it was not, after all, the betrayal of a hard-won cause to make use of applied decoration.

The two churches shown in this section illustrate some of the arresting decorative possibilities that are being explored in modern church architecture today. One concentrates on surface ornament, the other on stained glass. Both are intricately patterned and subtly colored, imparting a feeling of richness unusual in contemporary buildings.

Like the work of the engineer-scientists in the realm of structure, such frank use of ornament shows a welcome relaxation of the rigid rules that governed much of modern architecture at its inception. Although not equal in significance to structural innovation, this new enrichment opens yet another door toward freedom of expression in contemporary design.

7. CHURCH OF ST. ANTHONY THE ABBOT

Recoaro-Terme, Italy; Construction begun 1949
Giuseppe Vaccaro (b. 1896), architect

"[*Certain theories of modern architecture*] ... *seem to me to wish to restrict the vast and variegated field of harmony to one single aspect.*" — GIUSEPPE VACCARO

The Church of St. Anthony the Abbot, designed for a small village in northern Italy, is unquestionably a masterwork of modern architecture. Like most masterworks it breaks precedents that had been considered sacrosanct. In the hands of a lesser architect, the result might have been chaos. But here the brilliance of the executor has outwitted the rulemakers. Seldom has such a profusion of materials been encountered in one modern building: reinforced concrete, stone, fluted brick, hollow brick, marble of various colors, stained glass, clear glass, glass brick, copper sheeting. Four or five of these would be considered the limit by most modern architects. But with typical Italian exuberance, Giuseppe Vaccaro has used them all.

Structurally, too, the building is an anomaly. A reinforced concrete frame has been used, not to allow thin curtain walls, but to provide necessary stiffening for a massive infilling of stone. Springing from this weighty and all but conventional bearing wall are thin, reinforced concrete vertical arches — a most advanced structural concept — that support the roof and are exposed on the interior as a ceiling. The contradictions are carried further by the fact that this most modern of ceiling arcades acts to produce an atmosphere of traditional churchly grandeur.

However, this is only part of the story of this remarkable building. Its design calls for every wall surface to be overlaid with a mosaic of repetitive rectangles and stripes of richly colored Verona marble. Contrasting with the pattern and sheen of marble walls, the arched concrete roof of the church is surfaced on the exterior with sheeted, ribbed copper. Stained glass, using an almost medieval treatment of figures, forms a wall of window for one of the confessionals. In a lateral nave, to the right of the main nave, are placed four sixteenth-century altars with fluted columns and intricate carving,

saved from the old church that formerly occupied the same site.

It is still not difficult to recall what an architectural heresy such lavish decoration would have represented 30, or 20, or even 15 years ago — at least among the purists of modern design.

Like the profusion of decoration, the plan, too, follows no accepted rule of order. Although primarily a basilica, reminiscent of fourteenth century Franciscan churches, it is nevertheless not symmetrical. One side of the nave is enclosed, the other opens through a series of archways to a subsidiary lateral nave. The apse of the sanctuary is polygonal; so is the baptistry that extends out from the side wall of the church toward the front.

The great elliptical arches of the ceiling in the main nave, the vaulting of the lateral nave, and the polygonal spaces of apse and baptistry recall the Byzantine and Medieval architecture of Venice. But these forms and spaces have been used quite independently of historical antecedent. Both structurally and by their disposition within the total design, they are new and original concepts. Their similarity to ancient forms is more a resonance of the spirit of the Italian past than it is any attempt to reproduce it. In the same way, the exterior of the church, which looks almost Romanesque in its curves and rich decoration, cannot literally be linked to that historical style.

It would appear that Giuseppe Vaccaro, tired of the strictures modern architecture had placed upon itself, determined to use any form, any plan, any structural system, any decorative device that he felt would contribute to a grand and noble edifice, regardless of the traditional roots of these various elements. Such lack of self-consciousness and freedom from cant is one of the newer manifestations of modern architecture.

The Church of St. Anthony the Abbot is set in park-like grounds on a site that dominates the ancient market square of the village of Recoaro-Terme in the mountainous region of northern Italy. It has replaced an old and deteriorating church that once occupied this same location, but that was demolished to make way for the new edifice. In this traditional setting, flanked by the buildings of centuries past, a severely modern structure would have been entirely out of key. Instead, Vaccaro has designed a church rich in adornment and evocative in form, so harmonious with existing architecture that its modernity, although quite obvious, is not discordant.

There are other reasons underlying such an approach. Religious feeling is very strong in this part of Italy and the townspeople consider the church to be their most important building. It is truly the center of village life, primarily as a house of prayer, but also as the most hospitable meeting place for the entire community. In this, their major public building, the villagers seek an atmosphere of dignity and even of grandeur. Since Recoaro is a holiday resort of considerable importance, the church, too, will be the focus of architectural interest for all visitors. For these reasons it has been made, above all, an imposing edifice, noble of form and handsomely decorated.

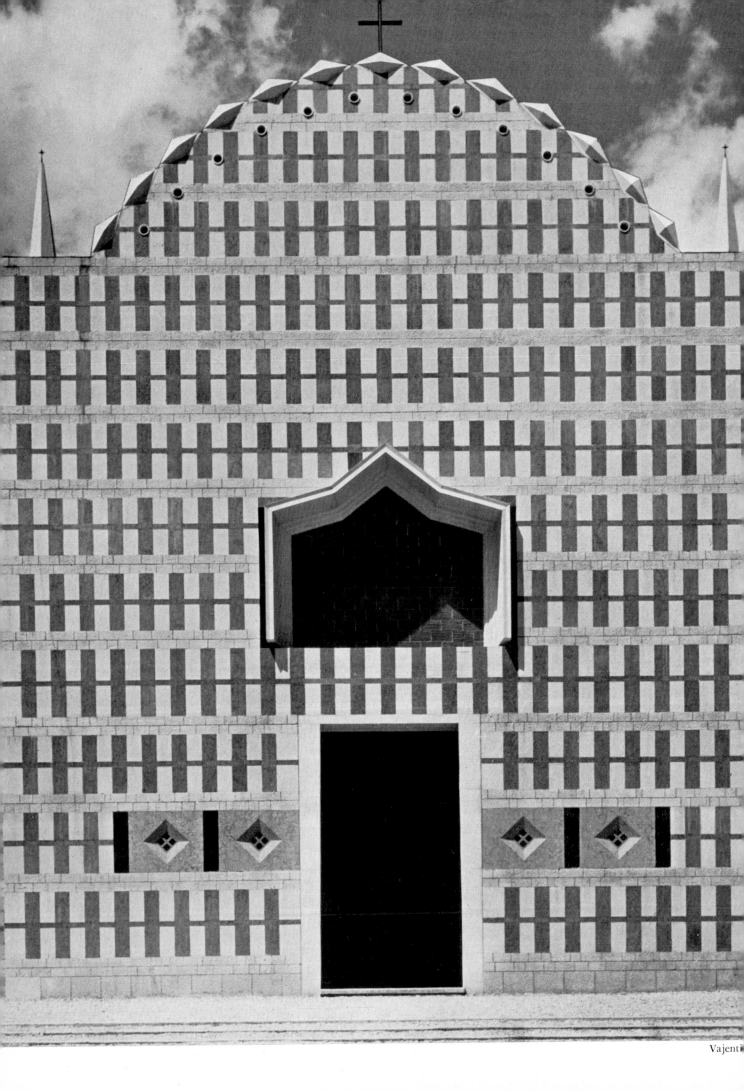

Direct front view of the Church of St. Anthony the Abbot shows the striking surface pattern and the bold forms that give it dominance over surrounding buildings.* The forms are not arbitrary, but clearly express the structure of the church. The curve atop the entrance wall, for instance, follows the structural curve of the roof arches behind it, recalling the famous roofline of Notre Dame du Raincy (No. 1), and echoing also the Romanesque arch. Wall surfaces are inlaid with Verona marble in shades of beige and earth-red. White marble is used for the door frame and the decorative window hood, and is repeated again in the diamond-patterned frieze and two obelisks that top the entrance wall.

This richness of form, pattern, and color, though copying no historic artifice, carries on the ecclesiastical

* In this view the scale of the church is not apparent; the huge entrance portal seems to be the size of a standard door opening, making the church appear much smaller than it is. Actually it towers above the neighboring three-story buildings.

tradition of the community to which the church belongs. As architect Vaccaro explains:

"This church was built in great part by the contribution of the townspeople, not only of the rich, but also the poor. Workers even gave their gratuitous help by turns. These people wish their church to appear beautiful, as it is an offering they have made to God. Therefore, I wanted to give to the exterior a certain aspect of richness, adorning it with inlaid work of colored marble chosen among those of the region."

This statement expresses the sentiment behind the unique design of St. Anthony the Abbot — a sentiment that could never have been satisfied by the stark severity of early modernism, nor by a small church of inexpensive construction and simple design. The majestic form and rich patterning of this church represent a sympathetic expression of the religious feeling of its congregation and of the way of life of this community, just as the needs and aspirations of an entirely different group of people are mirrored in the rugged simplicity of St. Sylvester (No. 6).

G. E. Kidder Smith

Side views of the church show the walls still unfinished. Eventually, these will be surfaced with inlaid marble in the same pattern as that of the baptistry, which extends from the left side of the church, as shown. A one-story lateral nave at the opposite side of the church will be finished the same way. The pattern of these side elements has been subdued in order to emphasize the drama of the entrance wall, and also to prevent the distraction caused by a bold geometry used over too wide an area. However, certain lines of the pattern of the facade continue at each side, tying all surfaces together into a unified design.

Reinforced concrete fins at the top of side walls are lower portions of the vertical arches that support the roof and create the great arcaded ceiling exposed on

the interior. The roof is surfaced with ribbed copper sheeting that, upon weathering, will turn the lovely bluish-green of verdigris. This color will act a complementary foil to the tawny earth-red and soft beige of the inlaid marble.

The apse at the rear of the church is domed to overarch the altar; there is a glass lunette joining it to the lower level of the main roof. This device floods the chancel with light, reflected downward from the interior surface of the dome. The window above the front entrance portal illuminates a choir loft.

The octagonal building with a pointed roof — just beyond the houses in the foreground — is the oratory of the church, a completely separate structure, designed by a different architect.

Interior view, looking toward the entrance wall, shows the window of the choir loft, eventually to be filled with glass brick. Walls will be surfaced with rectangles of marble, as shown by the small portion at left, already finished. Between the roof arches, set in each side wall, are round, clear-glazed windows, one of which can be glimpsed at left. From ground level these windows are hidden by the arches, casting a softened light entirely devoid of glare. This illumination creates a subdued, devotional atmosphere within the church.

Vajenti

View of nave, looking toward the altar, reveals the canopy effect of the elliptical roof arches, patterned by reflected light from their round windows. Within the sanctuary, light is more intense, pouring down through a glass lunette set into a separate dome. The great arches that form the ceiling of the main nave are of particular structural interest. Designed as reinforced concrete girders stiffened with boards of hollow brick, they exert no thrust at the side walls. This arrangement permits the thickest part of the arch to be at its center, and the thinnest part at each impost — the re-

verse of traditional structural requirements. Here, Vaccaro has hewed to the modern rule of using structural elements to create a highly decorative effect.

Doors at left lead to sacristy and confessionals. At right, reinforced concrete archways connect the main nave with the narrow, vaulted, lateral nave that contains the sixteenth century altars. In this photograph, walls are unfinished, lacking the inlaid marble that will eventually surface them. Also absent are the benches that will soon provide seating throughout the main nave. This church is large, accommodating 2,000.

Bird's-eye view of exterior   shows the long rectangle of the main nave ending in the polygonal apse at rear. The polygonal form is repeated in baptistry at front left. To the right, at rear, the lateral nave connects by passageway with a separate oratory — shaped like an irregular octagon. The freestanding bell tower in front of the church is hexagonal. Part of the church property, toward the right, consists of a small park with walks leading to the oratory, the lateral nave, and around the side to the front of the church.

The design for this complex was chosen by competition, with Giuseppe Vaccaro, Furio Fasolo, and Giulio Roisecco declared joint winners. The contract for the church was awarded to Vaccaro; for the bell tower and oratory to Roisecco. The contract for a rectory (not shown) went to Fasolo.

The church alone contains 10,000 sq. ft. of floor area. The cost was $150,000. Such a church could not be duplicated in America for this amount, partly because the beautiful marble is native to its region, and partly because of the much lower cost of labor in Italy.

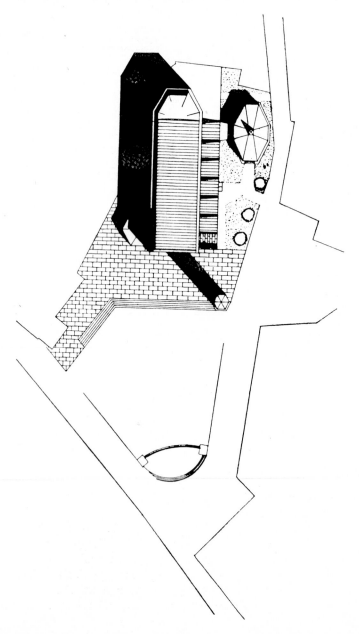

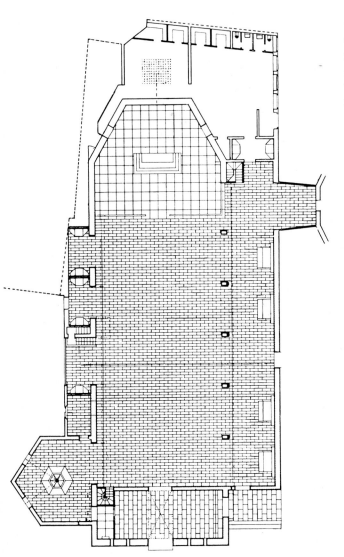

Cutaway drawing and plan show the disposition of the major elements of the church: baptistry, main nave, and lateral nave. The great elliptical ceiling arcade sets a tone of nobility, serenity, and grandeur for the entire church — this character being reemphasized in subsidiary elements and detailing.

In explaining his design, architect Vaccaro comments: "The Catholic Church, in its long history, has maintained within very different styles, some essential characteristics, both liturgical and psychological. I have tried to express these characteristics without, however, reproducing the building forms and systems of the past. Personally, and without reservation, I believe that religious architecture should be modern architecture. However, I feel that the Church would be wise to reject all formalized style, which is destined to lose its validity within a very short time. Rather than an anxious search after style, architecture should seek to be a sincere and lively expression of contemporary life and techniques of building. Such always were the greatest architectonic creations of past time."

References

Nestler, Paolo. *Neues Bauen in Italia.* Georg D. Callwey, Munich (1954).

Vaccaro, Giuseppe. "The Church of Recoaro-Terme," *Spazio*, No. 7.

———— "Principles of Harmony in Architecture," *Spazio*, No. 7.

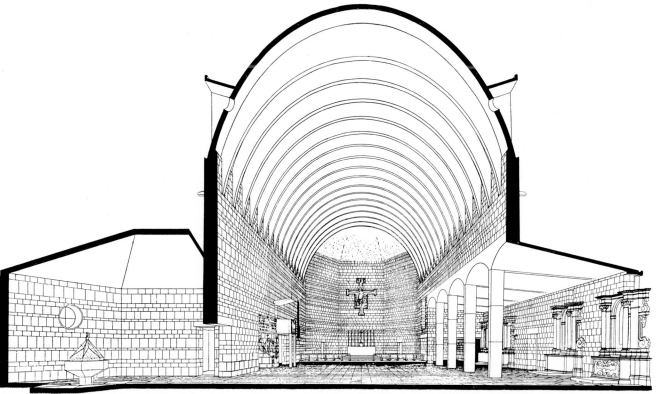

All drawings courtesy of *Spazio*

REPORT FROM THE CLERGY
Don Andrea Battaglia, Arciprete

We chose a contemporary design for our new church because we trust that modern art can also have its masterpieces. The clergy, artistically conservative, conceived a church only in classical style. We are now convinced that a modern church (excluding those "too modern") helps people in elevating their souls to God. Priests who declare themselves favorable to modern projects are becoming more numerous every day. The credit here is the architect Vaccaro's. He, from Recoaro, first showed the clergy the need to alter its original concept of the church.

We ourselves were not familiar with the field of modern architecture. We therefore followed the advice and guidance of experts, especially the Committee for Diocesan Art and the Pontifical Committee of Art. The actual design was chosen by national competition. Many interesting projects were submitted, but the winner, beyond any discussion, was Giuseppe Vaccaro. The major requirement laid down for the design of the church was its suitableness. It had to be a modern building, but adapted to its surroundings and conferring movement and majesty to the square in front of it. The experts guaranteed that the chosen design would meet these requirements.

The interior of the church also expresses our aims. In the center is the altar. Whoever enters our church immediately perceives the majestic apsis, where the altar and holy cross are located. The simple straight lines call the eye to the altar, where God is present. So the need for prayer is spontaneously born. To feel immediately the presence of God on the altar, and to start a prayer from the bottom of the heart, is a single act in a Catholic church.

The building also is suitable for its functions. All can see and follow the priest and the Holy Mass can be clearly heard. Thus, the faithful pray with greater devotion, they are suitably composed, and they feel a greater respect for the house of the Lord.

The faithful did have to be educated to this design. We did this through discussions and by trying to illustrate the advantages and harmony of modern architecture. As time passed they became accustomed to the new art and even the most stubborn opponents became convinced. Those who still feel hostile, are so because of ignorance, poor taste, or prejudice. But the majority are satisfied. Here are some quotations: "In this church we can breathe." "I feel I can pray better." "The more time elapses, the more I like it." The church still raises discussions among people who spend their holiday here. Many art lovers come to see it, and the design has stimulated the interest of the young people.

8. CHURCH OF MARIA KÖNIGIN

Cologne-Marienburg, Germany; Erected 1954
Dominikus Böhm (1880-1955), architect

"Only what comes from the heart, can find the way to the heart." — DOMINIKUS BÖHM

One of the most famous of Catholic church architects is the late Dominikus Böhm, who pioneered the movement toward modern design in German churches following World War I. Eclipsed with other colleagues during the Hitler regime, he emerged once more after World War II to lead a second renaissance of ecclesiastical architecture.

Probably in no other country has there been such a resurgence of church building as has occurred in West Germany during these postwar years. Particularly in the cities of Cologne, Frankfurt, and Saarbrucken, where bomb damage was greatest, new churches have sprung up by the hundreds, replacing the ruins of the old. In the diocese of Cologne alone, over 350 churches were built or reconstructed in new forms during the decade ending in 1958.

During this period Cologne was particularly fortunate in having as its archbishop Joseph Cardinal Fings, whose understanding of the meaning of church design led him to unqualified support of the modern idiom. Deeply concerned with the psychological uncertainty of the youth of Germany, he realized that the Church — if it were to recapture the drifting faith of a disillusioned generation — must show itself as a potent and vital new force in the life of the country. The most tangible expression of this vitality would be the physical buildings through which the faith expressed itself. For this task a moribund copying of the past was inadequate.

Archbishop Fings was fortunate, too, in having as residents of Cologne the leading Catholic church architects in Germany. Among them was Dominikus Böhm, famed as a structural innovator in his early designs. Böhm was inactive during the Nazi era, but, returned to ecclesiastical design after the war with a deepened feeling for the spiritual atmosphere of a church. This showed itself in a new richness of expression, nowhere more evident than in the Church of Maria Königin of Cologne-Marienburg.

In its decorative effect, this church is the precise opposite of Giuseppe Vaccaro's design for St. Anthony the Abbot. The church in Italy gains its richness from wall and roof surfacing and from the great structural arcades of its interior, while repressing windows to the point of invisibility. In Maria Königin, structure is held to the utmost simplicity and surfaces left entirely undecorated in order to emphasize the intricate patterning of a great wall of window, the focal point of the entire design. These two examples aptly illustrate the range of decorative treatment that can enrich and dramatize the architecture of the modern church.

Wall of stained glass extending the entire length of the nave is the glory of this design — probably the most beautiful of all postwar German churches. Its intricate pattern, a stylized leaf design, is executed in shades of silvery gray. No color is used except in fourteen small symbols of the litany which break the background pattern at irregular intervals. These accent points are fragments of antique glass, which blaze out in brilliant yellow, green, and red from the gray, modern glass surrounding them.

Except for these accents, the wall is semitransparent, and the outlines of several large trees, close to it on the exterior, can be glimpsed through the leafy pattern of the glass. Their shadows playing upon the glass add to the silvery, shifting, veil-like effect of this wall of moving light.

G. E. Kidder Smith

General view shows the interior of this church subdued to the point of severity in order to realize the full effect of its luminous wall. A square, open room with unadorned white surfaces, it acts as a receptacle for the shifting patterns created by the stained glass. The solidity of surrounding walls acts also as a contrasting element, a foil for the elegance and delicacy of the glass curtain.

The inspired use of glass for an entire wall enclosure is, of course, a direct result of modern building techniques that permit great voids between widely spaced framing members. Here, the frame is of steel, rather than reinforced concrete, a choice that permits the greatest slenderness of supporting columns. The four bearing columns exposed on the interior are painted a brilliant scarlet, the only color against white walls, and the only repetition of the glowing fragments of color within the window.

The church of Maria Königin demonstrates, to a remarkable degree, the subtle decorative effects of which modern design is capable when it seeks an enrichment appropriate to its own structure and esthetic.

G. E. Kidder Smith

Exterior view reveals the final touch of artistry that makes this church a magical construction. Here, silhouetted against the great glass wall of the nave is the small, circular baptistry entirely enclosed by stained glass. The repetition of the pattern of the larger nave wall unifies the two elements of church and baptistry despite their contrasting shapes. Note the shadow play on glass created by sunlight shifting through branches of nearby trees. This area of the church property has been made into a small park, equipped with benches where visitors may sit in quiet meditation, enjoying the play of light as sun and shadow move across the walls of the church buildings.

Interior view of baptistry is taken from the passage that connects it to the church proper. This passage is enclosed by clear rather than stained glass, in order to heighten the effect of entering the baptistry. Once inside, the feeling is that of being encircled by a web of silver light shot through with the colors of the rainbow.

Courtesy of *Architectural Record*

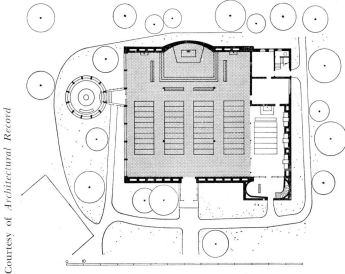

Plan of the Church of Maria Königin is square except for a slight curve at the apse, and a lateral extension that houses side chapel, sacristy, and stairways to the lower level. Position of baptistry and connecting passageway is shown at left. The square plan brings all members of the congregation close to the altar, an expression of the new liturgical requirements that are radically changing church design.

References

Elsen, Alois, ed. *Dominikus Böhm; ein deutscher Baumeister.* Josef Habbel, Regensburg (1943).

Smith, G. E. Kidder. "In the Rebirth of a Great Tradition," *Architectural Record*, June 1957.

THE SEARCH FOR PLAN: The Liturgical Revival

One of the aphorisms of modern architecture is the statement "form follows function." Most simply, this means that the function of a given interior space should determine the form of the structure that encloses it. If the function of a space is inadequately conceived, however, then both form and function, no matter how expressive of each other, remain in error. Until recently this problem perplexed the Church, although the most brilliant of modern architects were attempting to serve its needs. The continued use of the medieval church plan, even when its external style has been abandoned, is considered by many critics — particularly those who are themselves members of the ecclesiastical hierarchy — to be a basic error of church architecture today. Many of the designs shown in this book, even those exhibiting the most daring and advanced structural systems, commonly enclose a standard, rectangular plan.

During the past 50 years, the Catholic Church has gradually begun to change the traditional concept of church plan and function. This movement has been called the Liturgical Revival. In essence, this means a return to the more ancient concept of Christianity, lost during the Middle Ages, in which officiating priest and laity were intimately one within the mystical body of the Church. The liturgical effect of this concept is to bring the congregation into more active participation in the Mass. Its architectural effect is to bring priest and congregation physically closer together around the focal point of the altar.

The Liturgical Revival had its beginning under Pope Pius X who, before his death in 1914, attempted a basic reorganization of liturgical function within the Catholic Church. As explained by G. E. Kidder Smith:

One of his chief concerns was the growing estrangement, both spiritual and spatial, between the clergy and the congregation. His suggestions to counteract this and other faults were soon felt in church design itself, where any change in ritual or ceremony should be logically reflected.

The Pope asked first for a greater participation by the congregation in the church and its manifold problems, and then sought a more intimate relationship for them in the service itself. He wanted to break down the physical and psychological barriers between the nave on one hand and the pulpit and sanctuary on the other.... Many studies and investigations were made, and although few changes were realized until after the First World War, nearly all stem from Pius' initial efforts.

The liturgical and architectural recommendations of Pope Pius X were, of course, most immediately felt in Europe, gaining their first real impetus during the resurgence of church building in the 1920's. Particularly in Germany and Switzerland, and more recently, France, the above recommendations have been carried forward until today they stand as the basis upon which almost all of the newer modern churches to be found in these countries have been designed. Among those groups most actively sponsoring the new concepts is the Benedictine Order, whose efforts have been felt far beyond churches actually built under its supervision.

In America, as in Europe, the Liturgical Revival has found its most active support among the Benedictines. One of the most dedicated groups working toward the new expression in the United States is the Monastery of St. John the Baptist in Collegeville, Minn. (No. 36), the largest Benedictine community in the world today. Despite their efforts, however, the new approach to the liturgy has not yet been diffused widely enough throughout the American Catholic Church as a whole to have had much effect on church building in this country. But as long ago as 1930, the Baltimore *Catholic Review* wrote of the Liturgical Revival:

"If all of us could catch the enthusiasm of the Benedictines in making known the meaning of the Mass...of arousing a greater appreciation of artistic statuary and captivating architecture, the Catholic Church would be more admired and appreciated by our non-Catholic friends.... Indeed, the liturgical movement, as fostered by the Benedictines, is opening to tens of thousands of our Catholics vistas of which they have not known before."

However, the question of accepting the Liturgical Revival must remain largely academic until modern architecture itself is accepted as the proper means of expression for the Church. Gothic and Romanesque churches, based on the elongated rectangle and the cruciform, cannot easily accommodate the new liturgical concept. The plans indicated by this movement can properly be expressed only in new architectural forms. The Rev. Peter Hammond has written:

The reason why the typical medieval plan, with its elongated nave and chancel...is being so widely abandoned on the Continent today is the fact that it expresses an entirely different understanding of the liturgy, and of the function of the church building, from that now current in Liturgical Movement circles....

...a new kind of church has begun to appear: a church which reflects a new theological outlook, a deepened understanding of the liturgy which gives the building its raison d'être. The church is seen first and foremost as the place where the local Christian community gathers for the Eucharist. This is its essential function, to which everything else is subordinate. The liturgy itself is regarded not as something performed by the clergy alone but as a corporate action in which everyone has an active part to play. Hence the current experiments with novel types of church plans based on the square, the circle, the ellipse, the trapezoid. Such plans are not primarily the result of the freedom conferred by modern methods of construction. They are the outcome of the Church's new understanding of itself, and of the liturgy in which its essential character should be most fully realized and made manifest....

Though this movement is not confined to any one country or denomination, it is among continental Roman Catholics that its influence has been most widely felt. Significantly, it is in these countries of western Europe affected by the Liturgical Movement that church architecture is beginning to emerge from the depths of sterility and irrelevance into which it had fallen.

This section of the book presents four churches: two German, one Brazilian, and one Mexican, each with plans that are based directly on the ideas of the Liturgical Revival. To the tradition-trained eye, these examples look far less "churchly" than the other churches preceding them in this book. This sense of newness is the inevitable result of a changed function expressing itself in a changed form.

References

Catholic Review, 1930

Hammond, Peter. "A Liturgical Brief," *Architectural Review*, April 1958.

Smith, G. E. Kidder. *Switzerland Builds*. Albert Bonnier, New York (1950).

9. CHURCH OF ST. ANNA

Duren, Germany; Erected 1956
Rudolf Schwarz (b. 1897), architect

"To build does not mean to solve mathematical problems nor to create pleasing spaces; it means to place great communal forms before God." — RUDOLF SCHWARZ

In the small village of Duren, Germany, nearly leveled by bombing in World War II, this massive L-shaped church was constructed with the stones of its destroyed predecessor, which occupied the same site. The new Church of St. Anna was designed by Rudolf Schwarz, an architect ranking with Dominikus Böhm as one of the great innovators of modern church design in the 1920's and again after the second World War.

Although the plan of this church still contains an elongated, rectangular nave, effort has been made to distribute the congregation more evenly by including a second, smaller nave at right angles to the main body of the church. The L-shape thus formed has its point of conjunction at the altar. Fitting into the inner angle of the L to form a rectangle of the total plan of the church, is a large entrance lobby, or narthex, marked off by a lowered ceiling. With this plan, the sanctuary achieves a central position between two sections of worshippers, who have a direct view of the altar and a slanted view of one another through the open narthex, bringing all into intimate communion. Within each nave, space is unbroken as there are no separate side aisles and no columnar interruptions.

The sanctuary itself continues this unbroken space. It is simply a stepped dais in the corner of the L, placed directly against the walls of the church on two sides, without even an altar screen behind it. On the other two sides it opens directly toward each nave. Traditional sacristy, choir stalls, and ambulatory have been excluded from this area. Instead the choir is placed on another dais at the rear of the main nave, facing the altar. This arrangement, without loft, railing, or screening, emphasizes once more the communion of unbroken space. Priest, choir, and congregation are in direct view of each other and separated only by a difference in the level of their respective places.

Thus has Rudolf Schwarz expressed the major recommendations of the Liturgical Revival: close contact between altar and nave, and an unobstructed view of the altar — an open plan, with the fewest possible visual interruptions. Upon study, therefore, the design of St. Anna, far from being an arbitrary personal expression, is found to be thoroughly disciplined architecture, a thoughtful interpretation of the new liturgical concepts.

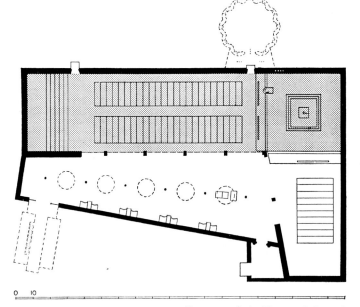

Courtesy of *Architectural Record*

Plan of St. Anna shows two L-shaped naves, joined by the large, low-ceilinged narthex, all disposed toward the altar. This compact, open plan gives congregation, celebrant, and choir a new sense of intimacy and unity. Main entrance is on the south side. Separate entrances have been provided also in the north wall, one near the sanctuary and one near the rear choir platform, so that priests and choristers can reach their places directly, and separately from the congregation. Eventually, a sacristy will be added, extending out from the north wall, near the sanctuary.

Exterior of church reveals the uncompromising honesty with which plan has been expressed in form. St. Anna is simply two high, flat-roofed blocks, joined by a lower one. Steel-framed walls of glass brick provide nave lighting. The lower-ceilinged narthex is illuminated by a series of round skylights. Close to the near corner of the narthex is the main entrance of the church. In the future this will be concealed from view by a freestanding bell tower that will break the block-like lines of the building, providing also a recognizable, traditional symbol of its function.

Artur Pfau

G. E. Kidder Smith

View from main nave looking toward the altar shows the open planning of the entire church, with the subsidiary nave glimpsed at right through the columns of the lower-ceilinged narthex. The stone walls of the church are tawny earth colors, lending warmth to the massive masonry. The floor is surfaced with black slate; the ceiling is of gray unpainted concrete; the altar of pale stone. Artificial lighting is provided by faceted glass globes hung in vertical groups of eight throughout both naves and singly behind the altar. Their crystalline delicacy acts as a counterpoint to the weight and solidity of the walls behind them. Brilliant color is entirely absent from this church, visual interest being provided only by the play of form and texture. This low key gives the church an air of great solemnity.

View of the interior is from the low-ceilinged narthex. The narthex is an unusually functional element in this design, because it opens along the entire side of each nave, allowing immediate seating in any pew. In addition, it serves the needs of St. Anna as a pilgrimage chapel, by providing standing room (with a clear view of the altar) for the great crowds that throng this church on special occasions. Esthetically, the narthex helps create a quality of affirmation, that sensation of soaring that is felt when going abruptly from a dimly-lit, low space to one of greater height and illumination. Behind the altar, stonework has been set in a pattern representing — as it extends upward to the ceiling — the tree of life, thus achieving integrally with the wall structure a quiet decorative effect.

View from within the sanctuary shows that the altar is square, presenting an identical appearance toward either nave. Although both plan and form of this church break all tradition, its interior — by modern means — conjures up the very spirit of the Middle Ages. Dean Joseph Hudnut of Harvard has written of this church:

"Its disdain of comeliness is almost feudal.... Within a vast and somber nave, the weight and mass of an unbroken wall of masonry is answered on the opposite side by a clean rigidity of steel columns framing wide areas of glass blocks. Thus, the great hall of a West-phalian castle is made hospitable to the advent of steel. It was in such a hall that the Emperor Otto assembled his barons to plan the conquest of Italy, a sword laid upon the altar...."

References

Hudnut, Joseph. "The Church in a Modern World," *Architectural Forum*, December 1958.

Schwarz, Rudolf. *The Church Incarnate*. Henry Regnery Co., Chicago (1958).

10. CHURCH OF ST. MICHAEL

Frankfurt, Germany; Erected 1954
Rudolf Schwarz (b. 1897), architect

"Church architecture is not cosmic mythology — rather it is the representation of Christian life, a new embodiment of the spiritual." — RUDOLF SCHWARZ.

The elliptical plan of the Church of St. Michael, Frankfurt, Germany, is actually an adaptation to the new liturgical requirements of a plan which has been common in Germany since the Renaissance. Here, Rudolf Schwarz, the architect also for the preceding Church of St. Anna, has reversed himself. St. Anna recreates the spirit of the Middle Ages in a new plan and a new form; St. Michael creates, within an old plan, a space and atmosphere entirely new.

This church, perhaps as successfully as any other in the book, achieves the spiritual feeling of one room, which has been advanced as an ideal by the Liturgical Revival. An elliptical masonry enclosure, massively framed by projecting concrete ribs, is lighted by one continuous window of glass brick that bands the entire edifice just below the roof. From ground level up to this window band, the towering walls are one solid expanse of masonry, broken only by low projecting entrance lobbies at front and chapels at rear.

It was the architect's aim to provide a "fortress" of enduring solidity and strength against the troubles of the outside world. But the great structural frame of exposed concrete and the mass of red brick wall that fills it, give way on the interior to a room of ethereal calm and beauty — a spiritual haven, protected and serene. Here, the walls have been stuccoed to smoothness and painted white, enfolding the interior in chaste and gentle curves. The vertical ribs of the concrete frame run from floor to ceiling, providing the only break in the interior surface. These ribs, which appear massive on the exterior where three of their sides show, look delicate on the interior where they present one slender edge, flush with the wall. They are painted a deep moss green, almost a neutral color. Floors are surfaced with dark gray slate and pews are a rich wood brown. Above white walls and neutral tones, the concrete ceiling, designed like a great floating canopy, is painted a heavenly blue, with ribs of gold.

Soft light from the high band of glass block suffuses this interior with a quiet radiance during the day. The final touch of artistry is in the night lighting: simple, white, elongated globes, which drop on thin gold rods from the high ceiling to a point low within the nave. That is all — no decoration, no stained glass, no color except the floating blue of the ceiling. The result, quite beyond the reach of photographs, is of a "peace that passeth understanding."

The plan upon which this lofty church is constructed consists of a major nave in an elongated oval, with projecting oval chapels at either side of the sanctuary. The oval is repeated once more at the other end of the church in two smaller, one-story, entrance lobbies, which also extend outside the nave of the church. With all subsidiary elements projecting outward, the main interior of St. Michael is truly an unbroken room surrounded by one continuous, gently curving wall. At the same time the side chapels are actually part of this space, since the wall simply curves outward, without a break, to enclose them.

Each of these alcove chapels is designed for a different use. The south chapel is occupied by the choir. The north chapel contains confessionals and the stations of the cross. The latter acts also as a subsidiary nave of small size and heightened intimacy for use on weekdays when the church is not filled. This allows direct communion between the priest at the central altar and a small body of worshippers in the north chapel. On Sundays and holy days a larger congregation fills the main nave, with the overflow in this chapel. The location of the choir in the south alcove facing the sanctuary places this group also in intimate relationship to the altar. Moreover, by eliminating the traditional loft, the choir is placed on a level with the congregation, and becomes a part of it. The altar itself is square and placed so that the priest may stand at any one of its four sides, turning toward the small daily congregation, toward the choir, or toward the main nave as the occasion warrants.

Behind the altar is a large, curved bench, constructed of brick and surfaced with the same gray slate as the floor. This is used as a resting place by the priest and his attendants. Here also sit the *schola* of singers and the priests' chorus. St. Michael has achieved a reputation as the "Frankfurt oratorium" and special provision for choristers had to be made in its design.

Although the nave of this church is long and narrow, recalling elongated traditional plans, it achieves a feeling of oneness between priest and congregation by its extreme simplicity and by its enfolding curves. No side aisles, columns nor other extraneous elements break the continuity of this long and lofty space.

67

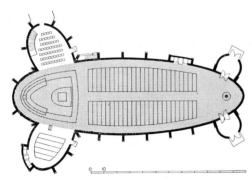

Courtesy of *Architectural Record*

Plan of St. Michael with its projecting side chapels is one which the architect calls the "open ring." Its central idea is the assembly of the congregation around three sides of the altar in a ring, the fourth side of the ring being the curved apse or opening behind the altar. Symbolically, this design is meant to express the turning of all peoples toward the altar as their "mediator," or "threshold," leading to the opening apse which signifies heaven.

Simultaneously, the placement of the altar as a center for four crossways symbolizes its centrality to "the four corners of the earth," a sign of the blessing of the universe. The position of the baptismal font is equally symbolic. On a direct line with the altar and between the two entrance doors, it represents entry into the Church, leading to the sacrament of communion, and, through this, to the promise of salvation.

The Church of St. Michael rises like a spiritual fortress in the midst of the workaday world of Frankfurt-on-Main. In this side view, one of the two projecting chapels is clearly delineated at left, and both of the small entrances are visible at right. The projecting ribs that boldly pattern the exterior are the concrete supporting frame.

Although the brick walls between them give the appearance of great mass, they are actually not thick, being only curtain walls bearing no weight. However, they have been made somewhat thicker than structurally necessary in order to provide insulation against heat, cold, and dampness. The architect chose this brick vaulting, rather than a thin shell of reinforced concrete, for two reasons: first, for its inherently superior insulating qualities; second, because it is almost insensitive to the irregular settling of foundations — a real problem in the many-layered soil of this difficult site.

The roof framework is an elliptical hoop of steel, slid in sections onto the tops of the inserted concrete pillars. The roof itself is a concrete shell. Although the appearance of this church is extremely unconventional, like St. Anna of Duren it will eventually be made more recognizable by the addition of a freestanding bell tower.

Artur Pfau

Interior view of this enormous room shows baptismal font in the near foreground on a line with the altar at the front of the church. The large curved bench for officiating priest and special choristers is behind the altar. Not visible in this view are the entrances to the choir's chapel, at right, and to the chapel for daily worship, at left, the latter containing also confessionals and the stations of the cross. Floors are dark gray slate, walls are white, ribbed with neutral moss green, and the ceiling is a celestial blue with ribs of gold.

Although the basis of this design is rooted in the liturgy, its particular expression came from another source. Upon a trip through the Aare Gorge, the architect, following a narrow path came to a spot "hemmed in by staring rocks and lighted only high up through a small gap to the open sky. I perceived this gorge as a common human experience: a menacing world towering all around with but a glimpse of the open sky whose silver light shimmers down from the highest region. This experience found its architectural expression in St. Michael's."

Reference

Schwarz, Rudolf. *The Church Incarnate*. Henry Regnery Co., Chicago (1958).

11. CHAPEL OF NUESTRA SENORA DE LA SOLEDAD

San Jose del Altillo, Coyoacan, Mexico, D.F.; Erected 1955
Felix Candela (b. 1910), structural engineer
Enrique de la Mora y Palomar, architect

"The imaginative use of structures of this type produce unsuspected interior and exterior forms. These may enrich the intolerably limited present vocabulary of cubical masses and spaces, pending new fields of thought for the architect." — FELIX CANDELA

The Chapel of Nuestra Señora de la Soledad, San Jose del Altillo, Mexico, for a comparatively new religious order in Mexico (the Missionaries of the Holy Spirit, founded in 1914) was jointly designed by Enrique de la Mora y Palomar and Felix Candela, the engineer-architect whose Church of La Virgen Milagrosa (No. 3) illustrates the structural principle of the warped slab.

In the seminary chapel shown here, the reinforced concrete slab, warped into a hyperbolic paraboloid, is used again, but much more simply and conventionally. Rather than comprising the entire structure, the slab-work here is limited to the roof (the only part of the building designed by Candela), which is supported by conventional loadbearing walls and posts. Although still a most unusual design of the highest technical interest, the chapel at El Altillo is less of a structural landmark than La Virgen Milagrosa.

However, there is a paradox. La Virgen Milagrosa's radical engineering has been used to enclose a quite conventional rectangular plan. But the somewhat less adventuresome structure of El Altillo encloses a bold, new plan, one of the most advanced interpretations of the Liturgical Revival — the concept of architect Enrique de la Mora y Palomar.

The geometric basis of this new plan is the rhomboid — a figure best described as an acute and an obtuse triangle placed back to back, pointing away from each other. The four-sided figure thus formed is broad at center where the two triangles join, and narrows toward the points of each triangle. It is a space admirably suited to the new liturgical requirements. The altar is brought forward almost to the center of the church. This allows three groupings around it, the major congregation of 350 in the base of the rhomboid, facing the altar, and two smaller groups of 50 each, flanking the altar along the sides.

This is a plan that could be adapted to a parish church. Indeed it is similar in idea to the tri-form grouping found in St. Michael (No. 10). But there are important differences. El Altillo has no projecting wings and its entire plan is more compact. Most important of all, the broad base of its rhomboid permits the seats to be distributed quite near to the altar across the width of the church — certainly a liturgical advantage over the oval of S. Michael.

As it stands, however, El Altillo is a specialized design not intended as a parish church. The rhomboid has here been tailored to fit the needs of a seminary in which choral singing is an established part of the religious ritual, the entire congregation of priests and seminarians joining in Gregorian chants. It is the seminarian choristers, therefore, who flank the altar in groups of 50. The general congregation faces both the altar and choristers. Behind the congregation, at the rear of the church, on a raised platform reached by exterior stairways, stands the main choir. Thus during a High Mass, El Altillo is literally filled with music, from above, from below, from the rear and front and sides.

This chapel has obviously been organized around the chorale and its design cannot be understood in any other context. For this purpose, the rhomboidal plan and the hyperbolic paraboloid of the roof are an ideal acoustical solution, since they present no parallel surfaces and therefore create no reverberation.

However, the rhomboid, as pointed out previously, is also a figure that leads inevitably to a close grouping of congregation about the altar, no worshippers being more than a few feet from this central point. For a parish church, the space flanking the altar could be developed, as it has been in St. Michael, for subsidiary seating of a small body of worshippers during the week, as well as for the choir. The intimacy achieved between sanctuary and nave, which are actually one compact unbroken space, separated only by their traditional names, appears to be close to the new liturgical ideal.

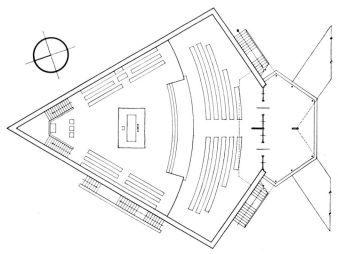

Side view of chapel during construction reveals how the doubly warped slab of the roof curves up from its center toward the back and front, at the same time curving down at either side. The major weight of the roof is born by reinforced concrete walls, which support the lower side corners of the roof. The rear and front corners are thus cantilevered, and supports at these areas merely provide stability. At the rear, the stabilizing element is a huge cross, extending downward from the tip of the roof through the choir platform to the ground. At front, steel posts act also as framing members for a large V-shaped window.

This photograph shows one of the two exterior stairways that lead up to the elevated choir platform at the rear. Walls are surfaced in volcanic stone with a black cast, and the roof with terra cotta tile, in a herringbone pattern. The roof structure is a 118 by 95-ft. shell of reinforced concrete only 1½ in. thick, although a vertical facing under its outer edge makes it appear thicker. Its true thickness can be seen in the extended edge itself.

The roof of the El Altillo chapel is a true rhomboid; the plan beneath it is broken at the rear to provide for the main choir loft. Note particularly the forward position of the altar and the closeness with which the congregation in the base of the rhomboid, and choristers at either side, cluster around it. The small area within the point of the acute angle behind the altar is utilized for stairways that lead to a lower level sacristy. Twin sets of exterior stairs at either side of the rear of the church lead up to the main choir loft. This platform is partly outside and partly inside the church, but entirely under the main roof. Fins extending out at rear are a continuation of the choir platform that here acts as a shelter for the main entrance to the church below. The interior space provided by the chapel is approximately 4,200 sq. ft. It was built in 1956 at a cost of $ 50,000, which breaks down to $ 11.90 per square foot.

Erwin Lang

Erwin Lang

View from nave looking toward the sanctuary shows
seminarian choristers aligned on either side of the altar.
This photograph was taken at High Mass on Easter
Sunday, 1956, while the church was still in the last stages
of construction. The huge windows meeting at the
point of a V, on a line with the altar, have since been
filled with stained glass. However, even in its unfinished form, the window provides an inspiring specta-
cle. Here is a panorama of natural beauty almost equal
to, although quite different from, the glowing colored
backdrop that has since intensified the mystical quality
of the interior. Churches that cannot afford stained glass
might well consider the loveliness of clear glass in such a
natural setting.

Erwin Lang

View of rear of interior during construction shows the great sweep of the roof and the "indoor-outdoor" choir platform, which is cut by the great slab of the exterior cross. The choir platform provides a lowered ceiling for the main entrance, and the vertical cross divides the entrance into two spaces. Note how close the steps that lead to the altar (right) are to the rear of the church. In this way the 350-person congregation is distributed in a broad grouping across the width of the church, all very close to the altar. Brilliant color will be used only in the chancel windows. Thus, a concentration of color, as well as the arrangement of the plan, will focus all attention on the altar, as recommended by the Liturgical Revival.

Jane Doggett/Dorothy Jackson

Views of the finished church show its two opposing window areas filled with stained and patterned glass
— at the "prow" as a jeweled backdrop for the church
service, and above the main entrance as illumination
for the choir loft. There are no other windows in the
church, and the light within the nave is therefore subdued, contrasting with the glow of concentrated illumination at front and rear.

These photographs also reveal the skill with which
the site has been made part of the total architecture.
At the side, broad terraces lead up the slope toward
the entrance, their steps and retaining walls forming a
linear composition of which the church is the climax.
Flower beds and trees relieve the severe geometry of
this design, making it an integral and harmonious part
of the landscape.

The deep overhead choir platform extends out in
two arms to shelter the walkways linking church to seminary buildings. The enclosure of the choir loft —
wood and patterned glass set in a wooden frame — forms
one of the major decorative elements of the entrance
facade. Of particular note is the harmony with which
the diverse materials of volcanic stone, natural wood,
geometrically patterned glass, and bare concrete have
been combined.

This building achieves a quality of fitness that tran-
scends stylistic catagories. The visitor does not instantly
classify it as either traditional or modern, but rather is
impressed with a general sense of harmony and pro-
priety. Despite its unusual plan, its bold form, its advanced engineering, and its striking combination of materials, this chapel gives the impresion that it has existed
always within the surrounding landscape.

References

Boyd, Robin. "Engineering of Excitement," *Architectural Review*, May 1956.

Candela, Felix. "Stereo-Structures," *Progressive Architecture*, June 1954.

Faber, Colin. "Felix Candela as a Contemporary," *Arts
and Architecture*, May 1956.

Jane Doggett/Dorothy Jackson

12. CHAPEL OF THE PRESIDENT'S PALACE

Brasilia, Brazil; Erected 1958
Lucia Costa (b. 1902), city planner
Oscar Niemeyer (b. 1907), architect

Courtesy of *Modulo*

"Most certainly we live in a great period insofar as urbanistics and architecture are concerned; this period, which began with the industrial revolution, will be recorded in history as one of the greatest stages, wherein technical progress modified and revolutionized everything, suggesting to architects a new world of unforseeable shapes." — OSCAR NIEMEYER (Left to right, above: Oscar Niemeyer, Lucia Costa).

One of the most dramatic and advanced designs to express the principles of the Liturgical Revival is the chapel that serves the President's Palace in Brasilia, the new capital city of Brazil being carved out of the wilderness 600 miles from Rio de Janeiro.

Brasilia represents one of the few opportunities in the twentieth century to build a whole city from the beginning, and as such it offers unlimited scope to both planners and architects. This opportunity has not been wasted. The master plan of Brasilia by architect Lucia Costa was selected in competition by an international jury. It embodies the most advanced theories of city planning, including the separation of pedestrian from vehicular traffic and the interlacing of business and commercial areas with parks and greenery. It embodies also the timeless concept of the artistic relationship of buildings to each other, to the site, and to the city as a whole. Dramatic open spaces and approaches set apart important structures, revealing their full power and meaning. At the same time all buildings are parts in a unified design, supporting and reinforcing each other in the varied, yet thematically consonant web of the city.

Oscar Niemeyer, the leading architect in Brazil and one of the most creative in the world today, was selected to design the individual buildings. He combines an unsurpassed technical knowledge with an artistic sense that is at once disciplined and original. As a result, his designs for Brasilia have carried the potential of modern materials and building techniques forward to a new expression; bold, fresh, vital, and, above all, starkly beautiful.

The design for the Chapel of the President's Palace is so simple that it appears to have been executed with a wave of the hand. Only an architect so sure of structure that he uses this knowledge instinctively could produce such an effortless work. Here, reinforced concrete has been curled like a shell, around a continuous, gently rising, interior space. Only the floor-to-ceiling entrance portal, and a similar floor-to-ceiling insertion of glass, which illuminates the chancel, break the continuum of the curving wall.

This unfolding spiral of a building, the outer wall of which rises to a sharp point against the sky, is set at the end of a promenade that fronts the President's Palace. Beyond, there is nothing but open space, for the chapel is the last outlying structure in Brasilia, thus concluding the city on a promontory, eventually to be surrounded by a great artificial lake, and planted as a park. Thus, no building can ever detract from the silhouette of the chapel, which stands out in full clarity against the flat, receding landscape.

The chapel is, of course, intimately related to the President's Palace, which it serves, acting as both repetition and counterpoint to the larger building. The chapel, with its curved form and solid enclosure, is the structural opposite of the palace, which is long, low, rectangular, and entirely walled with glass. The most dramatic feature of the palace, however, is a series of continuous exterior "columns" of reinforced concrete, in a curved, repetitive, dipping and rising design. These columns support the projecting roof like upstretched fingertips. The curve of these supports, which narrows almost to a point at the top, is repeated in the curve of the chapel, ending also in a skyward point.

The architecture of both chapel and palace is so thoroughly expressive of the country of Brazil and so much a part of the total design of Brasilia, that it would be out of context in almost any other setting.

Marcel Gautherot

The palace chapel here unfurls its smooth, curving expanse like a flag against the sky. Reinforced concrete structural walls are thinly surfaced with slabs of white marble, having a faint grayish cast, which is pleasanter in the blazing Brazilian sun than chalk white. These are the same materials used for the decks of the President's Palace and also for its dramatic columns, one of which cuts into the photograph above. The chapel is placed on a raised platform — a slab of reinforced concrete — which brings it to the same height as the palace loggia. The two buildings are connected by a footbridge, overpassing a sunken driveway. A second ramp to the left leads down to the level of the palace grounds. Eventual damming of the Parana River will create an artificial lake, surrounding Brasilia on three sides. It will be visible here in the distance as the definition of the palace grounds.

Plan of chapel is as simple as its exterior form. Entrance is between beginning and end of the continuous wall; nave and chancel are in the inner loop. No interior partitions break the free flow of space from the entrance around the broad curve to the sanctuary. In addition to the curve of the wall, the floor gently ascends,

reaching the height of its slope at the chancel, where it flattens to a horizontal. The continuous wall steps inward halfway around its loop-like path to allow the insertion of a vertical panel of glass for illumination of the chancel.

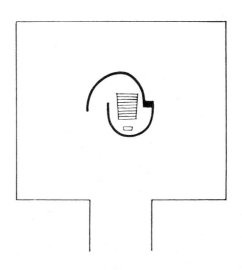

Courtesy of *Progressive Architecture*

Marcel Gautherot

Distant view of chapel beyond the President's Palace, shows the remarkable consistency of the two designs. The solid portions of each are of reinforced concrete, surfaced with marble. The dipping curves of the amazing columns, which partially support the roof structure of the palace, are echoed in the rising and dropping lines of the exterior chapel wall. At the same time the windowless enclosure of the chapel, a symbol of shelter and retreat, contrasts with the crystalline openness of the palace facade.

This is the main approach to the palace. Its formal entrance is at the center, where there are no columnar supports. The visitor approaches along the plaza, then traverses an open "corridor" between twin reflecting pools, up to the great glass palace doors. The loggia that runs the full length of the palace, as defined by its walls and exterior columns, connects with a footbridge to the chapel. The urbane elegance of these buildings contrasts strangely with the raw terrain that still surrounds them. Eventually lawns, trees, and formal gardens will tame the primitive landscape, creating a verdant park setting for these incisive designs.

The tremendous advances in the creative use of reinforced concrete during the past 35 years may be fully comprehended by comparing these two structures with Perret's church, Notre Dame du Raincy (No. 1). The palace shown here makes use of the same principle of the separation of concrete frame and curtain walls that was the pioneering gesture at Le Raincy. The chapel amalgamates frame and wall into one continuous skin structure, with consequent freeing of the building plan from a rectilinear prison.

Marcel Gautherot

Side view of chapel shows its fortress-like character, made more pronounced by the small skyhole in the "turret," like a firing slit in a castle wall. Atop the turret is a simple bronze cross, which carries the ascending wall of the chapel to its spiritual conclusion. This design makes of a small and simple building a bastion of religion, the quality of inviolability emanating from its every line. The solidity and serene strength of the encircling wall bespeak unfaltering protection for the sacred rite that takes place within. However, the expressiveness of this structure does not represent a straining after effect. It is part of a single concept in which the character of the enclosure and the functioning of the plan are indistinguishable.

Sketch of interior shows the great, center-hung entrance portal (right) as it looks when pivoted open to create a path on either side. The free flow of space into and within this building represents an unprecedented approach to church design. Traditionally separate elements of narthex, nave, and chancel are here all but eliminated in the continuity of interior space. All is open, unobstructed, and compact, thus fulfilling the requirements of the Liturgical Revival, and emphasizing the essential unity of priest and worshipper. However, there is nothing informal or egalitarian about this plan. The gentle slope of the floor to its height at the chancel imparts an all-pervading sense of ascent toward the Holy. At the same time, the curving, windowless enclosure creates an atmosphere of retreat and mystery, unfolding inward. This mystery, enhanced by the dim illumination of the nave, is dispelled at the chancel, where a shaft of sunlight enters like a benediction from the single, hidden window. With a different design, the lack of windows in this interior could have made it oppressive. But the movement of space within the curving, climbing room prevents the feeling of containment that would have been inevitable in a windowless rectangle.

Marcel Gautherot

Marcel Gautherot

Views of chancel reveal it as one of the most exquisite interiors to be found in any modern church. Here, richness is played against simplicity, the rococo against the severe, light and flame against shadow. Walls throughout are covered with gilded paper in a heavily indented vertical stripe. Wrought-iron candle stands line the periphery of the room, their ebony blackness etching a delicate pattern against monotone walls, while the flames of their candles turn the dull gilt of the wallpaper to glowing gold. Floors are of gray granite, uncovered by carpeting, but chairs and benches in the nave are cushioned and upholstered in velvet.

The lines of all furnishings — wallpaper, candelabra, chairs, even the altar — are spare and rectilinear, contrasting with the continuous curves of the building itself. In turn, contrasting with the stark black candelabra, and superimposed upon the disciplined striation of the wallpaper, is an antique figure of the Madonna, opulently carved, painted, and gilded. The beauty and richness of this ancient sculpture stands out in vivid counterpoint to the chastely simple lines of the rest of the interior. Its placement here represents the appropriate use of the traditional in our time: as authentic fragments from the past incorporated into designs otherwise contemporary.

The only other decorative element in the chapel is the great entrance portal, which has been repetitively pierced with small squares and inset with panes of glass, some clear, some colored. When closed, as shown in this photograph, the portal becomes a contemporary translation of a stained glass window. When opened, it acts as a decorative entrance screen, seen against the gilded outer wall of the chapel.

References

Niemeyer, Oscar, "The Contemporary City," *Modulo*, December 1958.

Richards, J. M. "Brasilia," *Architectural Review*, February 1959.

Marcel Gautherot

THE SEARCH FOR THE ARTIST:
A Revival of the Church as Patron of the Arts

During the same period in which modern architecture began to seek a new decorative enrichment for its stark surfaces and unadorned structure, a similar movement was taking place within the Catholic Church itself. However, rather than a return to ornament, which in fact the Church had never abandoned, the latter movement involved a rejection of the tasteless and sentimental liturgical art that had become almost standard throughout the Western world

For at least the past one hundred years, the usual statuary, stained glass, altarpieces, and other decorative church furnishings have been executed by artists of indifferent talents: copyists, rather than creators. But even as copyists these men have proved inadequate. Although their designs purport to follow tradition, they wholly lack the almost brutal power and majesty, the Gothic grotesquerie, the mystical distortion of the masterpieces of the past, their alleged counterparts. The artistic revival within the Church aims to replace such lifeless banalities with works of contemporary genius. This movement can, in essence, be compared to the Liturgical Revival, for it represents a return of the Church to a truly traditional position — that of patron to the leading artists of its age.

Like the Liturgical Revival also, this movement was conceived in Europe, but centered in France. The late Father Pierre Couturier, O. P., a Dominican friar who at the age of 27 gave up a promising career as an artist to become a monk, was the man most directly responsible for this revival of the arts within the French Catholic Church. Indeed, he dedicated his life to the realization of this goal. Before his death in 1954, Father Couturier saw the consecration of three churches * with blazing stained glass, tapestries, frescoes, mosaics, wood carving, metal work — all commissioned under his authority — representing the work of the foremost artists of modern France. Since his death, plans for other churches that he conceived have been carried forward.

As is usual in breaking new ground, controversy has surrounded Father Couturier and the churches under his sponsorship. The greatest criticism stemmed from the fact that most of the artists employed were irreligious men and indeed some of them were known anticlericals. Yet they have produced some of the most brilliant, profound, and moving ecclesiastical works to appear in centuries. It is significant also that, among bequests helping to pay for the art work of the first of Father Couturier's controversial churches — Notre Dame de Toute Grâce at Assy — he received a donation from the late Pope Pius XII.

The problem of the artist's irreligiosity did not exist during the great flowering of ecclesiastical art in the Middle Ages when all western civilizations were encompassed within the authority of the Church. Today, how-

* Notre Dame de Toute Grâce in Assy, and The Chapel of the Rosary in Vence (both shown), and Church of the Sacred Heart, Audincourt.

ever, the problem is an important one. Father Couturier has explained his views on it:

It was not theoretical reasons of doctrine but on the contrary considerations of a primarily practical nature that impelled us to summon these artists. We called on them purely and simply because they were the greatest — because, in fact, they were the best painters and sculptors of our day. We believed that it was our duty to procure for God and our Faith the best art of the present. That was our first reason.

We were tired of always seeing in our churches the most mediocre examples of painting and sculpture. In the long run, we thought, this mediocrity could only result in seriously altering the religious psychology of clergy and worshippers alike. We were also aware that unbelievers, comparing these works to the great Christian art of the past, would inevitably question the vitality of a Faith and a Church that could remain content with them. . . .

For more than a century, imagination — the true innovator of all new form — has remained completely outside of, and alien to, the Church. Life withdrew from the Church. The only great Christian artist alive, Rouault, had to wait until he reached the age of 80 before seeing one of his works admitted to a church — and that was actually at Assy.

These are very simple, very concrete facts which no serious person can controvert. I should add that never before in the entire history of Christianity has such a situation prevailed. . . .

Under these circumstances, if we wanted to work effectively towards a renaissance of Christian art, we had to go in quest of life where it existed, that is, among those who are today the true masters of living art. For it is only life that can be born, or reborn; and when rebirth is in question, one needs life which is as vigorous as the preceding decay has been long and profound. In such a crisis, lesser talents would never suffice. . . . In periods and societies where traditions are still living traditions, minor artists are enough to ensure the continuous production of whatever art religion may require. But they are not adequate to bring about a resurrection; that is entirely beyond their powers.

On the other hand, great artists — truly great men — are never very numerous. One must take those there are, wherever one can find them.

Thus, the first difficulty arose; the majority of these artists were not religious men. . . . For the record, we have consistently both believed and stated that the ideal way in which to revive Christian art would always be to have geniuses who happened to be saints at the same time. But under the actual conditions, since men of this kind did not exist, we believed that if we were to effect a revival of liturgical art it would be safer to turn to geniuses without faith than to believers without talent.

Still, this posed a real problem. One could certainly look for strong, vital works from men of this sort; but could one expect truly religious works? . . .

We believed that we could, and for the following reasons. . . . Our choice was between life and death. . . .

Where there is no natural life, there can be no supernatural life; and where there is no living art, no sacred art can be possible either, for actually there is no art at all.

We had further reasons for our confidence. In the first place, isn't it jumping to conclusions to say so quickly, "These men are not Christians?" After all, how does one know? Remember what St. Augustine said of the Church: "Many are outside who believe themselves to be within, and many are within who believe themselves to be without."

Furthermore, it is a grave error to think that art's true sources lie in the realm of conscious choices, deliberate decisions, and rational thought. This is not true. For every artist, the purest and most indispensable fountainheads arise from a certain inward realm in which reason and will lose their power — precisely from the secret and persistent realm of childhood. There lies that enchanted domain which great artists cherish throughout their lives as the purest, most precious part of themselves. Within that domain and in that obscure shade the deep, mysterious Christian sources never entirely deteriorate. Matisse once said to Picasso, "You well know that what we all strive to recapture in our art is the atmosphere of our First Communion."

Still another reason is that expressed by Delacroix when he said, "One should always bet on genius." Great artists are always inspired, and by the same token they have a natural disposition for spiritual intuitions. . . . No matter how casually one may have followed such matters, one cannot help having noticed how the gifts of great artists operate in them in a manner exactly analogous to the workings of what theology calls the "gifts of the Holy Spirit," which inspire the mystics and the saints, leading them infallibly to their goal without any rational explanation . . . .

Finally it was our conviction that even that very ignorance of religious matters with which one or another of these artists has been reproached could actually serve a useful purpose for a renaissance. In the midst of an age grown mature, it could provide a freshness, a virginity of thought and feeling, an atmosphere in which Christian themes might begin to renew themselves. And it must be said that our expectations have been fully justified.

Reference

Couturier, Pierre Marie-Alain, "Religious Art and the Modern Artist," *Magazine of Art*, November 1951.

NOTE: *To those American churches wishing to call upon the finest contemporary artists — either acknowledged masters or the newer talents — the authors recommend the advice of two men who are thoroughly familiar with the field and at the same time are unofficial spokesmen on artistic matters for their respective faiths. They are Maurice Lavanaux, editor,* Liturgical Arts, *7 East 42 St., New York, N.Y. (Roman Catholic), and Marvin Halverson, educational director, Department of Worship and the Arts, National Council of Churches, 297 Fourth Ave., New York, N.Y. (Protestant).*

13. CHURCH OF NOTRE DAME DE TOUTE GRACE

Assy, France; Consecrated 1950
Father Pierre Marie-Alain Couturier, O.P.
(1897-1954), patron
Maurice Novarina and Edouard Malot, architects
Exterior mosaic mural: Fernand Léger
Altar tapestry: Jean Lurçat
Tiled panel: Henri Matisse
Interior mural: Paul Bonnard
Stained glass: Georges Rouault, Jean Bazaine, Paul Ber-
çot, Paul Bony, Maurice Brianchon, Adeline Hebert-
Stevens, Father Pierre Marie-Alain Couturier, O.P.
Bronze tabernacle door: Georges Braque
Altar mosaic: Theodore Strawinski
Sculptured ceiling beams: Constant Demaison
Sculptured panel (yet to be executed): Jacques Lipchitz
Baptistry (paintings and stained glass yet to be executed):
Marc Chagall

*"We believed that it was our duty to procure for God
and our faith the best art of the present."*
— FATHER PIERRE MARIE-ALAIN COUTURIER, O.P.

The architecture of Notre Dame de Toute Grâce, Assy, France, is undistinguished and occasionally awkward. It is a modified and modernized version of the typical rustic chalet of the Alps Mountains, in the midst of which the church nestles. Built of rough blocks of greenish-gray granite — the local stone — its major virtue is that it blends well with the rugged terrain surrounding it. The major fault found with it by critics is its heavy exterior pillars, each a pylon of great granite blocks, which support nothing more weighty than the gable end of a wooden frame roof. The massive, 91-ft. campanile is also out of scale with the size of the church itself.

However, this rudely conceived piece of architecture acts as the setting for a blaze of jewels.

The entire entrance wall behind the great pylons is surfaced with a mosaic mural of heroic scale, in brilliant coral red, cerulean blue, golden yellow, and black. At night this facade is floodlighted so that it blazes, seemingly alone, against the deeps of earth and sky.

This same entrance wall is pierced with small, arched windows, six set low and six set high. From the exterior, appearing black, they act as repetitive accents within the colorful mosaic, and are in fact hardly discernible as windows at all. From the interior they reveal themselves as abstract portrayals of the saints, glowing with rich reds, purples, blues, greens, and yellows, heavily lined with black.

Upon entering the church one sees, across the dimly illuminated nave, covering nearly the entire wall above the altar, and flooded with light, a huge tapestry of grotesque apocalyptic themes in black, white, gray, scarlet, green, and gold, by the master of modern tapestry making, Jean Lurçat.

To the left of the chancel, visible through an arch, is a black line drawing of St. Dominic, on a lemon yellow background, designed and executed by Henri Matisse.

A small chapel dedicated to St. Veronica is separated from the nave by the gems of the stained glass collection: a head of St. Veronica, a bouquet, and a seated Christ, all by the late Georges Rouault. In these stained glass windows, tones of garnet, topaz, and sapphire smoulder against an almost black background.

Overhead in the main body of the church, heavy side beams, which brace the sloping roof, have been carved into the elongated and stylized likenesses of saints — dim shapes floating eerily above the quiet nave.

There is nothing pretty nor sweet about any of the works of art in this church. They are instead, powerful, bold, commanding, blazing; they strike the beholder with tremendous emotional force. To those accustomed to the saccharine statuary and stained glass that passes for art in most twentieth century churches, they come as an unnerving shock. Indeed today we are so unused to integrity in art that the works at Assy may at first be quite misunderstood. But a deeper examination reveals how suitable they are for expressing the stern and sometimes brutal Biblical passages from which their symbolism is taken.

Perhaps even more than the Liturgical Revival in architecture, these works of art deepen liturgical understanding, revealing the Christian faith as one encompassing the depths of suffering and the heights of majesty. They give to the Catholic Church once more a grandeur and authority largely suppressed since the Middle Ages.

Dimitri Kessel - *Life*. Copr. Time Inc.

Exterior of Notre Dame de Toute Grâce as it appears floodlighted at night. The tremendous blazing mosaic that covers the entire triangular entrance facade is based on the Litany of the Blessed Virgin — Notre Dame de Toute Grâce — to whom the church is consecrated. The focal point of the design is a head of the Virgin within a golden medallion, from which extend tongues of fire, the whole superimposed on a second circle of brilliant yellow, outlined in gold. This flaming circle recreates the apocalyptic text of the "Woman clothed with the sun," which forms also the basis of the Lurçat altar tapestry shown on the following pages. Above the medallion and the flames are two crosses.

The remainder of the design consists of geometric overlapping planes of color — coral red, deep blue, and yellow — also outlined with gold, and radiating out from the medallion of the Virgin. On each of the colored planes a different, mystical symbol of the Virgin is superimposed in gold: mystical rose, tower of David, tower of ivory, house of gold, ark of the covenant, gate of heaven, morning star. On each of the gold strips separating the planes of color, the appropriate mystic text from the Litany is inscribed in black.

In this emblematic work of art, even the choice of colors may be considered symbolic. The three primary colors — red, yellow, and blue — represent an artistic trinity, from which all other colors are derived. They therefore denote primacy, the first and, by extension, the source, the Creator. Taken individually, blue is the color of the Virgin to which is added red, the color of life, and yellow, the color of the sun, evoking once again the apocalyptic "Woman clothed with the sun" who brought forth life. The choice of these brilliant primary colors, rather than muted tones, is thus seen to be of sacred as well as artistic significance.

One of the most persistent criticisms of this church has been of its heavy columns, which cut across the mosaic and, some feel, detract from its effect. It is the opinion of the authors that these pylons, although they cannot be structurally justified, add to, rather than detract from, the impact of the mosaic behind them. The design is so powerful that it is in no way overborne by the massive silhouettes of the columns. Rather, the heavy striping of black serves to bring out the glorious color. In the daytime, against greenish-gray stone, the effect would be less dramatic, perhaps less pleasing.

Altar tapestry by Jean Lurçat, although wholly a contemporary work, catches the Gothic spirit of the Middle Ages.

Grotesque beasts, reminiscent of ancient gargoyles, contrast with a resplendent Virgin, clothed in the golden flames of the sun. Here and there, surrealistic symbolism recalls the work of the fifteenth century Dutch painter of heaven and hell, Hieronymus Bosch.

The tapestry is divided into four panels, and each symbolically portrays a part of the same awesome theme: the battle between Life and Death from the *Apocalypse of St. John the Apostle.*

On a dead black background, in configurations of white, black, gray, scarlet, and gold, the major panel depicts the dragon of Satan and the Virgin with Child. Of these figures it was written in the *Apocalypse*:

"And a great sign appeared in heaven: a woman clothed with the sun, and the moon was under her feet, and upon her head a crown of twelve stars. And being with child, she cried out in her travail and was in the anguish of delivery. And another sign was seen in heaven, and behold, a great... dragon having seven heads and ten horns, and upon his heads seven diadems. And his tail was dragging along the third part of the stars of heaven, and it dashed them to the earth; and the dragon stood before the woman who was about to bring forth, that when she had brought forth he might devour her son. And she brought forth a male child, who is to rule all nations with a rod of iron; and her child was caught up to God and to his throne."

This text of the *Apocalypse* then continues in the narrower subordinate panel at the bottom of the tapestry. Here, upon a background of purest white, St. Michael is depicted battling with, and defeating Satan, the same seven-headed dragon shown in the major panel above. The dragon's defeat is accomplished through the

blood of the Lamb and the word of witness, each depicted symbolically within the two interlocking circles superimposed upon St. Michael.

"And there was a battle in heaven; Michael and his angels battled with the dragon, and the dragon fought and his angels. And they did not prevail, neither was their place found any more in heaven. And that great dragon was cast down, the ancient serpent, he who is called the devil and Satan, who leads astray the whole world; and he was cast down to the earth and with him his angels were cast down.... And they overcame him through the blood of the Lamb and through the word of their witness, for they did not love their lives even in face of death."

When this photograph was taken, the tapestry had not yet been completed. Another vertical panel has since been added at the right side, balancing the vertical panel at left and carrying the apocalyptic text still further. Here on a verdant green ground, now rises the tree of salvation, symbolizing Christ and his mystic genealogy, the fruit of the dragon's defeat. The *Apocalypse* proclaims:

"And I heard a loud voice in heaven saying, 'Now has come the salvation, and the power and the kingdom of our God, and the authority of his Christ; For the accuser of our brethren has been cast down, he who accused them before our God day and night....'"

The fourth and remaining panel, placed vertically at left, represents the culmination of the battle between Life and Death. On a ground of deep blood red rises the tree of life everlasting, the fruit of salvation, awaiting him who overcomes the dragon:

"He who has an ear, let him hear what the Spirit says to the churches: Him who overcomes I will permit to eat of the tree of life, which is in the paradise of my God."

Dimitri Kessel—*Life*

Seated Christ is one of three stained glass windows by the late Georges Rouault, recognized as the greatest twentieth century interpreter of religious themes. Both a great modernist and a devout Roman Catholic, Rouault devoted his life to exploring the depths of the Christian faith in his art. But the church at Assy is the first and only church to make use of his unparalleled talents. Because of his devout faith, Rouault presented these windows without charge to Notre Dame de Toute Grâce as a gift to God. Critic Jerome Mellquist has said of the Rouault windows:

"All glow with the subterranean fires of this artist, graphic in their black leadings, opalescent in their gleaming. Particularly the mutilated Christ somehow touches the very core of pity. These provide a matchless repose and hushed atmosphere for the church."

After a pilgrimage to Assy, the Rev. James Douaire wrote:

"Perhaps the most effective of the Rouault windows is a superb Seated Christ mocked and crowned with thorns. All the love and humility of a suffering Christ is pressed into the burning glass. Only the consummate artistry of a man of Rouault's stature could accomplish a work as decorative and truly profound. Here at last the greatest religious artist of our times has been employed in the decoration of a church."

References

Douaire, James. "Pilgrimage to Assy — an Appraisal," *Liturgical Arts,* November 1950.

Mellquist, Jerome. "Chapel at Assy: A Twentieth Century Canterbury," *Art Digest,* December 1951.

14. CHAPEL OF THE ROSARY

Vence, France; Erected 1950
Henri Matisse (1870-1954) artist and designer
Auguste Perret, architectural supervisor

*"When I see a picture, I forget what it represents; all
that is important is line, form, and colors...."*

— HENRI MATISSE

Since its consecration in June of 1951, the Chapel of
the Rosary, built for a nursing order of Dominican Nuns
in the small village of Vence, France, has become one
of the famous modern churches of the world. Like the
church at Assy, shown on the preceding pages, it too
was executed under the sponsorship of Father Couturier
as part of his crusade for the revival of liturgical arts.
But the two churches could hardly be more different.

The church of Notre Dame de Tout Grâce (No. 13),
set amidst the towering peaks of the French Alps, demonstrates in terms of modern art the ancient majesty
and apocalyptic power of the Catholic Church. By
contrast, the tiny Chapel of the Rosary, in the south of
France, high above the shimmering Mediterranean, is
a celebration of Christian joy.

There is another difference: the importance of Notre
Dame de Toute Grâce lies in its use as a rough and
rugged setting for artistic jewels by fifteen different modern artists. The Chapel of the Rosary is instead a
unified concept, a single, polished work of art which,
from architecture to priests' chasubles, was designed by
one man. That man was the late, great Henri Matisse
who, during his lifetime, gained recognition as the master
colorist of the modern age.

In this, his masterwork, Matisse has played the almost
pulsating brilliance of electric blue, emerald green, and
lemon yellow, in stained glass windows, against floor,
ceiling, and wall surfaces of pure white, the latter broken
only by simple black outline drawings of St. Dominic,
the Virgin and Child, and the stations of the cross.
No red, purple, or orange is used within the church and
no color at all except in the windows. By these calculated
omissions, the interior becomes a lambent pool of re-
fracted light, gradually shading with the changing position of the sun from predominantly celestial blue to
an underwater green. The extraordinary light within
the chapel appears to be almost a living presence, and
yet it is nothing concrete that one can touch or even
see except as a vapor of color. While glowing with life,
this atmosphere is at the same time ethereally serene,
an artistic paradox precisely expressing the combination
of earthly and otherearthly radiance that is the polarity
of Christian joy. The contrast between chaste white
walls and the exuberant colors of the stained glass — not
obscured by the subtler coloring of the air itself — seems
to repeat in stronger and more extreme terms the paradox sensed in the quality of the light.

Matisse considered the Chapel of the Rosary "a chance
to apply the researches of my whole life." And in
describing these researches he explained:

"Thus it is that simple colors can act upon the inner
feelings with all the more force because they are simple.
A blue, for instance, accompanied by the shimmer of its
complementaries, acts upon the feelings like a sharp blow
on a gong... and the artist must be able to sound them
when he needs to.... In the chapel my chief aim was
to balance a surface of light and color against a solid
white wall covered with black drawings."

Matisse further described what he hoped to achieve
in the chapel as "the lightness and joyousness of springtime which never lets anyone suspect the labors it has
cost."

Nutzenberger

White chapel interior conveys a sense of delicacy, of purity, of ethereal serenity. Within this chaste retreat, the blue leaves and yellow blossoms of the stained glass altar window reach toward a golden sun like a burst of springtime. Behind the flower-like patterns, a field of green shades upward into celestial blue near the sun disk, heightening the effect of ascendant movement. At the same time, the containment of this movement within the relatively small window embrasures suggests a contrast between earthly limitations and the spacious calm of colorless infinity.

The only other decorations in the chapel are simple black line drawings — reductions of the human form to a spiritual essence. Seen here is the huge figure of St. Dominic facing the transept seating of the nuns across the sanctuary. Father Couturier himself was the model for this Matisse condensation of saintly character.

As an expression of the Liturgical Revival, the sanctuary is entirely open to the nave and is raised just one step above its floor level. This tiny chapel provides space for only 20 nuns in the transept and 80 worshippers in the nave. No pews have been included in the latter space since this is not a parish church and the nave is often unoccupied.

View of carved wooden stalls, designed for daily use by the Dominican sisters, shows their close relationship to the altar in a shallow transept. This placement shields the nuns from sight of visiting worshippers.

The altar is in the western end of the building, placed on a diagonal half turned toward the transept, half turned toward the nave. In order to face east, as is the tradition in the Catholic Church, the priest stands behind the altar, turning toward the congregation rather than away from it during celebration of the Mass. This is an unorthodox position, but one which was the norm in the great Roman basilicas of the fourth and fifth centuries. Presumably, it was used here in order that Matisse's concept of color and light — dependent for its success upon the relationship of windows to sun — might be realized.

Drawing of Virgin and Child overlooks the nave and is washed by blue, green, and yellow light from the facing series of stained glass windows. Lines here are flowing and ample. But the severe frontal position of the Madonna and the outstretching arms of the Child, which form the cross, give a suggestion of indomitable

prescience to the two figures. Father Couturier reports the remark of an old woman of Vence: "It is much better that the Holy Virgin should have no face — that way each may see her as he wishes."

In sharp contrast to the rounded grace of the Virgin is the almost brutal execution of the stations of the cross at the rear of the church. These drawings recall the cipher-like graffiti found in grottoes of the primitive Church. Alfred H. Barr, Jr. comments on these drawings:

"The drawing is almost savagely abrupt, scratched and rough, the whole effect painful and antidecorative as befits a picture of the brutal and heroic story of Calvary. So concentrated and elliptical is the style that for the non-Catholic, who does not know the iconography of the stations by heart, a written gloss is almost necessary before some of the scenes become legible; but to most Catholics, generally conditioned by the banal sweetness of ordinary modern stations, Matisse's version though intelligible must be shocking in its terse austerity. Obviously it was not Matisse's intention here to please."

Hélène Adant

Hélène Adant

←

Confessional door, the most beautiful architectural detail of the chapel, is carved wood painted white. The circle and diamond shapes recall the Persian folk designs incorporated in many of Matisse's secular paintings. Here, however, they have been artfully organized into a new composition, the panels of which are bounded by the Christian cross.

This confessional is also a testament to Matisse's genius with color. The evanescent vapor of green light which fills the nave produces a complementary effect of pinkish mauve within the confessional. This color serves as the background against which the white latticework of the door is silhouetted.

Two of the vivid chasubles which Matisse designed for this chapel, using his famous "cut-outs" of pure color. These silken vestments represent the only departure from the blue-green-yellow scheme of the chapel interior — except, of course, the complementary wash of light in the confessional.

Green is the predominating color of those worn at ordinary Masses, forming an unbroken harmony with the chapel itself. But high holy days and special services are set apart by striking contrasts. A clear scarlet is used for the feast days of the martyrs; violet and rose signify the penitence of Lent; a vibrating gold on pure white the joy of Easter. Masses for the dead are said in mourning black with white appliques.

Note the delicate candlesticks and slender, elongated crucifix. Like everything within the chapel, these, too, were designed by the artist.

Hélène Adant

Exterior views of the Chapel of the Rosary show altar windows; near and far views of the transept windows. The architecture of the church is, fittingly, subordinated to the stained glass, acting primarily as a sounding board for its gong-like colors. No effort has been made, nor could it have been made by Matisse, the artist, to explore the structural possibilities of his building material, reinforced concrete. The chapel is therefore little more than a smooth concrete envelope, unbroken except by the slender, round-headed windows, and painted white on the exterior as well as the interior.*

However, even though the Chapel of the Rosary is undistinguished from a structural point of view, artis-

tically it is exquisite. The plain, whitewashed walls reflect the strong sun of the Mediterranean, making the building stand out in brilliant clarity against surrounding greenery. The roof of the chapel is surfaced with blue tile in a geometric saw-tooth pattern; this blue is an opaque repetition of the transparent blue of the stained glass windows. Atop the roof rises a spire and cross of black wrought iron, a delicate and yet sharply definitive silhouette against the sky. From distant view the chapel looks as though it were part of a larger landscape painting, consciously designed, as doubtless it was.

References

Barr, Alfred H., Jr. *Matisse: His Art and His Public*. Museum of Modern Art, New York (1951).

Flanner, Janet. "King of the Wild Beasts," *The New Yorker*, December 22, 1951 and December 29, 1951.

"Henri Matisse," *Life*, November 26, 1951.

* Conceived by Matisse, the design of the building was technically supervised by the late Auguste Perret, famous French pioneer in reinforced concrete, whose own masterpiece, Notre Dame du Raincy, begins this book.

15. CHAPEL OF ST. PIERRE

Villefranche-sur-Mer, France; Consecrated 1957
Jean Cocteau (b. 1889), artist

"As an artist I wanted to create a chapel in which the poet, without losing any of his prerogatives, would become immediately accessible to fishermen and simple people." — JEAN COCTEAU

The Chapel of St. Pierre, Villefranche-sur-Mer, on a wharf jutting out into the blue Mediterranean, shows the transformation that can be worked on an existing structure by the hands of an artist alone. This modest building, which dates from the fourteenth century, had been used for generations by local fishermen as a storage and mending place for their nets. But today, by artistic alchemy, it has been transformed into a mystical temple to God.

Jean Cocteau, the celebrated French surrealist, has decorated the whole of the interior of the little building with strange and disturbing frescoes, symbolically depicting episodes from the life of St. Peter, the patron saint of fishermen, to whom the chapel is dedicated.

The chapel had in its favor the rounded interior arches typical of the Romanesque period. These have been incorporated as part of the background for the continuous painting, giving separation and depth to the episodic, linear tracery that now covers nearly every interior surface. Cocteau has explained the design:

"The chapel offers the aspect of an iridescent bubble, or of a vast net of significant lines. The very pale colors are cousins of the mother of pearl, of the pearl, of the egg, of Piero della Francesca.... [This chapel is] the crown of my work. In doing it I did not use my mind but my heart."

The stories told and the symbols used have been taken from theology, but many find their counterpart also in the recesses of the human subconscious. Indeed, the Chapel of St. Pierre suggests that the branch of modern art entitled surrealism is well suited to expressing the mystical concepts of the Church that, if too realistically portrayed, are not portrayed at all. Unlike abstract art, which devotes itself primarily to line, form, and color — often without reference to real objects — surrealism portrays the real, but distorts it by unreal juxtapositions into a symbol. This art form consciously attempts to tap that source described earlier by Father Couturier as an "enchanted domain ... a certain inward realm in which reason and will lose their power."

It is interesting to recall that, in less self-conscious periods of the past, "surrealism," although unnamed, was so taken for granted as a part of the human psyche that it was unhesitatingly used to express allegorical concepts beyond the surface reporting of realistic art. Indeed, the greatest examples even of realistic art have a touch of the unreal, a heightened emphasis, which is one of the qualities that makes them great.

Today, the scientific plumbing of the subconscious has made this mystic realm both more and less accessible to the Church. More, because it has been brought out into the light of conscious scrutiny as never before. Less, because of the schism between psychoanalytical and ecclesiastical interpretations of this realm.

But the fact that the Catholic Church differs from science in its view of the subconscious does not mean that it should abandon the field to secular interests. Symbolism is, and always has been, inseparable from religion itself. And it is true also that the symbolic in story, song, or picture, creates the deepest and most lasting impact, reaching as it does beyond conscious thought to the most mysterious realm of being.

View of exterior partially obscured by scaffolding during the renovation of the chapel, shows the modest character of the original architecture.

View from entrance looking toward the altar, reveals the artistic transformation that has been wrought upon the interior. Existing arches have been exploited as definitive elements within a continuous fresco. Dark traceries against pale, mother-of-pearl background colors are the means by which Cocteau has achieved this magical atmosphere.

Photos: Marc Riboud—Magnum

Entrance to chapel is guarded by huge ceramic candlesticks which culminate in "the eye of God." The watching eye is a characteristic device of surrealism, here doubtless symbolizing that all earthly actions are seen and judged. This view is taken from behind the altar, which is on a direct axis with the entrance portal, and thus under its guardian eyes. In the foreground, upon the altar, is a copper dove designed by Cocteau as a tabernacle for the Eucharist. The dove is the traditional symbol of the Holy Spirit, here depicted with wings outspread over the eucharistic receptacle, from which radiate rays of copper. Ceramic altar candlesticks echo the design of those flanking the entrance.

→

Altar fresco behind the altar portrays Christ reassuring St. Peter as an angel helps the frightened fisherman to walk on the waters. Other fishermen look up in fearfull wonder. Although this mural portrays recognizable figures from the Biblical text, it conveys also the generalized idea of calm in the midst of turbulence. St. Peter and the waters appear almost to quake upon the wall, while the figure of Christ is poised in serenity and assurance.

Detail of altar fresco shows watching fisherman as he gazes upward at St. Peter and Christ. Unlike them he has fish for eyes, perhaps signifying that he sees only through the blinders of his own limited experience. This is a typical surrealist hieroglyph, by which attention is arrested and allegorical meanings suggested to the beholder.

Figures in betrayal of Christ register lustful hatred, anguish, indifference, and sly enjoyment. Seldom has the range of man's cruelty been more vividly and yet simply portrayed. The effect is heightened by the contrast between the dark outlines of the figures and the pale, ethereal background upon which they are imposed. In this way, the tension between worldly suffering and otherworldly benediction has been expressed through the very colors employed.

The artistry by which this interior has been transformed into a web of beauty and meaning, suggests a solution for many American churches. Those congregations that, for a variety of reasons, cannot move from outmoded quarters, could work a similar transformation upon the existing church. Secular buildings could be purchased economically and changed into churches by the artist's touch. Moreover, there are in this country scores of artists of the highest talent and with a great range of stylistic approaches who would be eager to undertake such work, but who have never been asked. Here lies an unusual opportunity for the Church to reassume her traditional position as patron of the arts.

Reference

"Cocteau in the Chapel," *Newsweek*, July 15, 1957.

INTEGRATION: Toward a New Church Architecture

It becomes evident that five major streams of development have been following their separate but parallel courses: the renewal of the liturgy that demands new plans and forms in architecture; the investigation of structure by which new plans can be most forcefully expressed in new forms; the regaining of the traditional position of the Church as patron of contemporary arts; the search for simplicity in architecture, which can make of the church building a subordinate background to both liturgy and works of art; and, finally, the expansion of the contemporary philosophy of design to permit suitable decorative enrichment.

In each of the churches shown previously, one of these five developmental streams has taken precedence, although the other four have seldom been entirely neglected. Moreover, in many church designs it will always be necessary to emphasize one over another. A limited budget or a strong vernacular building tradition can make regional simplicity the only logical aim in design. The choice of modern materials such as reinforced concrete or steel may push the structural system to the forefront of importance. A strong urge by clergy or congregation toward the visual, symbolic representation of mystical concepts may lead to a subordination of architecture to works of art. Or a wish to return to the fundamental meanings of the liturgy may make the plan of the church its major concern.

Even so, it is to be hoped that these five streams, which have been developing in relative independence during the past 30 years, may merge and fuse to produce a fully realized ecclesiastical architecture as expressive of our own age as the Gothic was expressive of medieval times.

This trend does not mean that all modern churches might eventually be designed in one stye as immediately recognizable as the Gothic. When medieval builders pushed stone to its ultimate potential in Gothic cathedrals, the potential was clearly in one direction. Today, the potential of reinforced concrete for example, lies in many directions.

Furthermore, modern architecture does not care to limit itself to one material. The form potentialities of steel, although few in comparison to reinforced concrete, nevertheless represent a challenge almost as exciting and entirely different (see the German Stahl Kirche No. 18, by Otto Bartning). New techniques of laminating and molding wood have given this ancient material some of the plasticity of reinforced concrete (see the Zion Lutheran Church, No. 19, Portland, Ore., by

Pietro Belluschi). At the same time, traditional methods of building with wood, brick, and stone can still be utilized to produce contemporary designs of integrity and beauty.

If truly great church architecture is to emerge in our age, however, it will inevitably incorporate all the developmental streams the authors have attempted to trace in this section of the book. Great architecture is a balanced creation, as opposed to a simply structural feat of engineering, no matter how arresting the result of this limited approach may be. That is why the position of the architect must be elevated over that of the structural engineer even when he himself happens to be the engineer. It is his balancing of the varied elements of design, his ability to encompass and resolve possibly competitive elements into a harmonious whole, that distinguishes him as an architect, in the full meaning of that word.

The pilgrimage chapel of Notre Dame du Haut at Ronchamp, France, shown on the following pages, represents as nearly balanced a work of church architecture as any thus far constructed in the modern age. It was designed by Le Corbusier, one of the giants of modern architecture.

In his early career, Corbusier was a leading exponent of the stark, rectilinear, and unadorned International Style that took its inspiration from the machine and from the cubistic art of the early twentieth century. But over the years Corbusier departed from his original conception of design. Always a master of reinforced concrete, he began to handle it with ever greater boldness, fluidity, and movement. A sculptor and painter of talent as well as a great architect, he has partially amalgamated these different disciplines, bringing more of the quality of sculpture into his architecture and bringing his painter's command of line and color into play to provide a decorative adornment thoroughly integrated with his building concept.

It is hardly surprising, therefore, that a church by Le Corbusier — incidentally his first and only church design — should blend within it several of the streams of development that other church architects have expressed more one-sidedly.

As a result the Chapel of Notre Dame du Haut is a study in the plasticity of reinforced concrete; a study in the integration of art and architecture; a study in the new liturgy of plan and form. It resembles nothing as yet devised by the mind of man, and yet the atmosphere it creates is as ancient as religion itself.

16. CHAPEL OF NOTRE DAME DU HAUT

Ronchamp, France; Erected 1955
Le Corbusier (b. 1887), architect

"The key is light and light illuminates shapes and shapes have an emotional power...." — Le Corbusier

Set atop a wild and windswept foothill of the Vosges Mountains of France, the Chapel of Notre Dame du Haut — Our Lady of the Height — is capped by clouds, and itself caps the lower-lying vistas that surround it and extend from it into the blue distances of the horizon. This Haut Lieu, High Place, is an observation post in the Belfort Gap, the key invasion route through France, and chapels built upon the height have time and again been destroyed by war — the last chapel meeting its traditional fate in 1945, during the closing year of World War II.

It was inevitable that Notre Dame du Haut should be built again, for its hilltop has been considered hallowed ground almost since time began, the site of ancient pagan as well as later Christian rites and pilgrimages. Several unsuccessful attempts were made to design a fitting church for this site before Le Corbusier, the leading, but also the most controversial architect in France, was persuaded to undertake it. Some felt that the bold and machine-like style of Le Corbusier would not be appropriate to this sacred spot and this country setting. Although now considering Notre Dame du Haut "the pearl of my career," Corbusier himself at first protested that his system of handling reinforced concrete "should only be for utilitarian structures."

After a visit to the site he changed his mind. If the design of the chapel waited upon Corbusier, it would seem also that Corbusier's talents were waiting upon the chapel. For it was not until Notre Dame du Haut that the sculptor in Corbusier broke entirely free from the rectilinear mold of his earlier architecture. Never, until this church, were his art and architecture so fully integrated. And never did his interpretation of function in form achieve more inspired expression.

Architectural Forum has stated that "Ronchamp may well become the most influential church of our time." The *Architectural Review* calls it "The most influential contribution by an acknowledged master to nonrectangular design." And Dominican Father Regamey, of Ronchamp itself, describes the chapel as "hard and soft at the same time, like the Gospels.... It shows a way back to the truth and clearness of Christianity."

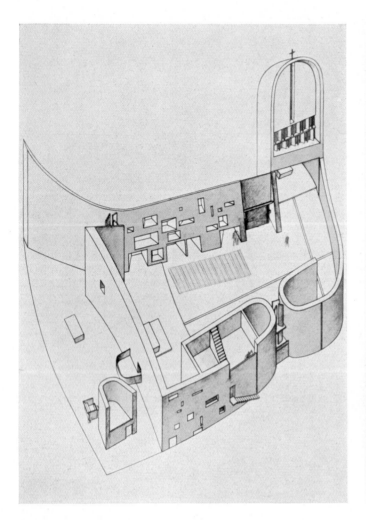

The unusual plan of this remarkable chapel is best grasped from the bird's-eye drawing. The nave opens out from rear to front to reach its widest point at the sanctuary. This blunted trapezoid insures that all worshippers will be near the altar. Furthermore, the sanctuary is entirely open and is but one step above the floor level of the nave. There are no separate choir stalls. An atmosphere of unity and sacramental intimacy is the inevitable result of such an arrangement.

Subsidiary elements of the plan include: along the north wall, two small alcove chapels and a sacristy; in the south wall, toward the rear, a third, larger alcove chapel. The entrance door — next to the third chapel — is one great panel, pivoted at center, which can be swung entirely open for processionals.

Circulation within the church is excellent. Pews are placed along the south wall, immediately reached from the entrance door. This leaves the rear and north side of the nave free — for processionals, for overflow worshippers, and as an access path to the three chapels.

Because it is a pilgrimage church, pews are provided for only a few people, although the nave can hold 200. The secluded chapels are used by single individuals or by small groups of pilgrims. A third place of worship, for the large gatherings that occur periodically is provided out-of-doors. This outside sanctuary backs up against the main sanctuary of the interior, and opens out onto a broad meadow where as many as 10,000

pilgrims can congregate. Direct access between inner and outer sanctuaries is provided by a small door between front and side walls of the church, toward the south.

The entire structure and plan of the chapel, both vertically and horizontally, has been laid out on Corbusier's "modulor," a system of standardized dimensioning which keeps everything in proper scale. With this system, certain spaces can be reduced to very small size without visually appearing so. In fact, Corbusier defies anyone to give offhand the dimensions of the different parts of the building.

Sculptural forms of Notre Dame du Haut change and flow and develop as one walks around the building. The side view, with the roof like a cresting wave, is that seen by pilgrims as they approach up the hillside path. The front view reveals the secluded porch that is equipped as a permanent outdoor sanctuary for great gatherings of pilgrims on the adjoining meadow. At the rear the towers of Notre Dame take precedence, jutting from the main curvilinear bulk of the church like proclamations.

Because the forms of this church are unprecedented in religious architecture, they are not easily read by the uninitiated. But to the informed eye they are a model of clarity, vividly articulating the areas within. The three round-headed towers, one large and two small, mark the three secluded alcove chapels that rim the nave. The main body of the church is seen to increase

Lucien Hervé

G. E. Kidder Smith

in height from rear to front, indicating the progression from nave to main chancel to outdoor sanctuary. The final upward and outward thrust of the south wall marks the point at which it leaves the church enclosure and becomes a screen for the outdoor sanctuary.

The difficulty of this amazing building lies — of course — in its endless curvilinearity. It is apparently impossible to find a straight line which does not somewhere bend into a curve; nor is it possible to find two major walls where lines are truly parallel. Formal balance is entirely lacking. Instead, the chapel is a flowing sculpture, its shape dependent upon the fluidity that is the unique property of reinforced concrete. But only an architect who possessed "command of his material so complete as to be almost subconscious" could have produced such a work.

G. E. Kidder Smith

The walls of Notre Dame du Haut prove conclusively that the concrete frame has not been outmoded as a vehicle of modern design by newer structural concepts. Rather than the more radical warped slab used by Felix Candela in the Church of La Virgen Milagrosa (No. 3), Corbusier has here chosen a modification of the classic post-and-lintel system. In his hands the supposedly rectilinear frame has been made to perform with a fluidity and movement equal to, although quite distinct from, that of the continuous vaulting of La Virgen Milagrosa.

But this is a concrete frame with a difference. Unlike the usual concept of the frame as an element to be exposed and separated from the curtain wall it supports, Corbusier's approach amalgamates reinforced concrete

columns and stone infill into a solid wall, surfaced with a membrane of sprayed concrete that entirely hides the inner structure. The result is a continuous, thin, and yet stable construction that can be smoothly curved or bent as desired.

A modification of this system — without the stone infill — is used for the great south wall. This is the major wall of the nave and one of the most remarkable structures to be found in modern architecture. Slender at top, massively thick at bottom, its depth is punctured by a multitude of large and small embrasures (see exterior and interior photographs). The supporting framework for this wall is a series of thin, flat, triangular slabs of reinforced concrete, set so as to cut vertically through the wall (see drawing of construction). These "columns"

slant from an apex of only $15\frac{1}{2}$ in. at the top of the wall to a depth of as much as 12 ft. at the bottom. Horizontal strips of reinforced concrete connect and brace these verticals and act also as a framework for window openings. The entire wall enclosure — bays between columns as well as embrasures that cut through the wall — are of expanded metal sprayed with a $1\frac{1}{2}$-in. membrane of concrete. The result is a wall that appears massive as a fortress, but is comparatively as thin-shelled as an egg, and diminishes to almost nothing at top. Here, the inner concrete columns extend a few inches above the wall to support, like outstretched fingertips, the roof shell above. This device leaves a sliver of open space between wall and roof, a narrow band of window, above which the roof appears to hover.

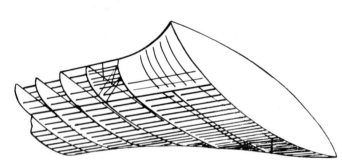

Drawings of construction: Martha Mayer

The great sheltering roof that caps the chapel like a nun's coif, is actually a hollow shell of reinforced concrete. It is built like an airplane wing, with interior struts and partitions bracing an exterior skin (see construction diagram). The skin itself consists of two, curved concrete membranes, an upper and a lower, each less than $2\frac{1}{2}$ in. thick. The top surface of the roof is sprayed with waterproofing and further protected by aluminum sheathing. Rain is directed by the curving shape of the roof and by its slanted position atop the building, to a single waterspout at the rear of the church.

The sum of the complexities of Notre Dame du Haut — in plan and form, in wall and roof structure — is, paradoxically, an esthetic of pristine simplicity. Rough-textured, whitewashed walls, thick, tawny-brown roof, and silo-like towers give this church something of the character of vernacular peasant architecture, particularly that of the Aegean Islands, well known to Le Corbusier. This character — at once primitive and sophisticated — weds the chapel also to its own French countryside. In addition, such studied simplicity forms an effective backdrop for decorative details that transform this into a manifold work of art.

Copyright by Bernhard Moosbrugger

Functional sculptures — utilitarian structures that have been raised to the status of abstract art — here form an inseparable part of the total design. A dramatic rain spout and trough perform in bold silhouette against the curvilinear white wall. Rugged pews of wood and cast concrete are a sculptural adornment to the nave. Large, curved forms of balcony and of freestanding sacristy, in the outdoor sanctuary, combine with angular stepped pulpit to make an abstract composition of the highest artistry.

One of the greatest achievements of the chapel is this: wherever one walks, on the exterior or interior, all elements, large and small, resolve themselves into perfectly proportioned compositions. This is not facade architecture to be viewed from one direction only. Nor is it solely a building contradicted by the afterthoughts of "applied features." Instead, everything is part of a fluid work of art which moves and changes with each change in perspective.

Hubmann

G. E. Kidder Smith

G. E. Kidder Smith

Integral Painting adds color and pattern to selected areas: the main entrance door of the church; the windows of the south wall; the two smaller alcove chapels. These three concentrations bring into vibrant life an enclosure otherwise limited to white, natural grays, and browns.

The entrance door uses a technique never before applied to architecture. It is surfaced with eight panels of sheet steel, which have been enameled by Corbusier and then fired at 1,580° F. to provide an absolutely permanent, waterproof finish. The background of the panels is white; the designs are executed in black, red, blue, and yellow. This huge door, containing the only vivid color on the exterior of the chapel, stands out like a flag against plain wall surfaces, boldly announcing the entrance to the church.

The windows of the south wall represent another special Corbusier technique. Considering leaded, stained glass to be too much a part of the Gothic tradition, Corbusier has instead surface-painted clear panes of glass in various symbolic patterns. With this method, even the colored parts of the windows remain transparent, and the out-of-doors is faintly visible through their tints and patternings.

Balancing the color of the south windows are two spots of color at the north side of the nave. The interior wall of one of the small alcove chapels is painted a clear scarlet; the other violet. All remaining wall surfaces within the church are white. These two colors are only glimpsed from the nave, but they add the balancing grace notes which make of the interior a unified artistic concept. When the scarlet, purple, and gold of ecclesiastical vestments is further added at the sanctuary, the interior of the chapel becomes a neutral vessel, punctuated on both sides and at the front by repetitive accents of rich and brilliant color.

la
mer

Interior of Notre Dame du Haut contains the key to this complex and mysterious design. Preceding descriptions of plan, form, structure, and decoration have given only glimpses of its character. But inside, as one turns to look down the nave, the meaning hidden within this enclosure begins to come clear; the characteristic movement of space begins to be felt. Even so, subsidiary movements such as the central dip of the roof (see rear view of nave) and its upward slant toward the south wall (see front view of nave) tend to obscure the general shape of this room. Thus, the visitor senses, rather than sees, that both side walls splay out, that the floor slopes slightly down, that the roof lifts gently up. These four simultaneous movements — subtle and obscured though they be — open out the interior of the church like a trumpet (Corbusier has called the chapel "an acoustic component in the domain of form"). The narrowest and lowest part of the chapel occurs at the rear of the nave; the widest and highest at the sanctuary.

This "opening out" appears to be the major theme of the church. It is played in different places and in different media. For instance, the outdoor sanctuary, delineated by the inward curving front wall of the church, the outward curving south wall extension, the upward

curving roof, and the faintly sloping porch floor slab, is a continuation of the trumpet shape of the nave, opening out onto the clear stretch of meadow and sky.

A variation on this theme is found in the changing shape of the great south wall. As described previously, this wall splays out from apex to incredible thickness at ground level, echoing in the very structure of the church, the opening out of space within the nave.

The most remarkable repetition of the theme, is in the fenestration that pierces the south wall. Beginning as small rectangles at one wall surface, windows open out in four directions as they cut through the masonry. Tiny slits become great embrasures, revealing the massive depth of the wall and creating an explosion of light and color within it. Clear crystal, laced with fuschia, fiery red, soft pink and green, and golden yellow, with here and there touches of deep brown and black, are the lights, deeps, and colors that vibrate against the rough, whitewashed tunnels framing them. The total effect of this wall is of a mighty fortress, pierced by shafts of light, and creating, here the quietude of shadow, there the glowing radiance of reflection, and again the stab of intense, fiery color. Here, a mystery begins to be illuminated.

In the great south wall of the Chapel of Notre
Dame du Haut, religious feeling is expressed in a way
entirely new to the world, yet conveying a timeless sense
of its ancient sources. Here, the underlying theme of
the chapel, only subtly visible in plan and structure, is
crystallized, intensified, and revealed for all to see. One
can only assume that, consciously or subconsciously, Corbusier meant this theme to symbolize the opening out
of the human soul toward the passion and mystery of
the Christian faith.

Three times Corbusier repeats this theme: in form,
in structure, in fenestration. Three times, too, he plays
a counterpoint to it.

116

In opposition to the gradual opening out of nave and wall and windows stand the three chapel towers. Here, like a symbol of solitary religious experience, space shoots upward, heavenward, within slender columns. Here, the opening is not out, but up, the Church's final declaration of human destiny. And here, windows set high in the tower walls cast light down their shafts, making each tiny chapel glow with a soft radiance, the source of which is not immediately discernible.

References

Boesiger, W., ed. *Complete Works of Le Corbusier*, Vol. 6. George Wittenborn, New York (1957).

Boyd, Robin. "The Engineering of Excitement," *Architectural Review*, November 1958.

"Europe's Great New Churches," *Architectural Forum*, December 1957.

Hammond, Peter. "A Liturgical Brief," *Architectural Review*, April 1958.

Hudnut, Joseph. "The Church in a Modern World," *Architectural Forum*, December 1958.

Le Corbusier. *The Chapel at Ronchamp.* Frederick A. Praeger, New York (1957).

17. CATHEDRAL OF BRASILIA

Brasilia, Brazil; Project
Oscar Niemeyer (b. 1907), architect

"The project of a cathedral is, without doubt, one of the most attractive of themes for the architect. Its study permits the greatest freedom of conception, due to the simplicity of the program with relation to the sacred ritual. It is not concerned — and this is a fundamental point — with the treatment of small areas, to which any system of construction might be applied, but with the creation of the great free spaces which characterize a cathedral. The problem is thus brought into the sphere of great structures, consequently offering the chance of employing the most advanced techniques."

— OSCAR NIEMEYER

The authors had intended to close the Catholic section of this book with the Chapel of Notre Dame du Haut at Ronchamp by Le Corbusier. Subsequently, however, they encountered another church — a project not yet built — which changed their plans and reopened the section. This church was the Cathedral of Brasilia, Brazil, shown on the following pages. It is the sole exception to the rule that only finished, or partially finished, work be included in this collection. Its creator, Oscar Niemeyer, the leading architect in South America, has long been known as a follower of Le Corbusier and at the same time a brilliant and original designer. In this work he at least equals and possibly surpasses his master. In fact, of course, Notre Dame du Haut and the Brasilia Cathedral cannot be compared, since the one is a small pilgrimage chapel, the other a vast structure seating 4,000 people. The chapel at Ronchamp is perfect for its size and function, but it also serves to point up the achievement of the Niemeyer design.

The Cathedral of Brasilia exhibits all the architectural virtuosity of the Ronchamp chapel, plus one thing more. It declares itself. It is immediately recognizable. Ronchamp is mystery and surprise, looking from the exterior like a piece of vernacular peasant architecture. It does not look like a traditional church.

This has appeared to be the choice open to modern designers: either to rely on simplified versions of bell tower, spire, or arch — or to accept the fact that a more creative design, lacking these symbols, will not immediately declare itself to the viewer.

The Cathedral of Brasilia — entirely rejecting what now appear to be feeble traditional symbols — is incontrovertibly a church, a Christian church, a Roman Catholic church, a great cathedral. Here for the first time in our era a new architectural synonym for religion has been coined.

It has been said that we can no longer build cathedrals; that the spirit of our industrial, man-centered society negates the very idea of a cathedral. Certainly a number of embarrassing attempts at modern cathedral design have shown only how far short we fall of the Gothic inspiration. But the Cathedral of Brasilia, a design which could have been conceived only in the twentieth century, fulfills the promise of our new techniques as a medium of spiritual expression equal to the challenge of these great structures.

A crown of thorns. This is the symbol that will rise upward within the new capital city of Brasilia. Set in a great open plaza to one side of the main esplanade, this building will achieve much of the dominant character of the Gothic cathedral that reared its spires at the heart of the medieval market town. Although the modern city of Brasilia is not designed around the cathedral as a focal point, the building is nevertheless so centrally located that it will be strikingly visible, and convenient to both business and residential districts. As shown in the model, the flat sweep of surrounding plaza seems almost to gather itself up without break into the gradual ascent, the swift outward curve, and finally, the jagged blossoming of the cathedral structure. Reaching even higher, from the roof of the crown, is a delicate metal cross with a radiating center, the final symbol atop a heavenly diadem.

This design is as open and direct as the chapel at Ronchamp is obscure and mysterious. Seldom in modern architecture have both plan and structure been revealed with such clarity. The interpenetrating structural and spatial elements of the Ronchamp chapel require paragraphs of explanation. The structure of the cathedral can be described in one sentence: a depressed circle is framed with concave bents of reinforced concrete, anchored at ground level in a circular concrete band, secured near the top by a smaller band, and inset with glass. Except for subsidiary underground elements, that is all. This design has the simplicity, regularity, and inevitability of a flower. And it seems as effortless. If greatness at any task be defined as economy of means in achieving the goal, then this is great architecture, measured against that of any period.

Here is combined the ancient, aspirational mystique of the Catholic Church with the new openness and intimacy of the Liturgical Revival. The circular plan brings clergy and congregation — even a congregation of 4,000 — into close communion under the soaring framework of the cathedral structure. The choir is located in a tall, oval stall, visible to the far left of the interior in the photograph above. From this elevated position, silhouetted against the sky beyond the glass walls, the choristers will resemble a heavenly choir, their voices reverberating into the highest reaches of the tower and down into the deeps of the sunken nave. Whether such symbolism was calculated or not, this design embraces, in its subterranean floor level and soaring upper structure, the polarity of earth and heaven, with "a multitude of the heavenly host" appearing to hover in between.

There are no street-level doors in the cathedral. To enter the sanctuary, the worshipper descends a ramp in the plaza, walking underground, through a sloping, dimly illuminated passage. Emergence into the open, transparent nave is thus a reenactment of the spiritual passage from darkness into light, a statement of religious rebirth.

This symbolism is furthered by a separate baptistry, the round, windowless structure visible at left. A horseshoe ramp gives underground passage to baptistry from the plaza and a second subterranean passage connects it directly to the cathedral. This arrangement is even more explicitly symbolic of the rebirth of the new Christian.

Much thought has been given to the enclosure of the cathedral itself. Because the great expanses of glass, if clear, would make the interior unbearably hot and glaring, they are to be of fumed-brown refracting glass. This will reflect the direct rays of the sun while still maintaining the transparency and floating openness which is the beauty of this design. The brown coloring will create a soothing atmosphere, at once softly glowing and serene.

In shape, the enclosure is similar to a cooling tower and it will function in much the same way, scooping warm air upward to be released at the top of the tower. Thus, both functional and symbolic aspects have been treated at one stroke in this condensed solution to manifold problems.

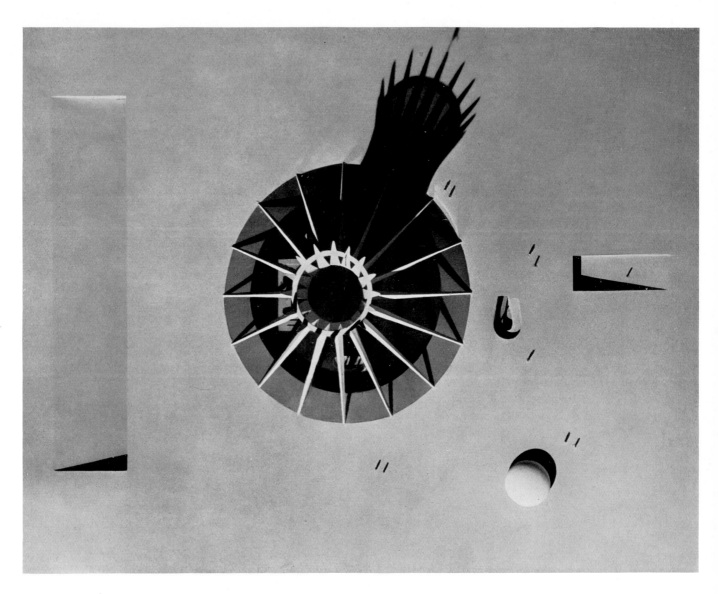

Air view of model reveals the shadow of the crown of thorns that will circle the cathedral as the sun moves across the sky, etching this symbol of the eternal Christian sacrifice, like a spiritual presence, upon the plaza. Even the shadow of this church thus becomes a part of its architecture, evoking the sacred rite that takes place within.

In this unusual plan, only those elements that are a part of the ritual of worship are placed within the great glass-enclosed sanctuary. All other ecclesiastical functions are hidden from view and connected by a network of underground passages. However, to one looking down upon the model, the subsidiary elements of the design are clearly indicated. The large, depressed rectangle at the rear of the cathedral delineates a subterranean structure housing sacristy and administrative offices. The baptistry is the flattened ball at lower right; the main entrance ramp, leading underground into the cathedral, is to the right center. The subsidiary horseshoe ramp, which gives secondary access to both cathedral and baptistry, is centrally located. By comparing this view of the model with the plan opposite, the viewer can see how the three major underground passages serve the cathedral.

In addition to the underground elements described above, thirteen small subsidiary chapels, in which priests celebrate private masses, also are placed outside the main circle of the cathedral. These are delineated in plan as the projecting cubicles which encircle the sanctuary except where entrance passages intervene. All are covered by one continuous roof, visible in the air view as a circular band at plaza level, just inside the cathedral enclosure. This arrangement makes the private chapels at once part of the sanctuary but outside its compass. Their low roof and windowless walls impart a sense of removed and sheltered meditation, in contrast to the openness, transparency, and soaring height that characterizes the place of public worship.

This main hall of the cathedral is simply one great open space. Traditional distinctions between nave, chancel, and narthex have been eliminated. The seating, the altar platform, the pulpit and the choir loft are all freestanding elements within an unbroken circle.

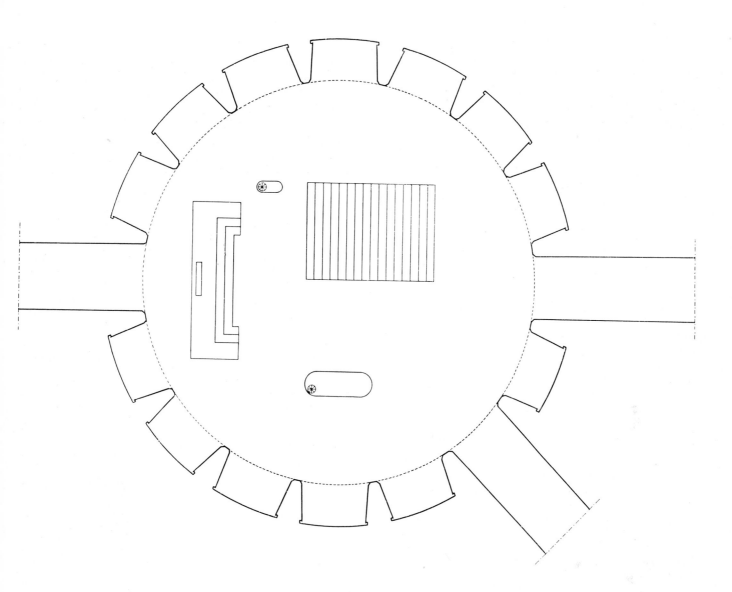

The plan clearly shows the arrangement of all the elements. Seating is represented by a rectangle of parallel lines. The altar platform is the shallow, stepped U, with the block of the altar set back upon it. Pulpit and choir loft are identical in their capsule-like plan, the pulpit however, being much smaller in all dimensions including height. The tiny, flower-like diagrams within choir loft and pulpit represent circular stairways.

The freeing of all elements of worship from their traditional positions and their grouping together in the center of the cathedral permits generous open space around the periphery of the plan, space that can function in a variety of ways. Primarily, it is a continuous "corridor," connecting all parts of the cathedral: entrances, side chapels and each part of the central grouping. It will also be the path of the great processionals on holy days, a path that will encompass all worshippers in a liturgy of song and moving color. Near the main entrance, and at either side of the plan, the open, peripheral spaces are large enough to accomodate great overflow crowds that are expected to throng the cathedral for special services. Because of the circular plan, even those standing at the periphery will be near enough to the altar to see and hear clearly the celebration of the Mass, feeling themselves to be truly participants rather than distant watchers. Those passing by on the plaza can see, through the great transparent enclosure, what is taking place within. Nothing is hidden here. The unity of exterior world and spiritual domain is made manifest.

But the implication of this cathedral is more important than any one of its aspects. In this design, the structure, plan, function, and symbolism of a church are brought to a new unity. From experiments with modern materials and structural systems, from a reexamination of the liturgy, and from the search for integral symbolism, have emerged new concepts of space and form, here fully realized. The 30-odd years separating Perret's Notre Dame du Raincy, which opens this section, from the Cathedral of Brasilia, which closes it, represent a journey from the significant recent past into the future of modern ecclesiastical architecture. It is interesting to remember that both churches are examples of the reinforced concrete frame and lightweight curtain wall.

Reference

Niemeyer, Oscar. "The Contemporary City," *Modulo*, December 1958.

CONTEMPORARY PROTESTANT ARCHITECTURE

Dr. Paul Tillich

Professor, Harvard Divinity School, Cambridge, Mass.

Dr. Paul Tillich, eminent theologian, author, and since 1955, Professor of Systematic Theology at the Harvard Divinity School, has devoted much study to the symbolic meaning of religious architecture. It is this neglected aspect of church design that he stresses in the following discussion. Because Protestants, in general, have remained so unaware of the symbolic implications of their architecture, Dr. Tillich's thesis offers what will be, to many, a new perspective on the controversy between traditional and modern styles in church building.

Obviously, Dr. Tillich cannot speak for all of Protestantism, since there is no single Protestant viewpoint. He himself is a member of the Evangelical and Reformed faith, which recently merged with the Congregational Church and is close kin also to the Presbyterian. The more orthodox denominations, such as the Lutheran and Episcopal, may find some of his conclusions at odds with their sacramental liturgy. The liberal churches, particularly the Unitarian and Universalist, may consider some of his interpretations too mystical. Nevertheless, for all those who have reason to clarify their thinking on the subject of appropriate church design, Dr. Tillich's penetrating analysis should act as an intellectual stimulus and an artistic guide. Above all, his discussion focuses attention upon qualities that are uniquely Protestant.

The great periods of Christian art and architecture from which we draw our tradition have been, without exception, the great periods of Roman Catholic art and architecture. The church building itself — and the frescoes, stained glass, tapestries, and statuary for which it was the frame — were, during these periods, clearly expressive of the faith that they made manifest. The great basilicas and cathedrals of the past represent the Roman Catholic Church in all its mystery and majesty and hierarchical power.

With the emergence of Protestantism, this unity of spirit with its finite expression was severed. From its very beginning, the Protestant faith has been at odds with the visual artes, including church architecture. The predominance of the "ear" over and against the "eye" in Protestant thought resulted in Protestantism creating great music and great poetry, but not great architecture, painting, and sculpture.

In the period of the Reformation the existing Catholic churches were taken over and subjected to more or less radical purges of sculptural and pictorial symbols in order to make them more appropriate to the new faith. But the buildings themselves remained, and with them the expressive power of their style — Romanesque, Gothic, Renaissance, Baroque. This very fact created a tension between the principles and needs of a Protestant congregation and the symbolic meaning embodied in the architecture of a genuine Catholic church.

Attempts to overcome this tension were not lacking and they led to some original forms when new buildings became necessary, as seen for instance in the New England meeting house and in some European central buildings such as the great, but now destroyed, Frankenkirche in Dresden, Germany. But these attempts did not lead very far, because, since the eighteenth century, the general decline of religious art began in all churches and in the whole western world.

No new style in religious art appeared in painting, sculpture, or architecture, and the general "historicism" of the nineteenth century led to a repetition of styles of the past. One of the worst of these trends appeared in the wave of neo-Gothic church architecture, not only in Catholicism, but also within the Protestant sector of both the old and the new continent.

It is difficult to understand why the Protestant church leaders did not realize that there is expressive power in an artistic style and why they did not feel the impact of the Roman Catholic past in the contrast between the symbolism of the building and the symbolism of what was performed within it during a Protestant service. But, as already stated, Protestantism is a religion of the ear and not of the eye.

Certainly there are situations in which a house must be used for purposes for which it is not appropriate. Such emergency situations often occur in private and public life. And Protestantism, as with Christianity in general, is not bound to a special house, as is being shown by the store churches in slum districts. But if a new house is built, it is absurd to repeat intentionally, and without necessity, an emergency situation of the past. Every neo-Gothic, neo-Romanesque, neo-Baroque or other imitative church repeats the emergency situation of early Protestantism. It becomes an absurdity!

There is a defense based on the polarity of tradition and contemporaneity in all religions, including Protestantism. The Protestant protest itself is rooted in the Catholic tradition, namely the Paulinian interpretation of the Christian message. Both Protestant liturgy and Protestant theology retain many elements of the common Christian tradition: Why not church architecture?

The answer to this argument is that, until the past 100 years or so, continuity of religious tradition did not preclude changes in its visual expression. Symbols like the cross are present in every period in the life of the Christian churches. But the style by which these symbols are shown has changed continually. The same is true of architecture.

The request that new buildings be stylistically contemporary is rooted in the nature of creativity and in the ethical principle of honesty. A creative act is normally born out of a cognitive and emotional participation in many or few creations of the past. But when the creative power of the artist or architect goes to work, it breaks through to the new, expressing the creator and through him his period. After a certain inevitable resistance and hesitation, his contemporaries come to recognize themselves in his work.

If, on the other hand, the architect is asked to imitate the style of a period which is not his own, his creativity is undercut and his honesty of self-expression is destroyed. He has ceased to be a mirror to his contemporaries and instead prevents them from awareness of their actual being. He deceives them — even though often they like to be deceived.

In the great periods of religious art such deception would have been impossible. In the religiously disintegrating development of industrial society the deceptive function of religious art, including church architecture, has not only been possible, but largely desired. It is worthwhile to notice how uninhibited former generations were in adding sections in their own contemporary style to churches built in an earlier period. A feeling for their own age, for honesty, and for unhampered creativity, was stronger than the desire to produce a stylistically consistent work. The latter approach is typical only of our own history-conscious period.

In the light of these basic considerations we can now give some answers to the question of a church architecture that is adequate to the religious character of Protestantism. Essentially, the Protestant church building serves the congregation that is assembled to hear the message of the New Being and to answer in prayer and praise. As opposed to the Roman Catholic, there are two fundamental elements that distinguish a Protestant church service:

1. The predominance of the Word over the sacrament.
2. The predominance of the congregation over the liturgical leader or leaders.

These predominances are less marked among the orthodox faiths, but gain in importance as one traverses the range of belief until, among Christian Scientists, the sacrament and the ordained liturgical leader are entirely eliminated.

Accepting, then, the fact that these concepts will receive greater or lesser emphasis depending upon the denomination, it may still be possible to describe an architecture that could be termed essentially Protestant.

The plan of the church is, of course, of first importance. A plan adequate to the Protestant purpose would be, preferably, a central one in which members of the congregation look at each other, and in which the minister is among the congregation for preaching and leading the liturgy. The place for the altar should not be removed, but preserve the character of a table for the sacramental meal in which, ideally, all members participate.

Churches that retain a central aisle leading to a removed altar as the holiest place, separated from other parts of the building, are essentially un-Protestant. With the abolition of any kind of hierarchical dualism between laymen and clergy, between a secular and a holy role — in short, because of the fundamental Protestant concept of the priesthood of all believers — these remnants of the Catholic tradition are religiously inadequate for a Protestant architecture. No new church should have them, and existing churches should be transformed as much as possible away from this old direction.

But the quality of the church, its essential character, is more than the appropriate arrangement of seating and liturgical furnishings. The architect must aim at a particular effect to be imparted by his shaping of the interior — and at this point he encounters a conflict of two religious principles.

The first is the emphasis placed by many Protestants upon the infinite distance between the divine and the human, between God and the world, a distance bridged only by the divine Word. From this follows the ideal of "sacred emptiness," symbolizing this distance. The Jewish tradition, especially its prophetic line, represents this attitude, which was followed in Islam and partly in Protestantism. The sacred void can be a powerful symbol of the presence of the transcendent God. But this effect is possible only if the architecture shapes the empty space in such a way that the numinous character of the building is manifest. An empty room filled only with benches and a desk for the preacher is like a classroom for religious instruction, far removed from the spiritual function which a church building must have.

Yet there is also the opposite point of view. Like all Christian churches, Protestantism is based upon the divine self-manifestation in a personal life, at a definite time, in a definite place. This view justifies within the church a concrete expression of the holy, by means of "pictures" — pictures in the largest sense, comprising everything finite through which the infinite shines. Under the criterion of the manifestation of the transcendant God in Jesus as the Christ, the churches can be filled with symbolic objects of all kinds. All Catholic churches emphasize this side, and some Protestant denominations are more open for it than others.

Protestantism need not reject these elements of Catholic substance, but it should subject them to some definite criteria. First, nothing can be admitted that furthers idolatry or ideas and attitudes of magic. For this very reason, early Protestantism emptied the Catholic churches it took over — without creating in this way what we have called "sacred emptiness." It was simple emptiness, often painfully noticeable.

But if Protestantism today tries to overcome such ugly emptiness, it should not simply bring back the statuary and painting rejected so long ago. Individual, figurative pieces are too indicative of ancient idol worship to be countenanced in a Protestant church. Works of art that are actually part of the church structure would have no such connotation. Murals, for instance, would be far more appropriate to a Protestant ideology than individual canvases. They are elements of architecture rather than objects of veneration. Yet they may heighten the religious impact of the church building. In the same way, single pieces of sculpture would probably have no place in the church, but a sculptural organization of wall or door might be highly desirable.

The problem of using stained glass also requires scrutiny from the Protestant point of view. Color, pattern, and diffusion of light were prohibited in the New England meeting house, early Congregationalists considering clear glass, which emphasizes the rational element in religion, the only appropriate solution. Most Protestant denominations have long since abandoned this stricture and stained glass is nearly as common today in Protestant as in Catholic churches.

However, some recent designs have used clear glass in a new way, in large expanses, widely opening the church toward surrounding nature: trees, flowers, water, sky. The idea is, or should be, to draw nature into the sphere of the Holy Presence. But it seems that the opposite happens: the members of the congregation are drawn away from concentration on the Holy Presence to the outside world. The human situation, man's estrangement from himself, seems to prevent in actual existence what is true in principle; that the divine is not a sphere alongside others, but a dimension in all of them. Only in a state of fulfillment would man be able to experience in everything finite the infinite. But then church buildings would no longer be needed. God would dwell among us, as stated by the last visionary book of the Bible. Since every church building is an adaptation to man's situation of estrangement in which the holy and the secular are present side by side, it seems inadvisable to open the building too widely toward surrounding nature. However, a flood of clear light, if this is desired to emphasize the clarity of the Protestant faith, could be provided where it does not distract the worshipper. Opaque glass or glass brick might offer a workable solution.

Stained glass, too, effectively shields the congregation from outside distraction while shedding a deeper and more mystical illumination upon the interior of the church. Because it is an architectural element, even though technically not a necessary one, it conforms to the criteria laid down for Protestant religious art. Moreover it is one of the most effective ways by which the desirable numinous atmosphere can be imparted to a church. Certainly, today its use should not be prohibited, although its special qualities may be more appealing to orthodox than to liberal denominations.

But here there arises the question of style. Nowhere is this more important than in the handling of stained glass. In a period of cubistic and nonrepresentational art it is all but impossible — as many futile attempts show — to produce naturalistic forms that are convincing. The possibilities of Chartres are not ours. The great artists of our time have chosen a different means of expression. Protestantism need not be bound to unbroken daylight; it too can emphasize the mystical element of religion by means of colored light. But ideally the pattern of such light should not be that of representational forms.

Wherever possible, this same ideal should be extended to painting and sculpture. Abstract, nonrepresentational works can have great symbolic power, often far more than realistic forms. If a story is to be told, representation cannot be avoided — although a naturalistic or sentimental style should be. Great expressiveness can be achieved by means of lines that circumscribe and indicate bodily reality without showing it in overly elaborate detail. A good example of this approach is the expressionistic style of the early twentieth century, which in many ways is still contemporary.

In an attempt to eliminate the realistic from religious art, the traditional symbol is sometimes considered as a substitute. Religious signs and symbols were much used during the early periods of the Christian church, but with the Reformation their usage was drastically reduced. Despite some recent attempts, it is questionable whether they can be revived. Symbols that demand a learned interpretation to be understood are without the power of genuine symbols and should not be confused with them. If such are used, however, their long tradition as expressions of the holy should be respected. Never should they be used lightly as mere decoration without a certain functional necessity. This would be artistically dishonest and religiously repellent.

In contrast to the ancient, esoteric symbols, there remains, of course, the cross, the most powerful and meaningful symbol of the Christian Church. Most Protestant communions will choose to include this sacred object even though every other type of Catholic substance be eliminated. But even this ancient and living symbol should be considered from the Protestant perspective. The innate disapproval of figurative representation, which goes back to the roots of Protestantism, makes itself felt here, above all. The simple, non-naturalistic cross is unquestionably the preferable choice. A crucifix should be allowed only if the body of the Crucified is made one with the structure of the cross itself, and is executed in an expressive rather than a realistic style. In either case, the impression must be avoided that the sacred object is a real object alongside others in a world of finite things.

Today, genuine Protestant church architecture is possible, perhaps for the first time in our history. For the early experiments were too swiftly engulfed by eclecticism to act as evolutionary factors in developing a recognizable Protestant architectural language.

Even today, however, many congregations and ministers still assume that the choice between modern and imitative-traditional architecture is merely a matter of taste and preference. They fail to see that *only* by the creation of new forms can Protestant churches achieve an honest expression of their faith.

This expression should be made real, even if many experiments are necessary and some end in failure. An element of risk is unavoidable in the building of sacred places, just as a risk must be taken in every act of faith.

LUTHERAN

On October 31, 1517, when Martin Luther nailed his document of 95 protests to the door of the castle church in Wittenburg, he had no thought of founding a new religion. He hoped only to rectify certain malpractices within the established Christian Church of his day. But Luther's attempt at reform exploded into the Reformation. Thirteen years later, with the Augsberg Confession of 1530, Protestantism was brought into official existence.

Except for some obscure dissenters, such as the early Waldensians, Wycliffites, Anabaptists, and Hussites, the Lutheran Church is the oldest of the Protestant denominations. It has also remained the largest. Today its membership numbers approximately 70 million adults and children, over 8 million of whom are in the United States. It is the officially recognized state church of Norway, Sweden, Denmark, and Finland, and is widespread in Germany, the Netherlands, and other parts of Europe.

In America, the Lutheran Church is divided into a number of separate bodies or synods, mainly as a result of the immigration of Lutherans from different European countries, each with its own national variant of the religion. Until fairly recently, this strong, nationalistic tradition was carried on in the American churches, Lutheran services being conducted in German, Swedish, Norwegian — whatever language was common to the immigrant group. Although Lutherans settled in America as early as 1624, the flood of Lutheran immigration did not arrive until the nineteenth and even early twentieth century. Thus, Old World ties remained stronger among the Lutherans than among other Protestant denominations.

Today, however, Lutheranism in the United States is experiencing a tremendous resurgence, and is breaking the bonds of nationalism that had held it apart from the general American community.

Recent mergers have significantly reduced the number of independent synods. During the 14 years from 1946 to 1960, the Lutherans gained more than two million new members, most of them converts.

The strength of the Lutheran appeal to modern Americans lies in a simple, clear-cut, and yet orthodox interpretation of Christian doctrine, based squarely upon the Bible as the divinely inspired word of God. In an uncertain world beset by wars, crime, juvenile delinquency, lax public morals, and the threat of nuclear annihilation, the Lutheran dogma — that the natural sinfulness of man can be erased only through God's gift of grace — provides a clear and uncompromising answer.

The sacrament of Communion, through which God's grace is received, is given an almost Catholic prominence in the Lutheran service. The focus of the church is upon the altar, where Christ is truly present in the Eucharist — although spiritually, rather than bodily as in Roman Catholic doctrine. The sacrament of baptism is also of primary importance. The *Small Catechism* of

Martin Luther stresses that only through baptism do sinful human beings become heirs to salvation, entering Christian life in which human nature "is to be drowned and destroyed by daily sorrow and repentance, together with all sins and evil lusts...."

In contrast to these emphases, retained from the Catholic, is the doctrine of "the priesthood of all believers." This is the single most important concept distinguishing the Roman Catholic from all Protestant branches of Christianity, because it destroyed the mystical authority of the priestly hierarchy. Instead of the sacrifice of the Catholic Mass, in which the priest is the instrument of transubstantiation, the miracle of Christ's presence in the Eucharist and its saving grace is achieved by the faith of each individual communicant. Furthermore, each individual Christian can reach God directly through prayer, without priestly or saintly intercession, and is free to read and construe the scriptures without a priestly interpreter.

Luther's daring act of bringing the Bible to the people and his reliance on the word of God as the final spiritual authority, gives the pulpit a place of special prominence in the Lutheran Church. Although the altar retains the central position, the pulpit is placed nearer to the congregation, stressing the primacy of the scriptures, rather than the mystical Church as the repository of spiritual truth.

In addition to its emphasis upon the sacraments and upon the word of God, Lutheran worship is characterized by formal ritual. Ministers always wear vestments. A major part of the service itself is a musical rite, responsively chanted by minister and congregation. Indeed, the clarity and majesty of Lutheran music is as much a part of the heritage of this church as its clear and uncompromising theology. The stately masses and choral works of Johann Sebastian Bach were written for the Lutheran Church. "A Mighty Fortress is Our God," composed by Luther himself, remains to this day the most famous of Protestant hymns. Carrying on this heritage in contemporary America are Lutheran choirs and *a capella* choral groups, many of them world renowned.

Traditionally, Lutheran churches have expressed their faith in forms that emphasize the sacramental nature of their liturgy. The chancel in these older churches is often as richly adorned as any Roman Catholic sanctuary. Dark woods and ornate decoration are typical of many interiors. The national heritage of the specific Lutheran congregation has also been commonly expressed in its architecture, especially through Germanic and Scandinavian wood carvings.

One would expect this Church, so orthodox in theology and so conscious of its Old-World origins, to cling more tenaciously than any other to traditional forms in architecture. Instead, Lutheran congregations have led the way in the contemporary approach to religious design, often electrifying conservative communities with their modern churches.

It is hardly surprising that European Lutherans were among the first to experiment with modern architecture, especially in Germany and the Scandinavian countries, where much of modern design originated. But in tradition-bound America, the modernism of the Lutherans comes as something of a shock. It is, however, a logical part of the great transitional movement that is changing this denomination in the United States from a church of the past to a church of the present and future. The central elements of the Lutheran service remain constant, whether embodied in old forms or new. But expression of these elements in contemporary terms has given them a dynamic and vital quality that is meaningful to the men and women who worship today.

NOTE: *The following sources were drawn upon for the discussions of the various Protestant denominations*: "The New Lutheran," *Time*, April 7, 1958.

Rosten, Leo, ed. *Religions of America*. Simon & Schuster Inc., New York (1955).

Spence, Hartzell. *The Story of America's Religions*. Holt, Rinehart and Winston, Inc. (1960).

Welshimer, P. H. *Facts Concerning the Disciples*. The Standard Publishing Foundation, Cincinnati (1935).

Wilber, E. M. *A History of Unitarianism*. Harvard University Press, Cambridge (1947).

The World's Great Religions. Time Inc. and Simon & Schuster Inc., New York (1957).

For those interested in obtaining additional information on Protestantism, the authors' recommend the following references:

Bainton, Roland H. *The Reformation of the Sixteenth Century*. The Beacon Press, Inc., New York (1956).

Brauer, Gerald C. *Protestantism in America*. Westminster Press, Philadelphia (1953).

Nicholas, James Hastings. *Primer for Protestants*. Association Press, New York (1947).

Sweet, William Warren. *The History of Religion in America*. rev. ed. Harper and Brothers. New York (1950).

Welch Claude and John Dillenberger. *Protestant Christianity*. Charles Scribner's Sons, New York (1954).

18. STAHL KIRCHE

Essen, Germany; Erected 1928
Otto Bartning (1883-1959), architect
Elizabeth Coester, artist

Courtesy Lambert Schneider

"It is wrong to believe that by using modern materials and building techniques we secularize church construction. There is a spiritual quality in any material. It is our present task to find this spirit and put it into the service of religion." — OTTO BARTNING

The design that leads off this section on Protestant churches was chosen as a counterpart to Auguste Perret's famous Notre Dame du Raincy, which opens the Catholic section. Just as Perret's French church is a landmark in the use of reinforced concrete, so Otto Bartning's German church is a landmark in the use of structural steel. Together these churches sum up the essence of modern architecture insomuch as it is based on two uniquely modern materials unavailable to builders of the past.

The Stahl Kirche was designed for the *Pressa-Austellung*, an exhibition in Cologne in 1928, to demonstrate the potential of modern materials in ecclesiastical architecture. Its designer, the late Otto Bartning, was unquestionably the leading Protestant church architect in Germany. Granted an unusual opportunity for free experiment, Dr. Bartning created not only a masterpiece of ecclesiastical architecture, but a laboratory in the technique of modern building.

Here, for the first time in a church, the steel frame was used according to its true nature. Instead of concealment beneath a mass of unnecessary masonry, it was exposed as the supporting skeleton of the building. The enclosing walls then became mere lightweight curtain panels, fitted into the modular steel grid. The nave, except for a low strip of wainscoting, was enclosed entirely by glass within the spiderweb of steel. In contrast to the curving, continuous, crystalline wall of the nave, other parts of the church were made completely windowless. But here, too, the unique possibilities of modern technology were explored. The solid walls of bell towers and narthex, and the strips of wainscoting, were prefabricated sandwich panels, consisting of an interior finish of ash wood, a core of insulation, and an exterior finish of

sheet copper. These completely self-contained wall panels were inserted into the steel frame like the panes of glass in the contrasting area. The roof was simply precut planking surfaced with copper sheeting.

With this system, the Stahl Kirche anticipated the most advanced techniques of standardized, prefabricated, panel construction — techniques that only now are being applied to steel frame structures. This ingenious system also meant that the Stahl Kirche was the first, and possibly still the only, completely prefabricated and demountable church of any size and pretension.

After the *Pressa-Austellung* closed in 1929, the church was dismantled, shipped 52 miles to the city of Essen and there reerected. According to Dr. Bartning, this was the first case in the history of architecture in which a church was so erected, dismantled, and built up again. This remarkable feat was made feasible only because of the extreme simplicity of the entire structure and the ingenious way in which the steel frame and prefabricated panels were fitted and joined together. Such a demountable church, truly a unique twentieth century phenomenon, might well be of interest to American congregations that must contend with the population shifts and the rapid urban growth and decay characteristic of contemporary parishes. Whether the quality of mobility is desired or not, the application of the steel frame and glass curtain wall to church design deserves far more attention that it has received.

Today, Bartning's masterwork is gone. After its move from Cologne to Essen, the Stahl Kirche served as a parish church for 14 years. In 1943, this magnificent example of modern technological design, yet to be equalled in clarity of structure and in the inspired use of glass as an enclosure, was destroyed by bombs.

Front view of Stahl Kirche shows its most famous feature: the steel frame and glass curtain wall that surrounded the nave. During the day, as pictured here, the church achieved a commanding presence by virtue of its blunt honesty of form and structure. At night, when lighted from within, it stood out against the black sky like a great, glittering jewel.

From the interior of the nave, the effect was one of weightlessness, of an enclosure seeming to float, suspended in air. This was a wall that changed and moved, glowed and darkened, with the changing exterior light. Its delicate patterning — clear glass with an intricate tracery of blue and crimson — heightened this effect. The atmosphere thus created — out of I-beams, steel mullions, clear and colored glass — was in its quiet and serene way as spiritually evocative as any Gothic cathedral.

One might well surmise that in the quality of its illumination the Stahl Kirche closely approached the goal of the Gothic. It is common architectural parlance that, in the Gothic style, stone was pushed to the limit of its potential, and the devices whereby stone could be opened up to admit interstices of stained glass were explored to their final limit. But the important point is that the expanse of glass and the magical quality of illumination was the major goal; the style known as Gothic was merely the best available means of achieving it. The modern steel frame of today far exceeds the potential for openness of stone, making this fundamental goal of the Gothic builders possible for the first time.

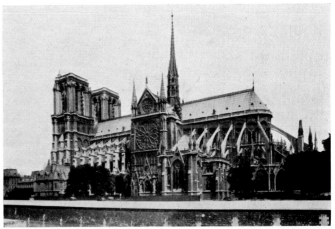

Nowhere is this achievement more strikingly illustrated than in the Stahl Kirche that, in actual fact, repeated the major form, the twin bell towers, and the roofline of the typical Gothic cathedral, minus the buttresses, arches, and intricate stone work that were necessary to allow the insertion of large areas of glass in these structures. Note, for example, the striking similarity of form between this church and the Gothic Notre Dame de Paris, shown here. Symbolically, therefore, the Stahl Kirche may be considered an exact expression of orthodox Protestantism. Like that faith itself, it retains the basic form of the Catholic church that preceded it, but a new and more direct supporting structure has created a new edifice.

H. Schmölz

Side view of church from inner court shows steps leading up and turning left toward the church entrance located at the rear. The wainscoting panel of the nave is here clearly seen as it cuts across the glass curtain wall of the church. The glass wall below this paneling enclosed a ground floor, multipurpose room, used for an adult Sunday school, for meetings and social events. These two levels of the church, nave and social hall, were differentiated by the style of their stained glass. Graceful expressionistic forms were used for the nave, while a geometric pattern was used for the more matter-of-fact meeting room below it.

The main body of the church was surrounded by a subsidiary one-story structure of reinforced concrete that joined the church at front and rear, but stood away from it at either side to create sheltered courtyards, one of which is seen in this photograph. The low periphery structure (see also the preceding exterior view) contained space for administrative offices, Sunday school rooms, a pastor's study and, when desired, living quarters for the minister and his family. Glass panels opened up most of these rooms to the inner court, while walls facing the street were entirely windowless. This is a particularly workable solution for urban churches, simultaneously solving the problems of outdoor privacy, noise, and separation of functions. It was also Dr. Bartning's aim to emphasize the difference between the heavenly element, expressed in the high central church, and the worldly element, embodied in the low, peripheral structure.

Rear view reveals the majesty of this church as it built up from the low peripheral wing to covered entrance area, to narthex blocks, to bell towers. This visual progression was echoed in the path of the churchgoer: from the front of the church, through the courtyards, up the side stairs, to the high rear entrance. It encouraged a gradual shift of mood, a feeling of "rising up" toward the Lord's house. Although barely visible from the angle of this photograph, a great steel cross rose between the bell towers to form the highest element of the church, proclaiming its dominance over the building below.

This is the view of the church that opened out before the worshipper as he entered. As with Notre Dame du Raincy, no photograph can capture the luminous atmosphere which enveloped this interior. In the dedication ceremony for the Stahl Kirche in 1928, Otto Bartning explained this design: "The glass walls close us in and at the same time open up the inside to the outside and hold us in the magic spell of the changing light of day and night."

Whereas Notre Dame du Raincy gives the impression of sparkling prismatic light, filtered through a lace of concrete, this church was all light, filtered only by its own colors and leadings, and dramatized by the black slashes of steel columns. As symbolic of the light shed by the Christian, and particularly the Protestant faith,

this glass wall was an expressive achievement, yet to be surpassed in church architecture.

The plan of this church and the placement of its liturgical elements were symbolic too. Both pulpit and altar were placed on the same central axis, directly opposite the entrance, thus indicating their equal importance to the communicant. The altar was placed beyond and above the pulpit to show its more mystical character; the pulpit was brought forward toward the congregation indicating its centrality to the Protestant faith. The plan was a parabola with altar and pulpit set in its curve. The sides of the parabola slanted outward toward the rear of the church, symbolically reaching into eternity. The space so created radiated from altar and pulpit like the radiation of Christian life by the sacrament and Word.

Twin choir lofts were placed at the rear of the church, overlooking the congregation and directly facing the sanctuary. The space of the entirely open interior was dropped step by step from the choir into the nave and thence rose up again to the pulpit and up once more to the altar. This variance in level emphasized the different elements of choir, congregation, and sanctuary, while bringing all into organic unity.

In the interior of the Stahl Kirche, one gained the feeling that a space had been created within a space. The structure was supported by twin rows of steel columns, the outer row forming the frame for the walls, the inner row defining the aisles at either side of the church. Above these aisles was a flat roof but over the nave proper the roof was pitched, giving a sense of added height to this "inner room."

The concentrated strength of the steel columns, and their exposure without any attempt at beautification, imparted a sense of the integrity, endurance, and purposefulness of the Protestant faith. In counterpoint, the delicate glasswork radiated an atmosphere of the mystical — of the sensed but not seen. Note the continuous pattern of angelic forms not clearly delineated, but appearing to hover on outspread wings about the holy place.

Josef Josuweck

The exterior detail shows the extreme simplicity with which stained glass panels were set into the steel frame. Each square of glass was composed of separate pieces, leaded together, but the pattern continued beyond mullions and framing members, creating expressionistic forms on a very large scale over the whole wall surface.

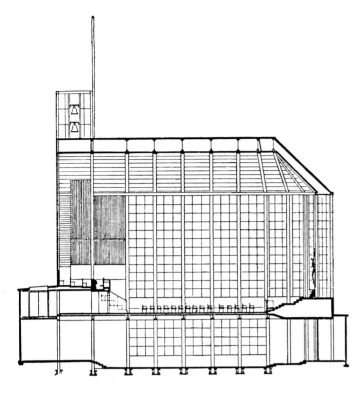

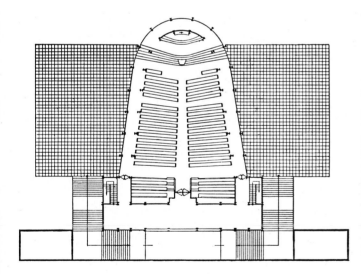

Plan and section of the church show how entrance was made through the courtyards, up the turning stairs, and into the narthex at rear. Passage into the nave was by either side of the choir lofts. Stairs led down to the multipurpose room on the lower level. The one-story structure that enclosed the church grounds at front and sides is not shown in this second-story plan. It contained subsidiary elements, such as classrooms, offices, pastor's study. The cost of the church in 1928 was 500,000 marks (approximately $143,000) but to this figure must be added the cost of bells, organ, steel girders, and copper sheathing, all donated to this church because it was a demonstration project.

Reference

Girkon, Paul. *Die Stahl Kirche*. Beratungsstelle für Stahlverwendung, Düsseldorf (1958).

18 a. Geodesic dome, originated by engineer-scientist Buckminster Fuller, carries the metal frame and transparent curtain wall into the realm of higher mathematics. By using a skeleton of aluminum tubing set in repetitive tetrahedrons, and an enclosure of weatherproof plastic, Fuller has created a demountable structure of the lightest possible weight and the lowest possible cost. This kind of metal skeleton is know as a "space frame", because all stresses are absorbed within the framework rather than concentrated at the joints as in conventional post-and-lintel. In some versions of the dome, a stressed metal skin helps distribute the load to the framework.

Variations of Fuller's famous dome have been used to enclose a railroad roundhouse, an automotive laboratory, an exhibit pavilion, and myriad other commercial and domestic functions. There is no reason why such a dome could not be incorporated into the design of a church, combined with a solidly enclosed lower structure of different size and shape. With panels of translucent plastic attached to the metal frame, it could provide a domed ceiling of unparalleled luminosity and color at absurdly low cost. The photograph shows part of the headquarters building for the American Society of Metals. This building combines a semicircle of conventional structure with a much larger dome. The framework of the dome has here been left uncovered, as its function here is purely decorative.

18 b. U.S. Pavilion at the Brussels Worlds Fair
of 1958 illustrates an unusual variation of frame and
curtain wall construction. Here, a continuous circular
enclosure of metal grillwork is set entirely free of
slender supporting columns. The effect created is similar to that of the walls of Notre Dame du Raincy,
which were executed in concrete. This design docu-
ments the versatility of metal and glass construction.
It suggests, also, one more way to capture luminosity,
a quality especially desired in churches. The pavilion
is the work of the distinguished American architect
Edward D. Stone, who has made the grille his hallmark
during the past several years.

19. ZION LUTHERAN CHURCH

Portland, Ore.; Erected 1949-50
Pietro Belluschi (b. 1899), architect, landscape architect,
and interior designer
Miles K. Cooper, structural engineer
J. Donald Kroeker, mechanical engineer
Grant R. Kelley, electrical engineer
Frederic Littman, sculptor

"The modern architect has found that his integrity will prevent him from building with the tools of the past, or to use deception in forcing old architectural forms onto modern materials; yet he has found that he must respect and preserve that feeling of emotional continuity which is the very essence of religion."

— PIETRO BELLUSCHI.

Zion Lutheran Church, in Portland, Ore., is a member of the Missouri Synod, the most orthodox body within the American Lutheran communion. Originally organized in 1847 near St. Louis, Mo., this synod has since established churches throughout the United States, growing rapidly over the years. Today, the name does not designate the Lutheran Church of a specific region. But it still carries with it the connotation of strong, confessional Lutheranism upon which the Missouri Synod was founded.

The Zion Lutheran Church of Portland is the mother church of the Missouri Synod's Northwest District, which comprises the states of Washington, Oregon, and Idaho. The first services in this region were held in Portland in the year 1871 soon after the Lewis and Clark expedition had brought pioneer settlers into the northwest. Eighty years later the congregation completed another pioneer venture when it erected the modern church building shown on the following pages.

Zion Lutheran Church — a design consisting of a wooden frame and a brick curtain wall — represents a phase of modern architecture not yet discussed in this book.

Wood frame construction is one of the earliest building systems to be devised by man. It was Auguste Perret who first grasped the fact that this system is more appropriate to reinforced concrete than traditional methods of building with masonry. And it was the early modern architects of Europe and America who realized the potential of the structural frame when steel was used for supporting members. These modern materials brought to an ancient building system a strength far greater than that possessed by wood, permitting buildings of a height and span that the wooden frame could not have supported. This strength also permitted the separation of structural frame from enclosing walls and the reduction of the wall itself to the thinnest of curtaining membranes.

With Zion Lutheran Church, this development comes full circle. For in addition to developing entirely new materials, the industrial age has made also a new material out of the traditional substance of wood, imparting to it some of the qualities of steel and concrete.

During World War II, new methods of lamination based on high-strength plastic glues were developed for the construction of lightweight airplane parts. The lamination process greatly increases the strength of wood. In addition under heat and pressure, it imparts the quality of pliability to this naturally rigid material. The subsequent application of these developments to the building field means that, today, laminated wood can be molded into arches, vaults, thin shells, and other structural shapes once the sole prerogative of masonry. Although still not equal in plasticity to reinforced concrete, nor in strength to steel, wood is now capable of a far greater range of performance than ever in its past. One result is the development of an entirely new kind of wooden frame, based on the arch rather than the ancient post-and-lintel system.

It is this arched frame upon which architect Pietro Belluschi has based the design of Zion Lutheran Church. Moreover, the separation of frame and enclosure has been here as clearly articulated as in the steel church by Otto Bartning or Perret's Notre Dame du Raincy, constructed of reinforced concrete. An interior arcade of laminated, bent wood arches soars up from ground level to an apex at the gable ridge of the church, supporting the major weight of the roof structure. This exposed skeleton stands entirely free of brick curtain walls, the legs of the arches being grounded 3 ft. from the outer walls to create the side aisles of the church. The result is a design that clearly reveals the new-found power of the laminated wooden arch.

The major advantages of wood in such a structural system are first, the visual "warmth" of its appearance, and second, its economy. In the Zion Lutheran Church, Belluschi has taken full advantage of both these characteristics. The cost of all eight of the wooden arches framing the church was only $ 2,500. This undoubtedly represents one of the major reasons why Zion Lutheran, seating a congregation of 400, was built for a total cost of only $ 100,000.

No less important is the visual effect of the wooden arches. With a typical economy of concept, Belluschi has made the structural arcade act also as the major decorative element of the interior. The exposure of the great skeletal arches and the rhythmic repetition of their pointed shape creates a Gothic atmosphere of aspiration without copying the Gothic means toward that end. At the same time the warm brown color of the natural wood lends a richness to the entire design.

The exterior of the church gives no hint of the structural system exposed on the interior, being simply an enclosing envelope placed like a tent over the great frame within. The character of the exterior is established by a gabled wooden roof, surfaced with redwood shingles. Protective eaves extend beyond the walls of the church at either side and, at front, shelter a broad entrance porch which runs the width of the church. Above the roof rises a simple wooden spire, proclaiming the function of the building beneath it.

Exterior of Zion Lutheran Church plays tawny brick side walls against a facade of rough-sawn board and batten, stained a deep brown. From this dark, rough-textured background, the entrance doors gleam out, surfaced with sheet copper and sculptured into a bas-relief of hovering angels.

The form of this church, with its simple spire, recalls the village churches of peasant Europe. It is also rooted in the wood vernacular of the American Northwest. However, even more important than its evocation of a tradition of building is its delineation of the character of a religious faith. By some alchemy, Pietro Belluschi is able to extract the essence of a particular denomination and express it in architecture. Such sensitivity is rare indeed, even among designers of the highest talent. The Stahl Kirche by Otto Bartning, for example, would be equally appropriate to a number of Protestant denominations. But the Zion Lutheran Church — why, it is not quite possible to say — looks like a Lutheran, and only a Lutheran, church. This elusive talent of Belluschi's is vividly illustrated by comparing the above design with his Episcopal church (No. 23), his Presbyterian church (No. 27), and his church for a Catholic monastery (No. 38).

Interior of Zion Lutheran Church clearly shows the separation of the structural frame from walls and roof which are merely enclosing envelopes. The placement of laminated wooden arches 3 ft. from the outer walls not only creates side aisles, but also reduces the width of the interior space that this arcade must span. Consequently, the trajectory of the arches can be more vertical, their curves less abrupt, and their effect more Gothic than if they were brought down on a line with the outer walls.

In this church, Belluschi has chosen to ignore the possibility of glass curtain walls so dramatically used in the preceding steel-framed church. Instead, he has devised a most unusual solution: brick walls that admit daylight only through individual glass blocks, set flush into the expanse of masonry in a geometric pattern.

There are a number of reasons why glass-bejewelled brick walls were preferable to all-glass walls in this church. The great exposed arches and the gabled wooden roof which they support are visually "heavy" elements, concentrated overhead. Unless a balancing mass was provided by the walls, this construction would have appeared topheavy. In addition, the visual impact of the structural arcade would have been drastically reduced if large areas of patterned stained glass had been introduced in competition to it. The interior as a whole would have lost its focus. Finally, this city church, located in a busy section of town and fronting directly on the street, needed a shield from the distractions of urban life that eddy around it. From the standpoint of the church service, glass walls would have been an unfortunate choice.

However, with a minimum of fenestration, Belluschi has achieved interior lighting that is both functional and beautiful. Spacing of the glassed apertures has been carefully calculated to provide subdued illumination without glare. So effective is the placement that, on sunny mornings, the windowless nave requires no electric lighting, a condition seldom achieved by churches with traditional window openings filled with stained glass.

To enhance this unusual method of daylighting, the cavity of each glass block has been lined with copper sheeting. The metallic surface of the copper reflects and amplifies the light, giving it a warm roseate hue, akin to the tawny brick and rich wood browns of the interior. This color is repeated and intensified in the east chancel wall that is composed entirely of stained glass panels in shades of rose and amber. Through this glass curtain, rays of sunlight strike the burnished surfaces of a great brass cross, an altar sheathed in copper, a copper baptismal font, and delicate brass candelabra. The warm coloring thus starts at a low key in the nave, heightens into glowing rose and amber at the chancel window, and then culminates into shining copper and gold. The only contrasting color accent in the entire church is a soft green rug that runs the length of the aisle up to the altar.

Although the photograph shown gives an accurate idea of the structure and furnishings of the church, it fails to reveal the true atmosphere of the interior when

in use. Concealed electric lights here flood the nave with light. Most Sunday services, however, are illuminated only by natural daylight filtering through the glass blocks. The ceiling appears to recede, the arches melt into shadows, and the sanctuary, by contrast, stands out in a glow of brilliance. Depth and mystery, opening out into a diffused radiance, and then intensifying into gleaming light upon the holy objects, is the special illusion of this church.

Timber Structures, Inc.

Close views of the chancel show the contrast of texture, light, and color that gives this area much of its beauty. Rose and amber panes of glass, set between structural arches and framed with narrow wooden mullions, flood the chancel with a softly colored light. The diffused rays are caught, intensified, and reflected by smooth surfaces of brass and copper, focusing illumina-

tion on the most important liturgical objects. Cross,
altar, and candlesticks shine out against the rough textured, light-absorbent, redwood battens of the wall
behind them. This textured wall also provides a sound-
absorbent surface directly opposite the choir loft in the
rear of the church, counteracting the sound-reflective
quality of brick side walls.

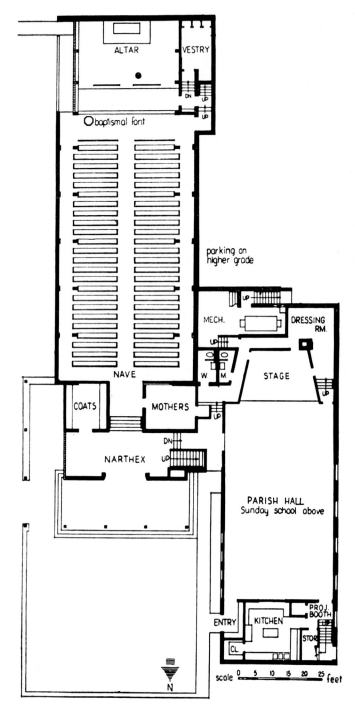

19a. Central Lutheran Church in Portland, Ore., designed by Belluschi almost simultaneously with Zion Lutheran, proves that the laminated wooden arch can be used to produce more than one exterior form. Here, the roof is flat, the nave a long rectangle. Consequently, the interior arches that support the structure differ in shape from those of Zion Lutheran Church. Rather than curving vertically to a peak, the arches follow the wall line straight up, then curve abruptly to meet the roof, straightening into a nearly horizontal line. This almost rectangular shape, set close to walls and roof, reduces the importance of the arches as a decorative element. Richer wall treatment than that of Zion Lutheran becomes appropriate.

One wall of the nave, here seen from the exterior, has therefore been designed as a latticed wooden screen, inset with panes of colored glass, which range from a muted grayish-blue through clear blue and violet to a brilliant red. This creates a wash of subdued violet light throughout the nave. Note also the delicate latticework bell tower, which together with the shape of the church and its rich stained glass, makes this design a modern translation into wood of the Gothic stone cathedral. The main entrance, placed at the side of the church, echoes the lattice work of bell tower and wall by means of a graceful wooden canopy. This large church — which seats 1,000 people — plus a lower-level parish hall and a separate Sunday school building, were built in 1949 for the incredibly low total cost of $250,000.

19b. Lutheran Church of St. Paul in Sarasota, Fla., designed by Victor Lundy, illustrates yet another form inspired by the laminated wooden arch. Here, the curve is reversed, traveling inward and upward to a dramatic spire-like peak over the center-line of the church. Steel piers, faced with coquina stone, support the arches at their outermost edge and act also to define broad, covered porches formed by the roof extension. The same stone is used for solid portions of the church enclosure, both at the entrance (see photo) and at the

Plan of Zion Lutheran Church reveals the extreme simplicity of its concept: one large, open room, a small narthex, and connecting porch. This is a typically Protestant design, eliminating as it does the separate elements of baptistry, chapels, side altars, and confessionals commonly included in a Catholic church. The 50-voice choir loft is simply a narrow balcony that extends the width of the rear wall above the entrance doors. Sunday school, social rooms, and offices have been relegated to an adjoining parish hall. The cost of the latter building was $100,000, equal to that of the church. The fact that as much money was spent for the parish hall as for the church itself highlights the emphasis on auxiliary church activities — a characteristic of most Protestant denominations.

George Cserna

chancel. Between these front and rear areas, side walls of the nave are sliding panels of clear glass, that can open the church interior to the porches for overflow seating, an appropriate solution in a mild climate.

This design is the work of a young Florida and New York architect who has made laminated wood his particular medium. It was built in 1959 at a cost of $ 80,000 and seats 350 at capacity. Of his unusual solution, the architect writes: "The roof shape of this church is not a derived shape out of the past; it is a symbolic shape. There is an attempt here in the form of the church to symbolize God and man — God in the central high areas reaching and pointing upward, man in the low horizontal side areas that hug the earth."

References

Belluschi, Pietro. "Church Architecture," *Liturgical Arts,* November 1950.

Blake, Peter. "Architecture and the Individual," *Architectural Forum,* June 1958.

REPORT FROM THE CLERGY
The Rev. Edwin C. Zschoche, Pastor, Zion Lutheran Church

I was not here when this church was built, but members of the congregation have helped me to answer the questions. Planning a new building for Zion Lutheran Church extended over many years. As early as 1929, a Portland architect was engaged and preliminary plans prepared for a building in the traditional style. But controversies among the members about rather unimportant details repeatedly halted progress; and finally the depression of the 1930's terminated all activity.

When a younger pastor succeeded to the position of the departed elderly predecessor in 1942, the idea of building a new church was revived. This time the congregation was urged to employ a St. Louis architect who had achieved prominence in designing churches. Again preliminary plans were prepared and an apparently acceptable layout was submitted, but the design remained

traditional. Difficulties in dealing with an architect at such distance brought the undertaking to a halt again, and the congregation decided to engage a local, but nationally known architect — Pietro Belluschi, of Portland.

Mr. Belluschi accepted the appointment and soon submitted his first design. It failed to be accepted. Criticism expressed was that the building would resemble a factory, being rectangular in shape. Mr. Belluschi counseled with the congregation and was amenable to suggestions. A second drawing was soon ready. This was again designed with a flat roof and the plan was not accepted.

The chairman of the building committee conferred privately with Mr. Belluschi and urged that a gabled roof be employed and that the tower be integral with the building. Mr. Belluschi was agreeable but warned that this was the last design he would submit. When the third creation was completed, the chairman was invited to Mr. Belluschi's office to view it, and acceptance was immediate with the words, "This I can sell to the congregation."

Evidently, in dealing with three architects and considering five plans, the congregation had developed a new concept of church design, suitable for its needs and yet more than an imitation of the past. Mr. Belluschi crystalized this conception by conditioning his acceptance of the assignment on the premise that the building be designed to express modern trends in architecture and materials. His first two sketches carried the modern trend to extremes, and though the members of the congregation did not accept these, they were inculcated with new developments in architecture while studying these plans. When a less extreme plan was submitted all reservations had been overcome....

To me, as pastor of the congregation, the knowledge that the church edifice attracts many visitors fills me with a sense of humbleness and deep responsibility. The church serves as an inspiration to me to proclaim the word of salvation in a manner so vivid that all my hearers will know the way of salvation even though they may never attend another church service.

The members are deeply rooted in their loyalty; many of them pass churches of our denomination recently constructed in the vicinity of their homes. Some travel the entire breadth of the city for their regular Sunday worship in our church. Their happiness is contagious and attracts new members. During the period of decline in the old church building there were few additions to the membership. Today the great influx has completely changed the makeup of the membership. Formerly old people predominated; today the membership gives the impression of youth. Formerly mothers and children were seldom seen; now they are numerous.

The Sunday school enrollment has grown to such proportions that accommodation of classes is becoming a problem, but our other church organizations have ample, complete facilities for their varied activities. We have no members now who object to the design of the church. On the contrary, all are well satisfied and happy to worship in such elevating surroundings.

20. CHRIST CHURCH LUTHERAN

Minneapolis, Minn.; Erected 1950
Saarinen, Saarinen & Associates, architects
Eliel Saarinen (1873-1950)
Hills, Gilbertson & Hayes, associated architects
Bolt, Beranek & Newman, acoustics

Harvey Croze

*"On sensing the fundamental characteristics of the time
and on giving these characteristics the truest interpretation — hinges the greatness of any really great man."*

— ELIEL SAARINEN

Like the Oregon churches that precede it, Christ Church Lutheran in Minneapolis, Minn., is a member of the theologically orthodox Missouri Synod. Since World War II, this most conservative of Protestant bodies has erected more outstanding modern churches than any other religious denomination in the United States, Protestant or Catholic.

Christ Church, shown on the following pages, is one of its finest achievements. Commissioned by a parish of middle-class families in a far from fashionable or wealthy section of Minneapolis, this church shows the functional beauty that is within the compass of any congregation daring enough to reach for it. Designed by the late Eliel Saarinen, the great Finnish architect who, after 1924, made his home in America, it is considered by many to be his masterwork. Recently a poll of 35 leading architects, editors, and specialists in church design, conducted by the National Council of Churches, voted Christ Lutheran in Minneapolis the best church erected in the United States during the preceding 25 years.

In Christ Church, Eliel Saarinen chose one of the more salient of Lutheran characteristics and designed his church around it. This characteristic is the almost equal balance between sermon and ritual that places the Lutherans, like the Anglicans, at a mid-point between the Protestant and Catholic faiths. Although the preaching of the Word is given a typical Protestant prominence in the Lutheran service, it is prefaced and followed by an altar-focused rite, with the lighting and capping of the candles to token its beginning and end. The ritual music is no less important. The Lutherans are known as a "singing church," and the beauty of their chanted service is unsurpassed among Protestant denominations.

Visually, therefore, Saarinen conceived Christ Church as the setting against which the liturgical drama is unfolded. Aurally, he conceived it as an instrument for the projection of the Word of God and the ritual of music.

Because he felt that nothing should compete with the visible rite for the attention of the worshipper, he has reduced the interior of the church to a background of unadorned simplicity, brought into brilliant focus by the use of lighting as a basic element of design. And as acoustics are important to the apperception of both musical liturgy and sermon, the control of sound has been made the organizing factor through which most major and many minor elements of this church take their shape.

The result is a structure without precedent in ecclesiastical architecture. But because the architect was here an artist as well as a scientist, Christ Church achieves a rare beauty, giving no hint of the practical and infinitely painstaking calculations upon which it is based. This church is proof of one of the more telling arguments for modern architecture: that only new forms can take full advantage of recent developments in acoustics, lighting, and other basic building sciences — and that these new forms can be just as compelling as the old forms that they supersede.

The traditional styles, so sentimentally appealing to most congregations, were actually based on quite primitive concepts of sensory phenomena. In the Gothic cathedral, for example, the acoustics were extremely poor.

The long, narrow nave, constructed on all sides of hard, sound-reflective materials, acted as a giant echo chamber for the sounds produced within it. Fortunately this characteristic was not a disadvantage to the religious services of the Middle Ages. The clear audibility of the Latin Mass, which few could understand, was considered of small importance. The emotional impact of the great medieval processionals was actually heightened by the reverberation of the choristers' voices within the great hall of the cathedral.

Today, in our smaller churches, and with our changed concept of a religious service, the acoustical effect of borrowed Gothic can be distinctly unpleasant. At best, it takes no advantage of the superior potential of our age. In the same way, the glorious stained glass windows of the Gothic cathedrals, although providing light of unparalleled color and mysticism, did little to clarify the service as it took place within the distant sanctuary.

Christ Church, dedicated to a more intimate worship and to a Protestant concept of visibility and audibility, offers an entirely new solution. The basic structural system of this church is an extremely simple one: merely a steel frame enclosed by stone and brick walls, the latter exposed on the interior as well as the exterior. But the organization of these elements to achieve the acoustical and visual goal is a more complicated matter.

The major instrument of sound control is the shape of the building itself. Since sound waves reverberate back and forth between parallel surfaces, such surfaces have been avoided in the design. The flat ceiling, hung from a roof of steel decking, is canted slightly downward from side to side, thus presenting a surface that is not parallel to the floor. The north wall of the church is splayed out from front to rear, angling away from the straight south wall at the opposite side. Toward the front of the church, this north wall melts into the chancel wall as a gentle, continuous curve, thereby eliminating the right-angle meeting of wall surfaces that is ordinarily a focal point for echoes.

The asymmetrical shape thus formed by canted ceiling, splayed side wall, and curved chancel wall is further broken by a lowered roof level at either side of the church where seating extends out from the main body of the nave. In these lower "aisle" spaces, walls are of glass, but reflection of sound waves from this hard surface is broken by a series of vertical wooden baffles. At the rear of the church, even so small a detail as the railing to the choir balcony has been considered. To prevent an echo from its hard surface, it has been tilted slightly forward, rather than placed upright on a parallel with the chancel wall.

In addition to the shape of the church and the tilt and angle of surface details, the materials used in the interior have been chosen for their acoustical properties. They apply the principle that, to provide clear tones without reverberation, a sound-reflective surface should be opposed by a sound-absorbent one. The hard floor and hard wooden surfaces of the pews are opposed by a suspended ceiling of perforated acoustic tile, backed at strategic areas by 2 in. of insulation. The solid brick

south wall of the nave is opposed by the north wall, patterned with open brickwork repetitively splayed in and out from the wall line. The open space thus created behind the brickwork is backed by sound-absorbent material.

The solid brick chancel wall is opposed at the rear of the church by a "curtain" of open-weave plastic fabric, which separates the choir balcony from the organ loft behind it. This is a special device, not sound-reflective, but not sound-absorbent either. The smooth plastic strands allow sound waves to pass over their surfaces and through the material without being muffled as they would be by a natural textile. In this way, organ music flows forth into the nave, clear and free of distortion. At the same time the reverberation between two hard-surfaced walls is eliminated. Sounds from chancel and nave pass through the plastic fabric and are absorbed within the organ loft behind it.

Because of Saarinen's concern for sound control, starting with the basic shape of the building and extending to minor details, the acoustics of Christ Church are probably the finest of any religious building in the United States. The tone and clarity of music within it is incomparable. Although not small — it seats 600 — every syllable spoken by the minister is as clearly audible in the last row as it is in the front of the church. In effect, the congregation is "within" the service, at its acoustical center, rather than being merely a crossover point in the path of reverberating sound.

The illumination of the church has been given equally conscientious attention. The only two sources of daylight are the glass walls of the side aisles and a narrow, vertical, window strip lighting the chancel. The main area of the nave has no windows at all. However, because interior surfaces are of the palest coloring, this limited amount of daylight is reflected rather than absorbed, providing a soft yet ample illumination throughout the church, intensifying to radiant whiteness at the chancel.

In most instances, devices that provide acoustical control are designed also to control light. The sound-absorbent ceiling, for example, is reflective to light, its white expanse redirecting light waves from the chancel down into the windowless nave. The wooden baffles at side aisle windows, which break the reflection of sound in these areas, are designed primarily to shield congregation and minister from the glare of direct sunlight.

Such amalgamation of function is most dramatic at the chancel. Here, light enters through the vertical strip window in the south wall, shielded from view of the congregation by a wooden baffle, extending the entire height of the church. Striking across the chancel, the rays of the sun are cupped and reflected by the white, curved, north wall, shaped to diffuse sound, but serving with equal importance to diffuse and deflect rays of light. The effect thus created by hidden light source at one side and curved reflecting wall at the other is a subtle illumination, its beginning and end invisible. At the center of the sanctuary, the rays are caught and intensified by a huge aluminum cross which sends forth a silvery concentration of pure, colorless light.

Starkly simple sanctuary of Christ Church is equally conducive to private meditation or to the clear apperception of the formal ritual. In order to heighten the visual impression of the rich purples and reds of ecclesiastical vestments and altar linen, all elements within the chancel are colorless, or nearly so. Walls are of white painted brick, the altar of pale marble, the cross and candlesticks of brushed aluminum, the communion rail of natural wood.

Note how the curved, brick wall cups and intensifies the light that strikes it from the opposing south window. The architect's original plan called for stained glass to be substituted for clear glass in this window when funds permitted. This would have added the sole touch of color to the church, washing the white north wall with a brillant mosaic. However, when money became available the congregation voted against the addition of stained glass, fearing that it might spoil the colorless purity which they had found so moving.

This purity is the result not only of the radiant whiteness of the chancel, but also of the fact that no other decorative elements have been introduced to distract attention from the cross, the altar, and the candelabra upon which the ritual focuses. The Christian setting ubdued richness to the interior. Ceilings are white acoustic tile, and the brick chancel wall is painted white, heightened to brilliance by the flood of daylight that washes over it.

In addition to the natural illumination from chancel and side aisle windows, a flexible artificial lighting system has been provided. Soft, general illumination is achieved by means of recessed ceiling fixtures. As a substitute or a supplement, strong, indirect lighting is provided by spun aluminum "spoon-lights" that are also the major decorative element in the nave. Their silvery gleam echoes the silver radiance of cross and candelabra in the sanctuary. The window sash is also aluminum, one more consistent detail in the unity of this design.

Photos: George Miles Ryan Studios Inc.

View close to acoustical wall of nave shows how the open brickwork is splayed in and out projecting 4 in. beyond the wall line at its outermost points. Space behind the brickwork is filled with sound-absorbent material. The architect has also provided an ingenious solution to the problem of the baptismal font which, in Protestant doctrine, must be at the front of the church in full view of the congregation. The usual solution is merely to place the font near the communion rail. Here Saarinen has created a separate baptistry by utilizing the open space in front of the aisle seating at left. In this way, baptism is architecturally defined as a sacrament distinct from that of the Lord's Supper. The aluminum font, designed by the architect, once more repeats the silvery gleam of holy objects in the sanctuary. Note how the great aluminum cross is here haloed in a white radiance.

Exterior view of Christ Church clearly reveals the separate elements of the interior. At the far left is the narrow vertical window that illuminates the chancel. The low wing projecting from the main building block contains the aisle seating. Panels of opaque glass, which protect the congregation from street view but still admit light to the interior, are framed by vertical aluminum sash. The bell tower is connected to the church proper by a narrow glass gallery. Together these two elements house the stairways leading to upper and lower levels within the church. This placement frees the interior of the church from space-consuming service elements.

The main facade of the church, not visible in this photograph, is of large stone blocks, not the brick of the side walls. This expanse of solid wall is broken only by one vertical window that lights a subsidiary chapel off the narthex. The main entrance is at the far side of the church, reached by means of an arcade, which is parallel to the street and connects the church to the parish house beyond it. It is regrettable indeed that this noted masterwork was built upon such a small plot of ground, for it is difficult to see the church from any distance and it is thus difficult to appreciate the elegance of the exterior.

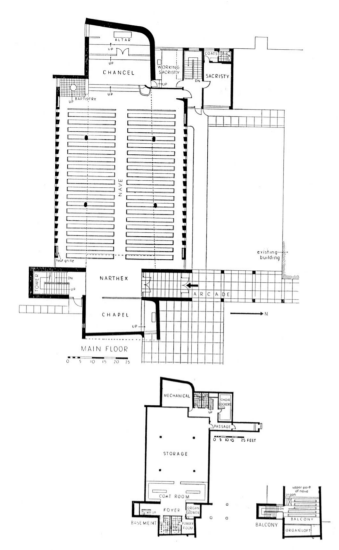

MAIN FLOOR

0 5 10 15 20 25

0 5 10 15 25 FEET

Plan of Christ Church shows the relationship of the nave to narthex and subsidiary chapel at the rear of the church. These rooms can be thrown together to provide additional seating as needed for special services. The choir balcony and organ loft are above them. Stairs leading up to balcony and loft, and down to the coat room, storage area, and rest rooms in the basement, are housed in the bell tower and its glassed gallery. Sacristy wing at the front of the church extends north from the chancel and can be separately entered from an inner court between church and parish house.

This spacious church was constructed for the remarkably modest sum of $300,000. Such economy was due entirely to the ingenuity of the architect. The structure of the church is simple. Exposed brickwork eliminates the cost of surface finishes. The double use of some spaces, such as the narthex and subsidiary chapel, further shrinks the costs. Even the seating arrangement in the nave is an economy. By continuing the pews without break into the aisles, the interior space has been utilized to its full seating capacity.

Christ Church thus represents economy as the result of painstaking planning, rather than reduced quality. The design as a whole and in detail achieves a harmony and beauty far above that of churches that cost much more.

REPORT FROM THE CLERGY
The Rev. William A. Buege, Pastor

When we undertook the project of building a new church, neither I nor the congregation were acquainted with the field of modern architecture. In fact, I had seen only the more grotesque examples, which were enough to frighten one even from contemplating such a design for spiritual purposes. But we did come to feel that only a contemporary approach would have relevance in an effort to interpret our message to the present age. Our Gospel is as honest as it is simple, and we felt that the building should express these qualities. This led us to dissatisfaction with a Gothic design which had already been prepared for Christ Church before I took up my pastorate there.

Looking back, I find it difficult to explain what moved me to this search for honest building and how I happened to think of going to the best archiect to design our church. I recall that I did seek the advice of Prof. Roy Jones, the head of the architecture school of the University of Minnesota. He suggested that I visit a number of architects, especially Eliel Saarinen, then head of the Cranbrook Academy of Art. Through a good friend I was advised to look into what had been done in the Scandinavian countries, particularly Finland. Fortunately, this limited the choice of men greatly, almost exclusively to Saarinen. We looked for the best and by God's guidance were led to Saarinen. Those who do not believe in God and his guidance would call it luck.

I cannot say today that I went to Bloomfield Hills, Mich., fully acquainted with the meaning of my mission. And I cannot say — as I would like to — that I knew the reputation of this world-famous man whom I was going to ask to consider our problem. No, I can only remember, with embarrassment, the questions I did ask and the suggestions I made as we discussed the nature of our goal. My own education began after Eliel Saarinen accepted our commission and began to educate me and our church officers. It was, for all of us, a beginning.

Why did he accept this challenge? I can tell you very simply. Eliel Saarinen consented to create our design — for very little money — because we gave him a program which, he said, compelled him to create it. In simple terms what we said was this:

"We want a house of worship reflecting our faith in our day and in our way. We want to praise God with our own hearts and hands."

Eliel Saarinen began to question us about our needs; the incubation period when the design took shape in his mind brought us into close communion with one another. It was a most rewarding association because I learned to know the greatest and the humblest man that I have ever met. I am still able to draw most heavily on that association for understanding.

At the end of the year, Eliel Saarinen was truly a member of our congregation. More than that, he was a teacher of us all and I can see why he used to say, "An architect must first of all be an educator." To further our education, we called in a competent theologian to present the history and development of church architecture so that the congregation could know that the presently accepted forms were not designs of God nor the only forms in which the church had worshipped. When Saarinen's prospectuses were ready, we used an entire week in presenting them to the congregation. I believe that these studies were important in opening the minds of the congregation to acceptance of an entirely new church design.

When the church was built, it fulfilled our requirements more perfectly than we could ever have hoped or dreamed and more perfectly than I have ever seen anywhere else. Moreover, I believe that our church would have been good at any time in history, if this type of expression had been possible with the materials then to be had. Our church ties in firmly by its basic floor plan with the churches of all time, because ours and all must meet certain liturgical requirements. It is the superstructure that expresses our life today. Church design must always have very firm roots in the past, otherwise it is merely an aberration.

Christ Church expresses the central fact that our justification, our salvation, everything is the work of God in Christ. This is most simply stated in John III: 16 — "For God so loved the world, that he gave his only begotten Son, that whosoever believeth in him should not perish, but have everlasting life." Our building shares the simplicity of these words. I doubt if anyone could be very comfortable in our church if he would not know what to do with the cross because everything comes into full focus upon it. Beneath the cross is the altar, centrally placed and perfectly lighted by God's own light as a reminder that our light is from Him and also as a symbol that the gift of Christ's Body and Blood in the Sacrament is from Him and could in no way be duplicated by us. Baptism receives its full due through beauty of design and placement of the baptistry. These are the two sacraments — baptism and the Lord's Supper — that we acknowledge as a means of grace.

Preaching of the word of God is central to our worship. This is well expressed by the size and prominence of the pulpit and made meaningful by perfect acoustics which allow direct communication without an interfering microphone. During our discussions, Mr. Saarinen mentioned, half jokingly, that if he designed the church, I would preach better sermons. But I believe that this was the literal truth. The building challenges you always to do only your very best. Sometimes I even wonder if there is anything idolatrous about my regard for this church. It has become the standard by which I judge almost all other buildings, especially those in which I preach and worship, and without any prejudice (I think) the others are found wanting.

My people react in much the same way without knowing it. A little girl walked in on the day of dedication and told her mother that it was so beautiful that she could cry. After being in the church for some months, a lady who had not been too pleased about the project, mentioned that she had been to another church and could not understand why she became so nervous there. I did not dare tell her that she had become accustomed to a single focus and was no longer used to having a variety of distractions, many different centers vying for her attention.

When we began to build, our congregation was small, and I'm afraid, quite uninspired. I remember that there were almost no members from the University of Minnesota, located across the ravine only a few miles away. After our church opened we received national acclaim, of course. But more important to us, we began to receive new souls in communion and in membership. At the end of a year we had enrolled 100 new members, many from the university. We now have many young people, people who have not been married too long. This is unusual in a congregation that is nearly 50 years old.

The merit of the form of our church is manifest to all of us because it can truly be said that this honest expression brought us a new means to reach salvation. It sharpened the wits of the old members and it brought stimulation to the new. Originally there were many who objected to the design. Two who objected left the congregation although it is doubtful even now whether it was the design or the cost of the new church that prompted their action. Others who objected remained and have since become convinced that this is the best church in the world. They are now quite willing to say so. Perhaps more than anything else showing the loving acceptance of the congregation is the fact that they paid for the church in the incredibly short space of seven years when the loans were set up on a 20-year basis. No sooner did they pay for the church than they voted to expand its facilities with a new multipurpose building. So well pleased were they with the church that they would hear of no other architect than Eero Saarinen, the son of the late Eliel Saarinen, and he has agreed to do the new work.

This church is a symbol of our faith; all of us feel that this is so and we thank the day when we were given the inspiration thus to express the best in us.

References

Christ-Janer, Albert. *Eliel Saarinen*. The University of Chicago Press, Chicago (1948).

Saarinen, Eliel. *The Search for Form*. Rheinhold Pub. Corp., New York (1948).

21. TRINITY LUTHERAN CHURCH

Walnut Creek, Calif.; Erected 1956
Pietro Belluschi (b. 1899) and Skidmore, Owings &
Merrill, architects.
Nathaniel Owings (b. 1903)
John B. Rodgers (b. 1905)
Margaret Wentworth, artist

Kaufmann & Fabry Co.

"We tried for, and think we attained, elegant simplicity, or perhaps, you might say simple elegance. We used materials of our country here — stone and redwood. The doors are symbolic of the basic principles of the Lutheran Church and set the key to the entire structure." — NATHANIEL OWINGS (Left to right, above: Nathanial Owings, John B. Rodgers)

In 1951, when Portland architect Pietro Belluschi was appointed Dean of the School of Architecture and Planning at Massachusetts Institute of Technology in Cambridge, Mass., he closed his Oregon office and entered a partnership with Skidmore, Owings & Merrill to facilitate the handling of his West Coast work. The design of Trinity Lutheran Church in Walnut Creek, Calif., is a result of that partnership, executed in the San Francisco office of Skidmore, Owings & Merrill. Although it shows the Belluschi touch unmistakably, it is equally the creation of the partner firm.

Skidmore, Owings & Merrill is one of the largest and most famous architectural offices in America, and one of the few that is set up on a nationwide operational basis. Its far-flung practice is handled by four offices — in New York, Chicago, San Francisco, and Portland, Ore. Each of these is run as an autonomous office with resident partners, rather than as a branch of the original New York firm. Nathaniel Owings, one of the founding architects, is today partner with John B. Rodgers in the

San Francisco office that handled the design shown here.

Trinity Lutheran Church represents something of a departure for Skidmore, Owings & Merrill. This firm has specialized in city planning and in the largest and most technical architectural projects: factories, office buildings, laboratories, shopping centers, huge government installations. During World War II, this firm planned and designed the then secret, but subsequently famous town of Oak Ridge, Tenn. (except for the atomic installations). Probably its most famous single building is the glassy, terraced Lever House skyscraper, which has become one of the sights of New York City, although the Company Headquarters Building at the dramatic new Air Force Academy in Colorado Springs, Colo., is becoming equally famous.

Trinity Lutheran Church represents one of the few ecclesiastical assignments to be undertaken by this firm. The result proves once more that fine architects are capable of designing any type of structure, and can temper their approach to suit whatever problem lies at hand.

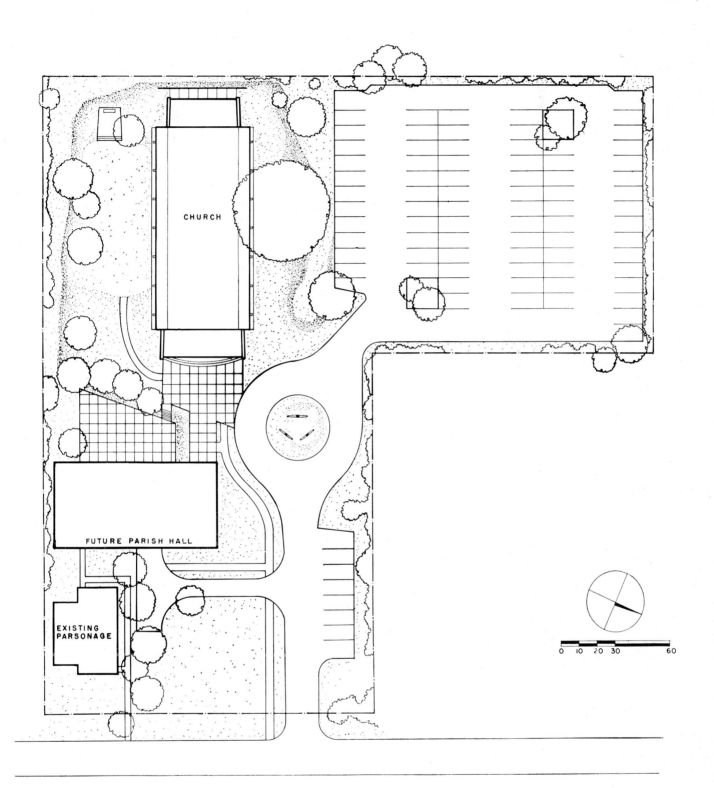

CHURCH

FUTURE PARISH HALL

EXISTING
PARSONAGE

0   10   20   30   60

Trinity Lutheran Church is as fine an example of site planning as it is of architecture. This design reflects the increasing concern, especially among Protestant denominations, with the use of the out-of-doors as an adjunct to church buildings. Located in Walnut Creek, a rapidly growing community near San Francisco, it shows the possibilities open to suburban churches that can obtain larger acreages and pleasanter sites than are available within a city. A meditation court is included at one side of the church; a social court on two levels between church and future parish hall.

The approach has been carefully planned to establish a gradual transition from the public street to the church interior. The church is placed on high ground, to the rear of the property. Consequently the approach is an ascending one, past the parish hall, culminating in the paved entrance court at the height of the property, in front of the church. As the churchgoer walks or drives upward, he sees always ahead the bold form of the church and its three towering crosses, silhouetted against the sky. Entrance is through a low, projecting, glass-fronted narthex, into the great open hall of the nave, the climax of the upward journey.

The front wall of the church, above the narthex, is stained glass, set in closely spaced redwood louvers that allow light to penetrate the glass, but cut off direct rays of the sun. The three rough and powerful crosses, planted in the circle of the driveway, are symbolic of both the Trinity and the three crosses of Calvary. They were hand-hewn by members of the church from telephone poles, a remarkable example of architectural ingenuity and congregational devotion. They are unstained and will be left to weather to a silvery gray, echoing the gray color and rough texture of the stone walls of the church.

Photos: Morley Baer

Side view of Trinity Lutheran Church, a surprising change from its bold and dramatic facade, reveals this as one of the most serenely lovely designs in the book. It is the essence of simplicity, and yet there is a softness and warmth about it entirely different from the stark, geometric simplicity of the European modern style. This church is unmistakably a part of the American countryside, evocative once more of Belluschi's "beautiful barns."

One of the most interesting features of the design occurs at the juncture of roof and lower wall on each side of the church. The roof extends beyond the wall and is joined to it by a horizontal glass panel, which runs the entire length of the nave. Through this panel, light is reflected up from the stone walls to illuminate the interior.

The supporting frame for the roof is a series of laminated wooden bents, here seen as they descend outside, and entirely free from, the lower walls. On the interior these bents are exposed as a structural arcade. The lower walls are of reinforced concrete, surfaced with gray

sonoma stone on both the exterior and interior. This stone is predominantly gray but includes enough other colors to give the expanse of masonry a lively variety in contrast to the monotone boards of the roof. The latter are of Port Orford cedar which, like the pine crosses at the front of the church, will weather a soft, silver-gray.

Trinity Church presents an interesting contrast with the Zion Lutheran and Central Lutheran churches (No. (19 and 19 a). The earlier churches emphasized the particularity of their denomination. They look like Lutheran and only Lutheran churches. This design has captured instead the generalized quality of Protestantism. It is excellent as a Lutheran church. But, with minor interior changes, it could serve equally well as a church for the Episcopal, Presbyterian, Methodist, Congregational, or even the Baptist denominations. This is partly due to its rejection of traditional features, such as bell tower and spire, that inevitably recall a particular historic past. Instead of reliance on such forms, this design has been made as simple as early Christianity itself, unencumbered by formal customs and symbols.

Interior of church looking toward the chancel, reveals a design of utter serenity and simplicity. Despite the use of natural materials and the exposure of the great structural frame, there is no sense of rusticity within this church. The composure of its lines and delicacy of its detailing — as well as the muted colors used throughout — create an atmosphere of restrained elegance.

Stone walls are a medley of gray and other earth tones. The framing bents are natural cedar. The wall and roof enclosure is of fir plywood, surfaced with narrow, horizontal, fir purlins, both stained a light ash color. Pews are of ash. Contrasting with these pale woods is the reredos of redwood, a deep reddish brown in color, and the chancel railing of dark walnut. Cathedral glass windows, which flank the reredos, are a translucent gray, shedding soft illumination upon the muted coloring of the interior. Their tone is repeated and intensified in the gray of the aisle carpet.

Occupying the central position in the sanctuary is a cream-colored marble altar on a black marble base, with the symbol of the Trinity inlaid in jade. The solid block of the altar contrasts with the delicate framework of the raised pulpit which seems to float in space at the right side of the chancel. Pulpit, candelabra, baptismal font, and altar candlesticks are all plated with brass, offering the gleam of golden metal against the rich wood of the reredos and the rough stone of the walls. The bowl of the especially designed baptismal font is colorless plastic.

The only brilliant color in this part of the church is found in the glass mosaic cross above the altar. Here, clear light blues and greens form the background, with small insets of deep blue and red. Because the interior is otherwise subdued, the glittering cross stands out as a symbol of vibrant, triumphant life.

The predominance of blue and green in the cross contrasts with the coloring of the large stained glass window that opposes it at the rear of the nave. The glass here is essentially lavender-pink and pale amber. However, like the cross, it is inset with small pieces of more brilliant color: deep red, blue, and green. Choir loft and organ chamber project out front of the rear stained glass window, which thus forms a glowing backdrop for the choristers.

Chancel cross is mosaic of glass strips, predominantly pale shades of blue and green with accents of deep blue and red. Note that a concentration of inserts, just below the cross bar, suggest a stylized lily, giving this cross the quality of resurrection as well as sacrifice. Small ceiling spots cast a dramatic glow upon the cross, while the vertical redwood paneling, thus illuminated, creates an effect of descending rays of light, reaching toward the altar.

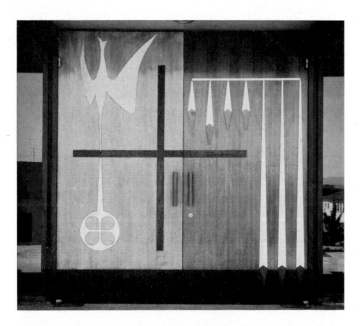

Entrance doors are of quarter-sawn walnut, one bleached and one stained a medium brown. The abstract inlays are of burnished metal: steel, aluminum, and brass. All are symbolic. The central cross dominates the group, with the Holy Spirit in the form of a descending dove at left, and in the form of seven lamps at right. These doors are among the most beautiful to be found in any modern church, illustrating the remarkable potential of abstract design for expressing the inexpressible.

Illuminating strip at each side of the nave is made of panels of obscure wire glass, set in wood frames. During morning services it admits natural daylight. At night, or if the day is overcast, the same effect is achieved by means of fluorescent tubes concealed beneath the glass. In addition to softly illuminating the nave, these panels cast light upon the walls above, intensifying the chiaroscuro of wooden purlins as they project out from their plywood backing. This unusual surface finish, which functionally strengthens and braces the plywood enclosure, serves also as integral decoration, adding textural interest to an otherwise plain interior. With the arcade of wooden bents it acts to draw the eye inevitably forward toward the chancel, the focal point of the church.

The cost of this church, erected in 1956, was a mere $125,000, including the organ, church furniture, and a warm-air heating system, as well as all landscaping and terracing completed to date. The church seats 300, but generous side aisles permit a larger congregation at Christmas and Easter. A total of 7,755 sq. ft. of floor area brings its cost to only $14 per square foot. The parish hall has yet to be erected, but its estimated cost is $150,000. It will be built on two levels of the sloping property, with the large social hall in the lower story opening away from the church, while classrooms in the upper story open toward the church, directly onto the social court that joins the two buildings. Also included in this spacious design will be a pastor's study, office, and garage.

It should be reemphasized here that the churches shown in this book were chosen solely on the basis of architectural merit without prior knowledge of their cost. The remarkably low cost of a church like Trinity Lutheran is proof of the large savings inherent in brilliant structural solutions as opposed to the few dollars that can be saved by substituting inferior materials in a basically wasteful design.

REPORT FROM THE CLERGY
The Rev. Alvin L. Rubin, Pastor

The following comments apply both to Zion Lutheran Church (No. 19), which is one of the oldest congregations in the city of Portland, Ore, and to Trinity Lutheran Church, a new congregation established only in 1946 in the "crossroads community" of Walnut Creek, Calif. I was pastor of both of these churches when they were designed and built.

The choice of contemporary architecture for these quite different churches stems from the same reasoning: a feeling that each generation should express itself honestly with its own forms. I am disturbed when the devotion of men is but a copy of that of past generations. I do not believe that the truth of God changes. But man expresses himself differently from age to age. When men use the same expressions of devotion to God — and a church is such an expression of devotion — it means to me that they have not discovered the truth of God for themselves, but are merely aping their forefathers.

I cannot point to a time nor to an incident which brought about the feeling that our houses of worship should be an expression of devotion in our own forms. Perhaps the fact that, as a youth, I learned to appreciate natural beauty, had much to do with it, for I was born and raised in the foothills of the Ozarks. I often wondered, as I began visiting different churches, why the natural beauty of God's creation, the texture of wood and stone, had to be hidden under plaster or paint. Do we sometimes think that we can do better than the Creator?

A few members of my congregation in Portland discussed the building of a church that would be an honest expression of our own feelings toward God. After a number of these discussions, I devised some questions that would embody their feelings and their approach to church design. We sought an architect who was a man of creative ability, a man who would seek to express the tenets of our faith in the design of the church, and a man who was sensitive to a devotional atmosphere. To our questions Pietro Belluschi gave the right answers.

In subsequent discussions with the architects I insisted that the interior of the church was primary, not the exterior. It is inside the church that people worship. I asked them to study the doctrines of the church and to attend the worship of the people. Finally, they were given space requirements and the amount of money available. This, then, became the problem for them to solve.

In both instances, in Portland and Walnut Creek, the people were convinced that they were not to interfere with the architects, as, for instance, by demanding certain forms. We agreed that the architects should be left free to create, and that the congregation would have the right to accept their work or to reject it. This would be done "in toto." We would not make changes in certain parts of the church to suit our own notions.

However, people are naturally disinclined to venture. I, myself, tried to approach the building of each church without preconceived notions. But as far as the congregation was concerned, these churches took a great deal of persuasion. Perhaps we used some arguments that would not normally be considered valid — for instance, that contemporary design costs less. There were also meetings with the architect in which he set forth his reasons for designing a church that would be an expression of our own time. But even with this education, the church in Portland was passed by only one vote. And even after this there was a great deal of resistance. Many members were surprised, some shocked. There were numerous objections, the most common being, "it doesn't look like a church." However, after the erection of the church, none, of whom I know, continued to object, but all became proud of their church. They found that they could think of the new church without a picture of the old, traditional church in mind.

When Zion Lutheran Church of Portland was designed and built, there was little contemporary church architecture that I considered worthwhile, at least in the Northwest. In Trinity Church of Walnut Creek, we had the example of Zion Lutheran behind us. Also, the members of this newer parish were more venturesome. The vote in favor of the design here was unanimous. We still heard: "The exterior does not look like a church." But there was no real objection to it. Once people have worshipped in either Zion Lutheran or Trinity, all doubts disappear. We are still hearing some criticism from nonmembers, but in each instance it is definitely a matter of being bound by tradition.

From my point of view, the most important attribute of these new churches is that they provide the pastor with an atmosphere conducive to worship. The people, placed in such an atmosphere, are moved to worship, rather than simply "attend church." I feel that the honesty of expression in these churches is conducive to honesty in one's relationship with God. This makes

for spiritual growth. Do not misunderstand. Worship begins in the heart. But the church is definitely an aid to worship, perhaps even a nurse.

Especially as a concrete expression of spiritual ideas, architecture can be very important. It would require a great deal of space to show how the architects accomplished this, since the tenets of the Lutheran faith guided the entire design in each instance. I shall therefore mention only a few things that I consider important in my present church. In conformity with the "priesthood of all believers," the chancel in Trinity Church is not set apart from the nave in any way, but is actually a continuation of the nave — a part of the whole — saying in form that the pastor and the congregation are worshipping God together. Also the communion rail is open to the altar, inviting the people, as well as the pastor, to approach the altar. The doctrine of the Trinity is expressed in the three steps to the altar, and also in the symbol incised in the altar. The fact that we worship a living Christ is expressed by the empty cross and the lily growing out of it.

Although I do not believe that any new church building will, of itself, attract and hold the unchurched, nevertheless our new churches have attracted people, giving us the opportunity to make contact with them. Sometimes people of our faith coming into the community become members of our congregation because they like the fresh and living design. In Portland there was a definite change in the membership. After three years, the average age of the members was much younger. In Walnut Creek there has been no change in the type of membership, since the community, at least for the most part, is made up of one class of people, an upper middle class. Nevertheless, the young people are far more conscious of the fact that the church is a place of worship. The comments of worshippers express this feeling:

"Since we left Walnut Creek, we miss most of all our church there. There is something about Trinity that makes one want to worship when you are in it. I do not find that in the church here."

"For some reason, one feels like worshipping when one goes to your church."

"My friend and I worshipped at Trinity last Sunday. It was an outstanding experience for both of us. Allow me to compliment you on the atmosphere prevailing in your church, also on the liturgical excellence and devotion of your people. I frankly consider it to be one of the finest examples of the Lutheran tradition that I have found anywhere. The prospects for Lutheranism in your community are exciting because of this awakening."

The Protestant Episcopal Church is the autonomous United States branch of the world-wide Anglican Communion, which recognizes the Church of England as its spiritual fountainhead. Its world membership numbers some 40 million, with 3.2 million in the United States.

Brought to Jamestown, Va., by Captain John Smith in the year 1607, it became the first and the official church of the English crown colonies in this hemisphere. A number of the founding fathers of the United States of America belonged to the Church of England, including George Washington, Alexander Hamilton, James Monroe, and James Madison.

However, the conflicting loyalties of the Revolutionary War nearly destroyed the American Episcopal Church, so shattering its organizational and monetary status that it did not fully recover from the blow for over 50 years. Even then, this denomination did not show the rapid growth typical of the more evangelistic religions in an expanding America. Yet despite its comparatively small membership, the Episcopal Church retained always a certain prestige rooted in its historic link to the British Crown and the hereditary position and wealth of many of its members.

Furthering its sense of the established and traditional is the fact that this faith considers itself to be the true, Reformed Catholic Church, tracing the spiritual authority of its ordained bishops, like the Roman Catholic, back to the Apostles. Even the name of the American branch is derived from the Greek word *episkopos* meaning "bishop," thus emphasizing the importance of the apostolic succession. However, the break with Roman Catholicism came over just this question of spiritual authority. Under Henry VIII, the Church of England freed itself from the papacy with the words: "The Bishop of Rome hath not by Scriptures any greater authority in England than any other foreign bishop."

Because of its strong sense of continuity, the liturgy of the Episcopal Church retains many of the ancient traditional emphases. The High Episcopal service is comparable to the Roman Catholic Mass, with its focus upon the Eucharist and upon the chanted ritual, rendered, however, in English rather than in Latin. But there is a great variation in Episcopal services and the so-called Low Episcopal has little more in common with the ritual of its own High Church than the famous *Book of Common Prayer*. Moreover, in their reliance upon the Bible, rather than upon "the Church," as the final authority and testing ground for Christian doctrine, all branches of the Episcopal faith proclaim themselves as distinctly Protestant. This communion is, in fact, less dogmatic in its beliefs than many Protestant denominations that have made a more radical departure from Roman Catholic form.

This particular combination of traditional pomp with a moderate position on questions of doctrine and personal discipline may at least partially account for the sudden and rapid growth of this church within shifting religious loyalties of the last decade. Certainly, it is true that in these past few years, the Episcopal Church has at last come fully alive to its potential as a universal church, essentially Catholic in ritual yet truly Protestant in its freedom of individual thought and conscience. From 1950 to 1957, membership increased by over one-third, more than had been added in the preceding 55 years. More interesting even than this increase is the fact that the new membership includes many middle class and working people, attracted by the new Episcopal commitment to community service in crowded urban parishes and to forthright stands on social issues.

Traditionally, the Episcopal church has expressed in architecture the richness of its Anglican heritage. Austerity in religious ritual or in the churches that housed this ritual has not been an Episcopalian characteristic. While the New England Puritans were building their severe, box-like "meeting houses," stripped of all traditional symbolism, the Episcopalians enriched the interiors of their steepled churches with glittering chandeliers and crimson velvet hangings, sometimes including a throne for the Royal Governor.

In more recent times, Episcopalians have taken their inspiration primarily from the English Gothic cathedrals, or from the half-timbered style of English parish buildings. Some members of the clergy even encourage the idea that these English architectural styles are part of the Episcopal religious heritage — that an Episcopal church must be Gothic.

It is interesting to find, therefore, that when Episcopalians do take the step toward modern architecture, as in the examples that follow, they have produced some of the most advanced designs to be found in America. One of the three churches shown here is a modern translation of the English Gothic, with the soaring arches and glowing stained glass that epitomize the tradition of this church. But the other two make a radical departure from inherited style, returning to the stark simplicity suggestive of early Christianity.

22. CHAPEL OF ST. JAMES THE FISHERMAN

Wellfleet, Mass.; Erected 1956
Olav Hammarstrom (b. 1906), architect, landscape
architect, and interior designer
Marianne Strengell Hammarstrom, textiles and interior
design
Paul Weidlinger, structural engineer

"Man is always the focal point; architecture is his setting, background, and echo." — OLAV HAMMARSTROM (Olav Hammarstrom and Marianne Strengell Hammarstrom).

The modest and inexpensive Chapel of St. James the Fisherman, built by a congregation of summer residents at Wellfleet on Cape Cod, Mass., may well become one of the most influential Episcopal churches of the twentieth century. Here, as in a pilot project, fundamental changes in the Protestant Episcopal liturgy have been expressed through architecture. Like the several Roman Catholic churches shown earlier in the book, this chapel illustrates the Liturgical Revival as interpreted by a specific branch of the Christian faith.

Wherever it is found, the Liturgical Revival emphasizes a renewed intimacy between clergy and congregation as coparticipants within the religious service. But the Episcopal church here carries this concept to its logical conclusion, by placing the altar at the very center of the church, surrounded on all sides by the congregation. With this plan, the Episcopal faith shows its aim as the full return to the earliest and simplest of Christian concepts.

At the Chapel of St. James the Fisherman, the officiating priest and other participating members of the clergy are seated within the congregation, as near to their own families as possible, leaving these seats only as the service demands. The choir is unvested, and seated amongst the congregation, rather than in a separate choir loft. It does not perform as a group at all, choir members acting solely as "leaders" for the congregational chanting and singing which are integral parts of the entire service.

Not only are clergy and choir made one with the congregation, the laity is also elevated to participation in the clerical service. Three roles traditionally played by the clergy are here performed by members of the congregation itself. These include the reading of the Old Testament lesson and of the Epistle, and the carry-ing of the oblations of bread and wine to the sanctuary. Chosen laymen, different ones each Sunday, perform these liturgical roles and then return once more to sit with their families. A small but revealing detail is the fact that the bread used for the sacrament of Communion is a real loaf, baked each week by a different woman of the congregation.

This church follows the ancient belief that complete worship contains three elements: the service of the Word, the service of the Sacrament, and the fellowship of believers. The Sunday program always includes Morning Prayer and Holy Communion — or in medieval terms, Matins and Mass — followed by an informal social gathering outside the church, at which light refreshments are served. The latter represents the Agapé or "feast-of-brotherly-love" which always accompanied worship in the primitive church. The Word, the Eucharist, and the Agapé are viewed as one continuous service, emphasizing in three ways the communion of Christian believers.

These various changes in accustomed liturgy bring all worshippers into a religious discipleship that had been quite lost to the church. The Rt. Rev. James A. Pike, Bishop Coadjutor of California, and formerly Dean of the Cathedral of St. John the Divine in New York City, is the founder and one of the two priests-in-charge of the Chapel of St. James the Fisherman. As the moving spirit behind the liturgy of its design, he explains:

Within the Anglican Communion, the Reformation was never really completed, especially as far as architecture befitting our ideas is concerned. We meant to return to the early Catholic Church, but our buildings, through the centuries, have not expressed this ideal. Only recently has the trend of Episcopal Church building

Joseph W. Molitor

shown signs of promise in this regard. Here, in the Chapel of St. James the Fisherman, we have tried to portray the ancient and primitive meaning of Christian worship. Many clergy and laity attending from other places feel that we have accomplished this aim more fully than in vastly more expensive buildings.

The printed program given to each worshipper adds:

At the Last Supper, and in Christian worship in the early Church, the apostles were a part of the sacred drama, not mere spectators.... In being more modern than some services to which you have been accustomed, we are actually more primitive and more ancient. And this likewise applies to our chapel building....

Since those of us who worship in St. James come from many communities throughout the nation, we have had a somewhat larger hope than simply the desire to provide a suitable home for our summer services. We are hoping that we may provide a stimulus to renewal of simple, realistic, and corporate liturgical worship, not only within the Episcopal Church but in the Christian Church generally. We are not alone in this aim: one of the most refreshing developments throughout the churches in recent decades has been the reexamination of what we should be doing in worship so that our weekday life may be indelibly impressed of the meaning of the Christian gospel.

Chapel of St. James the Fisherman is approached up a sloping unpaved road which leads to a court adjacent to the Agapé House and the church proper. The simple aspirational form of the spire, which rises from the center of the square building, proclaims the presence of the chapel to all who pass on the highway below. Because of the high ground upon which the chapel is placed, this spire acts also as a beacon to sailors and fishermen off the shores of Cape Cod. In this way, the consecration of the chapel to the patron saint of fishermen and sea voyagers is visibly emphasized.

The elevation of the spire, with an open space between it and the roof, allows direct skylighting of the altar, concentrating interior illumination upon the sacred center of the church. Its form vividly recalls the ancient prototype of European peasant churches, particularly those of Switzerland, Finland, and the Scandinavian countries.

The architect of the church, Olav Hammarstrom, was one of the leading younger architects of Finland before making his permanent home in America in 1948. In the United States he first worked as a designer in the office of Eero Saarinen, gifted son of the noted Finnish architect Eliel Saarinen, who designed Christ Church Lutheran (No. 20). Hammarstrom now maintains his own offices in Bloomfield Hills, Mich., and in Wellfleet, Mass.

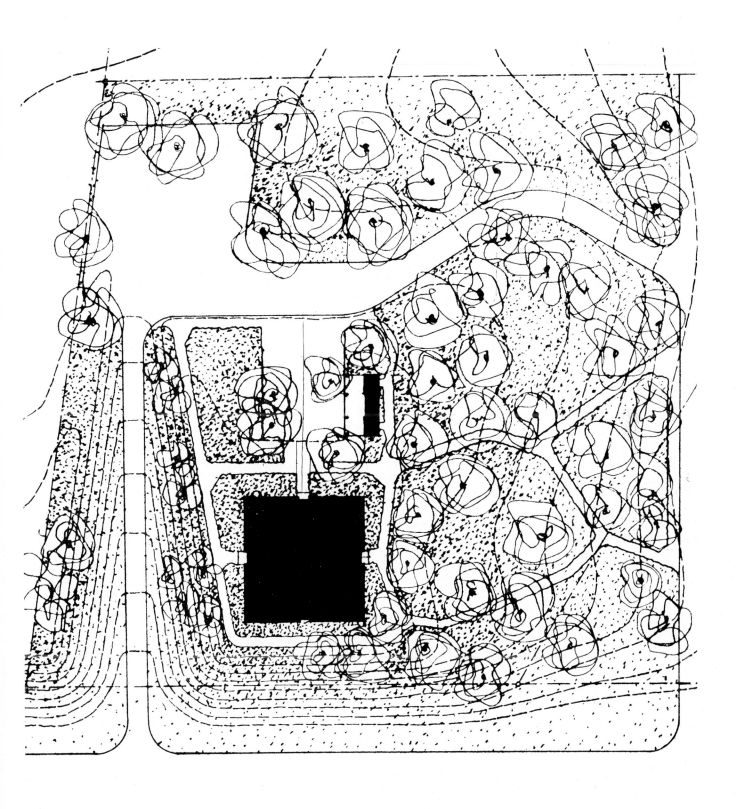

His approach to design centers on the use of local materials to produce structures of native simplicity. Characteristically the Chapel of St. James the Fisherman is built almost entirely of wood by local Cape Cod carpenters in a simple system of bolted beams and rafters. As reported in an interview in the *Worcester Sunday Telegram* for August 25, 1957, Hammarstrom remarks of this chapel: "It looks as if it belongs here. That is always the first test for me. It looks as if it has been here for ages."

Site plan shows the approach to the chapel from the highway below it. Parking space for automobiles will be provided to the north of the pine-wooded hill. Courtyard, Agapé House, and chapel are linked by pedestrian walks, which will eventually be continued though the woods as shown.

This chapel has three identical entrances, each centered in one wall of the square building. Shown here is the main entrance that faces the courtyard. Opposing it, in the fourth wall of the chapel, is a fixed window that acts as a backdrop for the pulpit. Doors are wood except for glass transoms set in narrow, wooden sash. The square roof of the chapel is "turned" so that corners project over entrance doors, rather than following the position of the building underneath. This feature creates the illusion that the chapel is a hexagon, rather than a square, and prevents the box-like appearance that a parallel roofline would have imparted.

The major source of ventilation is a continuous strip of clear glass panes set in operable sash along the bottom of each wall. These windows are also a source of light, almost invisible to the congregation.

William Neufeld

During the service of Holy Communion and at other times, the clergy leave their congregational seating to perform traditional roles at altar, pulpit, and lectern. When a layman reads the Old Testament lesson and the Epistle, and when the entire body of worshippers sings the service together, clergymen retire from the sanctuary to become part of the congregation. There is no separate choir or choir loft.

Illumination of the seating area of the church has been kept purposely dim so that attention will not be distracted from the sanctuary to a view of the congregation surrounding it on all sides. Only the sanctuary itself is more brilliantly lighted from above. There are no electric lights in this simple church, but a member of the congregation reports: "I have been there as late as 9 P.M. and the light was still glowing on the altar."

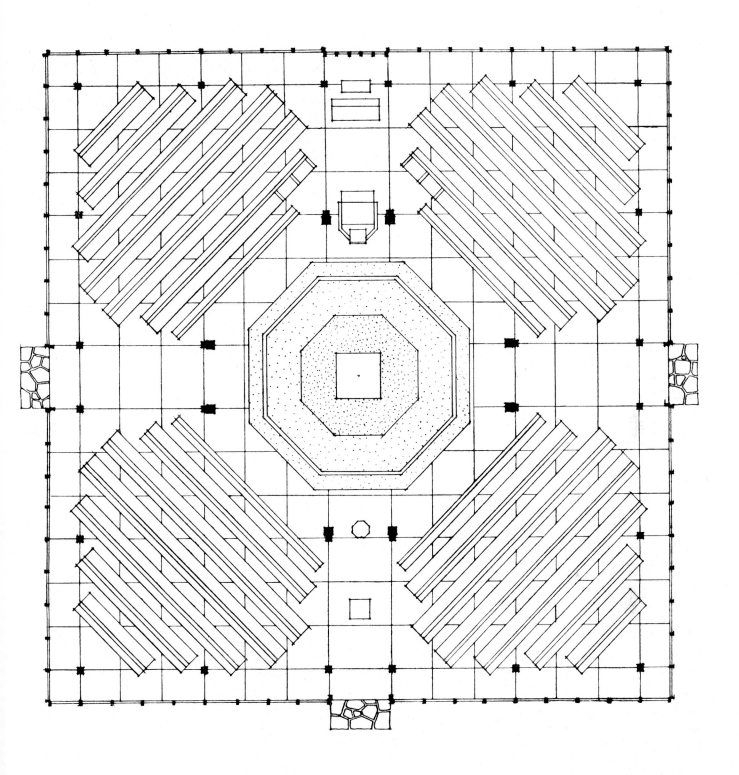

Plan of the chapel is a simple 58-ft. square, a dimension repeated by the 58-ft. central spire. Diagonal lines show how groups of pews are set at a 45-degree angle in each of the four corners of the chapel, thus surrounding the sanctuary, but allowing space for an aisle between each two groupings. With this compact arrangement, seating is provided for 300 to 320 worshippers in the surprisingly small space of 3,250 sq. ft. Because of the simplicity of its plan (which makes the best possible use of space) and because of the simplicity of its structural system (exposed without surface finishes or trim on both exterior and interior), this chapel was built for the remarkable sum of only $ 26,000.

The plan, however, is more than simply functional and economical. It is also symbolic. The grouping of pews around the altar emphasizes the centrality of the religious rite and the continuum of its participants. The altar is square, presenting the same view from any of the four groups of seating. The centered aisles, in plan, form the shape of the cross. The main entrance (bottom of plan as shown here) faces a fixed window (top), with baptismal font, pulpit, and lectern on this same axis at opposite sides of the sanctuary. This placement emphasizes the progression from baptism to Sacrament to Word, behind all of which shines the clear light of the sun.

Side view of chapel shows clearly its exterior structure and form. Unusual new materials and methods of building have purposely been avoided as inappropriate to the rustic Cape Cod setting. Instead, the chapel is built entirely of wood fabricated at the site by local carpenters. Walls are simply a sheathing of tongue-and-groove spruce boards, set vertically and without additional trim. The frame for the central skylight, and the spire above it, are both surfaced with cedar shingles like those of the older Cape Cod cottages native to this region. Even the interior furnishings of the church — pews, pulpit, altar, and lectern — were built by the contractor on the job.

Close view of spire shows its finish of cedar shingles, now patined by the sun into a mosaic of subtle colors. In this photograph, the plastic skylights that illuminate the sanctuary are clearly visible. They are set in equal rows of five, to form a square. Each dome is 2 ft. in diameter, making a square of slightly more than 10 ft. on each side — the size of a small room. These plastic domes and the glass ventilating panels are the only manufactured elements used in the entire design.

Joseph W. Molitor

Joseph W. Molitor

Joseph W. Molitor

Joseph W. Molitor

Interior view taken from main entrance aisle shows how structural elements of the chapel frame a view of the sanctuary. Slanted posts continue through the roof to support the spire. Uprights support the roof beams. Both the wooden frame of the church, and the wooden sheathing that encloses it, are exposed on the interior. All are creosoted a deep brown.

Thus, the visual impression of this chapel is that of a dark, rough-hewn backdrop, surrounding a sanctuary of pale radiance. White light pours through the skylight upon an altar covered with white linen. The carpeting of the sanctuary is white tweed, flecked with black. Suspended over the altar is a cross, hand-chiseled of wood by the architect and stained the color of old gold. The only brilliant colors in the entire church are found in an altar pillow of shocking-pink rough tweed, and the pulpit cloth of a similar tweed.

On a direct axis with the altar, the baptismal font echoes, at a smaller scale, the pale coloring of the sanctuary. Its pedestal — also chiseled by the architect — is stained the same gold as the cross. A large scallop shell, which serves as the font, repeats the white of the altar linen. The scallop shell is both the official emblem of the village of Wellfleet and the traditional symbol of St. James the Fisherman, to whom the chapel is dedicated. This choice therefore spans the centuries, emphasizing once more the ancient and yet contemporary character of the ceremonies enacted here.

Agapé House from which fruit juice and crackers are served to the congregation is set close by the church. It functions also as a sacristy and robing room for the clergy before and after the service. In this photograph, the priest-in-charge and participating clergy are preparing for their entrance to the chapel a few steps away. The setting for these buildings, in the midst of a beau-

tiful pine grove atop a hill, enfolds the worshipper in the everlasting natural creation, far removed from a transient, man-made environment. It thus establishes a mood of quiet reverence, reminding all who come of the fundamental nature of the God who made the world.

Reference

Sandrof, Ivan. "Adventure in Architecture," *Worcester Sunday Telegram*, August 25, 1957.

REPORT FROM THE CLERGY
The Rt. Rev. James A. Pike, J.S.D., S.T.D. Bishop of California; Co-priest-in-charge, Chapel of St. James the Fisherman

This church was founded only 10 years ago to serve Episcopalians and others who spend their summers in the Wellfleet-Truro area of outer Cape Cod. We are a transient summer church and therefore have no large official membership.

Prior to the erection of our own church in 1957, we had worshipped in the local Congregational church at an earlier hour than their regular service. The vestry and I discussed the question of building a church for several years before the decision was made, and the entire congregation talked a good deal about the liturgy of our church and its meaning for contemporary man. The concept of the building evolved naturally from these discussions and from our wish to speak to people of the present day in terms both ancient and modern.

The requirements laid down for the architect were basic liturgical concepts, the centralized plan being an idea stemming from our congregational discussions. The matter of economy of the building also helped dictate its plan and structure. I believe that Mr. Hammarstrom fulfilled our requirements and more. Our only trouble is that whereas we had an attendance averaging about 100 before we put up the new church, we now have 300 to 400 on a Sunday and we did not plan a large enough building. But the vestry, the architect, and I have managed to fit in more people.

This building expresses the belief that worship is not merely sitting in an auditorium and listening to a minister, however talented. Worship is the involvement of the whole group in action. Also, we have followed the best lines of the Anglican Communion in believing that complete worship includes the service of the Word and the service of the Sacrament. We have Morning Prayer and Holy Communion every Sunday at our one service, at 9:30.

The service begins with the traditional opening sentence followed by the versicles and responses. Then the congregation sings the Venite and the psalm — all together. Here, the minister does not read every other line *at* the people — we sing the psalms because they are simply parts of the Jewish hymnal, and there is no more reason to read psalms *at* people than to read hymns *at* them.

Next, a layman rises from his seat with his family and reads the Old Testament lesson out of the Bible, after which we sing the canticle.

Then, the celebrant, still in choir, with the people, begins the Collect for Purity and the summary of the Law. The congregation sings the Kyrie eleison, and the celebrant salutes the congregation with the *Dominus vobiscum* and receives their response *et cum spiritu tuo* — all this of course in English — and says the Collect for the day.

Then, another layman rises in his place and reads the Epistle. After the Gradual hymn, one of the clergy ascends the ambo (pulpit) and proclaims the Gospel. Then we all recite the Nicene Creed and the preacher ascends the pulpit. After his sermon he makes the anouncements for the week, calling on members of the congregation if they have reports to give.

Then begins the service of the Sacrament. The four clergy taking part in the service go inside the rails. The offertory sentence is announced and a hymn is sung, during which alms are collected and laymen come up to one side of the rails with the alms and the oblations of bread (a whole loaf) and wine. The Offertory follows with the rest of the Eucharist, the three clergy being on three sides of the Holy Table. The service is completed as usual.

After worship within the church, everyone repairs to the grounds, where, from the Agapé house, refreshments are served. An hour or so of visiting completes the pattern of the early Church: the service of the Word, the Eucharist, and the Agapé.

This is our revised concept of the Episcopal liturgy, upon which the design of St. James the Fisherman is based. The architect's approach caused no change in the original concept of our worship; but he made it possible for us fully to implement this concept. His architecture served to make more vivid the best liturgical objective.

23. CHURCH OF THE REDEEMER

Baltimore, Md.; Erected 1958
Pietro Belluschi (b. 1899) and Rogers, Taliaferro &
Lamb, associated architects
Archibald C. Rogers (b. 1917)
Francis T. Taliaferro (b. 1922)
Charles E. Lamb (b. 1926)
Gyorgy Kepes, artist
Ronald Hayes Pearson, sculptor
E. Bruce Baetjer, landscape architect
Henry Adams Inc., lighting consultant

"In sensitive and skilled hands, space creates suspense and drama; the light it receives, with its accents and its shadows, gives a hint of mystery and becomes a means to deepen space itself, while texture and color may provide a moving poetic experience." — PIETRO BELLUSCHI

The little Chapel of St. James the Fisherman (preceding), shows the Episcopal Church at its simplest and most direct. By contrast, the Church of the Redeemer in Baltimore, Md., represents the Episcopal Church in full panoply. Here are all the glory of stained glass, the soaring arches, the dimmed nave, and mysterious glowing altar that link the modern church with its Anglo-Catholic heritage.

Despite its evocation of the traditional, however, this church, like the Cape Cod chapel, has based its plan upon the new concepts of the Liturgical Revival, emphasizing an intimate union between clergy and congregation. The symbolic starting point of the design was the central altar, representing the communion table about which the parish family is gathered. This idea, which was carried out "in-the-round" by the small Chapel of St. James the Fisherman, here presents a far more difficult problem. The Church of the Redeemer is a large city church, with a congregation that has grown to over 2,100 communicants. The new church had to accommodate a minimum of 800 worshippers with provision for handling 1,000 at a later date.

Providing a sense of intimacy for such a large congregation would be quite impossible within the standard rectangular church plan. Furthermore, the circle or the square, used so successfully in the Chapel of St. James the Fisherman, would here present insoluble conflicts with existing buildings, executed in traditional style. The solution chosen was the cruciform plan with generous transepts at either side of the chancel to supplement the main nave.

The cruciform plan is an ancient one, used in both the Romanesque and Gothic cathedrals. It is also the plan of the existing church within this building group.

But in the new church it has been so modified — by shortening and widening the proportions of nave and transepts — that it becomes a new design.

The long, narrow, hall-like interior spaces of the Gothic cathedral emphasized the immense distance between worshippers and the remote high altar. Here, the altar is brought forward into the crossing and placed so that all worshippers are disposed closely around it. Transepts, as well as nave, are used for seating, carrying out the symbolic circle of the parish family, with the congregation at three sides of the communion table and the priest behind the altar at the fourth side, closing the circle.

The rector of the church, the Rev. Bennett Sims, has commented on the surprising closeness he feels to the congregation during a service, while at the same time experiencing a sense of "verticality" and mystery over the altar. This plan illustrates the remarkable ability of Pietro Belluschi to transmute the traditional symbols of an ecclesiastical heritage into a functional design, wholly expressive of the religious spirit of the twentieth century.

By echoing traditional form and detail, Belluschi also has related the new design to the existing, century-old Gothic church — which henceforward will serve as a chapel — and to a parish house built in traditional style during the 1930's. A new administration building and church school have also been integrated with existing buildings. Such an exercise in harmony between old and new has seldom been accomplished with the grace seen here. In this difficult task Belluschi has been ably aided by his associates, Rogers, Taliaferro & Lamb, a comparatively new office of talented young architects in nearby Annapolis, Md.

M. E. Warren

The Church of the Redeemer, although copying no historic style, awakes echoes of a varied Episcopal tradition in architecture. Without planking or plaster, it evokes the Elizabethan half-timbered style adopted by so many of these parish churches in the early twentieth century. Without spire, bell tower, or fanciful fretwork, it suggests the Gothic aspirational line. Above all, it looks English. The Church of the Redeemer could be set down in the English countryside and, despite its modernity, look as though it has been there always. In this manner the heritage of the Anglican communion is subtly yet clearly stated. Also, the new church achieves harmony with the English Gothic style of the old church, which remains as a reminder of the parish past, its spire still dominating the building complex and providing its architectural climax.

In order that the old and new should in no way compete, the major entrances to each are on opposite sides of the church property. However, the two churches are linked at transept entrances by a fenced courtyard as shown. This direct, rear view of the new church shows north and south transepts as they extend at either side from the central chancel. The projecting gabled element at center houses the sacristy and robing rooms.

The understated exterior of the Church of the Redeemer gives little hint of its majestic interior, even though the plan and form of the church are clearly delineated. A framework of laminated wooden arches supports the roof, giving it the gabled form seen here. On the interior, these arches are exposed to create soaring arcades in all wings of the church.

The lower wall of stone bears no weight. Because it is a curtain wall, structurally separated from the arch and roof system, it has been possible to insert a ribbon window of stained glass between the wall and the roof, encircling the church. Contrasting with this jeweled

Joseph W. Molitor

band are huge gable windows set with amber glass that provide muted illumination in each wing.

Entrance to the north transept (above), like all entrances, is set back within a broad, sheltered porch. The large louvered transept window is of the identical design used in all four gables of the church. A similar louvered screen at the center of the porch below forms a small, exterior narthex. The heavy arched framing member that cuts through the transept window is not an applied decoration, but one of the laminated wooden arches that are used as structural supports throughout the church. The smaller wooden members above it constitute one of the sets of struts that secure each arch to the roof beams. Here again is illustrated the principle of integral decoration, in which the pattern of the structure itself acts to "decorate" the building.

The main entrance loggia to the new church is visible at far left, sheltered at front by an open portico.

Entrance to the south transept is identical with that of the north transept that opposes it at the other side of the church. However, the approach here is through a paved, planted, and fenced courtyard — called St. John's Court — that connects the new church (left), the existing parish hall (rear), and the old church (out of photograph at right).

Stone used for the walls of the new church is identical with that of the parish hall in the background, erected during the 1930's. Gabled roofs of the new church repeat the gables of the parish hall and also those of the original church, built 100 years ago, so that the buildings appear to have been designed as parts of a unified whole. In these ways the architects have created a subtle harmony between old and new without compromising the contemporary design. The courtyard itself acts as a transitional area between the three buildings. It will be used also for outdoor services, sheltered from street view.

Looking into the main entrance court from the driveway, one is struck by the dramatic horizontal lines of the portico, repeated in the roof overhangs of adjoining buildings, and punctuated by the verticals of supporting stone columns. This entrance creates a sense of protection and shelter that is more than visual, because all roofs connect without a break to provide continuous, sheltered, circulation around the periphery of the courtyard.

Straight ahead, as one ascends the courtyard steps, are the doors to a narrow gallery — in traditional termi-

nology, the ambulatory — connecting the church at right with the administration building at left, and leading also to the parish hall at rear. In addition, the ambulatory opens into an interior meditation court, between it and the parish hall.

The ambulatory and administration building are more severe than the church itself, containing large areas of clear glass in a rectilinear framing system. However, their design is linked to that of the church by sloping, overhanging roofs and by the V-treatment of planking used to surface exterior walls.

Joseph W. Molitor

View across courtyard shows the main entrance to the church, flanked by ambulatory and portico. Although the gables of the existing parish hall — one of which is visible behind the ambulatory at left — were disturbing elements in the design of this courtyard, the architect's skill has made them part of the harmonious whole. The gable of the new church repeats their lines; the stone of courtyard columns echoes their stone construction; the continuous roof of all new buildings acts as a unifying line, tying the parish hall into the total design. The result is a thoroughly integrated composition.

When this photograph was taken, courtyard planting had not yet been completed. Eventually flowers, shrubbery, and a fountain will soften the continuum of paving and structure.

Unlike the transept entrances, the main doors to the church are not set behind louvered screens, but approached directly. They open into a broad narthex beneath the lower roof level, lighted only by a strip window of deep-toned stained glass. From this dim, low-ceilinged lobby, the church-goer enters the main nave to a view of soaring arches and, at the far end of the church, behind the chancel, a brilliant stained glass altar screen that is the visual climax of the interior.

Joseph W. Molitor

Stained glass altar screen is the most beautiful and most significant feature of the interior. It represents one of the first uses in this country of stained glass in a concrete frame — a system arriving 33 years after Auguste Perret introduced it in his famous church of Notre Dame du Raincy (No. 1). However, the screen in the Church of the Redeemer goes beyond the church at Raincy because concrete is used also as the delineating element in the design itself. The concrete has been cast into squares of intricate openwork, the interstices of which are filled with glass. This lacy patterning of concrete serves as an abstract over-all design within which another design is created by the subtle manipulation of color and light. Predominating are brilliant orange, red, and yellow with an intermingling of blue and green. These vivid hues partially give way to white, forming a luminous cross within the window. The delineation of the white cross is so subtly done that it is not immediately apparent, but tends to grow upon the observer like the materialization of a mystery.

In front of the screen, standing out against its brilliant colors and framed by the dark wood of the church interior, is an altar of white marble. The pure whiteness of this block of stone concentrates into solid form the evanescent whiteness of the cross above it, which, by contrast, assumes almost the quality of a vision.

In order to realize the full impact of altar and screen,

the rest of the church has been held deliberately to a low key. The wood of arches and ceiling is stained a deep brown; pews are black afarra wood; floors, wherever uncarpeted, a dark cork tile. Stone walls are neutral in coloring, and their rough-textured surfaces reflect no light.

Further heightening the focus on the altar and its vivid backdrop is the visual progression of lines within the nave and transepts. The great, brooding arches repeat the shape of the stained glass screen and lead the eye inevitably toward it. Cutting between the pews, like a ribbon of color toward the altar, is an amethyst carpet.

The final touch in the unique atmosphere of this interior is the artificial lighting, which allows unusual flexibility in the creation of moods and emphases. It consists of three separate systems: spotlighting of altar and chancel; backlighting of the altar screen; and general illumination for the nave and transepts, operating on a dimmer system. The effectiveness of these lighting systems lies in their relation to each other. Almost any combination of intensity and quality can be achieved through adjustments between them. In addition they can be keyed to either day or night conditions. The architects have commented: "Some of these effects are very moving indeed, and there is no question that the lighting arrangements greatly enhance the mystery and religious quality of this church."

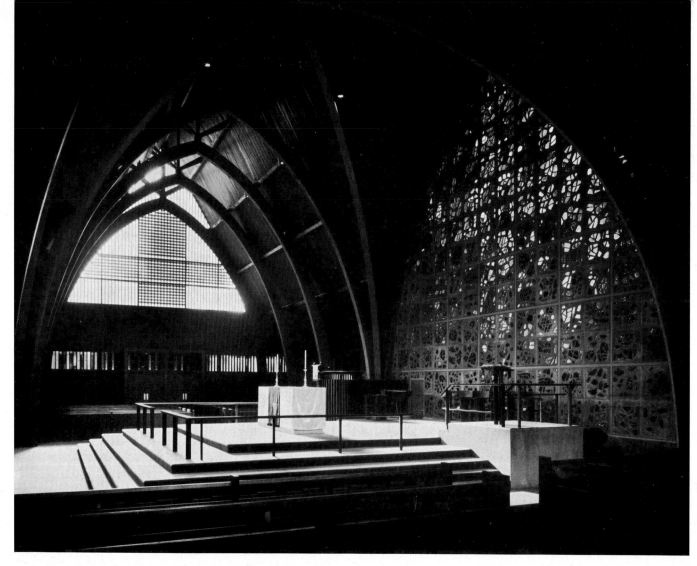

View of north transept from the south transept shows three treatments of stained glass used in the Church of the Redeemer. In the altar screen, a lacy, abstract patterning of concrete frames a predominance of brilliant orange, red, and yellow, highlighting the altar. The large transept window — one of four identical gable windows — consists of small rectangles and squares of antique German glass in a soft amber color set between slender wooden louvres. These windows provide muted illumination to each wing of the church, patternless except for the louvered cross. Encircling the entire church is the ribbon window, a series of narrow, vertical panes of glass, also framed in wood. It is executed in deep tones of magenta, purple, and blue-green, which admit very little light, but form a jewel-like band between stone wall and roof.

This view of the interior also reveals much of the symbolic power of the church design. The Rev. Bennett J. Sims, explains the confluences that meet at the altar:

The Episcopal Church is unique in Christendom, standing at the mid-point between the great churches of the reformation (such as Lutheran, Presbyterian) and the great church of the Middle Ages (Roman Catholic). We are a faith that holds in tension the valid emphases represented by Protestantism on the one hand and historic Catholicism on the other. The centrality of the freestanding altar in our design pulls into a single symbol both the Protestant and Catholic essence. The Protestant conviction is emphasized by the congregational character of the location of the altar in the midst of the worshipping family. The Catholic con-

viction is emphasized by the very fact of our paying such attention to the altar itself, believing as we do in sacramental worship. Also symbolic of our Protestant-Catholic heritage is the relationship between the altar and the two other major items of furniture in the chancel: the pulpit and lectern.

These occupy elevated positions at the upper corners of the chancel. They are illuminated for worship and are used at all services whether morning Prayer (a preaching service primarily) or Holy Communion (a sacramental service primarily.)

There is further and perhaps deeper symbolism in the relationship between pews and chancel and between the whole floor plan and the roof structure. The roof, supported as it is by the soaring arches, suggests the mystery-filled verticality so characteristic of Gothic design. The floor plan, gathering a large congregation (800) around a central chancel, works to draw people together on the horizontal plane. The result is a church building that almost instantly speaks the two indispensable dimensions of the Christian faith — the vertical in terms of our relationship to God, the horizontal in terms of our relationship to one another. This is another way of enunciating the summary of the law, using architectural forms instead of words — the summary being: "Thou shalt love the Lord thy God with all thy heart, and with all thy soul, and with all thy mind. This is the first and great commandment. And the second is like unto it; Thou shalt love thy neighbor as thyself. On these two commandments hang all the Law and the Prophets."

New church school provides many-windowed classrooms for all from the nursery to the young people's levels. Except for its gabled roofline this building makes no attempt to follow the style of existing buildings. It could not do so and still provide the light, airy classrooms that the banks of windows make possible.

The upper story contains eleven classrooms for the older age groups. In addition to four classrooms, the ground level houses an auditorium, crafts room, choir room, office, and separate play pen and crib rooms for the youngest children. A wing connecting the church school to the existing parish hall contains a large service room and kitchen serving both buildings, and opening onto the "kitchen court." The approach to the school is separated from the older structure.

M. E. Warren

Air view shows how closely the architects have related the new buildings to the old. All have similar pitched roofs and most are based upon the cruciform plan or a modification of it. The 100-year-old Gothic chapel is at upper left; the new modern church at upper right. Even the detailing of arches beneath the gabled roofs of these old and new churches is almost identical.

The large, multiwinged parish hall erected in the 1930's is now in the center of the building group. Always connected to the old church, this parish hall, by means of three of its wings, now also joins the new ambulatory, which in turn joins the new church and administration building. At left, this central parish hall also connects with the new church school. In this way the three new buildings and the two old ones have been made into one continuous construction. It is not necessary to go out-of-doors to reach any building from any other.

Note that the church school has been given a spacious, fenced play yard, seen in the immediate left foreground. Even nearer the camera is the large church parking lot.

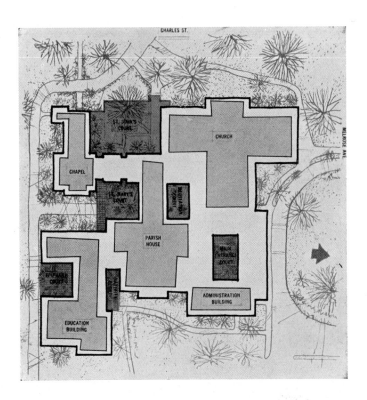

Plot plan shows more clearly than the air view the disposition of the six courtyards. These serve as approaches from the different street frontages, and most act also as links between buildings (the new ambulatory is not shown in this plan). An interior meditation court is the only one entirely cut off from the street.

The main entrance court, partially sheltered from sun and rain by periphery roofing, is a delightful plaza in which churchgoers congregate before and after services. The large, fenced St. John's Court, between new church and chapel, will be used occasionally for outdoor worship. Access to the new service wings between the chapel, parish hall, and church school, is by way of St. Mary's Court, the "kitchen" entrance to the entire complex.

The cost of this new church campus, although higher than most in the book, is still remarkably low for the great amount of space provided and for the magnificence of the church proper. The total cost of all buildings — including courtyards and other site improvements, plus necessary remodeling of the existing parish hall — was $800,000, with an additional $100,000 for furnishings and decoration.

The cost of the church alone was $387,000, brought up to a total of $500,000 by the altar screen, furnishings, carpet, and organ. For this price, 12,300 sq. ft. of space was provided — averaging out to $28 per square foot.

The cost of the administration building with attendant courts, corridors, and lobby was $85,000 for a total of 9,100 sq. ft. of interior space, $9.34 per square foot.

The cost of the church school, which provides 15,800 sq. ft. of space, including boiler room and kitchen addition, was $220,000, or less than $14 per square foot.

In view of the fact that no effort was spared to make the sanctuary a design of artistic splendor, this church group, erected so recently (in 1958), is a model of economy.

REPORT FROM THE CLERGY
The Rev. Bennett J. Sims, Rector

In 1954 we discovered that we must make a fresh approach to the problem of space both for worship and education. We had nibbled by degrees at the problem over a period of some ten years, making additions to both the church and the parish house. The rector, with vestry sanction, appointed an architectural committee. This committee then canvassed the knowledgeable people of the congregation asking for suggestions about architects. From this canvass a list of fifteen architects in this part of the country was drawn up. It was a deliberately representative list; it included some designers of the traditional and some of the contemporary; some local and some out-of-town firms. All fifteen of these firms then received a twelve-page brochure of both photographs and written text describing our problem. All fifteen were requested to come for an interview if they were interested in a commission. We also told them as a precondition to such a commission that we needed the help of an architect to decide whether to continue to modify and expand existing buildings or whether to be bold and build entirely new buildings that would connect with the old.

Eleven of the fifteen firms came to us in the course of some ten or twelve weeks. We chose the first architect we interviewed, Pietro Belluschi. We chose him for two reasons: first, of everyone we interviewed he had the most respect for the architectural integrity of the building that we were then using for worship — the century-old "English village Gothic" that seated about 300 people; second he showed the most willingness to struggle for a creative solution without reference to preconceived plans and ideas. In other words, Mr. Belluschi seemed to us the tallest man in understanding, artistic sensitivity, and humility of spirit. To work with him, we chose a local firm of young architects who had never done a church but were most eager for the opportunity to be associated with so eminent a man as Dean Belluschi. This was the firm of Rogers, Taliaferro and Lamb of Annapolis, Md.

It is important to understand that at no time was the leadership of the parish, either its clergy or its vestry, committed in advance to traditional or contemporary solutions. We simply tried to have an open mind and chose that architect whom we felt was most willing to be our friend and fellow sufferer in a difficult problem. However, it was our experience that the most exciting and intelligent men were the contemporary architects.

I personally was not at all inclined to accept a contemporary design, but I became thoroughly persuaded of its worth during educational and inspirational encounters with Mr. Belluschi and his associates. Once I had gotten beyond the point of fearing the inevitable controversy in the congregation, I didn't for a minute regret the choice of a contemporary architect, and now that the project is completed and in use, my heart sings for joy.

You ask also whether the congregation needed to be educated to accept a contemporary design. The answer, of course, is resoundingly "yes!" We did so first by introducing Mr. Belluschi to the congregation through the medium of a large parish meeting, which he was good enough to address one evening shortly after accepting our commission. He used slides and delineated his approach to the problem of architecture generally. This meeting was a terrific shock for a good many of our most conservative people. So convulsive was the shock to some that one or two families have never really recovered and are even yet deeply repelled by our new church building.

However, in a congregation of over fourteen hundred families only one family left the congregation because we chose contemporary architecture. Incidentally, they paid their building fund pledge before departing. All the others responded fairly well to the process of education.

We held another series of congregational meetings some 10 months later after the architects had had an opportunity to study the matter with great care. After another year a scale model of the entire complex of buildings was prepared and put on display in a central place and in as attractive a way as possible. The congregation was then urged to inspect the model over a period of some three months, to let the whole thing sink in, and to have as much hostility as possible either gotten over or vented upon the model. At the end of these three months a third set of congregational meetings was held at which Mr. Belluschi and his associates explained the architecture, as represented by the model, in great detail and the rector did his part to interpret it from the historical-theological standpoint.

Incidentally, there were some sermons on the subject from time to time during this two-year period of study. I did not want to jam this thing down the congregation's throat when they were a captive audience for Sunday worship, but I did take occasion, whenever it seemed good and right, to bear witness to my growing conviction that architecture, like sermons themselves, should attempt to enunciate the old truths in as contemporary and living an idiom as was possible.

On the heels of this third set of meetings we held another plebiscite giving the congregation an opportunity either to choose the Belluschi solution or request that the vestry hire another set of architects. This was the showdown and fortunately we received a 76 per cent vote in favor of the Belluschi solution. But the real decision was made by the vestry itself as soon as the tallies were in. The vestry met in a special session to receive the results of this important balloting, and it was discovered in the course of that meeting that the vestry as individuals had voted in inverse ratio to the vote of the congregation — in other words, the vestry was 75 per cent against the Belluschi solution.

In the Episcopal Church a vestry is not legally bound to honor any such plebiscite on the part of the congregation, but recognizing their grave moral responsibility, the vestry voted unanimously to honor the congregation's wishes. This was a great act of selfless leadership on the part of many of these men, voting as they did against their private desires in order to exercise a real steward-ship in behalf of a great congregation. This selflessness pulled us back together again and prevented any serious breach in the parish family. We still continue the process of education by conducting guided lecture tours of the buildings after the services of worship on Sunday mornings. The rector ordinarily does this and it is surprising and heartening to find these lectures attended often by as many of our regular members as by visitors to the church.

However, there are still a few who find the design offensive. I would say the reason for this is that in most cases they became so emotionally involved in rebelling against the idea of a contemporary church that it is now impossible for them to separate the standing result from their original emotional revulsion. In other words, the existing building itself has become a symbol of a dreadfully repugnant issue — a symbol of victory for a cause deeply opposed by people largely unaccustomed to losing.

It seems a little too early to judge whether the church will be a factor in attracting new members. We have used the new building for only 10 months. However, it is fair to say that it has noticeably increased the regularity of Sunday attendance on the part of many of our families.

Your question whether the new church has increased the interest of young people is an interesting one. We have found that our young people have responded as conservatives to this new building and have had to receive as much kindly education as we've tried to give the older folks. The young people seem not to have been attracted by the architecture. It was our exceedingly large group of younger and middle-aged parent groups that responded with enthusiasm to the new architecture.

Reference

Belluschi, Pietro. "The Churches Go Modern," *Saturday Evening Post*, October 4, 1958.

24. ROBERT F. CARR MEMORIAL CHAPEL

Illinois Institute of Technology, Chicago, Ill.

Dedicated 1952

Ludwig Mies van der Rohe (b. 1886), architect

"Less is more." — Ludwig Mies van der Rohe

The Robert F. Carr Memorial Chapel, which is part of the integrated campus plan for the Illinois Institute of Technology in Chicago, is a building the untrained eye would be quite apt to pass over. It is small, it is unpretentious, and it does not look like a church; yet as an example of a philosophy of modern architecture, it is one of the more important churches in this book. It is designed by Ludwig Mies van der Rohe, a man whom some critics rank among the three greatest architects of our day, the others being Frank Lloyd Wright and Le Corbusier.

In his approach to modern design, Mies is the antithesis of these other two giants who have dominated advanced thought in their field; Corbusier for over forty years, Wright for over sixty. These two men, superficially quite unlike, are both personal artists of the highest order and their solutions to architectural problems are always individual. Mies, too, is an artist in his clarity of expression, his purity of linear and formal relationships, and his infinitely meticulous detailing. But in his approach to design he is bluntly a builder. The solution he seeks is not an individual response to a particular problem. It is instead a system of building, universally applicable to all structures of whatever type, function, or size, and universally appropriate to our technological age.

This is an age from which the traditional hand craftsman is disappearing, the cost of labor is signally high, and the greater part of construction occurs in cities far removed from the immediate sources of traditional materials. The logical answer to this building problem lies in standardized, factory-fabricated elements that can be shipped easily to the site, and there easily fitted together to produce structures in a variety of sizes, on a module capable of extension either vertically or horizontally. Moreover, these standardized building components should be compatible with modern mechanical equipment, such as elevators, heating and cooling plants, bathroom and kitchen fixtures, ducts, shafts, and conveyors — most of them rectilinear, or at least fitting most easily into rectangular spaces.

The system Mies has developed is therefore repetitive, rectilinear, and modular. The basic materials with which he works are precast steel and other metals, reinforced concrete, glass, and brick. He rejects the exploitation of the plastic qualities of concrete or laminated wood as incompatible with a rectilinear system. He rejects also the use of a natural material such as stone, since it is too irregular to fit easily into a standardized module, and is not a manufactured substance, universally available.

The limited palette to which Mies has deliberately held himself finds its primary expression in the skeleton frame combined with a lightweight curtain wall — a reduction of structure to the bare bones of building. This is indeed one of the basic building systems of the twentieth century. The towering skyscrapers, which represent its most dramatic use, are buildings that proclaim themselves unique to our day, unprecedented in the history of the world, and probably the building type by which our age will be remembered, just as the marble temple is inextricably Greek and the stone cathedral inextricably Gothic.

Mies van der Rohe is not the originator of this system. It was developed in nineteenth century America, and was brought to its first pure expression by Louis Sullivan, the Chicago architect who dared to reveal the framing pattern of his multistory buildings and to expand their windows to nearly fill the grid. This honest expression of structure, at a time when other architects were burying the steel frame beneath heavy masonry walls and intricate applied moldings and cornices, came to be known as the Chicago School, and its originator as the father of modern architecture in America. It is doubtless coincidental, but certainly appropriate, that the German-born exponent of the International Style, Mies van der Rohe — who is considered the foremost practitioner of the architecture of the exposed frame — is today carrying this concept to its ultimate expression in the same city in which Louis Sullivan conceived it.

However, the contribution of Mies van der Rohe is not limited to the furtherance of a concept originated by another man. Mies has taken the grid and expanded its application beyond that of frame and curtain wall construction. In certain small buildings to which the frame is inappropriate (including the Carr Memorial Chapel shown here), Mies may substitute brick bearing walls, incorporating this different system of building into his repetitive, box-like pattern without so much as breaking his architectural stride. By the discipline of the grid, he has been able to resolve the contradiction between different materials and methods, conferring upon each the gift of consistency. Yet within his rectilinear pattern, great flexibility of height, breadth, transparency, or opacity can be achieved merely by an extension of the module or a shift from one material or structural system to another.

Mies van der Rohe's intensive study of the rectangle and the module represent an attempt to bring order out of the multiplicity of materials and techniques that act to diffuse the practice of architecture in the twentieth century. But his search for order goes beyond structure to include also a universality of function, thereby placing him squarely in opposition to much of accepted thinking in modern architecture. "Form follows function," the famous phrase of Mies's predecessor, Louis Sullivan, is one of the most widely accepted axioms of contemporary design. Such a theory inevitably demands a particular solution, to fit a particular function, in a particular time and place.

But one of the salient characteristics of our age is obsolescence. Cities thrust outward, old neighborhoods decay, what was once a residential community changes into a section of business and industry. As these changes occur, stately old houses are converted to stores or rooming houses, a church is demolished to make way for an office building. And even in the new office building, a change of tenants involves extensive remodeling to create spaces more appropriate to a different set of needs. Because of these facts of twentieth century existence, Mies van der Rohe has rejected the architectural theory that form should follow function. He explains:

"We do the opposite. We reverse this, and make a practical and satisfying shape and then fit the function into it. Today, this is the only practical way to build, because the functions of most buildings are continually changing, but economically the building cannot change . . . . We do not let the function dictate the plan. Instead let us make room enough for any function."

This, in essence, is the thinking behind the work of Mies van der Rohe. It explains, in at least one of its meanings, his famous phrase quoted at the head of this chapter: "Less is more." By a reduction of building to its basic function — that of shelter — he has vastly increased the functional potential of every building he designs.

The Stahl Kirche (No. 18) by Otto Bartning, which opens this section, was the first application of the steel frame and curtain wall to church building, and it was unsurpassed as a particular solution to a particular problem. But the Stahl Kirche was a church, only a church, and could never have appropriately been adapted to any other use.

In the Robert F. Carr Memorial Chapel, Mies has designed a church that does not look like a church — a church which could, in the common derogatory phrase, be a gymnasium. And of course it *could* be a gymnasium. That is the architect's whole point.

But it should also be added that such a gymnasium could be found nowhere except on the campus of the Illinois Institute of Technology. Although Mies has deliberately devised an easily copied system, none of his copyists have been able to equal the original. In the hands of this master of line, proportion, and detail, a generalized modular method of building achieves unequalled clarity and simplicity. Even when solid walls of brick are substituted for the steel frame, as in the Memorial Chapel shown here, the whole retains a delicacy and refinement seldom found in the work of other designers.

Mies's buildings achieve their restrained beauty to a great extent by what he leaves out. This ability to know when to stop, where to omit the "finishing touch" that could ruin the entire design, is rare indeed. It is one more meaning of "Less is more." In attempting to explain this phrase, Mies is fond of saying "God is in the details," signifying that the joints, trim, and projecting elements of a building reveal its essential excellence or lack of it. Certainly, in his design for the Memorial Chapel, it is the purity of Mies's detailing, more than any other factor, which gives a subtle, spiritual quality to a building that is nothing more than a flat-roofed rectangle without bell tower, spire, or other identifying feature than a small exterior cross.

The Robert F. Carr Memorial Chapel is but one consistent element in a campus plan designed in its entirety by Mies van der Rohe. As head of the Department of Architecture at Illinois Institute of Technology from 1938 to 1958, and sole architect for its long-range building program, Mies has, for twenty years, enjoyed a unique proving ground for his theories both academic and practical. These theories have influenced a whole generation of American architects, far beyond those he has actually taught. Buildings in the "Mies manner," notably offices, factories, and skyscrapers, are today found in cities from coast to coast. This is as it should be, since Mies has been concerned, not with personal expression in architecture, but with devising a characteristic way of building for our age.

Nowhere, however, is the Mies system better illustrated — both in its discipline and in its subtle variety — than on the Illinois campus itself. The building vocabulary is here limited entirely to structural steel, concrete, glass, and brick. Most of the buildings are steel frame and glass curtain wall, with occasional opaque panels of nonbearing brick. However, to impart a sense of seclusion to the chapel, distinguishing it from the nearby classroom and dormitory buildings, the architect has here used solid bearing walls of brick to support a steel-framed roof of precast concrete. The steel framing of the plate glass portion of the entrance facade bears no weight. These materials are, of course, the same ones used in the other campus buildings. Here, they are employed in a structurally opposite way, but in an esthetically similar manner. Identical with the other buildings is the Mies concept of a simple, rectangular enclosure within which the space can be arranged to fit whatever needs arise.

Although the chapel is thus held to the generalized concept of space that governs all Mies work, he has subtly particularized it by means of structural details. Note that the steel frame of the roof is exposed on the interior, repeating the steel framing grid of the glass entrance wall. Both of these grids are consciously designed to repeat in structure the pattern of the large cross suspended over the altar, and also the identical pattern of a small, black, exterior cross, centered atop the roof, which had not yet been applied when this photograph was taken. These repetitive crosses and the sheltering walls of brick are the only obeisance made to the religious character of the building.

However, the meticulous detailing typical of work by Mies van der Rohe does carry its own spirituality of economy, purity, and restraint.

The fact that the aluminum frame of entrance doors has not been painted black to match the black steel grid attests to the honesty of the Mies approach. The doors are different elements, not framing members, and so should remain differentiated from them. However, if these strips *had* been painted black, something would have gone wrong with the design. By such a small change the framing grid would have lost its subtlety. This is a good example of Mies van der Rohe's

Torkel Korling

ability to stop before the "finishing" touch. What is "less" here is only a coat of paint. What is "more" by this omission is the refinement and delicacy of the entire facade.

Such restraint is also carried over into the color scheme. Except for the black outlining of the steel framing members and a black-and-white terrazo floor, the chapel is executed throughout in shades of beige: buff, unglazed brick; a travertine marble altar; raw silk altar hanging; choir and sacristy screens and pulpit of clear, rift-sawn oak. The cross and communion rail are of stainless steel. This quiet monotone is brought into vibrant life during services by a wash of warm light

which makes the altar curtain and brick walls of the interior appear a tawny, almost orange color, while the exterior remains a neutral frame. No attempt is made, however, to dramatize the altar or to provide a sense of mystery by subdued illumination in the seating area. All is one unbroken space, open, clearly visible, and as rational as the architecture that contains it. By this means, the chapel symbolizes what some theologians consider to be the essence of Protestantism, as opposed to the mystique of the Catholic Church.

However, this is not a generally accepted Episcopal concept. The chapel was agreed to only reluctantly by the Episcopal Diocese of Chicago. Although this body had already conceded that the chapel should conform to other campus buildings, a detailed explanation of the design had to be given by the architect before consent was granted and funds provided. However each of the several pastors who have served this chapel came to be proud of the church as a building. The authors therefore advise the reader to turn back to this design occasionally after looking at other churches. Because of its severity and its complete lack of traditional symbolism, its spiritual beauty is not immediately apprehended. But whereas the more obvious expressions of spirituality may pall, this is a design of which one can never tire.

Probably in no other church have the altar and its platform been reduced to such utter simplicity as in this small Episcopal chapel. They are simply solid blocks of marble, undecorated except for the modest inscription at one side. By contrast, the silver candlesticks, themselves quite simple, appear richly ornate. The solidity of the altar is in striking contrast to the crystalline delicacy of the glass wall at the front of the church and to the graceful drapery of the altar hanging, emphasizing — merely by the material used — the purport and solemnity of the sacramental table.

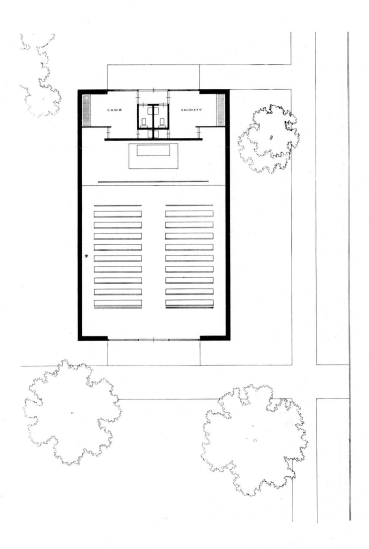

The plan of this chapel is just as simple as its structure: a rectangular, open room, with choir and sacristy flanking utilities behind the altar curtain. Pews shown on this plan have not yet been installed. The chapel accommodates 150 students in a total area of 2,300 sq. ft. At a cost of $ 75,000 — or $ 30.50 per square foot — the Memorial Chapel is probably the most expensive church in the entire book. However, although the cost of space is high, the cost per seat is low — only $ 500. This is because there is no waste space anywhere in the design: no narthex, no large and intricately designed chancel, no separately partitioned, subsidiary rooms. By far the greater part of the interior can be used for seating.

The major expenditure — $ 64,000 of the total — was for the structural shell. This attests to the high price of perfectionism, and also to the fact that technology has not yet caught up with Mies van der Rohe. His designs typically start with a redesigning of the basic manufactured elements that make up the building. This chapel is therefore truly a "custom-built" design, comparable in cost to a specially designed car in the automotive industry. However, more and more Mies-designed elements, from framing members to hardware, are today being offered as stock items by industry. Eventual mass production and mass sales could considerably lower the cost of a building designed in the Mies manner.

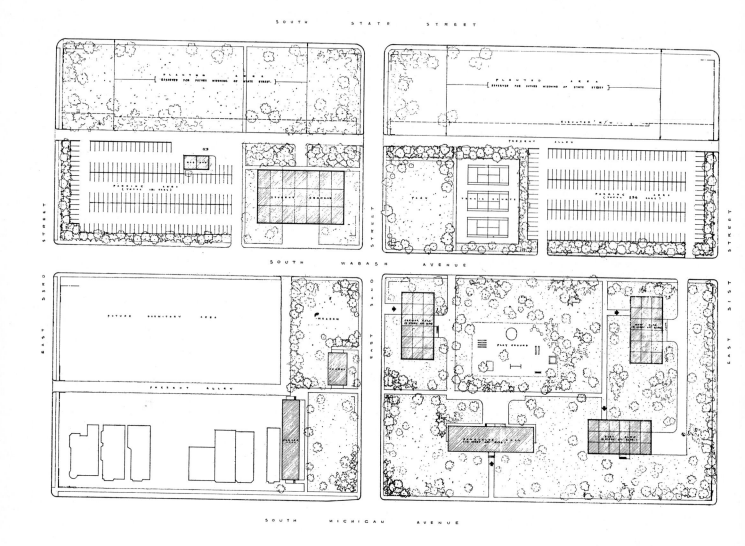

Site plan of a portion of the Illinois Institute of Technology campus shows the chapel centrally located near the Student Commons, and a group of four tall apartment houses, beyond East 32nd St. This is a convenient location adjacent to living quarters and student meeting places. The academic buildings of Illinois Institute of Technology are not shown here; they lie to the left, beyond East 33rd St. A total of 18 buildings have been completed. In this part of the plan, buildings indicated only by outline are existing structures that will eventually be torn down. Note the difference between these buildings, with various juts, and awkward massings, and the simple, clearly spaced rectangles of Mies van der Rohe.

The unique feature of this campus plan — indicating the lengths to which Mies will go in his search for order — is its modular basis. All buildings, no matter what their size, are designed on a repetitive module, with bays either 12 or 24 ft. in breadth and depth and 12 ft. in height. But not only the buildings are designed on this basis. The open spaces between them are also based on the same module. In this way, if buildings must be connected at any future time, the space between them can merely be filled in with more of the standard modular elements.

This provision for expansion is an incidental benefit, however. The primary aim of such meticulous planning is the achievment of a subtle, visual rhythm throughout the campus as a whole. Although all ground space is modularly calculated, there is no grid siting. Buildings, usually of different sizes, and grouped about open courts, are never placed entirely on a straight line or in a marching square. Instead, they are sited as though pushed slightly to one side, or forward, or back from each other. This provides a subtle variety that saves the similar design of the buildings from monotony. But because of the modular spacing, a basic order and regularity shines through the site planning, even though no formal or axial symmetry has been used.

The total effect of this campus thus adds up to much more than the sum of its buildings, each taken alone.

References

Blake, Peter. "The Difficult Art of Simplicity," *Architectural Forum*, May 1958.

Johnson, Philip C. *Mies van der Rohe*. Museum of Modern Art, New York (1947).

METHODIST

Methodism arose in England in 1739 as a society for good works and godly living within the established Anglican communion. It was not the intention of the founder, John Wesley, that Methodists form a new denomination, but rather that they remain communicants — even though rather special communicants — of the Church of England. The first break came when the Bishop of London refused to ordain priests to minister to the Methodists. A further break between English and American societies came by way of the Revolutionary War. Wesley vocally supported the Crown, thus leaving his colonial outposts to the sole guidance of the missionary, Francis Asbury. In 1784, after the Revolution, Asbury called a conference in Baltimore to establish an independent Methodist Episcopal Church in the United States, of which he later became the first bishop.

As part of their Anglican heritage, Methodists to this day maintain a heirarchy of church government similar to that of the Episcopal Church. They share also the Anglican belief in salvation through grace, as the gift of God freely given and uninfluenced by any propitiatory act of the individual. Once received, God's grace then permeates all the actions of life, directing it toward good.

However, within the Methodist Church, these outward manifestations of inward grace have traditionally been given more organized outlets than in the Episcopal, and indeed most other Christian communions. It is this fact that gave the emerging denomination its name. "Methodist" was originally a term of derision, fastened upon its early adherents because of the methodical way in which they planned their spiritual life and good works. So much time was allotted each day for church attendance, so much time for visiting the sick, so much for helping the poor, so much for prayer. Wesley also assigned each Methodist to a specific field of social endeavor, marshalling his forces where they were most needed to effect reform. Spartan codes of personal and public morality were outlined in the famous *Methodist Disciplines,* which guide church members in exact behavior while at the same time leaving them doctrinally free, as Wesley put it, to "think and let think."

The Methodist Church is thus unique among Prottestant denominations in that it arose, not as a doctrinal protest, but as an organizational "method" for creating a Christian society. There was a Methodist protest, but it was directed against the outward conditions of life as it was lived in eighteenth century England. That period was a time of lax morality and widespread drunkenness, stemming in great part from the cruel exploitation of the poorer classes in the mines and factories of a burgeoning industrial nation. The aim of the Methodist societies was therefore a reform of private morals, coupled with an attack upon the manifold social evils of the day.

In America, Methodist evangelists found the combination of personal and public reform ideally suited to the temper of a newly created democratic nation. Arriving later than most other Protestant denominations, the Methodist Church grew as the country grew, sending its missionaries ever westward to the most isolated pioneer communities. The Methodist circuit rider, who covered hundreds of miles on horseback to convert, to preach, and to baptize, was an inseparable part of the history of the American frontier.

These men preached in houses, in barns, in schools, on steamboats, and even, on occasion, in dance halls and saloons. When meeting houses were built in the more settled communities, they were usually bare and unadorned, the Methodists feeling no need for steeples, stained glass, chimes, organs, or anything that could be classed as an unnecessary frill. The unaccompanied singing of rousing hymns and the exhorting of the minister as he preached the gospel made up the Methodist service. Indeed, the Methodists may be considered the originators of the Protestant "revival" hymn.

Since those early frontier days, the Methodists also may be credited with the great change in American Protestant churches from sanctuaries alone to a complex of buildings including church, social hall, Sunday school, and a variety of meeting rooms for their manifold Christian endeavors. For the Methodists have always been the great "doers" of the Christian faith, and inevitably they expressed this character in their architecture. The organized activities of this faith ranged from church suppers and Epworth League meetings to reform movements against child labor, sweatshops, and racial inequality, as well as the famous prohibition campaigns of the Women's Christian Temperance Union. They produced a new concept of community service that has since been incorporated into the practice and the architecture of almost all American Protestant churches.

Probably because of its traditional concern for the rights of the underprivileged, coupled with a wide latitude in matters of theology and formal services, the Methodist communion in the United States is today second only to the Baptist, counting 12.3 million adults and unnumbered children as members. It can be considered primarily an American institution, as there are only about 7 million adult members in the rest of the world.

During the early days in America, the background against which Methodist services were conducted was of decidedly secondary importance to the business of saving souls and promoting public reform. These activities could be undertaken anywhere and the artistic effect during worship was hardly considered. When finally it was considered, the Methodists, like most other American churches, fell under the sway of the Gothic Revival. A claim could, perhaps, be made on this style as inherited from Roman Catholicism through the Anglo-Catholic Church of England. But that distant inheritance is largely negated by the actualities of Methodism. The Gothic style, evocative of the Middle Ages, of lord and serf, of mystic faith and unquestioning

faithful, contradicts the very fundamentals upon which Methodism is based.

Significantly, the two churches shown here reject entirely such traditional religious symbolism; the spires, bell towers, intricately patterned stained glass, and the cruciform or other Roman Catholic floor plan.

Moreover, these contemporary Methodist churches, one of them designed by Frank Lloyd Wright, represent an indigenous American architecture as opposed, for example. to the formal European modernism of Mies van der Rohe. In this choice, too, American Methodists are truly expressing their heritage of place and temperament.

However, no attempt has been made to recapture an early frontier severity. Apparently the time for bare necessity has gone, just as the exigencies of the early *Disciplines* have been relaxed over the years. This softening is in contrast to the Lutheran and Episcopal churches, some of which display a severity bordering on starkness as a background for their rich and colorful rituals (see churches No. 19, 20, 22). Possibly in reaction to the plainness of their theology and liturgy, the Methodists today favor a more decorative expression in architecture. The two examples that follow illustrate this point, particularly when compared with some of the preceding Protestant churches.

25. ANNIE PFEIFFER MEMORIAL CHAPEL

Florida Southern College, Lakeland, Fla.; Dedicated 1941
Frank Lloyd Wright (1869-1959), architect

Baltazar Korab ©

"As a matter of fact our architects are today building nine-teenth century buildings. We are still building the old steel frame. In other words, people who were accustomed to building lumber buildings, now build them out of steel lumber. All our famous modernists are still building steel-lumber buildings."

"Organic building is natural building: a construction proceeding harmoniusly from the nature of a planned or organized inside outward to a consistent outside. The place to be lived in is now the human reality of any building and in terms of space we will find the new forms we seek. Or lose them." — FRANK LLOYD WRIGHT

The year 1959 marked the death of Frank Lloyd Wright, the seemingly indestructible native American architectural genius. Wright was born in 1869 in Richland Center, Wis. His education as an architectural iconoclast began in 1887 in Chicago, in the office of Louis Sullivan, the only man he has ever acknowledged as a teacher. Since that time nearly every other modern architect in the western world, including even those European stylists whose work he deplores, have acknowledged Wright as their teacher. At a time when modern architecture was unnamed, and all but unknown, Wright evolved certain basic concepts from which have sprung the whole proliferation of contemporary expression.

Nevertheless, despite the debt all owe to Wright, there early appeared a schism within modern architecture that has deepened over the years and has yet to be obscured by additional new trends and currents. This fundamental difference in approach is summed up in the work of the so-called International Style, developed in Europe, as against the "organic" and essentially American architecture of Frank Lloyd Wright. Although Le Corbusier and Wright have usually been equated as

the opposing giants, it is actually Mies van der Rohe who stands most squarely in opposition to the concepts of Frank Lloyd Wright. It is therefore illuminating that the Methodist Annie Pfeiffer Memorial Chapel at Florida Southern College, shown here, represents the Wright approach to the same problem faced by Mies in the Episcopal Carr Memorial Chapel that directly precedes it: that of a college chapel within an integrated campus plan solely designed by the architect.

Needless to say, the two college campuses (the construction of both began in 1938) could hardly be more different. The Illinois campus is a series of precise and delicate glass rectangles, framed in steel and including only occasionally, straight walls of brick as a sheltering element. The Florida campus is constructed entirely of massive, reinforced concrete blocks, arranged in complex and irregular building forms, broken only occasionally by glass. But the difference is more basic than the choice of materials, and the formal as opposed to informal symmetry of the respective structural shapes.

Mies and his colleagues of the International School of modernists, including Le Corbusier, Walter Gropius, and Marcel Breuer (whose works are represented by churches No. 16, 28, and 36) are alike in regarding architecture as a synthetic, man-made construction. They therefore seek to differentiate their buildings sharply from the surrounding natural environment of earth and trees and plants.

Wright, on the other hand, conceives of architecture as part of nature itself, built of natural materials, even though these have been fabricated and shaped by man. He seeks always the closest integration between building and terrain and between interior space and surrounding nature.

In the Florida Southern College campus continuous, covered esplanades connect all buildings, providing outdoor paths throughout the campus, sheltered from both tropical rain and tropical sun. The buildings themselves bring the outdoors in with skylights, window slots, carefully placed expanses of glass wall, roofed terraces, and integral interior planting. The entire campus is, in effect, one continuous construction, here enlarging into a building, here diminishing into an esplanade, and everywhere laced with gardens.

It is on the interior of the buildings, however, that the difference between the "technological" and the "organic" approach to architecture is revealed in its most fundamental aspect. As described in the previous section, Mies van der Rohe approaches space as a rectangular void, defined by an arbitrary enclosure, and designed to be manipulated according to need by the inhabitants of a building. Wright considers space as the reality of architecture itself, the determining factor of both structure and form.

Probably the most penetrating analysis of this fundamental characteristic of Wright's architecture was made by Peter Blake:

"The reality of the vessel," says Lao-tse, "is the space within it." The space within it is also the most elusive, the most abstract, the hardest-to-define and the hardest-to-measure thing about the vessel. And, for that reason, it is the hardest of all to make beautiful.

Architects, like vessel-makers, can be divided roughly into two groups: by far the larger group consists of those who know how to make the vessel itself (some even know how to make the vessel beautiful); the smaller group knows also how to give life and beauty to that which is inside the vessel — the space within.

In the history of Western architecture there have been but few architects who qualified for this second group. And there has been no architect in the Western world since the great days of the Renaissance who has been so outstandingly qualified as Frank Lloyd Wright.... Wright's claim to greatness ... rests squarely upon a single staggering fact: Wright changed the nature of architectural space and, then, proceeded to change the nature of structure and form to fit his new spatial concepts.

The Annie Pfeiffer Memorial Chapel shows clearly this use of space as a creative force in the design. Only through an understanding of Wright's sense of space can his architecture, including this chapel, be comprehended.

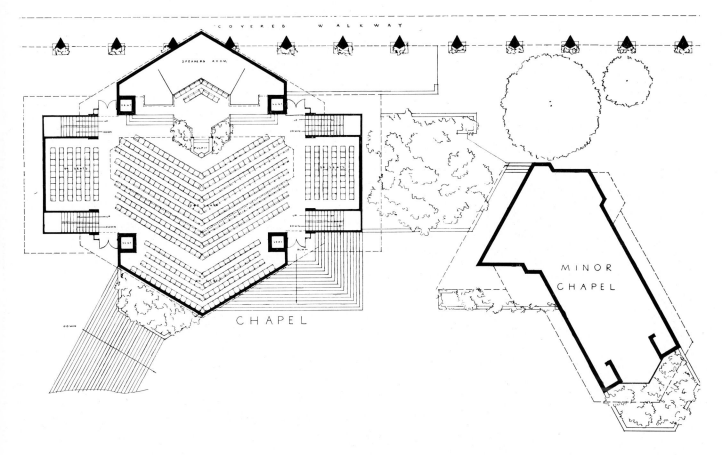

Plan shows the angled arrangement that is the basic theme of this chapel. Such a design depends upon a structural system that has come to be a hallmark of much of Wright's work. This system is the cantilever. Superstructures supported by columns are not held up at their corners, as in the traditional post-and-lintel system, but are cantilevered out from columns more centrally located. This application of an engineering principle was one of the basic changes in traditional construction initiated by Wright to give him his desired spatial freedom. The architect himself explains this development:

"When I looked at the hideous efflorescent boxing-in of humanity upon the Chicago prairies of the '90's, I soon realized that the corners of the box were not economical or vital bearing points of structure. The main load of the usual building, I saw, was on the walls and so best supported at points some distance back from the corner. Spans were then reduced by cantileverage... With the bearing points thus drawn in and clearly established aside from the corners...the walls themselves became individual screens for interior space. Space could now be handled freely to bring in or shut out the out-of-doors at will."

In the Annie Pfeiffer Chapel, Wright has brought supporting columns into the interior to do double duty not only in cantilevering the superstructure, but also to cantilever the balcony. Only four great columns bear the major weight of balcony, roof, and tower; hence their massive size. But by this system Wright has gained complete freedom to manipulate interior space and to enclose it by any means he desires.

Photos: © Ezra Stoller

Interior of chapel is executed in the clear tones of nature itself; pale beige concrete block, natural woods, and scarlet seat coverings, this warm color scheme accented by the cool, deep green of tropical plants. Planting areas are an integral part of most Wright designs. Here, some of them have been ingeniously built into the balcony, extending out like a bower of greenery above the ground floor seating. Also relating indoors to out are strip windows and skylights, unexpectedly located to permit glimpses of the tropical outdoors from within a cool, protected retreat.

These are the effects of Wright's architecture that have been most easily copied. Far more difficult, if not impossible for any follower of Wright to achieve, is his unique manipulation of space. In this chapel the restrictive box, which Wright so detests, is completely broken up into a rhythmic geometry of movement. Indeed, the entire design is based upon an intricate interweaving of vertical and horizontal volumes.

The major horizontal plane of space encompasses the whole of the ground floor seating and chancel area, with a minor horizontal plane encircling it overhead, in the form of a continuous, peripheral balcony. In

opposition to these horizontal movements, which create a feeling of intimacy and human scale, a major vertical plane of space shoots up at center, cutting from floor level into a tower, through which light floods down upon the interior. This vertical movement provides a dramatic sense of aspiration, transforming a building which lacks all traditional religious symbolism into a church.

To connect the low, broad bulk of the chapel with the narrow central tower, the wall and roof elements above the balcony at either side have been stepped inward, allowing a gradual progression, rather than an abrupt change from the horizontal to the vertical. Once again, this device prevents any feeling of a restrictive, rectangular box. At the front of the church, where the continuous balcony becomes a choir loft, the horizontal sweep is partially interrupted by an openwork screen of concrete block that shields the choir from view, but still allows a restricted horizontal movement of space through its interstices.

The final destruction of the box occurs in the ground plan itself, which is "pushed out" in opposing obtuse angles at both the rear and front of the church. Follow-

ing these lines, the two main groups of seating — and also that part of the balcony directly above them — are angled toward the chancel. The chancel and central pulpit, in turn, repeat this angle, jutting forward to parallel the angled seating. This arrangement, plus the encirclement of the entire chapel by the balcony, creates a sense of intimacy and unity between minister, choir, and congregation, expressing the aim of the general Liturgical Revival within the Christian Church. Esthetically, a balanced symmetry is achieved which, at the same time, presents ever-changing aspects as the eye sweeps over the chapel interior, or as one moves about within it.

Wright here achieved his freedom of spatial movement through use of the large steel-reinforced concrete block. This material — quite different from the ordinary builder's concrete block — is particularly suited to the creation of interlocking interior spaces. Unlike the conventional type, such blocks are as strong or stronger than slabs of reinforced concrete. In addition, they are stable in an upright position. Thus they can act either as supports or enclosures, changing their function as the design dictates. Their weight remains light enough to allow insertions of glass wherever desired. And as comparatively small building units, these blocks can be manipulated with greater facility than the large reinforced concrete slab.

For this particular chapel, they represent also an excellent solution to the problem of a tropical climate, providing an efficient insulation against the blazing sun, by means of their hollow masonry mass. Finally, during their fabrication these units can be perforated or imprinted with designs, yielding an integral pattern of light or line, as desired by the architect. Each of these effects is seen in the interior views shown here.

The Annie Pfeiffer Memorial Chapel illustrates to a remarkable degree Wright's insistence that modern materials and structural systems must be used in a way that is true to their intrinsic natures, yet subordinated to the higher aim of creating beautiful and appropriate spaces as a habitat for man. He sees the new technology of our machine age as a servant to man, a thing to be commanded by him, rather than (as in the work of Mies van der Rohe) a thing into which man must be fitted.

Exterior form of chapel which bears no faintest resemblance to any historic style, evolved naturally from the shaping of interior space and clearly expresses it. However, Wright, in explaining his organic approach to architecture, rejects the dogma "form follows function," proclaiming instead the deeper meaning that "form and function are one," developing together during the process of creation as a single, unified concept. Here, in this chapel, is an example of unified form and function, the vision of interior space seen to be inseparable from the unprecedented structural shapes which delineate it.

The main auditorium, with its stepped roofs, is the central horizontal block. Above it rises the vertical tower, lighted at the sides by windows which are shaded from direct sun by broad, angled overhangs. The roof of the tower, also, is skylighted. Cantilevered balconies extend outward from the building mass as well as inward into the auditorium.

This photograph was taken from beneath a roof overhang of a nearby building. Note how the covered esplanade melts into the buildings it joins together, forming a continuous construction throughout the entire campus. The reinforced concrete blocks of the esplanade give further continuity and unity to the design. The Florida Southern College campus is an excellent example of one of Wright's axioms: "The solution of every problem is contained within itself. Its plan, form, and character are determined by the nature of the site, the nature of the materials used, the nature of the system using them, the nature of the life concerned, and the purpose of the building itself. And always a qualifying factor is the nature of the architect."

References

Blake, Peter. "Frank Lloyd Wright: Master of Architectural Space," *Architectural Forum*, September 1958

"Frank Lloyd Wright: Florida Southern College," *Architectural Forum*, September 1952.

Gutheim, Frederick, ed. *Frank Lloyd Wright on Architecture: Writings, 1894-1940.* Duell, Sloan and Pearce, New York (1941).

Wright, Frank Lloyd. *An American Architecture.* Ed. by Edgar Kaufmann. Horizon Press, New York (1955).

——— *Genius and the Mobocracy.* Duell, Sloan and Pearce, New York, (1949).

——— "Prefabrication and the Role of Creative Man in the Machine Age," *House & Home*, April 1958.

26. FIRST METHODIST CHURCH

Midland, Mich.; Consecrated 1950
Alden Dow (b. 1904), architect

"The quality of a building, like the quality of a person, grows only through honesty." — ALDEN DOW

In both its architectural character and its history, the First Methodist Church of Midland, Mich., typifies the Methodist faith. The parish itself, now nearly 2,500 strong, grew from a four-member stop on an 1857 circuit-rider's route, when Midland City was a tiny crossroads settlement. Today the church building, although large in size and rich in detail, retains much of the flavor of the Methodist past in its sturdy brick construction and bold forms. Appropriately, it has none of the traditional features of ecclesiastical architecture which evoke, in more orthodox Protestant churches, their Roman Catholic heritage. Instead, its broad, horizontal lines suggest the limitless reach of the American prairie, which was a major background of this faith as it developed within a westward-expanding nation.

Like the chapel at Florida Southern College (No. 25), this church is an example of indigenous American architecture, one with the terrain and the region of its setting. Its designer, Alden Dow, a Columbia University architectural graduate, studied under Frank Lloyd Wright at Taliesin, and the Wright influence is still visible in his work.

But unlike the Florida Southern College chapel, which is limited in function, emphasizing primarily an auditorium for formal services, Dow's parish church encompasses a building complex that assumes much of the character of a community center. For above all, the Methodist Church is a church of fellowship and a church of action.

In order to accommodate its numerous activities, the church has been designed as a central block with subsidiary wings extending out from its four corners, and with a separate church school building to the rear at one side. A parsonage flanks the church at the opposite side. With this plan, space is provided for a youth center accommodating young people's activities, a church parlor for women's groups, a lounge for the men's meetings, and a memorial chapel, in addition to the usual Sunday-school rooms, choir room, administrative offices, and the large fellowship hall, which is located beneath the church auditorium. The placement of subsidiary group activities in corner wings makes for convenient access from the church proper, but gives each activity center complete privacy. Diverse activities — such as meetings, choir practice, and lectures — can be held simultaneously without in any way disturbing each other.

On the exterior, the various wings and buildings are connected by sheltered walks that lead through planted courts, in one of which is a large reflecting pool, bordered with flowers. The courts are protected from street view by the horizontal wings of the church at front and rear, at one side by a brick wall, and at the other by walkway, trees, and shrubbery. In this way, both church and grounds become an integrated design, usable both indoors and out, and with excellent circulation between all elements.

Since most American churches today, are expanding their subsidiary activities, this workable plan for a working church should be of interest beyond the faith it is designed to serve.

The First Methodist Church is built of red brick with fascias of copper that have weathered to a beautiful blue-green. These horizontal bands of color, sweeping across the facade of the church, are a striking example of integral ornament. So are the window mullions that, by the art of the architect, have been transformed beyond their function to become linear compositions in wood. They are inset with clear glass, occasionally accented by panes of color. Together the fascias and the patterned windows impart a quality of richness to an otherwise simple structure. Further breaking the severity of the design is the planting that tops the low roof.

This is the front view of the church showing, in foreground, the low southwest wing which contains the church parlor for women's meetings. Below it, at basement level, is the infants' nursery. These areas are directly reached from the entrance at the center of the church. Here the main auditorium rises to a height of two stories. The southeast wing, barely visible as it recedes into the background, continues at two-story height under the same roofline. In this way a lofty space is provided also for the memorial chapel that occupies the upper floor of this wing. Beneath the chapel, at basement level, is the lounge for the men's groups.

Hedrich-Blessing

The main auditorium of the church occupies the central position in the plan, with low, subsidiary wings leading inward toward the worship area. Like all rooms of this church, the auditorium is executed in muted natural tones: red brick, brown oak, and white plaster, accented by pale green carpeting and the deeper green of growing plants. The walls at either side of the nave are entirely of glass, set between brick piers. By extending these piers into the church, at right angles to the wall, the architect has been able to achieve the strength necessary to support the roof structure without enclosing the church in masonry. In this way he has created the unusual combination of a brick frame and glass curtain wall.

Cutting horizontally across the piers at either side of the church, and cantilevered from them, are twin balconies that serve a double function as overflow seating and also as a unique processional and recessional route for the choir. When the service begins, the choir enters from the rear of the church, filling these balconies, and then turns toward the congregation to lead the opening hymn. The processional then moves forward to the choir loft behind the altar. Here the choir is concealed by a brick planting wall, except when rising to sing.

Bradford-Lariviere

All lines within this church, whether horizontal or repetitive verticals, progress toward the chancel. The central overhead panel acts strongly to lead the eye forward. It is more than a visual device, however. Made of translucent plastic framed in oak, this panel conceals and diffuses the artificial lighting and houses also the ventilating system for the church. Over the chancel, this panel changes and opens to become a "sky window" flooding the altar with daylight and providing a view toward the "highest heavens."

The dominant element within the chancel is the cross, symbol of the perfection of man and of God's love for man. Beneath it, luxuriant planting indicates growth and life. Taken together, these elements — the

plants, the cross, and the window above them — symbolize the encompassing nature of growth from the humblest flower toward infinity. In fact, the architect has intended that the entire design of this church symbolize man's capacity for spiritual development. His use of clear glass in floor-to-ceiling doors and windows emphasizes that growth cannot be contained within the four walls of a church nor within rigid boundaries of any kind. At the same time, this transparency is meant to show that beliefs are not to be concealed nor transposed into a mystery. Such symbolism and such architecture could hardly be more appropriate to the Methodist denomination that places such emphasis upon man's own spiritual efforts and good works.

James J. Dion

Side view of the auditorium from within the walled courtyard, shows how the northeast wing, containing the youth center and part of the Sunday school, projects at right angles from the main body of the church. A large reflecting pool has been so placed that it casts a pattern of moving light up through the windows of the auditorium upon the ceiling within. The pool and the lavish planting that surrounds it can also be glimpsed from the interior of the church. In these ways the architect has made exterior light, water, flowers, and shrubbery an integral part of the interior design. This courtyard is completely shielded from street view by a high brick wall. It can therefore be used as a quiet meditation court and as a private outdoor space for churchgoers.

James J. Dion

Three of the many subsidiary rooms of the church are shown in these photographs. Above is the Sunday school for three-year-olds, in the northeast wing that opens to the walled courtyard. A portion of the window wall of the memorial chapel, across the court, is barely visible at far right in the southeast wing.

The view below, left, shows the interior of the memorial chapel. In addition to the window that flanks the altar, the entire side wall of this chapel is of glass, allowing a view of the adjoining garden court and reflecting pool. At night, the illusion of starlight can be produced in the chapel by means of tiny 10-watt bulbs, recessed into the ceiling. These different areas present a unity of design due to their exposed brick walls and their window treatment.

Right is a photograph of the stage and lower level auditorium, where business meetings, lectures, musical performances, plays, and holiday pageants take place. As in all areas of the church, special attention has here been paid to artificial illumination. Indirect lighting, recessed behind brick piers and planting walls, almost gives the effect of daylight to the basement room.

James J. Dion

Hedrich-Blessing

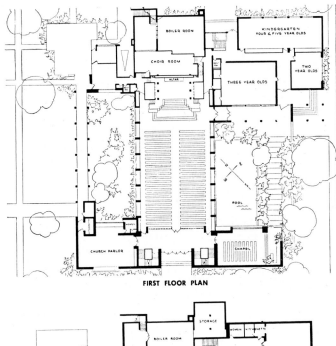

FIRST FLOOR PLAN

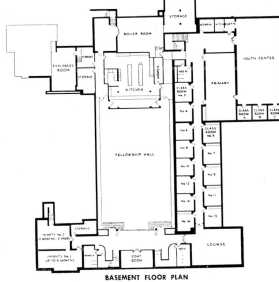

BASEMENT FLOOR PLAN

Plan of church complex shows the disposition of subsidiary wings at the four corners of the main auditorium. Upper level plan shows separate church school building to the rear of the church at right, and indicates also the planted courts that flank the church. The lower level plan reveals that the church school building and the youth center wing, separated from each other above ground, merge into one at basement level. Additional Sunday school rooms that flank the fellowship hall in the basement extend out under the reflecting pool in the courtyard.

The main auditorium of the church seats 950 persons, and the fellowship hall accommodates 500 for the church suppers that are so popular with this denomination. The memorial chapel seats 100, and the Sunday school handles an average attendance of over 900.

The cost of this entire church complex, exclusive of a new parsonage, was $632,000, providing 61,445 sq. ft. of floor area at an approximate cost of $10.28 per square foot. The church proper cost $317,000; the various added wings and church school, $315,000.

REPORT FROM THE CLERGY
The Rev. Orville H. McKay, Minister

I was not here when the church was originally built. I have served the church for the past seven years, and during that time we added the chapel, the educational unit, the parlor, and cloister walk. I have therefore relied upon the chairman of our board of trustees to answer a number of your questions.

Mr. Alden Dow, our architect, is a native of Midland, and had designed several homes and public buildings including a small church in our community prior to beginning the design of the First Methodist Church. We were, therefore, acquainted with contemporary architecture. One or two influential members of the church were particularly impressed with the architect's work and persuaded the other board members to give Mr. Dow's ideas consideration. The architect in his preliminary plans soon convinced the majority of the doubting church members. A scale model of the proposed church, constructed by the architect's staff, was very effective in selling the contemporary design. In laying down requirements for the church, special consideration was given to the size of the sanctuary, the size of the educational plant, the kitchen, and the dining hall. Beyond this, it was left to Mr. Dow to design the sanctuary with a worshipful atmosphere and a church plant of utmost utility to meet the requirements of an anticipated membership.

At first, there were a number of members who did not like the design and who objected to it. However, having worshipped in the church and used the entire building for several years, there are very few of the members who still object to the design in any way. We feel that the architect's approach has resulted in a new, creative concept of church architecture among our people.

One of the most eloquent words of witness to the beauty of our architecture came from an older member of the church. I called on her in a period of illness. She told me of the objections that she had to the design when it was under consideration and also under construction. Then, with a lovely twinkle in her eye and in a spirit of deep sincerity, she said to me, "Dr. McKay, I have asked the good Lord many times to forgive me for the things I said about that church while it was being built!"

From a personal point of view, as its pastor, I feel that the architecture has contributed greatly to the development of the church. It has created a worshipful atmosphere, brought a deep sense of pride in our building, and is a definite factor in attracting new people to the church.

Reference

Thiry, Paul, Bennet, Richard, and Kamphoefner, Henry. *Churches and Temples*. Reinhold Pub. Corp., New York (1953).

The Presbyterian Church, with approximately 41 million adult members, is one of the largest Protestant groups in the world today. In addition to foreign missions, for which the Presbyterians are famous, this world-wide total includes the Reformed Churches of Switzerland, Holland, France, Germany, and Hungary, which are virtually identical to, and officially allied with, the Presbyterian Church. In the United States, there are 4.2 million members.

Although it is generally believed that the Presbyterian Church came to America by way of Scotland, it was actually established here long before the eighteenth century wave of Scottish and Scotch-Irish immigration. Among the English Puritans who founded New England were a few Presbyterians as well as the more numerous Congregationalists. There were even Presbyterians among the colonists of Jamestown, Va., and the church they established in 1611 is officially recognized as the first Presbyterian Church in America, postdating the Church of England by only four years.

By the time of the American Revolution, Presbyterianism had become so widespread and numbered so many American patriots among its adherents, that the War of Independence was referred to in the British House of Commons as that "Presbyterian Rebellion." At least twelve of the signers of the Declaration of Independence were Presbyterians. One of the rallying cries of the Revolution was the prophetic statement of Scotland's great Reformation leader, John Knox, to the Catholic Mary Queen of Scots some 200 years earlier: "If princes exceed their bounds, Madam, they may be resisted and even deposed." Most important to history, however, was the fact that the Constitution of the United States, the foundation of our democratic government, was directly influenced by the Presbyterian organizational background of a number of the men who helped to frame it.

The name Presbyterian is taken from the Greek word *presbyteros*, meaning elder, and it refers to the system by which this church is governed. The "elders" of the church, elected by the congregation, determine in "session" the policies of the local church with the aid of the minister — the "teaching elder" — as moderator. Over the sessions are the "presbyteries," and over the presbyteries the synods, each representing a wider jurisdiction, and each composed of an equal number of ministers and elected elders. The Presbyterian system of elective congresses culminates in an annual general assembly, representing all member churches. This ecclesiastical legislative system is the model after which the United States system of congressional, representative government was largely patterned.

The Presbyterian predilection for law and order, if not for democracy, goes back to its roots in Calvinism. John Calvin was a French intellectual and the sternest of the Reformation leaders. Himself an exile in Geneva, Switzerland, he persecuted all who disagreed with his theology, particularly his theory of predestination, which states that all men are predestined to heaven or hell even before they are born. Today, most Presbyterians subscribe to this harsh doctrine only in modified form if at all. But Calvin's closely reasoned *Institutes of Christian Religion*, in which he systematically codified the Protestant viewpoint, remains the basis for the training of Presbyterian ministers to this day. A later revision of Calvinist doctrine, the Westminster Confession of Faith, framed in England between the years 1643 and 1649, is still the orthodox creed of the Presbyterian Church. However, the interpretation of this creed is no longer dogmatic and it has from time to time been officially amended. Presbyterians now enjoy a freedom of religious thought which would have appeared heretical to Calvin and have long operated under a democratic organization that would have been equally distasteful to him.

There have been similar changes in the architecture adopted by this faith. Mainly as a result of the views of the original Puritan reformers in England and Scotland, early Presbyterian churches were austere and plain, stripped of any artistic embellishment which might suggest the Catholic veneration of images and religious relics. Later Presbyterians relaxed this viewpoint, coming to feel that religious art, as a symbol of the holy, was not after all, idolatrous. However, with this change in temper, Presbyterians, like the Methodists and most other Protestants, fell victim to the widespread Gothic revival in architecture.

Today, the Presbyterian faith in no sense precludes richness and decorative effects in its churches, and those congregations desiring such an expression are quite free to carry it out. Nevertheless, it is interesting that, in recent years, the finest Presbyterian designs have returned to an earlier simplicity. To those unfamiliar with the history of church architecture, this appears to be a break with tradition, and certainly it is a break with the derivative styles of the recent past. But to Presbyterians, this is actually a renewal of their own early tradition, in new forms appropriate to life led in contemporary America.

27. FIRST PRESBYTERIAN CHURCH

Cottage Grove, Ore.; Dedicated 1951
Pietro Belluschi (b. 1899), architect

*"The materials used are humble ones, and the details
very simple, chosen more to convey the idea of purpose
than that of richness, and to prove that architecture is
an intrinsic art and not an arbitrary dress to be applied
at the designer's changing whim."* — PIETRO BELLUSCHI

The First Presbyterian Church of Cottage Grove, Ore., represents a complete departure from traditional ecclesiastical architecture. It is one of the few churches in this book that is devoid of all the usual symbols: spire, lofty bell tower, arch, or patterned stained glass. Their absence, however, is not based upon a negativistic rejection of the past. Instead, it stems from a positive attempt to express the essence of the Presbyterian faith, to which these symbols have little relevance.

Ironically, the very fact that this attempt has been so successful makes the First Presbyterian Church extremely difficult to describe. The essential character of a religion is by nature nebulous, an idea and a pervading spirit rather than a visible thing. When the forms by which this spirit is expressed are not the instantly recognizable ones of the past, the ideas behind them may remain obscure. The most important fact about the Cottage Grove Presbyterian Church is that it looks like a Presbyterian Church. But it is not easy to say why. The concepts that underlie this particular solution may therefore be of more than ordinary interest to churches facing the same problem, that of "significance" in architecture.

One of the hallmarks of Pietro Belluschi's churches is their appropriateness to their setting. Cottage Grove itself is a small town and the First Presbyterian Church is a neighborhood church located in one of its pleasant residential communities. The design is therefore modest and unpretentious, eschewing any attempt at grandeur, as this would have been out of place in such a setting. Rather than a scaled-down model of a large and imposing city cathedral, this church is a friendly center of community worship in which "people know one another and work together to do God's will."

Because Cottage Grove is at the center of the Douglas fir lumber industry, this design has been executed almost entirely of fir planking in a simple post-and-lintel structural system. Such use of a local material links the church with its own regional heritage, particularly the vernacular "barn architecture" of the Oregon countryside. The American Northwest is a rugged country far removed from the terrain and the tradition of the medieval cathedrals.

These regional and functional qualities, however, have not assumed priority in design. Instead they have been made contributory to the expression of the religious concept. Unlike the Lutheran and Episcopal denominations, which represent a continuing, though reformed, Catholic tradition, the Presbyterian Church rests upon a clear break with Catholicism, including its liturgy, iconography, ruling hierarchy, and theology. The elimination of spire, vault, arch, tower, and richly patterned stained glass is thus a relinquishment of architectural elements that are rooted in the Catholic tradition. Rather than the vertical lines of mystical aspiration, this church employs sweeping horizontals, designed to express a Presbyterian emphasis on the sovereignty of God and His reach out into the surrounding community "where the Christian responsibility lies." The flood of light that illuminates the interior of the church bespeaks the rationalism that is such an important part of Presbyterian doctrine. And the unadorned simplicity of the entire design echoes the straightforwardness and ritual simplicity of the traditional Presbyterian heritage.

It would appear that the Cottage Grove church is a pioneering institution. When founded in 1855, it was the first church in a new frontier settlement of the expanding American Northwest. Its new building, completed just four years short of its centennial, was the first contemporary building to be erected in the town of Cottage Grove. It may also represent a larger "first": the first church in the United States to achieve an architectural expression exactly suited to the Presbyterian faith.

Side view of the church shows the striking horizontality of all its lines. Subsidiary one-story wings and porches extend outward from the main body of the church and their flat roofs cut across it, as does the courtyard fencing. The most important element of the design, however, is the unprecedented roofline of the church itself. Rather than rising centrally into a gable and spire, this church progresses from rear to front, stepping gently upward and then leveling out once more in a continuous and mainly horizontal movement. The progressively rising roof height indicates the progression of space within the church: from utility rooms at the rear up to narthex and nave, and again from nave to the highest plane over the chancel. Even this final

shift in height, however, begins well back in the nave. By this means, the Presbyterian lack of distinction between secular and holy, laity and clergy, is echoed in architecture. At the same time, the subtle sense of opening upward from narthex to nave to chancel creates an atmosphere of serenity and devotion throughout the interior.

The church proper is encircled by subsidiary elements, including a small chapel at front, classrooms on the far side, parlor and parish hall to the rear, and a large, landscaped courtyard. Visible in the photograph are one end of the parish hall (left), and the sheltered main entrance, reached through the courtyard. Architect Pietro Belluschi has described this forecourt as "a tran-

sition area designed to dispose the churchgoer inwardly, and to create a feeling of space and expectation, both of which are such important and subtle elements in architecture."

The entrance gate, the railing at the top of the fence, and the large chancel window have all been carefully detailed to harmonize with one another. In addition, window and gate have been so placed that they break the solid wood of the rest of the walls at exactly the right juncture to create a balanced architectural composition. This is one of the simplest yet finest examples of integral ornament to be found in the book. It illustrates Belluschi's unusual talent for making even the smallest detail count as part of the total design.

"**I was glad** when they said unto me let us go into the house of the Lord." These words, inscribed on the great rock in the courtyard, greet the worshipper as he enters the gates of the First Presbyterian Church. This "Rock of Ages" is one of several rugged and unpolished stones which have been carefully placed throughout the courtyard in a manner reminiscent of Japanese gardens. Such a treatment is appropriate to the West Coast where Oriental influence is strong, and particularly to the Presbyterian faith, which has carried out such extensive mission work in the Far East.

The sovereignty of God, with its implication that all life — East and West, man and nature — lies under His rule, has been the central doctrine of Presbyterianism from its beginning. This theme runs through the entire design of the church. It is reflected in the dominance of the central nave and chancel over the surrounding one-story elements that house subsidiary church activities. It is seen also in the use of clear glass in the lower portion of one wall of the nave. This device links the interior of the church with the courtyard beside it, and makes the act of worship symbolically one with the secular life outside, rather than a thing apart.

A functional and also a strong compositional element in this design is the continuous, sheltered walkway that commences at the street entrance. becomes the porch joining parish hall and church at left, and then turns right to run the length of the church along the far edge of the courtyard. In rainy weather this arrangement shelters the congregation as it approaches or leaves the church, and in good weather the roof of the extended walkway protects the glass wall of the nave from direct sunlight. Note the surface finish of the church — vertical batten strips that seal joints while adding textural interest.

As a contrast to the natural coloring and rough texture of the wooden church, its entrance doors have been surfaced in copper, incised with a simple design of crosses and circles. The concentration of color and brilliance in a small area focuses attention on the entrance, reflecting a warm welcome to the passerby.

Front view of church shows the small, one-story chapel and beyond it, separated by a joint entranceway, a conference room. At the far corner is a small, subsidiary courtyard that adjoins the nursery classroom. The disposition of the various parts of the church complex, and the intersection of their vertical and horizontal planes, show the touch of a master hand. This design illuminates the meaning of composition in architecture.

The unusual bell tower, glimpsed within the main courtyard, shows also how a traditional element can be made appropriate to nontraditional architecture. The lofty and massive bell towers that dominated the facades of the ancient cathedrals could not have been made part of this unprecedented church without ruining its design and contradicting its symbolism. But church bells, "sounding the praises of God and calling the faithful to worship," enjoy a tradition so universal that they can be linked with no specific faith or period. The tower shown here, no more than a supporting frame for the bell, is a very personal expression of this particular church. Carved out of redwood posts by the minister, employing ancient Christian symbols as sculptural motifs, it represents "the craftsmanship of man dedicated to the glory of God."

The interior of the church is almost austere in its simplicity. Nave and chancel melt into each other without break. No attempt has been made to dim the illumination of the nave and set apart the chancel with a heightened radiance. Instead, large windows flood the whole of the interior with revealing light. This lack of distinction expresses the Presbyterian concept of God's encompassment of all things, rather than His mystical dissociation from man within a holy sanctuary.

However, a subtle, devotional quality has been imparted to the chancel by the rise in ceiling height, shown previously in an exterior view, and by the skilled use of reflected color upon off-white plaster walls. Rose-tinted, rather than clear glass, is used in the north chancel window and this casts changing shadows, at times warm pink, at other times lavender, across the chancel. The carpeting of the center aisle is a soft blue-green, and this color too is reflected upon the white plaster, especially toward the left of the chancel and

upon the side wall of the nave. The wash of delicate colors upon white walls brings an otherwise neutral interior alive with subtle tints and shadings.

The ceiling and the rear wall of the church are surfaced with strips of 1- by 4-in. fir flooring, finished in a natural lacquer. They have been grooved for sound absorption, thus solving the problem of reverberation common to a large rectangular room. The same material, but without the acoustical grooving, has been used on the north wall and for the curved screen, which shields the vestry, at the left of the chancel. The baptismal font is set into a rough hewn rock, similar to those in the courtyard garden.

In the Presbyterian Church there is no altar because, by its very name, it implies the concept of priestly sacrifice. Instead there is a communion table used for the service of the Lord's Supper. The table here has purposely been made large and approachable. On communion Sundays, the minister, congregation, and choir form a worshipping family gathered at the common table in the shadow of the cross. The unusual location of the choir is designed to help empasize this fellowship. Rather than a distant loft, the choir stalls (barely visible at left) have been placed next to, and on a level with, the congregational seating. In this way choir members become participants in the service rather than performers.

This church interior, which at first impression seems severely plain, is finally comprehended as a faithful expression of Presbyterian concepts. Its appropriateness becomes the more apparent when this church is compared to the preceding Zion Lutheran Church (No. 19) and the Episcopal Church of the Redeemer (No. 23) by the same architect. Each of these churches sets the sanctuary apart as a radiant holy place. Each makes use of the laminated wooden arch to create an almost Gothic atmosphere of aspiration. But for a Presbyterian Church, the architect has employed the concept of the undivided room. Instead of the medieval arch, he has used the ancient post-and-lintel system. In these ways the Presbyterian reform, creating a less mystical and less hierarchical concept of Christianity, has been made visible.

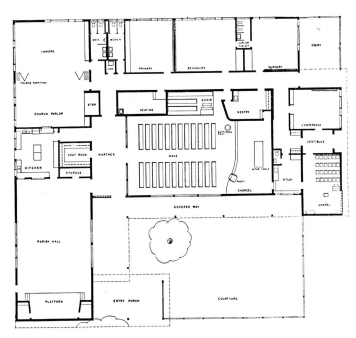

Plan shows the compact organization of subsidiary rooms and courtyards around the main body of the church. Interior circulation is provided by a minimum of halls, since the centrally located narthex connects all elements. Such economy of space is no accident, but a result of the thoughtful planning by which a good architect can cut costs without sacrificing quality.

This church complex was built for only $126,000. It includes 11,500 sq. ft. of floor area. The construction cost thus breaks down to a little under $11 per square foot, a figure many times lower than the cost of reproducing traditional styles. An additional $24,000 was expended on the organ, furnishings, landscaping, draperies, and other miscellaneous items.

REPORT FROM THE CLERGY
The Rev. D. Hugh Peniston, Pastor

The story of the planning of our church covers a period of more than four years. When I came to Cottage Grove the congregation was meeting in an old style frame building some 60 years old. Although there was $50,000 in the building fund, as yet no planning had been undertaken for the urgently needed new church. Our first step was therefore the appointment of a building committee.

This committee represented a number of different age groups and organizations within the church. We quickly found that all of us had different ideas of what the new church should be like. I myself was fresh from the Gothic halls of Princeton University and Union Seminary in New York, and it seemed to me that the Gothic style was the ideal. Others thought that a church had to be built of red brick. The only thing we agreed on was that it had to have a steeple and gabled roofs. We therefore decided that the sensible thing for all of us was to put aside our preconceived notions and ideas and start from the beginning. We spent a full year studying architecture together. Our committee met monthly, and between meetings individual members were supposed to think about the problems brought up and to gather material concerning new church buildings. Often we projected plans for new churches on a screen so that we could consider their advantages and disadvantages. We also obtained a great deal of literature about new church buildings. I myself started going into the city of Eugene on my day off, each Monday, to read in the library of the School of Architecture at the University of Oregon. Gradually we all found that our ideas were changing. We became familiar with the names of contemporary architects and noted the refreshing qualities of their designs. I quickly abandoned my liking for the neo-Gothic style which seemed to be fundamentally dishonest or at best merely imitative. We became more and more convinced that what we wanted to do was to build in terms of the materials and skills of our community, a building that would fit our own particular needs.

We were disappointed in many of the plans that we saw for new churches, feeling that most of them had an unimaginative similarity. The long narrow nave and divided chancel seemed to be standard. Yet we did not feel this plan was suitable for our Presbyterian tradition of worship. It seemed to us that our communion service in particular required a large, approachable communion table, which should be the center of attention for everyone — minister, choir, and congregation. This required a somewhat different placing of the choir than the divided chancel.

At the end of the year we started looking for an architect with these ideas in mind. We met several architects and saw the buildings which they had designed, but we were particularly interested in Pietro Belluschi. He was at that time considered a rather controversial figure. But as soon as I met him I realized that this was a man who was responsive to our problem and our needs.

Before our committee even met with him he told me some of the conditions under which we would have to work. First, we had to have an intelligent committee; second, we were to allow him plenty of time to work out a creative solution to the problem; and third, we should agree to work until all of us were satisfied.

I have just looked over the book of letters that I received from Mr. Belluschi during the three years when he was perfecting our church plan. These letters and my remembrance of our frequent meetings make very vivid to me again the great experience that our association was. This was a real education for all of us on the committee and in the congregation. At no point did Mr. Belluschi try to force us to a new opinion but I can truthfully say that at every point it was a real, cooperative experience and we were working together. He was amazingly responsive to our ideas, and persuasive in helping us to understand his. It is hard for me to explain to you the excitement involved in this experience of planning. You have to understand something of the atmosphere that prevailed in the Belluschi organization, as well as the feeling in our congregation that our little church was about to do something new.

During the years since we have had our new church we have had a continual stream of visitors from all over the world. The most frequent question asked me is "how did you persuade the congregation to accept such a design?" The answer to this question seems to me to be contained in the one word — time. The plan for our new church was not simply thrust upon us for our approval, but it grew over a period of time and we were involved in its growth. First of all we had many conversations with the architect concerning the history of our denomination and what it stands for. I think the main thing that our architect got from the conversations was an impression of the truly democratic spirit of Presbyterianism. I am sure also out of this he caught something of the spirit of the Presbyterian tradition of worship. Then we outlined for him a picture of the program we wanted to be housed in this new building.

The next step was the working out of a floor plan. I believe about seven or eight different floor plans were submitted. The most drastic revision was made as a result of a suggestion from one of the members of the committee that thrilled the architect and caused quite a revolution in the design.

After the completion of the plan the architect built cardboard models showing various possible designs for the exterior. When the final model was at last shown to the committee it was quite a shock to some. We decided that we could not truly judge it until we got used to it, so we talked about it for several meetings without making any decision. One member of the committee said to me "I don't really like it, and yet when you think of it, Mr. Belluschi has expressed in this plan simply those ideas which we wanted him to express."

Eventually we came to understand the plan better and it was approved by the committee and then submitted to the congregation. I tried to prepare our congregation for our final meeting with an article entitled "A Plea for Imagination." At the meeting color slides of various elevations were thrown upon the screen and Mr. Belluschi explained to the people the ideas we were trying to express. When a secret ballot was taken it was found that there was only one negative vote disapproving the plan. I might say that a number of people were not sure about the plan even then, but as they said to me afterwards, they had come to respect Mr. Belluschi so highly that even where they were not sure, they knew that if he said so everything would be all right. I do not know of anyone who dislikes the plan now. We are all naturally very proud of our church and the world-wide recognition it has received.

Our new building, of course, has completely changed the program of the church. It has become an important center in the lives of our people. It is used for many different types of activities, and it is used every day of the week. Our old church was used only for morning worship and for choir practice. We now have programs of recreation and study that carry out the community responsibility so fundamental to our faith. The released-time classes meet in our educational rooms, as well as Scout and Brownie groups. Many different community organizations use our facilities on one occasion or another during the year.

Of course our education program has been completely revolutionized, for we now have ideal facilities. One of the biggest changes is in our program for youth, which has grown tremendously. At the time of construction of our new building, we had many older people and few young families. But since then we have received many younger families into the church. And of course Sunday morning worship is much better attended and the spirit is altogether different. There is no question that the atmosphere of a church building makes a great difference. Many people find a certain serenity and peace simply through stepping into the nave. I believe that Mrs. Eva Holderman, the oldest member of our congregation, summed up the most important quality of the building when she said: "I was fond of the old church. But I feel closer to God in the new one."

References

Belluschi, Pietro. "The Churches Go Modern," *Saturday Evening Post*, October 4, 1958.

Stubblebine, Jo. *The Northwest Architecture of Pietro Belluschi*. F. W. Dodge Corp., New York (1953).

28. TRINITY PRESBYTERIAN CHURCH

Natick, Mass; Fellowship Hall erected 1955
TAC (The Architects Collaborative), architects;
Richard S. Morehouse, in charge of the project
Walter Gropius (b. 1883)

Walter R. Fleischer

"Standardization is not an impediment to the development of civilization, but on the contrary, one of its immediate prerequisites...The fear that individuality will be crushed out by the growing 'tyranny' of standardization is the sort of myth which cannot sustain the briefest examination...The most admired cities of the past are conclusive proof that reiteration of 'typical' buildings notably enhances civic dignity and coherence...The unification of architectural components would have the salutary effect of imparting that homogeneous character to our towns which is the distinguishing mark of a superior urban culture." — WALTER GROPIUS (Left to right, above: Sarah P. Harkness, Jean B. Fletcher, Robert S. McMillan, Norman Fletcher, Walter Gropius, John C. Harkness, Benjamin Thompson, Louis A. McMillen)

Behind a self-imposed anonymity, the firm which calls itself The Architects Collaborative conceals one of the great names of modern architecture: Walter Gropius. One of the famed group of European modernists whose work was later to be named the International Style, Gropius was the first to establish himself. As early as 1911, when he was only 28 years old, his steel, glass, and brick Fagus factory in Alfeld, Germany, heralded the arrival of a new architecture. The unusual transparency of this building, with its sheets of plate glass suspended on a slender steel frame, had been seen before in the fanciful Crystal Palace in London, England, designed solely for exhibition purposes. But the Fagus factory, at one stroke, proclaimed the practicality of the glass curtain wall, which was to become one of the more important elements of modern architecture.

As Director of Germany's famous Bauhaus, or Build-ing Institute, for the ten years from 1918 to 1928, Gropius introduced many other concepts which formed the basis for a new philosophy of design. These included: the standardization and prefabrication of building parts; the prototype design based on a modular repetition of these standardized, manufactured elements; the shift of the architect from the end of the design process to its beginning, through direct collaboration with the manufacturer in developing component parts; the training of the architect by actual experience with materials and manufacturing processes, rather than through artistic exercises on paper; the return of the painter, the sculptor, the textile designer, and the metal worker to their traditional role of architectural collaborators, rather than the individualistic artists they had become when industrialization cut them off from the building process.

These revolutionary ideas were so advanced that

none of them even yet has been fully developed in practice. Their goal was nothing less than a new system of design — applicable to every man-made object from a chair, to a building, to an entire city — based upon the new process of industrialized mass production. They represented a radical departure from the nineteenth-century concept of the architect as a manipulator of surface details, and adaptor of historic styles, an esthete far removed from the hurly-burly of building, manufacturing, and engineering. To Gropius must go full credit for the early recognition that a technological age required, for the realization of its potential, a fresh approach to both architectural practice and architectural education.

In addition to the pioneering concepts embodied in his own buildings, it was this fundamental and inclusive viewpoint on architecture that brought Gropius in 1938 the chairmanship of the Graduate School of Design at Harvard University, a post he held until mandatory retirement in 1952. Through the changes he made in the Harvard curriculum during these 14 years, Gropius may well have influenced the course of architecture in America as much as any other one man. Today, former Gropius students have carried his ideas into many of the leading architectural firms throughout the nation.

Concurrently with his teaching of the new principles, Gropius continued to test his theories in practice. In 1946, following a partnership with former Bauhaus colleague Marcel Breuer, he gathered together a group of young graduate architects, engineers, and other designers to form The Architects Collaborative, submerging his world-famous name in a cooperative enterprise. In this way he demonstrated his dedication to the concept of the design team, as opposed to an office in which draftsmen merely execute the designs of the head of the firm.

Gropius' precedent for this unusual operational scheme goes back to the building guilds of the middle ages, when design and construction were one process, cooperatively carried out. These teams of craftsmen, who built the great cathedrals, have been described by Gropius as follows:

"Most striking within the organization of these building guilds was the fact that . . . every craftsman on the job was not only an executing hand but was permitted to put his own design ideas into his part of the work as long as he abided by the master's guiding key of design . . . similar to the keys in musical composition. Preconceived paper design hardly existed at all; the group lived together, discussed the task, and built their ideas . . ."

The Architects Collaborative represents the modern counterpart of the medieval building guild adapted to today's specialized industrial conditions but still essentially a cooperative creative effort. The First Presbyterian Church of Natick, Mass., shown on the following pages, is an example of such collaborative design, guided by Gropius' key concepts of prefabricated component parts and the repetitive building module.

Joseph W. Molitor

Fellowship Hall is the first, and as yet the only, building of the church complex to be finished. Worship services are being conducted here until the church itself is built. When completed the master plan will include four separate buildings — church, Fellowship Hall, classroom building, and chapel — all connected by covered walkways.

Fellowship Hall is an excellent example of the technological approach to design. It is not a prefabricated structure in the same sense as the prefabricated houses that are sold as completed packages. Instead it illustrates the infinitely more flexible system of industrialized component parts, from which a variety of different designs can be made.

End walls are of standard concrete block, a hollow, manufactured masonry aggregate which combines cheapness with excellent insulating properties. A coat of acrylic-resin paint on the exterior makes it waterproof and gives a white finish to the concrete.

The framing of the entrance wall shown above, and the similar wall at the rear of the hall, is standard 2-by 3-in. lumber. Spaces between these framing members are infilled with plate glass, or with prefabricated wall panels combining acoustical treatment and finished surfacing in one sandwich. The ceiling is sand-finished plaster on joists between supporting beams of laminated wood.

The standard and prefabricated elements are dimensioned to fit together like the pieces of an erector set, thus reducing the wasteful and time-consuming site-cutting of materials that accounts for a good share of the cost of a traditional building operation. Instead, the major construction job takes place in the factory or mill before materials are shipped to the site.

Because this process, even today, is still in the developmental stage, the prefabricated panels and the laminated roof girders used here were especially designed for the job. When such elements become available as standard items in a sufficient range of type, size, and finish — as they eventually must — buildings can be designed merely by an arrangement of stock parts. Unable as yet to depend upon such a standard selection, Fellowship Hall follows Gropius' thesis that the architect should function as a creator of building elements for factory production, thus controlling design at its source.

Joseph W. Molitor

Interior view of social hall reveals its simplicity of construction. Each bay is marked by a wooden post which supports the heavy laminated roof beam directly above it. These exposed structural elements are distinguished from nonbearing members by their natural finish. Wood framing of window and wall panels, which bears no weight, is painted white.

The prefabricated wall panels are designed on a hidden frame of 2-by 3-in. lumber, with an exterior surfacing sheet of stucco on metal lath. The interior surface is clapboard, stained a dark walnut. In order to provide acoustical treatment, each clapboard is offset, one from the other, leaving a crack between each. The entire area behind the clapboards is sound-absorbent Fiberglas. Additional acoustical treatment is used in the end wall, where masonite punchboard panels are backed with Fiberglas. Ceiling panels of sand-finish plaster are putty colored. Floors are gray asphalt tile.

The cost of Fellowship Hall, which contains 4,200 sq. ft. of floor area, was $41,000. This breaks down to a low $9.70 per sq. ft., the direct result of the economical structural system and materials employed.

Joseph W. Molitor

Direct front view of Fellowship Hall reveals a carefully composed design. Natural wood doors and opaque wall panels painted light blue are interspersed with clear glass and outlined by white framing members. Heavier end walls and roof fascia, painted white, act as a definitive border for the composition. A narrow porch of natural wood, running the length of the building, adds the fourth border and finishes the picture.

The design as a whole is reminiscent of the straight-line compositions of Piet Mondrian, the famous Dutch modern painter. The resemblance is not accidental. An interaction between the work of modern artists and modern architects was one of the characteristics of the Bauhaus school of design, and the imprint of certain artists is still visible in the architecture that stems from this collaboration.

In such a simple, geometric arrangement, perfect proportion and delicacy of detail are all-important. As in the work of Mies van der Rohe, shown previously, a fault in the spacing of elements, or even in the width of framing membrers, would render the entire design clumsy and coarse. Although it appears to be simplicity itself, this type of architecture therefore requires an artist's eye. When attempted by builders or contractors without benefit of an architect, the result is a utilitarian structure entirely lacking the subtle and disciplined beauty of the building shown here.

The task of architectural composition is doubly difficult because it is tied to the function of the building rather than being an artist's free exercise on canvas. For instance, the changes in wall treatment, seen above, indicate changes in the interior use of space. The governing dimension is the 17-ft. bay, seven of which make up the length of the hall. From the left, the first four bays enclose one large room, the social hall. This hall, which is meant for church suppers, adult meetings, and study groups, is also being used for worship on Sundays until the church is built.

The fifth bay, infilled entirely with glass, provides needed lighting for a stairwell to the basement. This lower level will eventually be finished as a youth center. The sixth bay contains solid entrance doors that lead toward the stairwell at their left and church offices in the seventh bay at right. Here, again, glass provides excellent natural lighting for the close work done in these rooms. If expansion is desired in the future, one or more of the standard bays can simply be added to the end of the buildings. It is commonly found that an increase in membership follows the erection of a new church, often rendering its new facilities once more inadequate. An easy solution to this problem is here planned into the original building.

The small chapel, the next building to be erected, will be placed on this side of Fellowship Hall, connected to it by a covered walk that will join the hall at the double entrance doors to the right.

Model of Trinity Presbyterian Church shows disposition of the four buildings on a five-acre, wooded site. Walkways which connect each building to its neighbor also define their courtyards. The Fellowship Hall and chapel are in the foreground; Sunday school building to the rear; the church to the right.

The design of the church sets it apart from the other buildings, but like them, it is based at least partially on a system of prefabricated component parts. The supporting structure is a rigid frame of laminated wooden bents. These are similar in effect to the laminated arches of Pietro Belluschi's Zion Lutheran Church (No. 19), but here columns are brought down outside the church rather than inside. In both structures these supports are kept free from curtain walls that enclose the church. But whereas the arches of Zion Lutheran act to define interior side aisles, the bents of Trinity Presbyterian form an exterior colonnade, a sheltered walk at either side of the building. This treatment, which frees the interior from columns, also eliminates the Gothic atmosphere, which is so striking in Zion Lutheran Church, but which is hardly appropriate to the Presbyterian faith.

The design shown here is not the final one and changes will inevitably be made when the time comes to erect the church. However, the model suggests the probability of a large, louvered window, of stained or colored glass, to be set in the gable of the entrance wall. As now planned, side walls will be of stone below a bank of clear glass windows. This represents one of the few uses of natural rather than manufactured materials within the entire church complex.

The chapel, intended for christenings, small weddings, and private meditation, is completely windowless in contrast to the other buildings. The outgoing character of the Presbyterian faith is expressed by the large areas of glass in hall, church, and classroom units. But the need for private communion, sheltered from the exterior world, is recognized in the design of the chapel. The outside is allowed to enter here only through a small transom above the door and through the skylight which sheds a diffused radiance within the protected circle. Structurally, the chapel is a wooden frame and platform set upon a stone base and enclosed by a "drum" of vertical clapboards, painted white.

Instead of a traditional bell tower, a tall, slender cross dominates the approach to the building group, directly in front of the church. Similar smaller crosses in black wrought iron are used on the chapel (shown here) and on Fellowship Hall. This traditional symbol identifies an unorthodox church complex, and acts as a repetitive decorative motif, unifying the various buildings within it. Although entirely different in character from the Cottage Grove Presbyterian Church (No. 27), the order, discipline, and simplicity of the Trinity design makes it equally appropriate to the Presbyterian faith.

References

Giedion, S. *Walter Gropius, Work and Teamwork.* Reinhold Pub. Corp., New York (1954).

Gropius, Walter. "Gropius Appraises Today's Architect," *Architectural Forum*, May 1952.

—— *The New Architecture and the Bauhaus.* Branford, Newton Centre, Mass (1936).

REFORMED

The Reformed Church near Zurich, Switzerland, shown on the following pages, might logically have been placed in the preceding Presbyterian section. The two denominations have common roots in Calvinism, remain similar in doctrine, and are officially allied. However, the Reformed faith of Switzerland, as it developed through the teachings of Ulrich Zwingli, is slightly different in spirit from the Presbyterian, which reached America through English Puritans with a later admixture of Scottish and North-Irish immigants. The Swiss Church is more firmly rooted in the continuity of a single, national tradition, a fact that is evident even in the modern expression of its architecture.

The Reformed church also might have been placed in the later Congregational section. The Congregational denomination, too, traces its history through English Puritanism to Calvin. In its modern development, it is close to both European Reformed Churches and to American Presbyterians. Moreover, Congregationalists recently united with the Evangelical and Reformed Church in America, making an official link with one branch of the Reformed faith. There is also an architectural link. The Congregational building heritage is one of starkness, severity, and purity. In its display of these qualities, the Swiss design might be considered a modern equivalent to the Congregational churches of colonial New England, although on a much larger scale.

However, this Swiss architecture has a flavor all its own. In addition, it carries a religious heritage which reaches beyond these two major American denominations and their English and Scottish counterparts. As an indirect descendant of Calvin's early church, it may be considered a link with all the national variants of Calvinism developed in different countries over the years.

These include, besides the Presbyterian and Congregational, the Dutch Reformed Church, the French Hueguenot Church (now also called Reformed), and the Reformed Churches of Germany and of Hungary. Thus, while evoking the particular spirit of Swiss Protestantism, the Reformed Church of Zurich also expresses general religious characteristics common to the various denominations listed above. It may therefore serve as an architectural inspiration to any one of them, embodying as it does qualities appropriate to all.

29. REFORMED CHURCH

Alstetten, Switzerland; Designed 1938; Constructed 1942
Werner M. Moser (b. 1896), architect

"My philosophy of design is to tackle each problem as if it were never done before and study it off the ground — but still exploiting critically all present solutions on the subject, and incorporating as many future claims in the use of the building as possible. Knowledge and appreciation of outstanding historical solutions enter the design unconsciously." — WERNER M. MOSER

The Reformed Church of Alstetten in suburban Zurich, Switzerland, is one of only two European churches chosen for the Protestant section of this book, the other being the historic Stahl Kirche (No. 18) in Essen, Germany. G.E. Kidder Smith in 1950 called the Alstetten church "unquestionably the finest modern church in Switzerland, and possibly anywhere else." Although the great resurgence of church architecture after World War II has given this church many competitors, it still remains one of the loveliest and most evocative designs of our era.

Moreover, the church is interesting because its distinctive character is the result of difficult problems overcome — problems that are faced also by many American congregations.

Population growth, spilling over from the city of Zurich, had transformed the once rural village of Alstetten into a suburban community, thus rendering its local Protestant church inadequate. Rather than abandoning or demolishing its historic church, the congregation decided to build a new church on the same site, while retaining the old one as a small chapel for weddings, baptisms, and evening services. The new church was to be large enough to accomodate 1,000 people for worship, and provide also adequate Sunday school rooms, offices, and a large social hall — facilities entirely lacking in the older building.

This arrangement was sensible, but added to the difficulties of planning. The architecture of the new church, although modern, could not clash with the traditional Swiss style of the old church, which dates from the eleventh century. The new building would have to

dominate the site without overpowering its smaller neighbor. Even more troublesome, the disposition of its various elements was complicated by the position of the old church, which cut well into the available property.

To resolve these difficulties, an unorthodox solution was a necessity. The architect, Werner M. Moser, explains:

"To create a relation between the new and the old building without compromise for the new — just by careful proportions — was a special aim. It resulted in an asymmetrical shape, which was very individually fitted and just only to this solution."

For such a challenging assignment, Dr. Moser was eminently qualified. As one of the leading architects and town planners in Switzerland and son of that country's famous pioneer modernist, Karl Moser (see the Church of St. Antonius, No. 1c, at Basel), he was steeped in the entire development of Swiss architecture, past and present. The influence of his father, and behind him of Auguste Perret, can be seen in the handling of reinforced concrete in this church. In addition Moser had worked in Germany under Mies van der Rohe, the master of the rectangle, and in America under Frank Lloyd Wright, the master of asymmetrical space. These various influences in the background of Dr. Moser undoubtedly aided him in solving the problems posed here. But the Reformed Church of Alstetten — although it retains a faint echo of the Swiss past, and although it shows the subtle influence of several masters of modern architecture — is in no sense a derivative work. Established approaches to design have served as paths to the creation of a fresh and original architecture.

G. E. Kidder Smith

Soaring bell tower, 110 ft. tall, dominates the entire site. Like the exposed structural frame of the church, the tower is of reinforced concrete, painted white. Its alternation of solid slabs with open grillwork, in vertical panels, imparts slenderness and delicacy, changing what would otherwise have been a massive structure into one of floating lighness.

The pattern of the concrete grillwork is like that employed by Auguste Perret in his famous church of Notre Dame du Raincy (No. 1). This same ornamental motif has been found on seventeenth-century Swiss barns in the canton of Bern. Thus, while appropriate as a modern decorative device, it evokes the Swiss past.

Within the reinforced concrete frame of the church, curtain walls are of gray brick, offset to create an integral, textured pattern. This view shows the exterior of the rear wall of the nave, the main entrance to the church being at the right side just around the corner. The lower roofline that cuts into the main body of the church indicates a one-story wing that runs the full length of the nave, housing entrance vestibule, choir, and organ. The part that here projects toward the camera contains rest rooms, isolated from the main interior. In this way all working elements of the design are concentrated in the one-story wing, leaving the nave free of all obstructions.

Sheltered church entrance adjoins the bell tower, its latticework screen repeating the pattern of the tower grille. This photograph shows the one-story wing that houses the working elements of the church, concentrating them to one side of the nave. A small part of the high clerstory window that illuminates the nave is visible to the left of the bell tower.

G. E. Kidder Smith

This nave is one of the most attractive to be found in any modern church. Here the severe lines of the exterior are softened. The subdued coloring and the wash of sunlight across the chancel create an atmosphere of benediction. Walls are the palest of gray. Ceiling panels and window louvers are white, as are also the translucent, hanging light globes. Against this pale background, the plaque and cross which decorate the chancel wall, the pulpit and other furnishings, all of natural wood, appear the color of old gold. There are no bright accents anywhere to break the quiet serenity, only the inscription: "One is our Master, Christ, and we are all brothers."

This view of the nave is taken from the same direction as that of the exterior photograph on page 223. Note choir stalls and organ at right, which are housed in the one-story side wing. The clerestory window above is cut off from view by a shield of frosted glass. A large chancel window is equipped with deep vertical louvers, which shield the congregation from glare while permitting the movement of sunlight across the wall.

This church employs many of the acoustical principles that dictated the design of Christ Church (No. 20) in Minneapolis, Minn., by Eliel Saarinen. The front and rear walls are each canted slightly outward from the left to the right side of the church. The roof of the nave slants upward from left to right; the roof of the side wing upward from right to left. The asymmetrical shape thus achieved prevents the reverberation common between parallel surfaces.

As in the Saarinen church, several aims are amalgamated into one solution. The slanted ceiling deflects light as well as sound. The window louvers act to baffle sound waves as well as sunlight. Equally important to these functional requirements is the more nebulous one of atmosphere. The asymmetrical shape of the interior and its perfect proportions give this large church a character of intimacy and close communion. It is difficult to believe that it seats 1,000 persons.

This same asymmetry has been used as a religious symbol. In the Reformed Church, as in the Protestant faith generally, there is no coercion. Worshippers come freely and voluntarily to hear the word of God. An interior based upon the principles of formal balance suggests rigid control. On the other hand, the asymmetrical form suggests freedom and spontaneity. Thus, the arrangement that gives this church its excellent lighting and acoustical qualities is also the means by which its religious character is expressed.

Copyright by Michael Wolgensinger

Exterior view of left wall of the nave shows the
vertical chancel window and, in the lower story, the
series of large windows that light the social hall beneath it. The building is sited on a hill, with this side
of the social hall at ground level, the opposite side built
into the slope. In this way the nave, which is here a
story above ground, is at ground level on the opposite
entrance side.

The two stories have been differentiated by their structure. Rigid, tapered, concrete bents, exposed on both
exterior and interior, frame the social hall and support
the nave above it. A concrete slab forms the end wall
of the social hall. The nave employs a more conventional post-and-lintel concrete frame, infilled with flush-
set gray brick.

A separate entrance to the social hall is in the end
wall, at left. Beyond, at far left, the two-story Sunday
school wing is visible as it forms an L with the church
proper.

The tower is visible from every side of the church. Here, it gives the appearance of being centrally placed, making this view of the church reminiscent of New England colonial churches. A design similar to this would seem eminently appropriate to the New England region. Although this church is individually planned for this particular site and congregation, the character of its design might act as a stimulus to Congregational churches that are planning expansion.

Interior of social hall shows how reinforced concrete bents combine the functions of both posts and beams. The wall of windows is the one seen in the exterior view on facing page. The cool serenity of the nave gives way to a warmer atmosphere, created by the exposed structural members, painted white, and by ceiling and floor surfaces of natural wood, in a rich brown tone. Vertical half-rounds of wood surface the proscenium of the stage. This level of the church contains also a kitchen, a projection room, offices, vestry, and coat room.

Michael Wolgensinger

Over-all view shows how the disposition of old and new buildings creates a sheltered court within the property. The main church is in the background, with the Sunday school building extending from it into the foreground. The rear of the old church is visible at left. This photograph provides a particularly good view of the clerestory window in the new church, which runs the full length of the nave above the one-story wing.

Like the church proper, the Sunday school building also has a lower wing to the side, visible here in profile. The opposing, slanted roofs of the two classroom elements repeat the rooflines of the main church and its wing, and harmonize with the roof of the old church.

The slope of the ground from the direction of both church and Sunday school wing is up toward the old church, which commands the brow of the hill. With this hillside setting, it was possible to show only the upper story of the new buildings as they face the inner court, while still providing windows in the lower level down the slope at rear. In this way, the new church complex, large though it is, does not dwarf and overpower the older, smaller church.

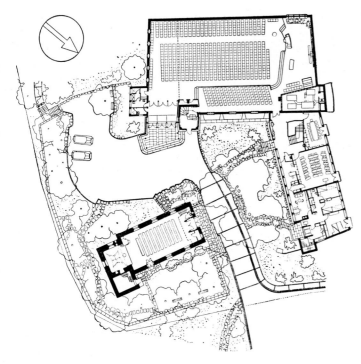

Upper level plan shows the old church outlined in heavy black at left, the nave of the new church at rear, and the Sunday school building extending from it, as seen also in the over-all view. To leave "breathing room" between the churches on a limited acreage, the new buildings were placed as far back toward the edge of the property line as they could go. This allowed plenty of space for courts, walks, and parking between the old and new buildings. The entrance road cuts the property into two distinct parts, setting off the old from the new, but at the same time parking space is equally convenient to either church.

The angle at which the new church and its classroom wing join is greater than 90 degrees. With the rising slope of the land this wide angle makes the new church buildings appear to "reach" for the old church.

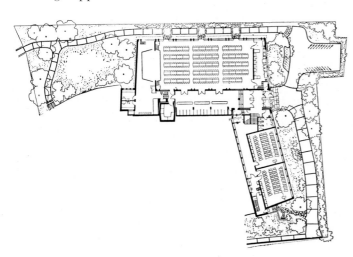

Plan of lower level shows the social hall with its stage, which is at the opposite end of the church from that part of the nave (above it) containing the chancel.

Two large classrooms occupy the lower level of the Sunday school building. The social hall (excluding the kitchen and offices) is 82 by 42 ft. and seats 500. The church proper, above it, is approximately 105 by 50 ft. with a capacity seating of 1,000. In comparison, the old one-story church seats only 120.

REPORT FROM THE CLERGY
A. Schmid, Pastor

The new building had to be erected so near to the old one that only contrasting architecture could be considered. I was acquainted with modern architecture, but most members of the congregation were not, originally, prepared for it. The architect was able to present it as the sole possible solution. This was not easy, as in our Zurich Reformed Church the final decision on church building lies in the hands of the general meeting of parishioners. The architect himself has stated that "the unusual shape of the church was accepted by clergymen and building committee only as a consequence of a long planning period, due to the difficulty of building during the war. This allowed enough time to educate and encourage the congregation for an individual, unconventional solution."

The parish is now proud of both their old and new churches, although the block-like rear wall toward the orchard is still considered by some as disturbing. However, the beauty of the church and the suitability of the community halls have increased activity in the parish. Each Sunday the spacious church attracts double the number of people that the old church did. Certainly the young people have flocked in greater numbers to the events organized by the church.

Since construction in 1941, the church buildings have answered their purpose in every way. They contain no unnecessary space or angle. It is a daily pleasure to perform my duties in these church premises. The symbolism of the architecture is particularly well realized. Our church is mainly the place for the proclamation of the Word. For this reason the organ was placed at the side . . . . The pulpit was placed to that it can be easily seen from all angles. From baptism one passes through the Word to Communion. This sequence is clearly revealed, as the font is placed at the side of the pulpit. On the other side is the Communion table, raised one step above the pulpit, in the middle of the chancel. The acoustics also are entirely adapted to the Word. Light enters from above, symbolizing the grace of God, which reaches us from above. At the same time, the enormous window on the side, next to the pulpit, reminds the minister of the contact with life outside the precincts of the church.

Reference
Smith, G. E. Kidder. *Switzerland Builds.* Albert Bonniers, New York (1950).

The Congregational Church is the historic church of the Pilgrim Fathers, who landed at Plymouth, Mass., on September 6, 1620, to found the first permanent colony in the New World. From this small band of 100 settlers, the Congregational community rapidly expanded to embrace much of New England in the stern morality of its Puritan doctrine. Even as it expanded, however, other denominations began to invade the chosen land of America. And although westward moving pioneers eventually carried this faith across the continent, the stronghold of Congregationalism has remained, through the years, in New England.

Today American Congregationalists number approximately 1.4 million, but a historic merger with the Evangelical and Reformed Church in 1957 has brought the combined membership to over 2 million and up to 7.2 million throughout the world. The new church is known as the United Church of Christ.

Despite its comparatively small present membership and its localized authority even in the seventeenth century, the Congregational Church is recognized as one of the major contributors to the development of a democratic America. From the beginning, its system of government made each church entirely autonomous, to be ruled by no higher authority than the vote of the local congregation — hence the name Congregationalist. Although today there is a Congregational General Council, the national body has no authority over local churches, and each congregation still adopts, or writes its own creed.

In colonial days, this ecclesiastical democracy was inseparable from the secular self-government of each Massachusetts village as planned by the church itself. Membership in the Congregational Church was prerequisite to voting in either church or village affairs, and the same group of men controlled both. The Puritan experiment was therefore a rigidly exclusive "church-state" allowing no disagreement with prevailing religious views. Nevertheless, it was the Congregational concept of "the rule of Christ as manifested through His people assembled" from which stemmed the American system of local, democratic self-government. This church gave its members practical experience in self-government and this idea was carried westward to the new villages and towns within an expanding American nation.

Under the rule of the Congregationalists, seventeenth century New England was also the first colony to set up a compulsory public school system, teaching — in addition to "horn-book, primer, psalter, testament, and Bible" — the subjects of geometry, Latin, and Greek. With this curriculum, they prepared their most promising students for Harvard College, a Congregational institution, which in turn prepared them for teaching and the ministry, thus completing the educational circle. Although the Congregationalists were in firm control of the schools, because church and village affairs were administered by the same men, the schools nevertheless were not officially church schools, nor did their funds come from the church. Thus was paved the way for the public school system that is also an integral part of America's democracy.

Historically, the Congregational Church is a branch of the Church of England, formed in protest against the authority of the Anglican bishops and based upon the tenet of congregational, rather than hierarchical rule. The emigration to America was not an act of separation from the established church, but a means to gain freedom from the demands of the bishops while still remaining nominally within the Church. The break came under Charles II, when that monarch required even of his colonists strict conformity to the *Book of Common Prayer*.

In its deviation from the Church of England, however, the Congregational faith was strongly influenced by Calvin. It is from this other heritage that the name Puritan arose, as descriptive of the stern precepts which early characterized this persuasion. The sober dress and austere behavior of the Puritans represented a protest against the worldly dissipation of the English court and secular life of the day. In the same way, their religious buildings represented a protest against the Catholic richness of ritual and accoutrement within the Anglican Church.

The early Congregational "meeting house," in which both church services and town meetings were held, was simply a bare, rectangular building without a distinguishing ecclesiastical feature of any sort. Even the later, steepled church, landmark of the New England village, kept much of this earlier simplicity, employing small-paned clear glass windows, an open platform for the chancel, and chastely white, undecorated interiors. These beautiful and historic buildings are still used throughout New England, and nothing could be more evocative of their religious heritage.

However, in building new churches today, Congregationalists might well wish to express the changes that have occurred within their faith over the years, transforming it from one of the sternest and most rigid of doctrines into one of the least dogmatic. Especially in other parts of the country where the New England architectural tradition is out of place, such a new expression is indicated. The chapel illustrated on the following pages shows how one congregation in California has met this challenge. Without sacrificing Congregational essentials, it has adopted an entirely new architecture expressive of a new position in time, in location, and in practical religious application.

30. CHILDREN'S CAMPUS, THE NEIGHBORHOOD CHURCH

South Pasadena, Calif.
Nursery school erected 1948; Chapel erected 1954
Religious education building erected 1957
Smith & Williams, architects
Whitney R. Smith (b. 1911)
Wayne Williams (b. 1919)
Eckbo, Royston & Williams, landscape architects
Kolesoff & Kariotis, structural engineers

"The religious education program of the church is centered around the relationship between the children's own lives and the religious content of nature. Our architectural philosophy matches this program closely. Structural systems, materials, and finishes must all express the natural fact of their function and by so doing will impart an atmosphere of peace and solidity."

— SMITH & WILLIAMS

The Neighborhood Church in South Pasadena, Calif., represents a common enterprise in which the Congregational and Unitarian fellowships have joined together. This is the type of neighborhood cooperation which can be undertaken by local churches when both are autonomously governed.

The new children's chapel, religious education building, and nursery school shown on the following pages, illustrate the concern displayed by both these denominations for the healthy spiritual and emotional development of their children. This concern echoes the intense preoccupation of the early Congregational Puritans with the religious education of the young. The buildings shown here, however, and the aims that produced them, strikingly reveal the changed attitude toward child development that has taken place within these two contemporary denominations both of which derive from a common Puritan root.

Today it is understood that children cannot be forced into respectful attendance at an adult service that they cannot understand and that religious attitudes are best fostered by experiences within the immediate mental and emotional grasp of the child. The long-standing Protestant custom of Sunday schools had this effect as its aim. Here in the Neighborhood Church this goal has been carried even further. The three new buildings represent a children's domain in which worship services as well as Sunday school lessons are geared to the different age levels, starting with the first grade. The guiding aim of the entire children's center is to make

religion such a vital and absorbing experience that it becomes a natural part of the child's awareness of himself and the world.

Because so much of the religious experience of children centers around the recognition of God in the wonders of nature, all buildings have been integrated with the out-of-doors. Play yards and pleasant courts and terraces, designed for use rather than show, are interlaced with the buildings, and connected by sheltered walks.

Whitney R. Smith and Wayne R. Williams, the architects chosen to carry out this aim in the new buildings, were admirably suited to the task. Both are native Californians, both are graduates of the University of Southern California and their office has been one of the leaders in developing the California style of modern architecture, which emphasizes the integration of the building with the out-of-doors, and the appropriate use of regional materials. In addition, Wayne R. Williams has been particularly active in the planning of public parks and recreation areas and in working with youth groups. In 1957 he was chairman of the Youth Conference in Pasadena, attended by 2,000 young people and sponsored by the school system, various departments of the city government, and youth service groups. Whitney R. Smith has served as chairman of a number of community planning and redevelopment organizations and also of the Housing Research Council of Southern California, Inc. This background, in addition to their architectural excellence, gave these architects a special understanding of the problems of planning for children.

Photos: Julius Shulman

The children's chapel echoes the form of the early Congregational meeting house that was simply a gabled hall with a small, projecting vestibule at the front. The decorative detailing, on the other hand, has a distinct flavor of the Orient. This, too, is appropriate. The Congregationalists early sent their missionaries to China and Japan, and interchange with these countries is a part of the heritage of the church. Such detailing is suitable also as a West Coast regional expression.

This chapel was built on a limited budget and some of its best features stem from certain enforced economies. For example, painted plaster was used for the walls of the chapel because it was the cheapest material that could give the required one-hour fire resistance rating. The plaster has been formed into reinforced, sectional panels, exposed on both interior and exterior. This is a new use of a material ordinarily employed only as a surface finish. The panels are supported by a frame of wooden posts, projecting out from the wall surface in a manner reminiscent of Japanese building.

The economical use of large, uninterrupted plaster

panels necessitated an unusual window system. Narrow, vertical strips of glass are set between post and plaster, running the full height of the chapel from floor to ceiling. Thus, from the exterior, the chapel appears to be a windowless retreat. On the interior, no wide views of the out-of-doors can distract a child's attention from the service.

Steps lead down from the chapel entrance to a central garden court about which all buildings, old and new, are disposed. This plaza can be used on pleasant Sundays as an outdoor classroom and also for the after-church coffee hour. It is large enough for special services, for church barbecues, and for children's plays.

Such a "working" courtyard is quite different from the fenced or walled courts previously shown in conjunction with other churches. The architects believe that the outdoors should be used and that grounds should "flow" around and between buildings rather than being chopped into parts. The major central court, therefore, continues under the covered walkways, melting into the smaller play yards and patios of surrounding structures.

Chapel door is decorated with ashwood sculptures depicting the themes taught in Sunday school. At lower left is the image of a child "admiring the objects of nature — a growing vine, a flower, a squirrel, and birds." This represents one of the major themes of first and second grade study, "Seeing God in the wonders of nature."

Above this group is a mother and baby, which represents not only the Madonna, but any mother's love for her child. This is another theme of the first and second grades, "Seeing God in the love of our homes." Complementing the mother figure, at the right side of the door, is a father-son sculpture. It represents the parable of the prodigal son, one of the stories taught to third-grade children who are starting their study of the Bible. It signifies also the love of father and child in the home, the father-love of God, and the forgiveness of man toward man, which are universal elements of every religion.

To the right of the Madonna is another woman's figure representing the arts — specifically the singing, painting, and clay modeling through which the children express their worship of God and develop their own creative powers. At the lower right is an irregular block with depictions of clouds, sun, stars, and planets in bas relief. This symbolizes the third-grade course "How miracles abound," in which the children are taught to see God through the wonders of science.

Tying the group together is the largest sculpture of all, the robed figure of a man with upstretched arms, symbolizing worship. This figure was not patterned after Jesus, but was purposely made universal in order to suggest the aspirational impulse which has stirred all men "since humanity began."

Latticed entrance wall of chapel permits a view of the courtyard while giving a sense of protection to the interior. However, its major function is esthetic. One of the architects explained the aim as follows: "When the sun passes through it, it will be like the sunlight falling through leaves." At night, when the chapel is illuminated from within, the same pattern of light stands out like a tracery against the dark sky.

In order to create the desired effect, the architects designed the grille at the site, experimenting with pieces of wood until the most effective light filtration was achieved. Although the latticework lends a feeling of luxury to an otherwise undecorated building, it was actually built from waste lumber as another cost-saving feature of the design. This building offers one more proof that beauty need not be expensive.

The chapel is designed to give even very young children the experience of ritual worship in a building inspiring by its beauty, yet not overpowering in scale. This interior view shows how the redwood grille of the entrance is echoed over the chancel where it is used to screen mechanical heating elements. The brick wall behind the altar represents an ingenious way of meeting a four-hour fire resistance requirement for this part of the building. The wall was set back from the main part of the chapel, creating a small garden space as a backdrop for the altar, and providing also separate exterior entrance to the chancel. Sliding glass doors immediately behind the altar close off this space in cool or rainy weather without obscuring it from view. This small "chancel garden" emphasizes the recognition of God in nature, an important theme of Sunday school in the lower grades. During night services, or whenever it is so desired, curtains can be drawn across the glass wall, which provides a very different but equally effective backdrop.

The color scheme of the interior is carried out in shades of brown and pale pink. Pews, latticework, exposed framing members, and altar are stained dark brown. The chancel wall is tawny red brick.

Plaster walls are painted a medium shade of brown, contrasting with the chancel draperies and carpeting of pale beige. Pink is introduced in the stained glass of the vertical nave windows casting a warm radiance upon the interior.

Particular attention has been paid to the muffling of noise, with floors of cork and ceilings of mineral acoustic tile. However, the atmosphere of the little chapel has been even more effective than its physical properties in quieting the children. After the first service in the new chapel, Mrs. Miriam Gorton, the director of religious education, wrote:

"Since I have been working with the children in our church school, I have never experienced so reverent and inspiring a service with them. The beauty of the place is felt even more by the children than by the adults, I believe. Not a child was noisy or ill at ease, and all responded to the mood set by the building and the organ music.... One mother said she had a lump in her throat, because the children's attitude was so moving."

Religious education building echoes the chapel with its broad eaves, plaster walls, and exposed wood frame. Covered walk at left, which connects it with the chapel, had not been built when the chapel photographs were taken. Trusses supporting the roof of this walkway are identical to those used as roof framing for both the education building and the nursery school, a visual repetition which unifies these different structures.

Covering most of each end of the education building are screens of redwood planking, which shield exterior stairwells from view. These stairways lead up to the balcony and down to front ground-level entrances, thus providing convenient exterior access at both ends of the building on two levels. The screening acts also as integral decoration, visually the most striking feature of the building. Guard railings for the balcony are also decorative, being of expanded metal mesh in a deep shade of blue.

Although the building, as seen in this photograph, looks like a simple, two-story rectangle, it actually con-

tains four levels and two subsidiary wings. The main part of the building seen here contains two stories. The one-story west wing, which can be glimpsed under the covered walkway at left, is elevated half a level above the ground floor of the main building block to take advantage of a sloping site. The corresponding east wing, at the far end of the building, adds the fourth level to a staggered building elevation.

All ground-level classrooms open upon paved terraces or play yards and all upper level rooms upon balconies. With this plan, trees and gardens are everywhere visible from the interior and rooms can actually be extended into the out-of-doors when glass walls are thrown open on pleasant days. At the same time, because of the several levels of the building and the different directions toward which the rooms face, privacy is maintained between each class and age group. Adult discussion and study groups that use the building during the week find its light, airy "garden rooms" as pleasant as do the children.

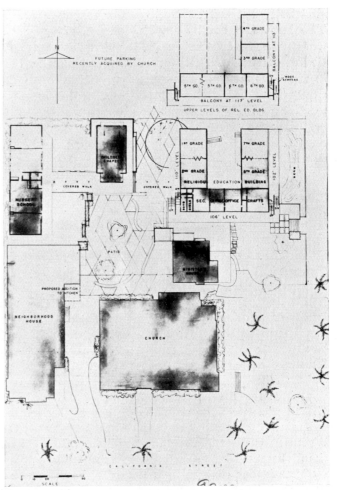

Nursery school looks more like a home than a school, thus providing the desired atmosphere for very young children. Here during the week the church conducts a nonsectarian day-care center, a community service today undertaken by many denominations. It is a natural outgrowth of the Protestant ethic, which considers the Christian responsibility a community as well as a personal one. On Sundays the building is used for nursery and kindergarten classes, separating these preschool children from older Sunday-school grades.

Like the chapel, this building combines a wood frame and plaster wall panels with brick end walls. Office, lavatories, pantries, storage rooms, and heating element are concentrated in a central core. This location considerably reduces the cost of piping and other connections, an important consideration because mechanical equipment accounts for a major part of the construction costs.

On each side of the "working core" is a large classroom which can be subdivided by a sliding partition. In this way, available space can be used either as two large open playrooms, or four smaller classrooms, to suit changing activities. Sliding glass entrance walls also permit the extension of classrooms into the out-of-doors.

Site plan of the Neighborhood Church shows arrangement of old buildings to the south and new buildings to the north, all centering inward upon the large open patio. Circulation between all buildings has been carefully plotted, with covered walks, paved terraces, and steps to connect the various levels.

Few churches have provided such extensive facilities for their children as those represented by the new buildings shown here. There is a total of 12,300 sq. ft. of space in the three structures, including their balconies, paved terraces, and covered walks, which were computed at one-half their nominal area. All this was provided for a total price of only $ 123,367.

The religious education building, the largest and therefore the most costly structure, was built for $ 75,755. However, its cost per square foot was the lowest of all: $ 9.96. The chapel, which seats 80 children, cost the most per square foot; its $ 20,182 total breaking down to $ 11.64. The nursery school cost $ 27,430, or $ 10.06 per square foot.

The economy of the religious education building is the more remarkable since it was finished in 1957, the last of the group to be built. Construction costs had nearly doubled since the nursery school was erected in 1948. The chapel, the second building in the new children's campus, was completed in 1954.

Reference

The Children's Chapel. The Neighborhood Church, Pasadena (1954).

REPORT FROM THE CLERGY
The Rev. Dr. Curtis Beach, Minister

Our church was originally called the First Congregational Church of Pasadena. It was founded and built in 1887 in what was then the center of town. Subsequently the city grew toward the east, leaving the church in a residential neighborhood. In 1900 a majority of the members wanted to move to the new civic center; those who remained in the old building took the name the Neighborhood Church, which is our name today.

Our new buildings are supplemental to the church sanctuary and parish house, built in 1887 and 1917 respectively, which are wood frame, brown shingle buildings. There seemed to us to be no point in continuing this nineteenth century style in the middle of the twentieth. We came to feel that a living contemporary design would better express the living contemporary spirit of our church and its faith.

However, our choice of a contemporary design was largely due to the influence of our architect. We chose him first and he sold us on the design afterwards. We became acquainted with Mr. Smith when he gave an illustrated talk on modern homes to one of our church clubs. When our building project was conceived, the committee felt he had the ability and imagination to give us what we wanted. We were not particularly familiar with contemporary architecture and architects. We made no special study. We chose our architect simply because we were impressed by his work.

Some in our congregation, especially the older members, needed to be educated to accept the contemporary design. Our architect sold us by giving an illustrated lecture on contemporary church architecture. Working with our architect over a period of ten years has been a constant process of education in the meaning and spirit of contemporary design. He has done a very good job of educating us. And although some of our people remained dubious before the building program was started. nobody has any doubts now. The beauty of our new buildings has converted them.

In outlining the building program, we laid down no requirements except functional ones — such as circulation needs and number, size, and use of rooms. These the architect has fulfilled admirably. We believe that religion must be functional — geared to serve human needs. Our functional architecture suggests this. But there is also more than funtion. We believe that religion is primarily the aspiration of the human soul toward God and the desire to serve people. We believe that God is present in all of nature and the human spirit. We believe in the dignity of human beings as sons of God. We think our architect has expressed this aspiration excellently, especially in the children's chapel.

Our new buildings, which are all related to religious education, have made possible a much more vital church school program, which has attracted many new families to this congregation. Our new members in recent years have been mostly young parents. I think our attractive, modern buildings have been a definite factor in drawing them.

The Baptist faith is one of the very few denominations that, today and in all of its past history, has stood for "full, complete, and unrestricted religious freedom," not only for itself, but for all others. Religious liberty, not as mere tolerance, but as inalienable right, lies at the root of the Baptist heritage. Such commitment to freedom of belief stems logically from the basic Baptist principle that the individual's relationiship to God is a wholly personal one, dependent upon no mediating agency of church, clergy, or even sacrament for the salvation of the soul.

Although not presuming to judge the salvation of others, including non-Christians, the Baptists nonetheless feel that their practice of Christianity comes closest to that of Jesus and his disciples. The name Baptist is taken from their ritual of baptism by total immersion,* a ceremony reserved for adults only, since they alone are capable of comprehending its significance: a symbol of the death and resurrection of Jesus Christ and of the death and resurrection of the sinner into a new Christian life. This was the ceremony by which John the Baptist baptized the adult Jesus and His followers. It was also the method employed in the ancient, pre-Roman, Christian Church, of which Prof. Hans von Schubert of Heidelberg has written: "It was not the general custom to baptize children; preparation for baptism and the baptismal ceremony were designed for grown persons."

Although there is no record of any organized body of Baptists until the Reformation, small groups throughout the centuries sought to preserve the simplicity of the early church. Among these were the Anabaptists, so-called because they insisted on rebaptism, believing that the original infant ceremony was void of meaning. It was from Anabaptist groups that the later Mennonites and Hutterites developed, and Baptists today consider these early dissenters from the established church to be their spiritual forebears.

The Baptist faith first emerged as a recognized doctrine in England in 1611, its notable seventeenth century figure being that of John Bunyan, a convert from the Church of England who wrote *Pilgrim's Progress* while in jail for his beliefs. In America the first Baptist church was established in 1639 in Providence, R.I., by Roger Williams, zealous proponent of religious freedom and founder of the state of Rhode Island, the only one of the original English colonies to offer complete freedom of belief to all its inhabitants.

From this small beginning, the Baptist faith has grown to be the largest Protestant denomination in America, numbering approximately 21 million adult members. On a world-wide basis it counts 40 million

members. These impressive figures must be due at least partly to the evangelical character of the Baptist persuasion. Although holding that religious error cannot be persecuted nor legislated out of existence, Baptists expect each church member to proclaim the Christian faith by his own actions, to seek the conversion of others, and to defend his convictions in "witness." The revival meeting and the exhortatory tract have played vital roles in Baptist development.

The phenomenal Baptist growth in America may be due also to the fact that this denomination is a "free church," and one therefore in fundamental concord with the temper of the country. Like the Congregationalists, the Baptists recognize no authority higher than the Bible and the individual local congregation. They have no official creed as a test of membership, no canon law, no compulsory compliance with ecclesiastical resolutions. Because of their concept of the personal relationship between God and man, Baptists recognize no sacraments as bearers of supernatural grace, but consider both the Lord's Supper and the baptism which is so central to their faith to be symbolic, commemorative rituals. Although traditionally puritan in their code of personal behavior, the Baptist line of development is thus toward a general, rather than a particular, communion, open alike to fundamentalists or liberals.

For such a denomination, any derivative, historic style in architecture, expressing as it does a restricted version of the Christian religion, is inappropriate. Even an attempt to emphasize unique Baptist characteristics could only defeat its purpose. For the central idea of the Baptist faith is that of universality. The generalized ideas of man's aspiration toward God and man's brotherhood toward man — concepts central to all religions — are probably the qualities most appropriate to Baptist expression in architecture.

Unfortunately, the Baptist churches thus far have almost entirely missed their architectural opportunity. Like other evangelical denominations, Baptists have preached the gospel in public meeting halls, in tents, and in the store churches of slum neighborhoods when occasion demanded. This is as it should be. But even among large and well established congregations, little if any consideration has been given to an appropriate architectural expression of Baptist religious attitudes. Throughout America, towering pseudo-Gothic edifices house a faith that lies at the opposite pole of belief and practice from that of the Roman Catholic Church that inspired this style. Until very recently Baptists have remained oblivious to the contradiction. The First Baptist Church of Bloomington, Ind. — a modern expression of ancient and universal ideas — therefore represents something of an architectural milestone for this denomination.

---

* Baptists consider this description redundant, since the word "baptize" is from the Greek word *baptizein,* which means "to immerse."

31. FIRST BAPTIST CHURCH

Bloomington, Ind.; Dedicated 1956
E. A. Sovik & Associates, architects
Edgar A. Sovik (b. 1918)

"We are traditional designers in the sense that we approach the problem with the point of view which has produced the greatest work of the past. This point of view requires that the best of technical knowledge and imagination be put into the service of the church."

— EDGAR A. SOVIK

Edgar A. Sovik, architect, and Stanley Pressler, chairman of the building committee, inspect the model of the First Baptist Church of Bloomington, Ind., which helped persuade the congregation to accept this design. The main body of the church is joined at rear by a Sunday school wing, ending at right, in a small meditation chapel. Tower, at left, is connected to the church entrance by a sheltered arcade.

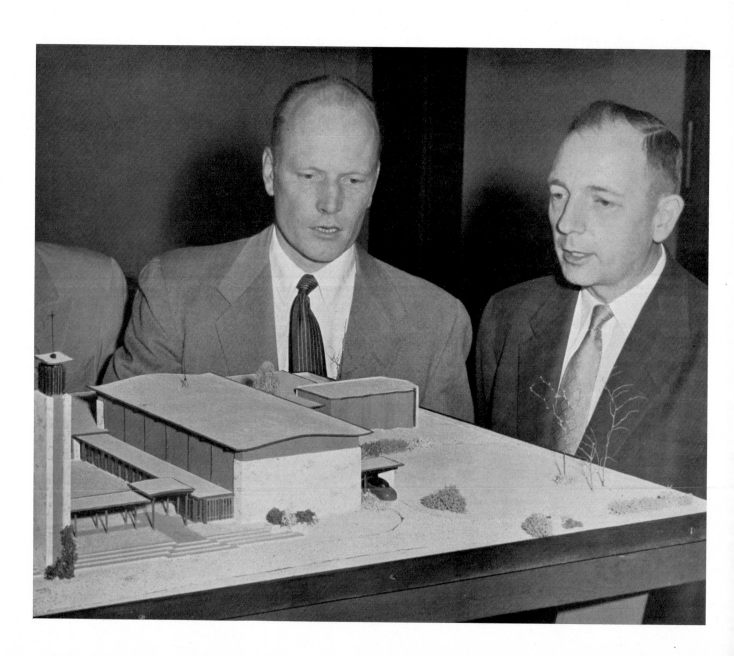

David H. Curl

Night view of the First Baptist Church shows the cross atop its tower shining like a beacon across the flat Indiana countryside. The missionary fervor of this denomination seems embodied in the soaring bell tower, boldly proclaiming the Christian position and beckoning all to come. The universal quality of aspiration is here dramatically expressed. At the same time, the tower appears as a symbolic guardian to the low-lying buildings that house the earthly activities of the church.

This grouping is actually one continuous building, divided into separate parts by changes in size and window treatment. The sanctuary is the large block at right; the one-story rear wing houses the fellowship hall, Sunday school, administrative functions, and a small chapel. Large sliding glass doors in the wing open onto a landscaped court, defined by the building L, the bell tower, and a canopied cloister walk.

The structural system throughout is a combination of masonry bearing walls with post-and-beam frame, using laminated timbers. The solid masonry used as end walls for both church and fellowship hall gives a sense of strength and protection at these areas. It is native Indiana limestone. Elsewhere, enclosing walls are curtains of cedar siding or glass.

All wood is stained a fairly dark shade of brown. This deep coloring plus the strong texture of the limestone give the building a rugged character entirely appropriate to the Baptist faith.

The bowed arch of the roof beams of the church, which adds to their strength, eliminates the need for interior columns anywhere within the nave. Their upward curve at either edge creates a rain trough, from which downspouts within the wall structure carry off the water. This bowed roofline also is meant to be a symbol, suggesting the yoke of Christ, who said: "Take my yoke upon you and learn of me."

Hartley Alley

Interior circulation is provided by a broad, one-story aisle that projects from the left side of the church, extending from the main entrance at front to the Sunday-school wing at rear. The photographs show this aisle as it appears from both exterior and interior, facing toward the Sunday-school wing. In addition to its function as a corridor, it is large enough to provide overflow seating for 150 to 200 persons at special services. With pews for 500 in the main nave, the aisle brings the seating capacity of the church to nearly 700.

Jerry Uelsmann

The right side of the church reverses the treatment of the left side. There is no aisle projection. The flat, unbroken wall is of cedar, with glass used only in a high, horizontal bank of windows and in narrow, vertical strips at either side of supporting posts. This reversal of glass on opposing sides of the church provides effective general illumination for the interior, the high windows in the right wall lighting its upper portion, and the aisle windows at left its lower area. The almost solid right wall seen here gives a sense of protection to the nave.

Clear rather than stained glass is used throughout this church, expressing the unbroken character of Christian action, in worship, and in the world. It emphasizes, too, the immediate, personal relationship of man to God, unobscured by ecclesiastical mystery or clerical intermediary. The honesty, simplicity, and straightforwardness with which all materials have been used, echoes this concept. The posts and the beams that support the building are exposed on the exterior as well as the interior, making the entire structure visible and understandable — a symbol of the unity of Christian thought and deed.

Henry H. Smith

Hartley Alley

The interior of this church is simply one large room. No attempt has been made to set apart the chancel as the focus of converging aspirational lines, nor to dramatize it through heightened illumination. Instead, all is open and clear, no part of the whole dominating any other. In this way the architects have expressed the concept of "the priesthood of all believers," which is common to Protestant denominations.

The interior also was designed to reveal the hardship of commitment to Christ. Particularly the chancel, paneled in cedar and decorated only by a large wooden cross and a quotation from the Bible, is plain to the point of severity. This treatment suggests discipline, even harsh discipline, the harder because it is self-imposed. But it also reflects purpose, vigor, and hope. The architects have avoided prettiness or anything suggestive of melancholy, which they consider to be affectations of the Christian spirit. Painted plaster walls and balcony panels in soft yellow, olive-green, and pale beige-gray, carry out this theme, being animated without undue drama or prettification.

The 16-ft. cross that dominates the chancel is of dark African mahogany, chosen to symbolize this congregation's belief that the twentieth century cross of cruelty is that of national and racial tensions. The quotation from *Matthew* reinforces this concept, emphasizing the Christian attitude toward these problems: "One is your Master, the Christ, and you are all brothers."

The design as a whole represents an attempt to express the essential character of Protestant Christianity without emphasis upon sectarian tradition. This approach is especially pertinent to an era in which the ecumenical movement dominates much of Protestant thought, pointing toward a growing interdenominational cooperation. With minor changes, the architects believe that this church could serve any branch of Protestantism.

Close view of the chancel shows one of the pools of natural daylight that enliven this interior. The unusual communion table and stools were designed by the architect. So also was the communion service — a tall, brass pitcher and a graceful, footed plate.

The Catholic concept of the sacrificial altar, centrally placed within the chancel, is today retained only by the Lutheran, Episcopal, and Methodist churches among American Protestants. In other denominations the focus of the communion ceremony is a table. It is becoming increasingly common to design this table so that clergy and lay leaders can be seated around it, with the congregation symbolically sharing the fourth side. The customary position is at the left side of the chancel,

balancing the pulpit to the right. The prominence of the scriptures is further declared by bringing the pulpit forward and raising it higher than the communion table. All these emphases are followed in the chancel arrangement shown here. The design of the table especially emphasizes the unique character of the Baptist service as a commemorative breaking of bread and sharing of wine without supernatural overtones.

The ceremony of baptism by immersion, which must be witnessed by the entire congregation, takes place in a baptismal pool, located within the chancel. The low, limestone parapet, which cuts across the chancel wall, forms one side of this pool. Steps behind the wood-strip screen connect this area with dressing rooms.

Nelson Smith

Jerry Uelsmann

David H. Curl

The small chapel seating 80 persons, which projects from the Sunday school wing to the right of the main church, is its opposite in design. Here, one side wall and the chancel wall are entirely of masonry, giving this interior an atmosphere of solidity that is in sharp contrast to the lightness and openness of the main nave. The only windows in the chapel are skylights and one floor-to-ceiling chancel window of leaded amber glass, which sheds a luminous glow upon the communion table. The lower part of this window is actually a door, providing the necessary separate access to the chancel.

The right wall of the chapel is a wooden screen, folded in and out in an obtuse repetitive V. This treatment breaks the otherwise rectangular shape of the small room. Another break is provided by a louvered light screen that projects at right angles from the masonry side wall to shield the ceiling lights from view.

This is a meditation chapel and its solid, protective walls and dim illumination create an atmosphere appropriate to such use. The only color in the chapel is a chancel wall hanging in varied shades of blue, blue-green, and green. Its soft folds and vivid coloring contrast with the rugged masonry wall behind it.

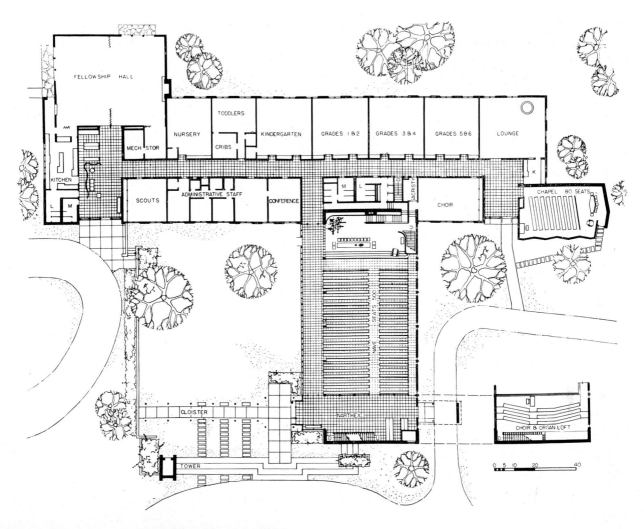

Following are the labels in the plan (clockwise/reading): FELLOWSHIP HALL, TODDLERS, NURSERY, KINDERGARTEN, GRADES 1 & 2, GRADES 3 & 4, GRADES 5 & 6, LOUNGE, MECH STOR, CRIBS, KITCHEN, L, M, SCOUTS, ADMINISTRATIVE STAFF, CONFERENCE, M, L, SACRISTY, CHOIR, CHAPEL 80 SEATS, K, NAVE SEATS 500, CLOISTER, NARTHEX, TOWER, CHOIR & ORGAN LOFT

Plan shows the excellent circulation provided on both the interior and exterior of this church. There are three major entrances: the narthex of the main church, and subsidiary lobbies at either end of the educational wing. A curving driveway serves both the narthex of the church and the subsidiary lobby at the right side of the educational building. To the left, the parking lot brings automobiles close to the Sunday school wing at its opposite end.

The left side aisle is a corridor designed to link the Sunday school wing and church. The balcony on the right side of the nave acts as a processional path for the choir. From its robing room to the right of the chancel, the choir ascends a screened stairway, thence proceeding along the balcony to the rear choir loft.

Included in the educational wing of this plan are two large social rooms, one for adults and one for young people. The fellowship hall seats 250 for church suppers and banquets. A folding partition can divide it into two smaller rooms, each with its own fireplace.

Focus of the youth lounge, known as Roger Williams Hall, is a large, open, hooded fireplace. Its lines are echoed in modern Scandinavian furniture. The exposed ceiling beams and the welcoming fireplace give the lounge an informal and almost cozy atmosphere, like the living room of a private home. A small kitchen and a grand piano are part of its equipment.

REPORT FROM THE CLERGY
W. Douglas Rae, D. D.

The project of building our new church was truly a congregational undertaking. For two years beginning in 1952, the congregation through the work of five major committees attempted to define the place and function of our church in the last half of the twentieth century. They composed a definition of fundamental Baptist beliefs and a statement of those concepts which we wished the new church building to express, as well as a detailed outline of functional requirements and space needs.

The architect was chosen in 1954 on the recommendation of the structure committee to the executive committee and finally by vote of the entire congregation. The firm chosen was that of E. A. Sovik & Associates of Northfield, Minn. Edgar Sovik, head of the firm, is a comparatively young architect who received his training at the School af Architecture, Yale University, graduating in 1949. The son of Lutheran missionaries, he had received his B.A. from St. Olaf College and had spent two years in training at the Lutheran Theological Seminary before transferring to the study of architecture. His firm has specialized in church and school design in the midwestern states.

The new church was completed and dedicated in 1956. At the dedication ceremony I described something of the process of study, work, and operational method by which this church was planned and built. Excerpts from this dedication service will show what a vital and meaningful experience building the new church has been for our entire congregation:

DEMOCRACY IN ACTION

One of the chief characteristics of the entire building program was the unusual use of the broad, democratic process. The architects were at first very dubious about the possibilities of allowing an entire congregation to make so many decisions. The best results in their judgment were achieved by turning the program over to a small committee.

In the building of the church all major decisions were made at congregational meetings and not by the executive committee — the method of raising funds, the choosing of the location, the selection of the architect, the acceptance of the contemporary design, the purchase price, the amount of the mortgage, the letting of the contract.... These decisions were all made after prolonged discussion ... [and] were carried by a large and significant majority.

More than this, each of the working committees — finances, structure, grounds, furnishings, and memorial gifts — was composed of ten members providing an honest cross section of the church: men, women, and young people....

THE PROBLEM AND THE NEED

The Structure Committee ... submitted the following statement for the approval of the congregation, and after being approved, it was submitted to the architect as a working statement describing the function and purpose of the church building:

"Provide a place of worship so challenging in its conception that the worship will not be sterile ... a place of Christian worship so designed that in its symbols, the worshipper will draw strength from the history of the whole church and from that of the Free Churches in particular ... a place so simple and meaningful and honest, that no one will be made afraid by lavish appointments or pretension in any form.

"Provide a preachig center ... of such a character that the sermon shall not only be a part of the worship service but shall bring both the community and the church under the judgment of the Word....

"Provide in the stone and wood of the building a Christian symbol which will speak of man's search for God in the forms and with the materials of our time ..., thus creating a religious symbol in the form of a building to symbolize the nonauthoritarian, Free Protestant Church in the twentieth century."

MONEY

The cost of the project including the price of property and the furnishing was $525,000. Of the families of the congregation, 286 participated in the financial program. For many of these families this meant giving at the level of personal sacrifice; for some it meant giving a double tithe. One nine-year-old boy, for example, gave up comic books for three years. Many families postponed the purchase of new cars and drove old cars well beyond the 100,000-mile mark. There was one large gift of $25,000. Most of the three-year pledges ranged between $500 and $2,000. The mortgage assumed by the congregation was for $140,000.

WORKING TOGETHER

Over 200 members of the congregation actually worked on the construction of the church.... These volunteer workers, in addition to doing other jobs, laid all the floor tile in the church and church school, 14,000 sq. ft. of tile. They also painted the interior walls of the entire project. The men assembled and anchored the pews. The grading, raking, and sowing of the grass was a work project of the fathers and sons of the church.

In summing up, this contribution of skilled and semi-skilled work brought a new sense of Christian community which was of far greater value than the actual money saved by the free labor.

A SYMBOL OF THE CHRISTIAN CONTROVERSY

The first thing that strikes most people when they see the church is that it is different. The design is not only different but it is controversial. Some think it is the queerest church they have ever seen. This we think is in keeping with the history of Christianity. When the Christian religion has been alive and growing it has been controversial. It has made people talk and think and act differently. The simple lines of this church will not always be as startling as they are now, but we hope that the thinking and living of the congregation will always strike the note of controversy, and never be completely at home in the world.

Reference

Sovik, Edgar A. "The Shape of Our Places of Worship," *Protestant Church Building and Equipment*, May 1960.

CHRISTIAN CHURCH - DISCIPLES OF CHRIST

If anything could be broader and simpler than the Baptists it is the denomination most commonly known in the South and Midwest as the Christian Church, and in the East as the Disciples of Christ. This denomination, or as its members prefer to call it, this movement, is the only one of the Christian sects that had its beginnings in America. The Christian Church building shown in this book is that of a 1,500 member congregation in Columbus, Ind. When writing their program for the architects, the building committee of this church explained the origins of the movement:

Our ancestors who settled this country were practical as well as religious, and they soon saw the impossibility of maintaining three or four churches in small pioneer communities that could barely afford one. Obviously, Christians living under these conditions should unite and worship in a single body; and so some of the leaders tried to outline a common belief that would be acceptable to all and that would serve as a foundation for union. After a good deal of struggle and some mistakes, they decided to discard all their inherited beliefs and to go to the New Testament with open and unprejudiced minds, determined to follow its teachings only. They felt that all Christians would be willing to unite on it and to accept the gospel as presented there, unhampered by human additions and divisions of later centuries.

Such a return to the New Testament produced a practice of Christianity closer to that of the Baptist than any other among the established denominations. Although there is no official creed, Christians and Disciples agree on the statement: "Whatever the Bible commands us to do, those things we do; what the Bible forbids, from those we refrain; where the Bible is silent, there is freedom of opinion." By Bible precedent, therefore, baptism is by immersion and is reserved for adults only. Predestination, original sin, the apostolic succession, and a systematic catechism of required beliefs are rejected as accretions upon the simple Christianity taught by Jesus. In accord with the custom of Christ's own disciples, meeting together after his death, communion is held every Sunday. This practice, although unusual in a Protestant church, is being adopted today by some congregations among the more orthodox faiths. One example is the Episcopal Church of St. James the Fisherman (No. 22).

Because of their faith in "the priesthood of all believers" the New Testament churches make little distinction between clergy and laity, and bow to no ruling ecclesiastical hierarchy. Indeed, in the early days there was so great a distrust of clericalism that ministers were called Elder rather than Reverend, and any elected elder of the congregation could perform ministerial functions. A demand later arose for ordained pastors and today 38 church-supported colleges, universities, and Bible schools prepare candidates for the ministries of the churches.

There is also an international convention that aids cooperation between individual congregations, but does not rule. In this convention, the names Christian Church and Disciples of Christ are used interchangeably, as they have been used also among many congregations since 1832, when these two, virtually identical groups officially joined. The total membership of both groups today has reached nearly 3.8 million.

Although their practices come closest to those of primitive Christianity, the Disciple movement is chiefly an ecumenical one, working to reduce the differences among all Christian faiths and to promote cooperation among them. It excludes no baptized Christian of whatever denomination from its communion service. "We are not the only Christians, but are Christians only," sums up their attitude, as does also the statement made by the Columbus, Ind., Christian Church:

"We attach much importance to our effort to preach and to practice primitive Christianity and nothing else, for we believe that in it lies the hope of the world."

Because of their rejection of accumulated ecclesiastical tradition, it might be assumed that the Christian Church and the Disciples of Christ would be more open than other denominations to simple, nontraditional expression in architecture. Some of their early meeting houses did express this religious simplicity. The first building of the Columbus Church, for example, was merely a blocky rectangle with a small cupola at one end. But this simplicity did not last long. Despite the grave contradiction between the belief and the building, New Testament churches, like most Protestants, accepted the Gothic and other historic Catholic styles in architecture as these became popular throughout America. Most still embrace these inappropriate architectural forms today. As early as 1942, however, one congregation took the decisive step toward a church architecture matching the fundamentalism of the faith. The result of this pioneering gesture is the First Christian Church of Columbus. Ind., shown on the following pages.

32. FIRST CHRISTIAN CHURCH

Columbus, Ind.; Erected 1942
Eliel Saarinen (1873-1950) & Eero Saarinen (1910-1961),
architects

*"Our endeavor has been to design a church which could
be lastingly appreciated rather than bring about a design
which might effect momentary excitement and early indifference."* — ELIEL AND EERO SAARINEN

Twenty years ago the late Eliel Saarinen, Finnish-Amer-
ican pioneer of modern architecture, wrote an autobi-
ography of design which he called *The Search for Form.*
In this title is summed up the aim and the accomplish-
ment of a distinguished career.

Unlike some of his colleagues, Saarinen never allowed
the new materials and techniques of building to become
primary determinants of his architecture. Instead he
employed technology as a means toward another end.
The exciting potentialities of the steel frame, reinforced
concrete, plate glass, and the other twentieth century building media were always subordinated to — even
though made an intrinsic part of — the larger concept
of architectural form.

As a result, Saarinen, perhaps more than any other
modern architect except Holland's Willem Dudok, is
recognized as the master organizer of building masses,
the manipulator of varied blocky shapes into a harmo-
niously proportioned whole. His designs are seldom
spectacular, but they are always solidly satisfying, tending
to outlast the more dramatic expressions in modern architecture. Some interiors achieve exquisite beauty.

The First Christian Church of Columbus, Ind., is
one of the finest examples of the Saarinen approach to
design. Here the various elements of sanctuary, bell tower, Bible school, and chapel each take a distinct form,
but all are organized into a single architectural composition of dignity and power.

Saarinen was one of the few architects of our time
who has been able to cope successfully with the problem
of monumentality, a concept that sometimes appears to
be alien to contemporary thinking. But public buildings, especially churches and government structures,
must have monumentality if they are to dominate an
urban scene composed of many competing sizes and
shapes of buildings. The First Christian Church achieves
such dominance by means of its great sanctuary block
and towering campanile. The bold outlines of these
building forms create an instantly recognizable silhouette
against the sky; park-like grounds insure that the building will stand alone, free from the distraction of neighboring structures. By his simple yet powerful forms
Saarinen has suggested also the uncompromising quality
of the beliefs and practices of a New Testament church.

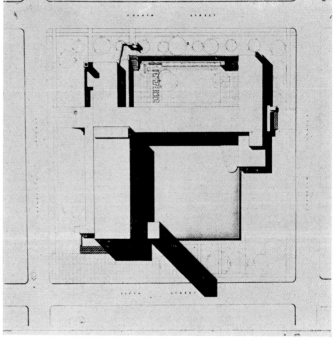

The First Christian Church balances vertical masses of sanctuary and tower with long, low, sweeping horizontals. Deceptively simple in appearance, it is actually a complex structure, interlocking interior and exterior space in a way that can be understood only by comparing the plot plan with the rendering.

The church to the east and the Bible school to the west oppose each other across a central, sunken terrace that gives direct access to the basement level of each building. Exterior steps lead down from north and south street frontages to this terrace. Conversely, the first floors of each building are elevated above grade so that all main entrances are reached by steps leading up from street frontages.

The most dramatic feature of the plan is an elevated wing or bridge that spans the terrace, connecting church and Bible school at their upper levels. This bridge also acts to shelter a terrace walkway between the two buildings. The church complex thus becomes one continuous construction, with convenient circulation between buildings at all levels.

The terrace itself is enhanced by a garden at rear and a reflecting pool toward the front, these separate courts being visually defined by the elevated bridge, but physically unobstructed by it. Dominating the entire composition is the freestanding campanile that rises from the water level of the reflecting pool to a height of 166 ft.

Photos: Hedrich-Blessing

View toward the left front of the building group shows only the church and the tower. The sunken garden and Bible school wings at right are obscured from view. However a wide, projecting side aisle of the nave is clearly visible at left. Its lowered roofline breaks the severe box of the nave and creates an exterior progression from aisle to sanctuary to tower. A small chapel can also be glimpsed as it joins the rear of the church.

The major structures in the building group are of brick curtain walls on a supporting frame of steel beams or reinforced concrete girders, depending on the area, and with a floor and roof system of reinforced rib slabs. In some of the smaller structures, masonry walls are loadbearing without a supporting frame. The tower, which measures 17 by 23 ft. at its base, is built entirely of brick except for reinforcing floors of concrete slab, set at intervals to provide wind bracing.

There is almost no applied decoration on this church except in front, where panels of Indiana limestone in a pale buff color are used as decorative surfacing. The grid pattern thus created dramatizes the facade and the light color offers a pleasing contrast to the darker buff of the brick used elsewhere. Superimposed upon the limestone panels is a large wooden cross, painted yellow. Limestone is used also to surface the columns that support the bridge (see page 254), thus creating visual unity.

View from sunken terrace shows the dramatic bridge that connects upper levels of church (left) and Bible school (right). Unlike the nave of the church, which has few windows, the Bible school and its bridge are almost entirely glass-enclosed, creating light, airy, and open classrooms. Basement rooms open directly upon the terrace, while all rooms in the bridge enjoy a beautiful view of reflecting pool and tower. The inclusion of private outdoor areas in the design of a city church greatly expands the scope of its activities. Church suppers can be held here in the summertime; classes can also be conducted out-of-doors if desired. Easter sunrise services and vesper choral services can take place in this impressive outdoor setting.

Artist's sketch of tower and garden side of the church, across the reflecting pool, shows a view similar to that seen from Bible school windows. The great campanile appears to rise straight out of the water, towering over the adjoining church, entrance steps, and retaining wall. In certain areas of the tower, the brickwork has been designed in a perforated, lace-like pattern, harmonizing with the narrow, leaded windows of the church. At the top of the tower, the openwork is repeated on both sides, creating a sounding chamber for the carillon. The chiming of the organ on the interior of the church can also be broadcast through this chamber. The narrow openwork strip illuminates the stairwell.

Serene and chastely simple church interior expresses the Christian faith reduced to its essentials. The design of the nave is remarkably similar to that of Christ Lutheran Church (No. 20), by the same architects. Both designs are asymmetrical, with the middle aisle slightly off center, and the side aisles of different widths. In each church, natural lighting is provided from similar sources: soft general illumination for the nave through a series of side windows, and a wash of bright morning sunlight from the single east window upon the chancel. Brick walls are exposed on the interior as well as the exterior, and colors throughout each church are muted —a pale harmony of buff brick and light wood, the latter used in pews, screening, and altar furnishings. The design of the pulpit and the spoon lighting fixtures of spun aluminum are also identical.

These striking similarities in churches as theologically different as the Lutheran and the Christian illustrates the Saarinen concentration on the essence of Christianity, rather than upon sectarian difference. With minor changes, either of these churches could serve any denomination.

However, the differences between Christ Lutheran and the First Christian Church, although small, are significant. Instead of the curved chancel wall of the Lutheran church, which suggests a mystical infinity, the chancel wall is here a straight, one-directional plane. The focus of the former church is on the altar, the only object in an otherwise empty sanctuary. The focus of

the latter is diffused between baptistry, communion table, choir, and pulpit, all grouped within the sanctuary. If any one of these elements is primary, it is the baptistry, here shown shielded by a wooden screen. When in use, central doors in the screen open to permit congregational view of the baptismal ceremony, in which the candidate enters at the west and arises toward the east, into the full flood of light from the chancel window.

Because the weekly observance of the Lord's Supper is central to this faith, the altar has been given a central location. However, unlike the Lutheran, it has not been made the focus of a mystical radiance. Instead, it is brought forward and assumes the typical Protestant character of a table, with chairs for the pastor and elders of the church.

The pulpit is equally large and prominent, brought forward to extend over the chancel steps almost into the congregation. This placement emphasizes the importance of the word of God as the final Christian authority, containing the means toward salvation.

Choir stalls are to the right of the communion table, partially shielded from view by a wooden partition, and facing across the chancel. The organ is opposite the choir, housed in a spacious chamber that projects out from the left wall of the chancel. In this church, therefore, all elements contributing to the liturgy have been given nearly equal importance. The sacramental mystique found in the Lutheran church is entirely absent.

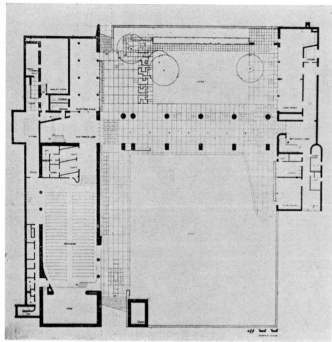

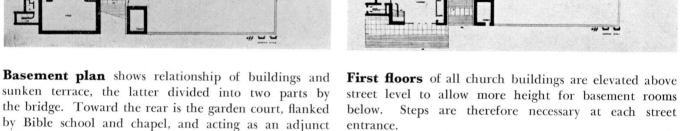

Basement plan shows relationship of buildings and sunken terrace, the latter divided into two parts by the bridge. Toward the rear is the garden court, flanked by Bible school and chapel, and acting as an adjunct to both.

The large reflecting pool occupies most of the fore-court. A bank of floor-to-ceiling windows opens the church social hall onto a long paved terrace adjoining the pool. In this way, summer entertainments can be extended out into the forecourt.

The reception room, at rear, is used for smaller women's meetings, with its own access to the rear courtyard. For unusually large gatherings, the social hall and reception room can be used together. Both are served by a central kitchen, cloakroom, and entrance hall. Their terraces also connect these two rooms by way of the out-of-doors, so that there can be a free flow of circulation both inside and outside the building. This appears to be a nearly perfect solution for the subsidiary activities that are an important part of any Prot-estant church.

First floors of all church buildings are elevated above street level to allow more height for basement rooms below. Steps are therefore necessary at each street entrance.

The building group and its grounds occupy an entire city block. Linked by the central bridge, buildings be-come one continuous construction, which can be entered from any of the four street frontages.

The bridge itself can be entered directly from the south, by means of one of the most interesting features of the plan. This is an elevated terrace, atop the roof of the reception room in the basement. The terrace functions as an outdoor "hall," linking street frontage, chapel, bridge, and the lower terrace gardens.

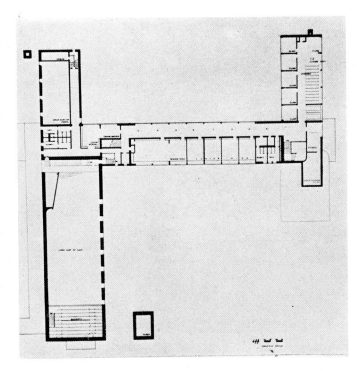

Second floor plan shows the third level of all buildings. Beyond the chancel on this upper floor are the choirmaster's room and robing room, separated from each other only by a folding partition. This arrangement allows the two rooms to be used as one space for choir practice. During services, the choir descends a stairway, entering the chancel directly from the side rather than forming a processional through the nave. The cost of this entire church group was $1,250,000 in 1942.

References

Christ-Janer, Albert. *Eliel Saarinen.* The University of Chicago Press, Chicago (1948).

Saarinen, Eliel. *The Search for Form.* Reinhold Pub. Corp., New York (1948).

REPORT FROM THE CLERGY
The Rev. T. K. Smith, Minister

The objective of our faith is to attempt to restore the simplicity of the church as described in the New Testament. There was no traditional architectural style that could be successfully employed for our purpose. None could fully express the grandeur and yet the simplicity of Christian faith unencumbered by human creeds and human symbolism. The only alternative was to find an architect whose creative genius would make possible the realization of such an expressive building.

We were not particulary familiar with contemporary architecture, but our building committee had seen some of the work done by Eliel Saarinen. They were so impressed by it that they chose Mr. Saarinen and, of course, this meant the architecture would be of contemporary design.

There was some education of the congregation and we did use slides and a brochure of the proposed building. But the people as a whole were willing to leave to the committee the decisions on architect and style of architecture.

We feel that the architect expressed our objectives very well in the design of the church. Because the building creates an atmosphere of "God being with us," it has made the work of the pastor, from the standpoint of worship, more meaningful. The architecture has played some part in attracting new members to the congregation and certainly the splendid facilities of our new building have played a most important part. Quite a number of our people have expressed their joy in worshipping in the sanctuary. They feel the architect has made a strong contribution to the worship of our Lord. They have been slow in becoming adjusted to the contemporary design of the exterior. I would say that there are some who perhaps still do object to the design, but by far the majority of the people have now become attached to the style of architecture and most of them seem to appreciate it. I think the primary reason for the objection is that it is such a departure from the accustomed church.

In the 18 years since the dedication of this building, hundreds of architects, students, and building committees have visited the church and incorporated many of its features into new church buildings over the country. Thus, the congregation feels that it is not only numbered among the pioneers in restoring New Testament Christianity to the world, but has pioneered in church architecture suited to these simple, basic teachings.

In the *Manual of the Mother Church,* Mary Baker Eddy, founder of Christian Science, stated the aim of this new faith: "To organize a church designed to commemorate the word and works of our Master which should reinstate primitive Christianity and its lost element of healing."

It is this emphasis upon healing which so distinctly sets Christian Science apart from the other branches of the Christian religion. Other sects may believe in miraculous cures and the "laying on of hands" as a spiritual antidote to disease. But none except Christian Science completely repudiates not only medicine and psychiatry, but disease itself, holding that sin, sickness, and death are material falsehoods, nonexistent in the face of spiritual truth.

Because they believe that God is divine Mind, and Mind is all that exists, Christian Scientists do not practice baptism in a material form, nor do they seek salvation of the soul in the orthodox sense. Rather they seek salvation from "the delusion of mortality" and its "illusion of disease and death." They believe in the Trinity, but this belief too differs from that of orthodox Christians. The unity of Father, Son, and Holy Spirit is not considered to be God in three persons, but instead the abstractions of Life, Truth, and Love as the "triune Principle called God." Christ they believe to be the master of the science of divine Mind, which is available to anyone through effective prayer, and is exact and scientific in its results — hence the name, Church of Christ, Scientist. Christ is truly divine, but in the sense that all reality is divine.

There are two "bibles" within the Church of Christ, Scientist. One is the King James version of the Holy Bible. The other is *Science and Health with Key to the Scriptures* by Mary Baker Eddy, which is believed to explain the true and complete meaning of the Bible. It is upon these two works that the Christian Science church service is based. After hymns and responsive reading similar to those in any Protestant church, the rest of the service is devoted to readings from the Bible and correlative explanations from Mrs. Eddy's text.

These are presented to the congregation by a first reader and a second reader, members of the congregation and preferably, but not necessarily, a man and a woman. There are no ordained ministers and no preaching as such, the readers acting solely as impersonal instruments for the dissemination of the prescribed Word.

Because there is no clergy, no sermon, no choir, and no traditional ritual in the Church of Christ, Scientist, there is also no altar, pulpit, choir stall, baptistry, nor cross — furnishings that serve as focal points in the design of other churches. Here there are only two lecterns as a focus of attention and these are not conceived as being set apart. Ideally, congregation and readers form an unbroken unity as they come together to hear and ponder on scriptural truth.

For this reason, even the older Christian Science churches are apt to be quite different in design from those of the more orthodox faiths. In the state of New York, for example, there are several circular churches built a number of years before Catholics and Protestants began their current experiments with such plans. The First Church of Christ, Scientist in Belvedere, Calif., shown on the following pages, is equally unorthodox, but its plan is essentially a rhomboid rather than a circle.

Although the Christian Science societies have been somewhat ahead of others in the architectural expression of their faith, today they might draw inspiration from some of the recent Catholic and Protestant churches that have been based upon the Liturgical Revival. The circle, the oval, the spiral, the rhomboid, the triangle, the square, all can express the unity that is fundamental to Christian Science. Although the plans that appear in this book retain traditional, Christian focal emphases and their enclosing structures are expressive of the more orthodox religions, they nevertheless offer a wealth of suggestion for Christian Science.* In turn, the Christian Science Church shown here should be of interest to other denominations seeking to express a new closeness between clergy and congregation.

* See churches No. 9, 12, 18, 22, 25, and 35.

33. FIRST CHURCH OF CHRIST, SCIENTIST

Belvedere, Calif.; Dedicated 1954
Charles Warren Callister (b. 1918), architect
August E. Waegemen, structural engineer
Robert Barnecut, mechanical engineer

"Architecture evolves from faith."
— CHARLES WARREN CALLISTER

The First Church of Christ, Scientist, in Belvedere, Calif., is an excellent example of what has been called the California Style of modern architecture. This usually implies a lavish use of glass and native redwood, handled in an informal and naturalistic way. Integration of indoors and out is a primary characteristic of this architecture, and buildings are usually fitted to the contours and general appearance of the site rather than set apart from it as a contrasting element.

The architect, Charles Warren Callister, who is one of the most talented of the many outstanding California designers, has here paid particular attention to an unusual site and to the unique flavor of the community in which the church is located.

The site was a challenging one, irregular in shape and steeply sloped. It is bounded by two roads that meet at an acute angle and then slant outward from each other and less sharply in again to create a roughly kite-shaped or rhomboidal property between them. The plan of the church echoes the shape of the property, being also essentially a rhomboid. The slope of the land is from the acute apex of the rhomboid down to the wider part of the land. The church has therefore been built into the hillside with only the upper story above ground toward the acute angle of the property. At front, down the slope, the lower level of the church emerges above ground, revealing it to be a two-story structure.

Because Belvedere is a coastal town and the site of the church is close to the scene of much nautical activity, this flavor has been incorporated into the design. The jutting angle of walls and roof at the front of the church cut into the air like the prow of a ship. The slender central spire is suggestive of a mast. However, this is merely a faint echo of nautical lines. No contrived attempt has been made to force the building into a shape alien to its function.

Before building the new church, the Christian Science Society of Belvedere had held services for many years in a log cabin — one of the earliest homes in this area — which had been very simply converted for church use. Because the congregation had become so attached to the cabin, the architect also was requested to incorporate something of its atmosphere into the new church. Compliance with this request is seen in the great ceiling beams which are exposed on the interior of the church, in its wooden walls and ceiling, in a large fireplace, and in the rough unpainted concrete of the central mast, wall piers, and floors, the latter purposely left uncarpeted. Thus, although the church is very beautiful, it displays at the same time a rugged character that links it with the traditions of both the local society and the community of which it is a part.

Side view of exterior shows the jutting prow-like roof and mast-like steeple which link this church to its nautical neighborhood. A graveled path leads from parking lot to church, giving direct entrance to the basement Sunday school. The angled stairway at left leads up to the second-story porch of the church and thence to entrances at either side of the triangular building front.

Although the porch serves primarily as an entrance gallery, it has also been made large enough to act as a gathering place after services, providing a beautiful view of church gardens and the lagoon beyond. When Sunday afternoon lectures are held in good weather, the porch is used as an outdoor auditorium, seating 150 persons.

The two side walls of the church are identical, and the apex of the obtuse triangle which they create at front contains the entrance lobby. The concrete wall seen at left marks the beginning of the church auditorium. It marks also the beginning of one of the most interesting features of the design. The auditorium has been enclosed on either side by a series of staggered, concrete piers, the first and longest of which (seen above) extends the plan to its widest point at the rear of the auditorium. Subsequent smaller piers step the width in once more to an apex behind the rostrum. Only the first piers are of solid concrete. The rest are concrete frame, inset with stained glass. Directly behind the rostrum, and connecting the last concrete frame on each side. there is a climax of stained glass, shading up into ethereal tints of blue and green toward the roof of the building.

This area is both the narrowest and lowest point of the church. From this apex, walls are staggered outward, and the roof slants up, creating a sense of expanding space from the central brilliancy of stained glass. Within the auditorium, the effect of this unique design is a combination of intimacy and spaciousness, shelter and openness, solidity and translucency, shadow and brilliant color. Such a pairing of opposites creates an interior at once serene and full of sparkling life.

Morley Baer

View of interior is taken from behind one of the rostrum reading tables looking toward the entrances. The centered mast is a column of reinforced concrete, on the interior a major support for the roof beams, on the exterior narrowing to become the steeple. With the angled door screens at either side, this concrete mast acts also as a shield between lobby and auditorium. On the lobby side it contains a generous fireplace, with concrete hood and open hearth, offering a glowing welcome to all who enter. By means of a small aperture in the mast, firelight also flickers through into the auditorium, creating a sense of "eternal light" as the core of the church.

The great Douglas fir ceiling beams and rough, unpainted concrete suggest the return to "primitive Christianity" advocated by Mrs. Eddy. The use of masonry "buttresses" and stained glass, but in an entirely nontraditional way, recalls Mrs. Eddy's continued use of the expression "new-old" in relation to her "rediscovery of the science of Christianity."

A note of luxury against the rugged background of the church is the velvet cushioning of the pews. These are executed identically on both sides of the auditorium, with matching pews in the two banks always of the same color. Shades range from mauve and purple to orange, cherry red, and various pinks. These colors have been placed to catch and echo the same hues reflected through the stained glass windows when the sun is in the right direction. Because of the subtle harmony of the shades used and their perfect juxtaposition, this liberal use of brilliant color does not appear too elaborate, especially when contrasted with the rugged, natural textures and muted tones of the church structure.

The aptness of the rhomboid as a plan that insures congregational closeness is here immediately apparent. Pews cluster about the rostrum, which in turn seems to project into the congregation. Breadth is provided exactly where it is needed to extend congregational seating. Where breadth is not needed, at rostrum, and opposing entrance lobby, the plan narrows. The two banks of pews are set at right angles so that members of the congregation face each other as well as the readers.

In addition to its functional excellence, the rhomboid helps to create the desired spiritual atmosphere. Especially as modified here by the staggering of wall panels, it gives a feeling of continuous space without an immediately identifiable beginning or end.

This continuity is furthered in other ways. The outdoors flows into this church by means of its many window panels. The interior and exterior of the building expose the same materials. Thus both plan and the details express the unity of all reality, which is central to the Christian Science faith.

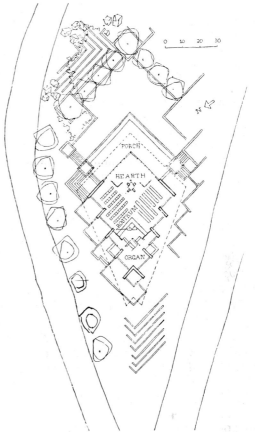

Courtesy of *Architectural Forum*

Plan, essentially a rhomboid, reflects the similar shape of the property. This is most clearly shown by the roof — dotted lines outside the staggered walls of the church proper. Outer wall lines represent the entrance porch at the far end and flower beds at either side of the church, delineated by low retaining walls.

Landscaping is an important part of this design which is so closely integrated with the out-of-doors. Terraced gardens are located at both front and rear of the property. Their retaining walls repeat the angles of the church structure, unifying indoors and out.

Unlike other Protestant churches, this building contains no social hall, no meeting rooms, no offices, and no kitchen, because the Christian Science faith supports neither clergy nor subsidiary church activities except the Sunday school. The elimination of subsidiary rooms partially accounts for its low cost: only $50,000. It is also a small church, seating no more than 100 people. The church was purposely restricted in size, with no provision for future enlargement, because the congregation feels that their society is more effective when small. If the church ever becomes overcrowded, a new society will be formed and another church built elsewhere in the community.

REPORT FROM THE CLERGY
Joseph B. Wallace, President, Board of Directors.

Less than ten years ago the members of the Society recognized the need for a large building, more centrally located and more easily accessible, if we were to be of greater service to our community, which is almost entirely residential and growing rapidly.

The members, who at that time were very few, appointed a building committee, entrusting it with the task of engaging an architect and supervising all matter relating to construction when the time should come for the actual building.

It was this committee of five persons who chose the architect — a young man who then had never built a church but whose predilection for contemporary design was well known. He was chosen after a number of other architects had been considered.

Throughout the period of planning and construction there was the closest cooperation between the building committee and the architect and the committee was thoroughly satisfied with his work. To quote from the report of the building committee:

The plan did not spring full-fledged from the thought of the designer. It developed step by step as he assimilated the various ideas that came to him while contemplating the problem from its many angles....

What eventually unfolded was a bold and original design conceived for the primary purpose of showing forth, to the greatest extent feasible, "the beauty of holiness" and of meeting the special needs of a Christian Science church. These needs are of course quite distinct and in many ways unlike those of other congregations.... Mr. Callister was acutely aware of these special considerations....

After Mr. Callister had completed the design of the church, a model was submitted to a general meeting of the members. To give you some idea of the attitude of the members toward the new project, we shall quote again from the report of the building committee:

Mrs. Eddy says in Miscellaneous Writings: *"Unity is the essential nature of Christian Science. Its principle is one, and to demonstrate the divine One demands oneness of thought and action."*

This oneness of thought and action ran like a golden thread throughout the whole fabric of our church building. It enabled the building committee to act as a compact and efficient unit. It inspired the members of the Society to give full and effective support to the church not only in metaphysical work but also in all the tasks in which they were asked to participate....

Something that happened at the meeting when members were called upon to decide the type of design for the new church will illustrate how the one Mind unfolded its decision in unity of action. A small-scale model of the church was exhibited together with the blueprints. There was no hesitation nor delay among the members. The thought of them all was expressed by one who exclaimed, "I just love it! Let us build it as quickly as we can!"

Someone asked if the steeple were really necessary.

It was removed and all saw clearly that something vital to the completeness of the whole had been lost. "Put it back!" said one member who had originally been in favor of a more traditional kind of church. His conversion to the new architectural concept made its approval unanimous.

These extracts from our report make it apparent that our church members did not need to be educated to like contemporary design. They were wholeheartedly in favor of it. We did not have to change the original concept of the building as shown in the model in any of its major requirements. There were minor changes in detail but these did not detract from the quality of the whole. The greatest improvement was the highly successful use of stained glass both in the church auditorium and in the Sunday school. It has greatly enhanced the beauty of the interior.

It is possible (but of this was have no proof) that there may be among those who have joined the church since its completion less enthusiasm for the design than among those who were instrumental in building it. The latter remain unanimous in their approbation....

We are very happy in the rapid increases in our congregation and in the enrollment of pupils in the Sunday school. The church is generally filled to capacity on Sundays and there is good attendance at the Wednesday evening testimony meetings. We think that, however pleased the newcomers may be with the beauty of the architecture, it is the spiritual inspiration they gain at the services that is the real attraction.

It may be of interest that practically half of those members admitted recently are young couples. They are taking an active and enthusiastic part in church work. This somewhat greater proportion of young people is about the only change in the type of our membership.

To quote once more from our building committee report:

First Church of Christ, Scientist, Belvedere, is definitely and unmistakably a Christian Science Church. It embodies all the needs of our particular mode of worship in a form that is unique. One might truthfully describe it as a pioneer in a fresh region of architecture. As such it will stand on its own conspicuous merits while possibly opening up vistas to be explored by other creative artists....

UNITARIAN - UNIVERSALIST

The Unitarian fellowship, one of the smallest denominations in America and in the world today, believes that its attitude toward the Trinity represents the ancient majority viewpoint within the Christian church. The belief in one God and one God alone was central to the Jewish faith from which Christianity sprang. This belief was carried on by the early followers of Jesus who regarded Him as the divinely sent Messiah rather than God Himself. In the early part of the third century the ecclesiastical writer Tertullian complained that the majority of Christians still held to a belief in the simple unity of God and were loath to accept the Trinity, a term which he first introduced. Not until the Council of Constantinople in 381 A.D. was the doctrine of the Trinity established as an official tenet of the Christian Church. This dogma, upon which all of orthodox Christianity is based today, was proclaimed only after a century and a half of bitter dissension over the exact substance of Christ and the equality or inequality of deity between Father, Son, and Holy Ghost.

Today the Unitarians and their sister denomination, the Universalists, are the sole groups of those acknowledging Christian antecedents who do not accept the doctrine of the Trinity.* Instead, they revere Jesus as an inspired and prophetic teacher, divine in the sense that divinity is to be found in all mankind.

Although they feel a spiritual kinship with the ancient followers of a simpler Christianity, Unitarianism as a distinct belief under that name stems only from the Reformation. In America it began as a progressive movement mainly within the orthodox Congregational Church of eighteenth-century New England. There were individual Unitarians prior to the Revolution, and the Episcopal King's Chapel in Boston became in fact, if not in name, a Unitarian church as early as 1787. However, it was not until 1825 that those holding Unitarian views officially declared themselves by forming the American Unitarian Association "to diffuse the knowledge and promote the interest of pure Christianity." †

The Universalists predate the Unitarians in America, their mother church having been established in Gloucester, Mass., in 1779 and an official Declaration of Faith adopted in Philadelphia in 1790. Unlike the Unitarians, they developed from a Trinitarian base. But their rejection of the Calvinist theory of predestination in favor of universal salvation under a God of justice and love, was equally revolutionary for that time.

However, even the early Unitarian and Universalist "heresies" bear little relationship to the beliefs and practices within these fellowships today. Doctrinal disputes

have long since become secondary to the practice of a way of life and mind based on "freedom, reason, and tolerance," and dedicated to the establishment of "peace, justice, and brotherhood" among men. Social reform, racial equality, and a responsibility toward less fortunate peoples throughout the world — uncoupled to missionary conversion — are the working principles guiding Unitarian-Universalist action.

The intellectual search for truth, even when the discoveries of science and archeology upset cherished religious beliefs, is not only a privilege, but is considered fundamental to man's expanding grasp of spiritual reality. In their quest for insight, both fellowships draw upon other great religions than the Christian and other great books than the Bible. In fact, Unitarianism has been defined not as a faith but as a search. To a great extent this description is true also of Universalism, although it retains perhaps stronger identification with traditional Christianity.

Today, however, the two denominations are close enough to have voted for a merger in 1960. This signifies an increased cooperation at the national level, more than it does an actual relinquishment of identity on either side, since local Universalist and Unitarian churches are both entirely autonomous. The combined groups number approximately 200,000 members in the United States and 500,000 in the world. However, it is significant to note that despite this small membership, recent rates of growth are among the highest of any denomination. Consequently many new churches are being built today and more will undoubtedly be needed.

Unitarians have, of course, shared in the architectural heritage of the Congregationalists. Throughout New England, especially in Massachusetts, many Unitarian fellowships today worship in churches that were built to express Congregational orthodoxy. The Universalist denomination, also, is heir to early churches that were erected when it was trinitarian in nature. Beautiful as they are, these steepled, box-like churches reveal little of the universality that characterizes the liberal religions today. Even more inappropriate are the later nineteenth- and early twentieth-century churches, designed in the pseudo-historic styles then popular throughout America.

Today, however, it is safe to say that few Unitarian or Universalist congregations would build any but a modern church. This direction is to be expected from fellowships dedicated to the future rather than the past, and containing a membership noted for its intellectual and artistic vitality.‡ It also indicates a growing urge to demonstrate a unique religious approach in a uniquely appropriate architecture.

---

* The Quakers are uncommitted on this point, believing religion as a way of life to be more important than dogma.

† Thomas Jefferson wrote: "I rejoice that in this blessed country of free enquiry and belief, which has surrendered its creed and conscience to neither kings nor priests, the genuine doctrine of one only God is reviving, and I trust that there is not a young man living in the United States who will not die a Unitarian."

‡ In proportion to membership, these two denominations have also more members in the Hall of Fame for Great Americans than any other denomination in America. Eminent Unitarians there include Thomas Jefferson, John Adams, John Quincy Adams, Ralph Waldo Emerson, Nathaniel Hawthorne, Oliver Wendell Holmes, Henry Wadsworth Longfellow, and Horace Mann. Famous contemporary Unitarians include Leverett Saltonstall, Adlai Stevenson, and the late Frank Lloyd Wright.

34. FIRST UNIVERSALIST CHURCH

Chicago, Ill.; Erected 1954
Schweikher, Elting & Bennett, associated architects
Paul Schweikher (b. 1903)
Frank Klein, structural engineer
Samuel Lewis Associates, mechanical engineers
Angelo Testa, Dossal Fabric, interior designers

"In wood, steel, concrete, or any other material I wish simply to enclose the needed space as directly as possible, avoiding compound curvatures or thin shells unless they are the only solution. I pay my greatest attention to spaces, both inside and outside, and to the way the building is put together, with no attempt to be impressive nor, as Mies van der Rohe says, even 'interesting' — just good." — PAUL SCHWEIKHER

The two churches shown in this section are as unlike as it is possible for two designs to be. The Universalist is plain to the point of severity; the Unitarian is complex in both spatial organization and decorative effect. The former is a solution to the problem of a city church in a central crowded area; the latter embraces the country in a calculated flight from city disturbances. Such extremes in architectural expression are entirely appropriate to denominations that place their greatest emphasis on individual freedom of thought, actually encouraging divergent views and searching argument among their membership.

Paul Schweikher who, with associates Winston Elting and Edward H. Bennett, Jr., designed the First Universalist Church, Chicago, Ill., is an exponent of what has been called "stick architecture" — the ancient post-and-lintel system adapted to modern materials. The acknowledged master of this architectural approach is Mies van der Rohe. Like the Mies chapel for the Illinois Institute of Technology (No. 24), the First Universalist Church is a study in rectangularity, but here adapted to a parish educational and service program rather than to student use for worship alone. The problem also differed because the church was an isolated building within a crowded city area, rather than part of a unified campus plan. As a result, the problem of privacy, especially in the use of the site, was a factor in the Schweikher church but not in the Mies chapel.

The solution was to divide the church into two rectangles, one for worship, one for educational and social activities. The twin buildings are separated by a planted court that is enclosed by a continuation of the outer wall of the buildings. From the street, the church appears to be simply a square of brick, like a high, continuous garden wall.

The minister and some of the congregation are not satisfied with this design, feeling that it fails to express the outgoing character of the Universalist fellowship. However, it is hard to imagine how the outdoors could have been utilized in this noisy, crowded neighborhood without shielding it from the street. When faced with certain difficult conditions, it becomes necessary to sacrifice one aspect of a design for another. Indeed, the great virtue of this church lies exactly in its quality of enclosure, creating as it does a quiet garden retreat in the midst of the busy metropolis. For those congregations that intend to build in the city rather than removing to the suburbs, it offers a felicitous solution to the problems of privacy and noise, while allowing full outdoor use of the site.

View of church interior reveals an atmosphere of serene composure. In contrast to the openness of the glassed parish hall (page 270), it is a quiet, almost window-less retreat. The street frontage has no windows at all. In the opposing courtside wall, only narrow, vertical strips of glass are used.

The major source of illumination is a glass end wall, mostly obscured by a large screen, as shown in the photograph. Directly behind the glass wall, on the out-of-doors, is the exterior courtyard wall that reflects sunlight through the glass, but cuts off direct rays and also shields the interior of the church from street view. Additional natural light enters at the rear of the church through the glass side walls of the balcony, above the narthex.

This combination of three light sources, plus the light-reflective quality of the pale colors used throughout the room, creates a soft general illumination without major emphasis or focal point. Walls and floor are executed in shades of gray and beige and the reredos is gray fabric, set in a frame of natural wood. This monotone effect is accented only by the steel framing of the glass end wall and by two delicate black lecterns that substitute for the traditional pulpit.

The small church seats 140 in the nave, 40 in the balcony and 20 in the choir, located at the rear of the sanctuary. With the parish hall, it contains a total of 10,430 sq. ft. of floor area. The cost of the church alone, exclusive of architect's fee and landscaping, was $ 135,000 — approximately $ 13 per square foot.

Exterior views show the dignity and serenity that can be achieved by the simplest of building forms through sensitive handling of proportion and detail. In keeping with the nonliturgical character of the Universalist Church, there is no suggestion of traditional symbolism. This is a church shorn of traditional beliefs and of the architectural elements — spire, tower, ascending space — that usually express them. Indeed, it is less a church than it is a meeting house, and only the lettered name and the small encircled cross beside the entrance indicate the function of the building. The horizontality of its major lines is appropriate to a faith concerned primarily with the needs of man, just as pronounced vertical lines imply aspiration toward a mystical God. The severe form and precise detailing also suggest the intellectual discipline of a fellowship that approaches religion in a spirit of scientific and philosophical inquiry.

Continuous, windowless walls of pale gray brick completely enclose both the buildings and the courtyard between them. Solid brick is used for the buildings themselves, while the courtyard is indicated by an openwork pattern. The architects would have preferred to use solid brick throughout, but the client insisted upon open brickwork for courtyard walls to reduce the sense of barrier between the church and the community it serves.

Also offsetting the closed character of the exterior design are its unusual entrances. These are grilles of black wrought iron, which reach the full height of the building and are inset with glass. The one seen in these photographs gives access to the parish hall. A similar grille, in the opposing twin building, leads into the narthex of the church.

The black used for grilles, cross, and lettering, as

an accent against the bland, gray brick, is repeated once more in the roof fascia. This narrow stroke of black atop the building gives a crisp delineation to its simple form and acts also to tie the whole design together.

Bird's-eye view, taken from the same direction as the photograph on page 268, reveals the church in the background, parish hall in the foreground, with the paved, planted, and fenced courtyard between. Eventually a small pool will be added to the courtyard with a bridge to connect the court entrances of the two buildings. The wall that encloses the church nave is of stucco paneling, with only narrow, vertical panes of glass between each panel. This arrangement shields the congregation from courtyard view while admitting some daylight to the interior. When funds are available, this wall will be decorated with a mural painting as suggested in the sketch.

The structure of the two buildings combines brick cavity bearing walls at the exterior with steel columns and curtain walls on the court side. For the church (but not the parish hall) supporting columns have been set out beyond the building line and the roof extended

to meet them, thus forming a sheltered porch. It can be used both as a gathering place after church and as a seating area for outdoor services or entertainments in the summer.

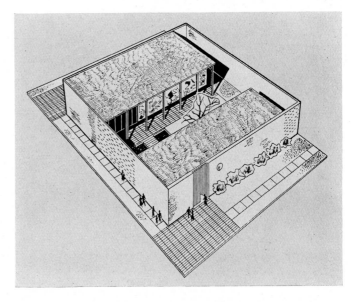

Night view of court is taken from the porch of the church looking toward the parish hall. A paved walk connects the entrance lobbies of the two buildings, but when this photograph was taken, no landscaping had been done. The upper story of the parish hall contains Sunday school classrooms. The lower story is mainly one large social room with its kitchen placed to the far right, beyond the entrance lobby.

Because this building group is distinctly "unchurchly" in appearance, all but obscuring its function from the casual viewer, it will not appeal to those with a strong, sentimental attachment to the older forms of ecclesiastical architecture. However, this generalized quality of design makes it an eminently practical solution for our present-day shifting urban pattern. With a minimum of change, these buildings could be converted into a school, a recreation center, a museum, a library, a small office group, a medical clinic, or even a shopping center, if the need ever arose to sell the property.

This universalization of function is basic to the philosophy of Mies van der Rohe and to those architects who have been strongly influenced by him. Their system of design rests on the belief of the inevitability of urban change and the necessity for sound investment in an uncertain market. As such, this type of design should make a strong appeal to city congregations. However, the fact of flexibility and practicality in no sense detracts from the present stature of this building group as a distinguished example of Universalist architecture, expressing many characteristics of that fellowship.

REPORT FROM THE CLERGY
The Rev. David Harris Cole, Minister

The First Universalist Church of Chicago was organized in 1836 and is the third oldest church in the city. Its second building, a beautiful Gothic structure, was destroyed in the great Chicago fire of 1871. It was known as the leading church in the city and numbered among its members many of the wealthy and prominent families, including several of the city's former mayors.

This fellowship has always been noted for its social service, achieving national fame for pioneering a community youth program in the last century. The church also organized the first school for Negro girls in Chicago and founded the Old People's Home. Through several relocations, the church has now become essentially a South Side institution. It has changed from being a church of the wealthy elite to a congregation of mixed races, mostly middle class and largely college graduates.

The First Universalist Church espouses a liberal religion, which rests upon the authority of reason and scientific discovery, freed from old superstitions and traditions. Old forms have been discarded and new forms evolved to fit the needs of modern man. Such a faith, centered in man and man's needs, could only be adequately housed in a new form of architecture. This was the line of reasoning of our building committee and it was a unanimous choice to have modern architecture. Other than general discussion and some articles in the newsletter, it was not necessary to educate our congregation. They readily recognized the compatibility of modern architecture with modern religion. One or two people felt that the obvious economy of the new design was the compelling reason, but this was not the primary concern of the majority.

In attempting to choose an architect, we got dozens of copies of architectural magazines and pored over them looking for designs that had originality and distinction. Although we interviewed a few architects recommended by friends, our study of the magazines was the decisive step, and it was through photographs of the work of Paul Schweikher that we came to feel that he was our man....

We gave the architect a completely free hand. We described the nature of our faith to him, some of the elemental functions of a liberal church such as worship, education, and fellowship and let him have complete freedom of imagination to design a building that would express the nature of a religion that is free, universal, man-centered, optimistic, rational, and progressive.

However, I feel that Mr. Schweikher did not completely grasp the feeling of our faith. He designed something that was radical, with great beauty and simplicity. Nevertheless, freedom is a basic characteristic of Universalism and he enclosed the church in a rigid enclosure. This suggests encumbrance, rigidity, withdrawal. Certainly not the openness of freedom. Being a suburbanite, he was distressed by the busyness of the city corner on which the church was to be erected, and this influenced him to design something that shut off the world and provided sanctuary from the tensions of the world. There is validity to the concept of sanctuary and withdrawal, but this is not the chief characteristic of our faith. There are also some members who feel that the building does not look like a church, that it is nothing but a big wall.

However, despite our objection to the enclosure, we have found the design to have many commendable aspects. Although Universalism grew out of Christianity, it no longer confines itself to the Christian tradition, believing that truth is to be found in many of the religions of the world. Festivals from other religious traditions are recognized in the worship service as well as the usual Christian holidays. The architecture of the church is such that it can be adapted for these purposes. There is a flexibility in the chancel that enables it to be used for several kinds of services from many world traditions.

There are other good points. The straight lines of the building are symbolic of man. The courtyard, which will one day have a great outdoor mural, allows a place for beauty, not only of nature and its growing things, but of man's own artistry. The originality of the design immediately suggests a modern faith, unique among religions.

The congregation has almost tripled in the three years since the building was built. The architecture of the church has been a compelling factor in this increase. Many have come from curiosity and stayed because they liked what they found. The membership also has changed toward a much younger congregation. Two-thirds of the members are married couples with young children. They come from all sorts of religious backgrounds, but show great enthusiasm for liberal religion. The children have increased by six-fold in the church school program. Young people of high school age have been attracted by the character of the church and its reputation in the community as a liberal and intellectually respectable institution.

35. MEETING HOUSE OF THE FIRST UNITARIAN SOCIETY

Madison, Wis.; Erected 1951
Frank Lloyd Wright (1864-1959), architect

"Truly ordered simplicity in the hands of the great artist may flower into a bewildering profusion, exquisitely exuberant, and render all more clear than ever. Good William Blake says exuberance is beauty, meaning that it is so in this very sense." — FRANK LLOYD WRIGHT

This Unitarian Meeting House near Madison, Wis., is an exuberant church. Here the warm, outgoing, and generously human qualities of a liberal religion are captured in a structure full of life and movement. The interplay of spaces, of textures, of solid and void, of light and shadow, impart to this building a dynamic quality characteristic of the work of Frank Lloyd Wright, making the more restrained designs of other architects seem static and lifeless by comparison.

Such a design unquestionably expresses the vigor that is characteristic of Unitarianism. However, Wright has also been more specific. If any one concept can be considered generally acceptable to individualistic Unitarians, it is the unity of man, nature, and God, however defined. This is the theme Wright has followed in the design.

The building is, of course, closely related to its natural setting, a rolling partially wooded site. Broad sweeping lines and natural materials, including a predominance of rough-set masonry, help to integrate the church with surrounding nature.

The theme of unity has, however, been carried well beyond the integration of building and site, binding together also the varied functions of the church itself. Here, Wright has amalgamated traditionally separate ecclesiastical elements of spire, sanctuary, and parish hall into one open and unbroken space. The foyer at the rear of the church, known as the Hearth Room because of its great open fireplace, represents the traditional parish hall, and it is here that most social functions take place. The larger portion of the building, toward the front, is the church proper, or sanctuary, in which religious services are held. The two areas are entirely open to each other except for a dividing curtain that can be closed when desired. The "spire" is actually a great upward sweeping prow which develops, by means of a rising roofline, from the rear of the church to a peak over the chancel.

The basic figure with which Wright has worked to create this condensed design is the triangle. The floor plan of the church is roughly a rhomboid, the union of two opposing triangles, with the broad base of each where nave and Hearth Room merge. From this widest part of the plan, the triangle enclosing the nave narrows to its apex at the chancel. And from this same wide point the Hearth Room also narrows to a secondary, blunted apex at the rear of the church. However, to achieve the rising prow, Wright has instituted an opposing progression of space on vertical and horizontal planes. At the same time that the width of the nave narrows, its height increases. The rear of the nave is thus broad and low-ceilinged, progressing inward and upward toward a triangular peak above the chancel.

Wright has described this building as "a church where the whole edifice is in the attitude of prayer." The Rev. Max D. Gaebler, present minister of the church, has written of this design: "Inside the church, as one faces the prow, the powerful focus upon the pulpit and the strong vertical thrust of the prow create a feeling of unity and elevation which surpasses description. Yet when one faces the Hearth Room, there is by contrast a warm and intimate feeling which suggests the flux of daily life."

In addition to this main body of the church, a spacious entrance lobby and Sunday school wing extend out from either side of the Hearth Room at its broadest point, adjoining the nave. Such a placement provides convenient circulation among all elements. Of equal importance, it unites varied functions of the church in one structure, emphasizing that all are part of a single whole. In writing of this design, Wright has explained: "Myself a Unitarian, brought up in the spirit of the unity of all things — the building I designed in that spirit — the building in itself an expression of reverential-unity over all."

Direct view of the prow of the church reveals the forward thrust of its triangular plan and the upward thrust of its triangular roofline. Explains Wright. "As the square has always signified integrity and the sphere universality, the triangle stands for aspiration." Here then is a church that conveys by the shape of the sanctuary itself, without applied spires or towers, the instinctive quality of man's reach beyond himself. The great glass-enclosed prow, which forms the symbol of the church, serves on the interior as a transparent backdrop, ascending upward behind the pulpit and choir loft.

Opposing this vertical movement are the low, horizontal lines of the wings, which visually anchor the fore-structure to the earth, and symbolically emphasize the Unitarian commitment to earthly concerns.

The entrance lobby is in the left wing of the church; classrooms, fronted by a stone-columned loggia, are at right. The latter wing ends in the minister's residence. Note "windov box," a small planting trough incorporated into the masonry of the prow, which further integrates nature with the building structure.

Photos: © Ezra Stoller

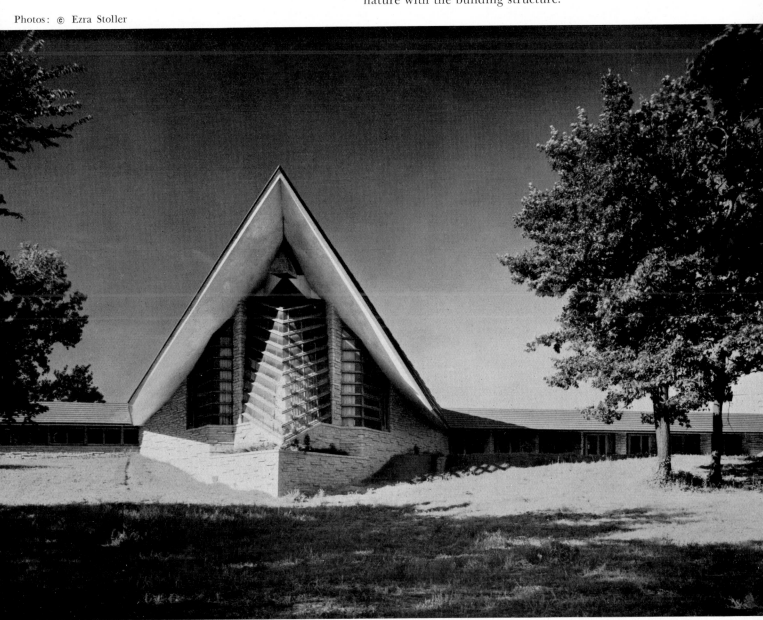

Side view of the Unitarian Meeting House reveals once more its dual quality of aspiration and protective shelter. The entrance lobby is shown here as it joins the main body of the church. Deep roof overhangs on all sides shield large windows from direct sun. The broad surface of the roof is finished with strips of copper, laid to emphasize the sheltering character of the design, and crowning the church with the beautiful blue-green typical of this material. The smooth surface and vivid coloring of the copper present a dramatic contrast to the rough texture and neutral tone of stone walls.

Although the roof of the nave appears from the side to have a center ridge pole, this is an optical illusion. The top part of the roof, not visible from front or side, is actually a triangle with its broad base over the rear of the Hearth Room, its apex at the prow of the church. Sides drop down from this top triangle to form smaller triangles at either side, one of which is the major roof element seen in this photograph. The apexes of all three roof triangles meet in a point at the prow. Note how the angled chancel window stands out in side view like a stiff glass veil from the peak of the copper roof above it.

This meeting house was planned as a country church, placed in a setting of Wisconsin farmland, overlooking a lake. Such a choice stems from Wright's own intense dislike of city congestion and noise. He persuaded the congregation to abandon the downtown site they had been considering in favor of these peaceful rural surroundings. Since the church was built, however, Madison has expanded to incorporate the site in its newer suburbs. This occurrence typifies the difficulty of maintaining a decentralized position within any reasonable distance of rapidly expanding cities. With four and a half acres of land, the First Unitarian Society is well protected. Other churches intent on such a location would do well to purchase a similar acreage to insure against the encroachment of new and possibly disturbing building, and to allow for expansion if it becomes necessary.

Interior, looking into the prow, shows the upward sweep of the roof and the powerful thrust of triangular stone columns supporting it. These columns jut out toward the bottom, forming a ledge from which the choir loft is cantilevered. Immediately above the loft is a sounding canopy that directs music outward toward the congregation, rather that allowing it to reverberate in the height of the prow.

There is no altar, since Unitarians recognize no sacraments. Instead, the massive stone pulpit is placed at dead center, in front of the choir, emphasizing the centrality of reason and enlightenment within this denomination. Seats are arranged around the pulpit, both in front of it and at the sides. Because the plan widens from the apex of the prow to the rear of the nave, it is possible to make the seating area broad and compact, reminiscent of an intimate family group. This arrangement is one of the great values of a plan based on either the triangle or the rhomboid. It expresses the unity of clergy and congregation that is fundamental to Unitarianism, but which is also a general Protestant concept as well as an aim of the Liturgical Revival in the Roman Catholic Church.*

However, the atmosphere created here. with its emphasis on "meeting together," rather than upon the observance of a formal rite, is unmistakably Unitarian. So is the emphasis upon nature as integral with man and his works. Throughout the church, stonework is set in irregular ledges, reminiscent of the natural outcroppings of unquarried rock.

Colors throughout are keyed to nature: the warm beige of stone, the natural wood brown of louvers and benches, rust colored carpeting, and upholstery of a soft, medium green, repeated in the planting boxes. Such a color scheme is quietly harmonious, rather than striking, interweaving the interior with the Wisconsin landscape as glimpsed through the chancel windows. The final unity of this design comes in the upward sweep of space itself, as the ascending roof passes over nave, pulpit, and choir loft, past rough stone and a view of trees to the "sky window" at the apex.

* See "The Search for Plan" in the Catholic section, the Episcopal Chapel of St. James the Fisherman (No. 22) and the First Church of Christ, Scientist (No. 33).

View across the nave toward the Hearth Room, from one side of the chancel, shows the two rooms entirely open to each other except for a central curtain that can be closed when desired. This curtain, in stripes of rich purple, copper, green, and tawny red is the one dramatic color accent in the entire church. It was designed by the wife of the architect and handwoven by women of the congregation from flax, sisal, rayon, banana rope, and metal ribbon. For regular Sunday morning services and for small meetings in the Hearth Room, this curtain may be closed, separating the two areas. For special services drawing a larger than usual congregation, or for large social gatherings, it is left open and the two rooms used as one. Overflow church seating can be placed in the Hearth Room, greatly increasing the capacity of the church.

In reverse, the nave becomes part of the Hearth Room when its capacity must be expanded. Facilitating this double use of space is the unique design of the pews. They are made of light plywood, easily movable and also folding for storage. This photograph shows them arranged for a church service. For lectures, pageants, concerts, or movies, they are reversed to face the Hearth Room, which then becomes a "stage" for performers, with the nave of the church acting as its auditorium. The curtain between the two areas is then used as a stage curtain. For dinners or other socials, the center pews are simply folded and moved to one side. Such a scheme makes the most intensive possible use of space. It is well worth considering by any congregation attempting to build on a limited budget.

Although the church is essentially one unbroken room, Wright has marked off spaces within it by means of dropped ceiling canopies. One of these is placed over the Hearth Room, giving this area a more domestic character than that of the higher-ceilinged nave. In the center of the Hearth Room, a six-sided dome cuts up through the canopy, from the sides of which artificial lighting is reflected down into the interior.

The other ceiling canopy is over the chancel at the prow of the church. Here, it lends added emphasis to an area that is the focus of the church interior. It also supplements the smaller "sounding board" above the choir loft, reflecting music out and down into the nave. Visually, it acts as a balance to the rear canopy over the Hearth Room, tying the two areas together in one more way.

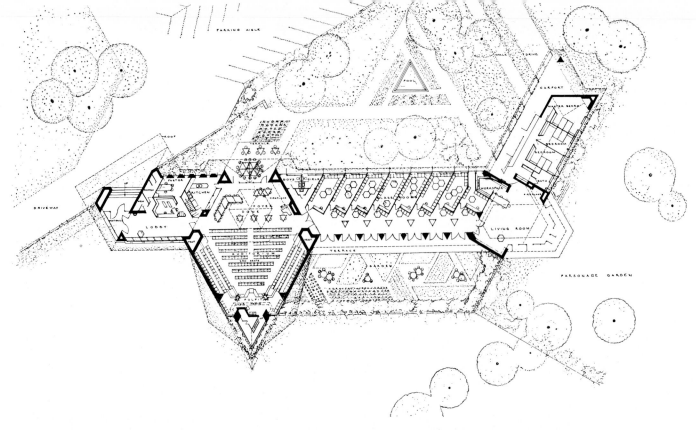

Plan shows the rhomboidal church flanked by lobby and classroom wings. The minister's residence angles backward from the latter wing at extreme right. The lobby at left turns backward to give direct access from the church parking lot.

Wright's masterly manipulation of interior space is indicated by this ground plan. One of his basic techniques is the playing of openness against containment, thus providing in some places a sense of enclosed shelter, in others surprising vistas. Here, the walls of the nave are solid masonry, breaking open only at the prow. The Hearth Room (labeled "foyer" on the plan), on the other hand, is mainly open, with a glass wall at rear, glass doors to lobby and classroom wings, and only two freestanding columns and the great fireplace wall of solid masonry. This creates a distinct change of atmosphere between two areas within the same interior space.

Consistency between plan and structure, indoors and out, is another distinguishing feature of Wright's work. The triangle, which is the basic figure of this plan, is repeated in the stone columns partially supporting the structure, also in the reflecting pool at rear, and even in flower beds in the church garden.

The cost of this church, which provides seating for 250, the eight classrooms, hearth room, pastor's study, and residence, was a low $165,000. However, costs were held down by considerable volunteer work. Members of the congregation loaded and hauled the 1,000 tons of stone needed for walls and columns from a local quarry some 30 miles distant. They also plastered the interior of both wings and applied the finish to floors and woodwork. Wright's apprentices acted as stonemasons for the pulpit and as plasterers for the assembly room. As mentioned previously, women of the congregation wove the handsome Hearth Room curtain. This church was therefore something of a communal enterprise. Even the architect was more than ordinarily involved, because his father had been one of the founders of the parish in 1879, and he himself was a long-standing member of the church.

REPORT FROM THE CLERGY
The Rev. Max David Gaebler, Minister

I was not here at the time our congregation voted to build this building, nor was I in Madison at the time of its actual construction. My impression is that the only hesitation to proceed with this plan arose from financial considerations. As to the design and the choice of an architect, there was never any significant disagreement so far as I know. After all, Mr. Wright is deeply rooted in this Society and we were extremely fortunate that he was prepared to undertake this project for us.

As to the results, at least in terms of what has happened to us as a congregation, I should like to mention that our resident legal membership has risen from 125 to somewhere in the neighborhood of 350 and that our Sunday school enrollment, which was expected to reach an eventual 100, is now something over 200. These are modest figures, but they represent substantial and continued growth ever since we moved into this building.

Moreover, our whole program has been immensely strengthened and diversified in this new setting. We sponsor a nursery school for three- and four-year-old children five days a week, as well as a remarkable program we call the Dance Fellowship on Saturday mornings. These and other activities keep our facilities in use seven days a week. This is possible primarily because of the remarkable flexibility of the space as Mr. Wright designed it. This multiple use of space is not, as I had at first feared, makeshift; rather the space is genuinely adaptable to a wide variety of uses. As a result, although our building is not large, we have more use per square foot than any other church building I have ever seen. There is absolutely none of it so specialized that it can be used only once a week. This multiple use, of course, requires extensive custodial service to arrange it properly for each successive occasion.

In this connection, one thing that rather concerned me when I first came and that I am sure startles some visitors, is the flexibility of our church auditorium itself. In effect, our major space is occupied by two rooms —

the auditorium and the Hearth Room. Each can be expanded to occupy as much of the total area as is necessary for the occasion. Far from regarding this multiple use of the church proper as an unfortunate necessity bordering on sacrilege, I have come to regard it as a wholesome and welcome symbol of the fact that religion is not a special set of activities reserved for a particular time and place, but a quality that can infuse all of life. Thus everything we do in the fellowship of our congregation is by implication religious, and this fact is represented in the very nature of the building itself.

Another way in which the building suggests meanings that are particularly appropriate to Unitarianism is in its use of diagonal lines. The great upward thrust of the roof is balanced by the delicate diagonals of the prow, so that we are pointed both skyward and earthward. This combination creates an atmosphere of adventure and openness characteristic of our approach to religion.

Moreover, the strong focus of the auditorium upon the pulpit combines with the side seats (which serve very much the same function as the facing benches in a Quaker meeting house) to produce a sense of genuine community among the people present that I have never seen equalled in any other church. We are aware of each other and of ourselves as part of the group. No church building I have ever seen so effectively transforms a collection of individuals into a congregation. Even the pulpit, for all its massiveness, really just completes the circle, so that the minister speaks not from on high but from within the circle of the congregation.

Perhaps my comment, printed in *Architectural Forum,* best sums up this atmosphere: "The utter simplicity of the assembly room is friendly, not austere. The large, clear glass areas, the warm colors, the closeness of the congregation to the pulpit — all this helps to create an atmosphere of directness and honesty, with no barriers of false formalism interposed between minister and congregation. It would be difficult to speak or think anything but the truth in such a setting. Mr. Wright has caught the spirit of liberal religion and has given it architectural embodiment."

References

"Churches," *Architectural Forum,* December 1952.
Wright, Frank Lloyd. *An American Architecture* (ed. by Edgar Kaufman). Horizon Press, New York (1955).

SUMMARY

This design by Frank Lloyd Wright for a Unitarian Meeting House closes the section devoted to Protestant churches, just as Notre Dame du Haut at Ronchamp by Le Corbusier closes the section of Catholic churches. (The Cathedral of Brasilia, the final project in the Catholic section, presents a different problem from that of a small church.)

Because Wright and Le Corbusier have long been equated as the opposing giants of modern architecture, a comparison of their churches may be of interest. Although the two designs could hardly be more different in atmosphere and in style of execution, they nevertheless show remarkable likenesses. Particularly, the spatial progression within each interior reveals the fundamental similarity between these two architects who, in all superficial aspects, are utterly unlike. Indeed, of all the churches in this book, only the very French chapel at Ronchamp and this thoroughly American church in Wisconsin display an equal grasp of spatial movement, on a multiplicity of planes.

Both show, in the nave, a simultaneous progression of vertical and horizontal space. The Corbusier chapel opens out in width as its height increases, to form a roughly trumpet-shaped interior. Wright's church narrows as the roofline ascends, forming a doubly pointed triangle. From the exterior, however, the gently lifting prow of the Ronchamp chapel and the more acutely angled prow of the Madison meeting house are similar as they develop from a low rear roofline to a frontal peak, in one unbroken sweep.

Another remarkable similarity, revealing the kinship of these two minds, is the repetition in structure of the basic figure of the plan. Wright repeats his triangle in stone columns and in angled chancel windows. Corbusier repeats his trumpet shape in the deep embrasures that cut through the massive south wall of the chapel, and also in the four-way thickening of the wall itself. It is interesting also that the major windows in each building are shaped to funnel space rather than cut it in a single flat plane.

Both architects have also played long, narrow spaces against the one large, open room of the church proper: Wright in his low, horizontal wings; Corbusier in his vertical chapel towers.

The sculptured ceiling canopy that Wright has placed over his chancel consists of two up-curving sheets, meeting at an angle at the center of the ceiling. Although Corbusier's ceiling is a single, unbroken membrane, the way in which it curves from side to side, and from back to front, gives it a visual kinship to the Wright canopy. Even the dome in the Unitarian Hearth Room, which cuts up and through the ceiling canopy in that area, is reminiscent of the upward-shooting space in the Ronchamp chapel towers.

With the manipulation of space, however, the similarities between the two designs abruptly end. In the Corbusier chapel, all is smooth, curved, sculptural, white. The Wright design makes a virtue of jagged angles, textural contrasts, rugged materials, and warm colors. The Ronchamp chapel is contained, mysterious, and suddenly a revelation; the Madison church throughout, is open and free. Each is the vivid expression of architectural talents, national cultures, and religious attitudes that lie at opposite poles.

These two leaders, Wright and Le Corbusier, employ the same rare talent for spatial thinking toward ends so different that their work seems scarcely to be encompassed by the same name — modern architecture. This diversity demonstrates the infinite variety open to designers who care to explore the potential of our own time in our own idiom.

MONASTERIES AND SEMINARIES

The design of a Catholic monastery or a Protestant theological seminary is a far more complex undertaking than the design of a parish church or even a cathedral. Such an institution embraces not only a church or chapel as its focal point, but also extensive educational buildings, recreational facilities, administrative offices, varied types of housing, and perhaps farm structures and craft shops. Essentially, it is a small town, with many of the attendant problems of land use and traffic flow.

Although the church is central to this complex, its design must harmonize with the other structures, a number of which are nonreligious in function. The church itself is not a parish church, but must accommodate the specialized needs of the monastery or seminary. Finally, the design and construction of a large theological group represents a projection of present needs into the future. Because of the large expenditure involved, such undertakings are often long-range projects, with a building schedule that can extend, as does that of the Benedictine Abbey of St. John the Baptist, over a period of a hundred years. Even those that are built at once must be carefully calculated to serve future growth and needs.

The traditional monastery, which has served so often as the inspiration for contemporary seminaries, was focused inward upon the cloisters, grouping the church, refectory, communal dormitory, and chapter house around this central court. Granaries, dairies, and other working buildings, operated mainly by lay brothers, were placed away from the main grouping and schools were either nonexistent, or decidedly secondary in importance.

This cloistered plan, reinforced by the massive stone building system characteristic of past ages, expressed the concept of complete withdrawal from the world into a life of religious contemplation. But few Catholic monasteries and no Protestant seminaries are so withdrawn today. The education and training of students for work in the world is one of their primary functions; many are centers for missionary operations that circle the globe. Their purposes and their reponsibilities far exceed those of the monasteries of a simpler past.

Because of these changes, the simple, contained, and essentially rigid site plan that served traditional monastic life so well is no longer a functional one. Nor is its fortress-like architecture expressive of today's religious outlook.

A solution appropriate to the spirit and the functions of the present must combine seclusion with openness. A more intricate site plan is demanded in order to accommodate teaching and other daily work as well as the religious rituals. The elements of worship, education, administration, and housing must be integrated in a complex that allows convenient access between buildings while it shields certain functions from conflicting ones.

The designs shown on the following pages have been chosen because they sympathetically serve the changed functional requirements of the modern theological community. Equally important, they are brilliant architectural statements of the spirit of religious life in the twentieth century, as valid for our age as were the cloistered monasteries for ages past.

36. ABBEY OF ST. JOHN THE BAPTIST

For the Order of St Benedict, Collegeville, Minn.
Monastic wing, erected 1955
Monastic church, erected 1960
Marcel Breuer (b. 1902), architect
Pier Luigi Nervi (b. 1891) and Farkas & Barron,
structural engineers.
Fred Dubin Associates, mechanical engineers
Sidney K. Wolfe & Walter Holtkamp, acoustical
engineers

"A building is a man-made work, a crystallic, constructed thing. It should not imitate nature — it should be in contrast to nature. Even where it follows free lines, it should always be clear that they are built — that they did not just grow. I can see no reason at all why buildings should imitate nature, organic, or grown forms."

— MARCEL BREUER

The Abbey of St. John the Baptist, on the shores of Lake Sagatan in rural Minnesota, is the largest Benedictine community in the world today. Founded in 1856 as a small mission to serve the flood of German immigrants to Minnesota and also to do work among the Chippewa Indians, its scope now encompasses a school of theology, a liberal arts college, a preparatory school, and dependent priories and parishes located in the United States, the Bahama Islands, Puerto Rico, Mexico, and Japan.

In accordance with the Rule of St. Benedict, which stresses manual labor and craft skills as part of the monastic discipline, the abbey maintains its own farm, stables, greenhouses, carpentry shop, and printing plant. These functions, extending far beyond the bounds of the traditional cloistered monastery, could not possibly be encompassed within its simple, rectangular plan.

However, there was no problem here of educating the client to accept a contemporary solution. An older campus, centered about a quadrangle, already had proved its inadequacy to the present monastic responsibilities. Moreover, the Abbey of St. John is a community of rare intellectual and artistic enlightenment, one of the pioneers in this country of the Liturgical Revival in art and architecture. Its members therefore decided on a bold, 100-year building program that, stage by stage, will replace the existing monastery with the best in modern architecture and planning. The attitude behind this decision is expressed in a letter written by Abbott Baldwin Dworschak to the various architects under consideration when the building program of St. John was in its formative stage:

"The Benedictine tradition at its best challenges us to think boldly and to cast our ideals in forms which will be valid for centuries to come, shaping them with all the genius of present-day materials and techniques. We feel that the modern architect with his orientation toward functionalism and honest use of materials is uniquely qualified to produce a Catholic work. In our position it would, we think, be deplorable to build anything less, particularly since our age and our country have thus far produced so little truly significant religious architecture."

The choice of Marcel Breuer as the architect to carry out these goals could hardly have been more felicitous. Breuer had received his training at the famed Bauhaus Institute in Germany, working with such masters as Walter Gropius and Mies van der Rohe. Here, he acquired that intimate knowledge of materials and craft skills — geared to modern technological processes — which was fundamental to the Bauhaus program. In America, after 1930, he taught at Harvard University's Graduate School of Design and entered a partnership with its director, his long-time colleague, Walter Gropius. Shortly after World War II, he opened an independent office in New York City.

Because of his training and association, the work of Marcel Breuer exhibits certain characteristics common also to that of his European contemporaries.

Unlike the organic architecture of Frank Lloyd Wright, which makes of the building a part of nature, this school of design sets the building up against nature in sharp contrast to it. In accord with the rationale of modern technology, the building is usually modular and the supporting frame is clearly delineated as an element separate and quite different from the parts that merely screen or protect.

However, within these general principles, Breuer, from the beginning, has exhibited an original approach to design. For example, he has never limited his vocabulary

to the rectilinear frame and to the manufactured materials that have become the hallmark of Mies van der Rohe. He early incorporated natural stone and wood into his designs, thus achieving a warmth lacking in most work of the International Style. Recently, in the Paris Headquarters for UNESCO, and also in St. John, he has experimented with the plasticity of reinforced concrete.

Even when working within the classic rectangle, Breuer developed a characteristic style. Rather than make the building a smooth, enclosing envelope, Breuer pulls frame and enclosure apart, projecting one, recessing the other, sometimes even balancing the building upon an under-frame that, structurally, is entirely separate. Unlike Mies van der Rohe, Breuer is concerned also with the expressive essence of particular buildings. His houses and other small structures are light, airy, and open. Large institutional buildings are usually given a massive character, verging on the monumental.

These qualities of his architecture, its discipline and its expressive clarity, coupled with a certain rugged solidity where this is appropriate, made Breuer a sympathetic choice to the monks of St. John. When choosing him, they recorded also that "Breuer is a man of recognized ability, unassuming, direct, easy to work with and yet not afraid to tell you if he thinks you are wrong. His quiet and humble manner, and his willingness to tell exactly what he thinks are the characteristics most in his favor."

The church is the focus of any monastic community, ancient or modern. Here the monks assemble four times each day, seven days each week, to chant the divine offices. The church at the Abbey of St. John functions also as a parish church for the surrounding region and as a student chapel for college and preparatory school. It is the scene of great processionals on holy days. As the *raison d'être* of the entire community, it sums up the purpose toward which all activities are dedicated.

In the new plan for St. John, the church will be the first building encountered at the entrance to monastery grounds. It fronts upon a public court, the remainder of which will be walled, to shield the educational buildings and living quarters of the monastery from public view. Facing the courtyard, the church will stand alone as a proclamation of the monastic community.

The symbol by which the ancient abbey church proclaimed itself was the bell tower, two of which flanked the main entrance. The form and structure of the ancient towers were integral to the fortresslike architecture of which they were a part. In addition to their function in sounding the canonical hours, these were originally watch towers, from which the tolling bells spread an alarm against approaching marauders. The latter function is, of course, long since obsolete. But the sounding of the hours is still a primary function within monastic life. The housing for bells, therefore, remains a logical choice as a symbol for the abbey.

In this design the traditional bell towers, protectively flanking the church have been transformed into a single, dramatic bell banner, whose supports still shelter the main entrance. With the exception of the Cathedral of Brasilia, no other church illustrated in this book has achieved such a forceful symbolism.

The 99-ft. bell banner soars high above the main body of the church, bearing within it, toward the heavens, the ancient symbol of the cross. Beneath the cross, in a horizontal slot, hang the bells, a decorative element within the starkly simple slab. This banner will act at once as a landmark of the abbey, seen from afar, and a portal through which worshippers enter, under the shadow of the cross and the music of the bells.

Beuer chose the cantilevered slab of reinforced concrete for this banner as a summation of building in our age, just as the massive stone towers summed up the structural essence of the past. In addition, its broad, flat surface serves a functional purpose. The facade of the church is a honeycomb of reinforced concrete, inset with glass. Because it was a necessity of site planning to face this wall toward the north, no direct sunlight can enter it at any time. But the rays of the sun, striking the bell banner, are reflected on and through this wall of window, flooding the church with a soft light. The effect is a diffused and glowing illumination that could never be achieved with direct sunlight.

The great springing support, upon which the banner rests, arches over the main entry to the church. This entrance is through the baptistry, a one-story structure placed outside the church proper yet connecting directly to it. Such an arrangement recalls the outdoor atrium of the early Christian basilicas. It reestablishes the importance of the baptistry which, in recent Catholic churches, has been relegated to a secondary position to the side of the choir or vestibule. Here it is placed on a direct axis with the altar, emphasizing the entry of the new Christian into the Church, through the sacrament of baptism, leading directly to the sacrament of the Mass, whereby the Catholic practices his faith. This symbolism is further carried out by the opening of the enclosed, low-ceilinged baptistry lighted only by skylight, into the immense and glowing interior of the church itself.

In side view of the church, the supporting wall structure is clearly revealed. Upon a lower framework of horizontal beam and freestanding piers, huge folded slabs of reinforced concrete rise to the roofline. Here they are joined by a similar under-roof structure of folded concrete, connecting where each wall and roof serration forms a V.

This structural system, exploiting as it does the plastic quality of reinforced concrete, is similar to that of the Priory of St. Anselm in Tokyo (No. 2), which, incidentally, is one of the dependent priories of St. John. Unlike those of St. Anselm, however, the folded wall slabs here are not separated into freestanding columns, but are joined in one continuous construction, actually a thin shell of concrete, similar to pleated paper. The effect of massiveness is deceptive, an illusion created by

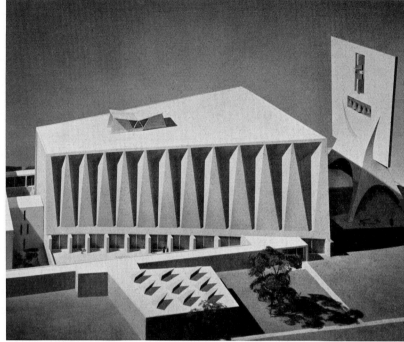

Warren Reynolds, Infinity Inc.

the depth of the fold, the reverse of which is exposed on the interior. However, with this pleated design, walls achieve such strength and the roof such stability that interior columns are unnecessary. The interior of the church can remain one great, unbroken room. In addition, since the entire support of the church is concentrated in side walls, the end walls can become mere screens infilled with glass. This creates a play of contrasts between delicate, crystalline walls at the front and rear, and powerful, protective masonry at the sides.

In the lower portion of the side walls, however, the functions of support and enclosure, amalgamated in the folded slabs, are separated once more. Between projecting concrete piers the wall enclosures, like the end walls, are entirely of glass. In this way the massive masonry envelope surprisingly breaks open into transparency at bottom, allowing, from the interior, glimpses of the cloister gardens that flank the church on either side. The projecting piers interrupt vision sufficiently so that the view toward the out-of-doors does not distract attention from the service.

At their outer boundaries, the two cloister gardens are defined by enclosed passageways, which also function to connect the church with the monks' living quarters at rear. The walls of these "cloister walks" are to be solid granite brick where they face away from the church, and clear glass where they face toward it. They are the routes of monastic processionals, which can be glimpsed by the congregation, through opposing glass side walls in church and passageways.

Projecting outward from one of the cloister passageways, as seen in the foreground of this photograph, is the chapter house, in which church business is transacted by the monks and their presiding abbot. In contrast to the church, which is variously opened up with glass, this meeting house is entirely enclosed except for skylights.

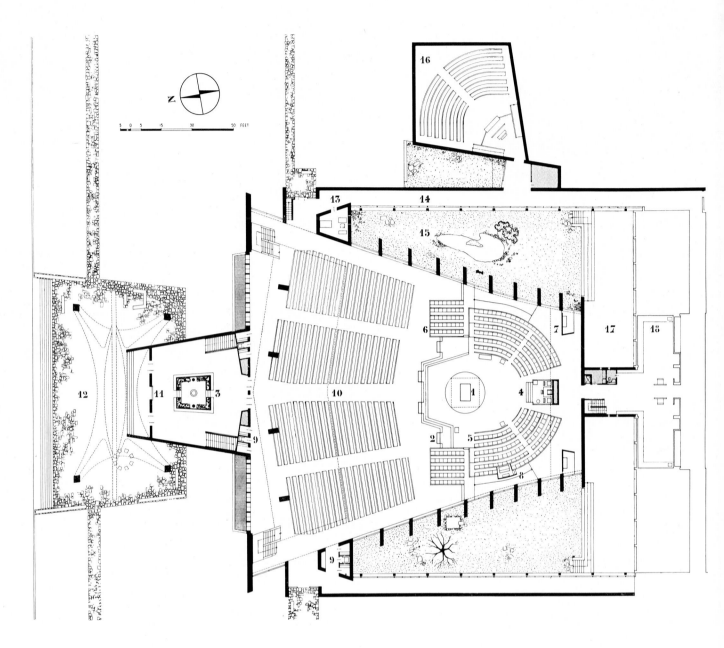

1. altar
2. communion tables
3. baptistry
4. abbot's throne
5. monastic choir
6. brothers' choir
7. private altars or shrine
8. organ console
9. confessionals
10. nave
11. processional door
12. forecourt
13. pastor's office
14. cloister walk
15. cloister gardens
16. chapter house
17. sunken garden
18. sacristies

The geometry of this entire design is based upon the trapezoid: a four-sided, symmetrical figure, wider at one end than the other. The trapezoid is first stated in the slab of bell banner, as it extends upward and outward. It is echoed — broadened and in reverse — in the facade of the church itself and its smaller rear wall. In elongated, vertical form, it appears in folded slabs of reinforced concrete that support the church at either side. It is used also in the various ground plans, including the terraced approach, narrowing toward the entry; the baptistry opening outward toward the church; and finally in the plan of the church itself. In the plan of the church the broadest dimension is at the entrance wall; the plan then narrows focusing on the altar and beyond to the stained glass at the rear of the church.

Such repetition, in both plan and structure, of a single, geometric motif is found also in the Ronchamp chapel by Corbusier (No. 16) and the Unitarian church by Frank Lloyd Wright (No. 35). This variation on a theme gives a subtle harmony and discipline to the entire architectural complex.

The main floor plan shows the repetition and reversal of the trapezoid in terraced approach, baptistry, and church. Enclosed processional passages at either side square the site of the church, delineating the cloister gardens and shielding them from public view.

The trapezoidal shape of the church and its interior arrangement, as well as the structural system, were dictated by the requirements of the Liturgical Revival. Intimate congregational participation in the act of worship calls ideally for one room, uninterrupted by columns. Such an unbroken space is achieved here through the strength of folded concrete side walls and roof, which require no additional interior supports. Only the freestanding cantilevered balcony, indicated by dotted lines across the rear of the nave, is supported by columns, but these are placed so far back within the church that they are behind the line of vision.

The major aim of the Liturgical Revival is to unite priest, choir, and congregation around the focus of the Mass, rather than separating them as celebrant, performer, and audience. This goal is particularly difficult to achieve in an abbey church, since it must serve two different functions: use by the monks alone during the week and by a full congregation on Sunday and holy days. At St. John the requirements were for 180 choir stalls plus 1,250 seats for the general congregation. The problem was to provide an intimate atmosphere for the former, while bringing the entire seating arrangement into communion around the altar.

The trapezoidal plan is the solution to this problem. The high altar is brought forward into the main body of the church, between congregation and choir. The widest portion of the trapezoid is used for congregational seating, allowing a short, broad arrangement of pews that brings all close to the altar. The main choir of monks is disposed in a semicircle behind the chancel, flanking the abbot's throne. The subsidiary brothers' choir is placed at either side of the chancel. In this way the entire body of worshippers is grouped about the altar, which is clearly visible to all. At the same time the monastic choirs occupy a physically separate, smaller area, providing a feeling of intimate worship, even when the nave is empty.

In addition to seating arrangements, other changes have been made in accepted custom. Instead of an altar rail, there are separate communion tables disposed before the chancel, leaving the chancel entirely free and open to the congregation. The placement of the baptistry on a direct axis with the altar emphasizes the polarity between the two fundamental sacraments of baptism and the Mass. In addition, the baptistry and the screen that shields the baptismal font are trapezoidal, thus appearing to open outward toward the church in symbolic gesture.

Few designs in this book have so sympathetically expressed the aims of the Liturgical Revival, nor so deepened the symbolism of the religious ritual.

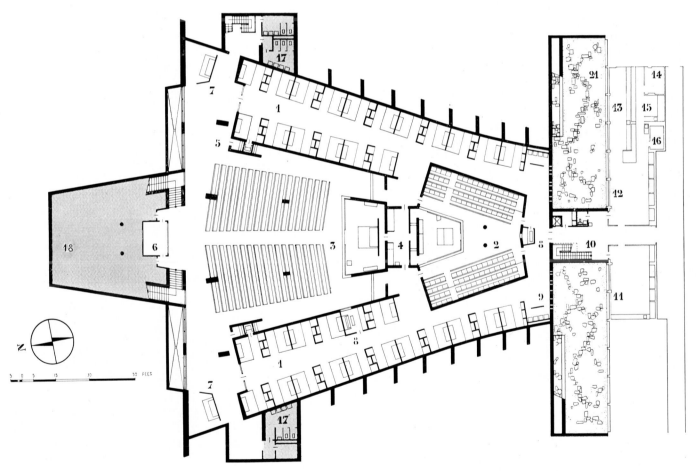

Lower level of church houses special chapels for parish and preparatory school, and for lay brethren, as well as the many individual chapels in which monks celebrate private masses.

1. private chapels
2. brothers' chapels
3. parish and high school chapel
4. sacristy
5. confessionals
6. crying room
7. shrines
8. organ console
9. lavabos
10. link
11. layserver's sacristy
12. sacristan's storage
13. flower room
14. wine storage
15. host bakery
16. vault
17. public restrooms
18. mechanical equipment room

Warren Reynolds, Infinity Inc.

Monastic wing, with its walls of rugged granite brick and its blocky silhouette, captures something of the massive quality of the traditional cloister. It was the first building of the new campus to be completed. The church, which now occupies the space directly in front of it, was second on the construction schedule. The large blank wall square toward the left indicates the place at which the church now joins this building. The west cloister passage joins this wing at the smaller one-story blank square immediately to the left of the group of monks. The east cloister passage joins at far left. Thus, as now finished, the church obscures part of the monastic wing from view.

In this earlier photograph, the entire north facade of the building is visible, showing clearly the "diagrammatic" style of architecture that is characteristic of Marcel Breuer. The church, with its plastic use of concrete, its canted walls, and dramatic bell banner, represents actually a radical departure for him. But the long monastic wing, with its interior spaces quite literally "diagrammed" on the exterior, is a typical Breuer design.

The reinforced concrete frame that supports the structure is used as the delineating element, projecting a foot beyond the wall line. Its horizontal members define the separate floors of the building. Vertical members define the rooms. These are spaced according to a 12-ft. module, which allows interior dimensions of one or more module depending upon room requirements. The 24-ft. spacing on the top floor delineates the clerics' dormitories, while the 12-ft. divisions in the second story indicate the monks' private bedrooms.

The building is divided into two unequal parts by a glassed entrance lobby, which cuts through the full width of the narrow structure, and can be entered from either side. The three monks in the photograph are standing directly in front of its north entrance.

On the ground floor, to the right of the lobby, are guest rooms for visitors, including a two-bay lounge. The abbot's private chapel and church sacristies are to the left of the lobby, their windows distinguished by lattices.

Such an arrangement places fathers' and brothers' living quarters, abbot's rooms, and sacristal elements in close conjunction to the church. This is a primary requisite in any abbey plan, unchanged since ancient times, but here modified to accommodate today's complex monastic life.

Warren Reynolds, Infinity Inc.

Lobby of monastic wing plays the tracery of a latticed teakwood screen against chaste, white walls and ceiling, and the rugged texture of a red brick floor. This combination is used in all public areas of the building.

This is the view that greets those entering from the north side of the monastic wing. Beyond the latticed screen, only members of the monastic community and ecclesiastical guests are allowed to enter. Lay visitors take the door glimpsed at right that leads to guest lounge and bedrooms, separated from the monastic enclosure.

The lobby, however, continues beyond the screen, providing the main focus of circulation for the monastic area of the wing. Note that the glassed, south entrance, leading to the rear grounds of the monastery, is visible in the background. To its right, screened by a perforated brick partition, is the main stairway connecting all stories. In addition, a central corridor traverses the length of the building. Thus, both vertical and horizontal circulation converges in this lobby. It is here that the monks will congregate before entering the church by the rear passage to carry out their daily offices. And it is here that the great processionals will form, proceeding thence along the cloister walks.

Warren Reynolds, Infinity Inc.

Abbot's private chapel adjoins the main lobby and connects also with the abbot's reception room beyond. Teakwood screens separate its outer vestibule from the sanctuary, echoing the screen of the lobby enclosure.

Although this tiny chapel is only 11 by 13 ft., it was designed as a preview of the architecture of the main church. The rough texture of red brick floors and concrete block walls, painted white, contrast with the polished granite altar and luminous window behind it. A suspended canopy, painted a clear, vibrant blue, diffuses artificial light onto a gilded ceiling. Solid entrance doors are painted the same blue. In the main church, similar materials and much the same color scheme will be used. However, brilliant color will be concentrated in the "lantern" above the altar, in the choir screen behind it, and in the stained glass wall at the entrance.

In this chapel, the stained glass window is completely colorless, a study in opalescent whites and grays. It is also an experiment with photosensitive glass, developed for this new use by the Corning Glass Co. Traditional stained glass appears black from the exterior during the day and black from the interior at night. The photosensitive glass reflects light as well as transmitting it, thus revealing the design both night and day from inside or out. The shift from natural to artificial light merely reverses its values, but does not obscure them.

Whitney Stoddard

South facade of monastic wing is both functionally and visually different from the north side shown preceding. Because there is no problem of direct sun from the north, the structural frame there projects only 1 ft. beyond the building envelope. Here, the frame projects outward 4 ft., acting as a sun baffle for the southern exposure. Its depth has been carefully calculated to admit the low winter sunlight, but shield rooms from the higher sun in summer. In addition, it creates a dramatic pattern of light and shadow upon the exterior, aptly illustrating the principle of integral decoration in architecture. This effect is enhanced by the textural contrast between concrete piers and granite brick walls. The latter is local stone, split into thin slabs by a new process and used for the first time in this building.

This south facade expresses interior space with the same clarity as does the north. The central lobby is indicated by solid panels of brick. These are shields for the interior stairwell, adjoined by glass entrance doors and, on the upper stories, by similar floor-to-ceiling windows. Bedrooms for retired monks on the first floor have private balconies, here distinguished by the perforated concrete guard rail.

In addition to clerics' dormitories and monks' cells similar to those on the north, recreation rooms are placed at the south side of the building, overlooking the private

monastery grounds that slope down to nearby Lake Sagatan. In these communal rooms members of the monastic community gather twice each day for short periods of talking, music, and relaxation. The clerics' recreation room is on the upper floor with their dormitories, distinguished here by curtaining (far right). The fathers' recreation room occupies the same three bays at ground level. The brothers' recreation room is in the basement, overlooking a sunken garden, delineated by the retaining wall in the foreground of this photograph.

Because it is part of the tradition of the Benedictines to do all possible manual labor in the community, they provided approximately 20 per cent of the labor for this monastic wing. A crew of clerics undertook the dirty job of dipping lumber in paraffin oil for the forms of the concrete walls. Another crew worked 12-hour shifts digging the footings. The brothers prepared more than 30,000 ft. of oak and maple flooring: cutting the trees on monastery land, sawing them, kiln-drying the lumber in the carpentry shop, and laying it.

The use of monastery labor and materials wherever possible was a stipulation of the cost-plus contract signed with the Wahl Construction Co. of St. Cloud. This arrangement saved money for the abbey and made the construction of the monastic wing a training course in building skills for the abbey community.

Warren Reynolds, Infinity Inc.

Fathers' recreation room has the red brick floor, white painted ceiling and walls, used in all public areas of the monastic wing. Sliding glass panels open the south side of this room to a shallow balcony and monastic gardens beyond. The room is divided in two by a double fireplace of bushhammered concrete framed in brick — one of the many beautiful modern fireplaces designed by Breuer for this building.

The smaller division of this recreation hall functions as a music room. Here, against a granite wall, is placed a large photomural of the fourteenth century mosaic "The Baptism of Christ" from St. Mark's Cathedral in Venice. These photomurals are the major decorative element throughout the monastic wing, and create a striking effect against the stark white interior. Another photograph of an ancient masterpiece can be seen upon the flat surface of the fireplace.

By this unusual decorating device, Breuer has brought the depth and richness of the Church's past into the present, without a false copying of earlier styles. Thus the traditional artistry of the Church becomes what it must when transposed to a contemporary setting: frankly an image.

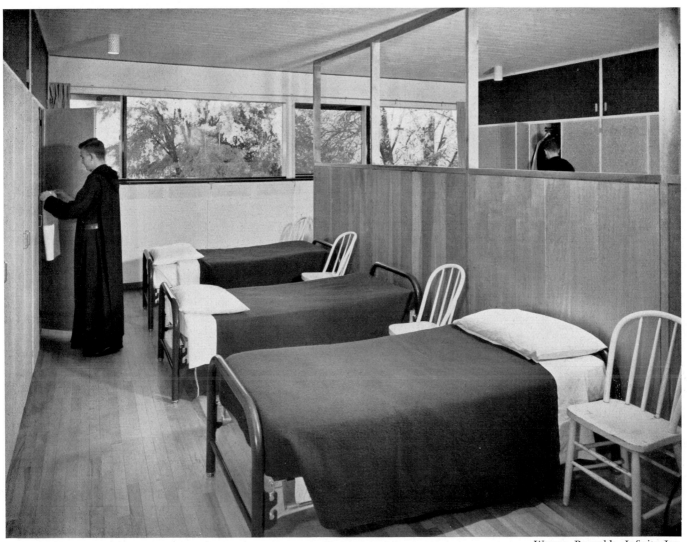

Warren Reynolds, Infinity Inc.

Clerics' dormitory is divided at center by a partial partition with a row of four beds at either side. Lockers are in the side walls. In accord with the Benedictine vow of poverty, furnishings of these dormitories are severely plain. The rooms themselves, although reduced to the functional essentials, are masterpieces of rectilinear composition.

These communal dormitories are used only by clerics serving their novitiate. Because the function of the monastery has now expanded to include teaching, administrative work, and other duties requiring individual study and different schedules, the traditional communal dormitory is no longer practical for ordained monks. The fathers have therefore been given private rooms. These are divided into an entrance and a study-sleeping cubicle by an ash panel. Three walls are painted white; one is colored. For the latter, monks were allowed a choice of blue, cadmium yellow, gray, or vermilion red. These are the only colors used throughout the monastery, their clear, vibrant hues providing a vital spark to the predominating white walls and muted natural materials. The use of a strong primary color in a limited area, surrounded by neutral tones, is typically Breuer.

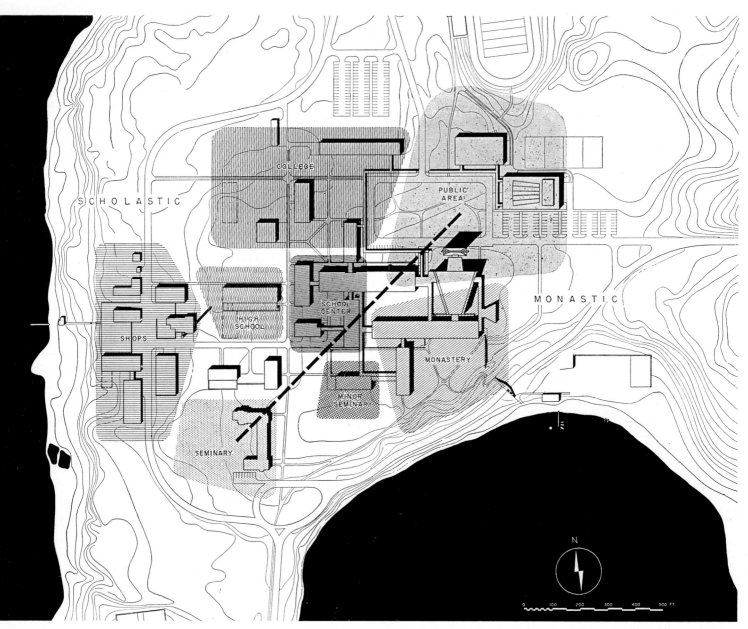

Site plan shows the coordinated scheme for the entire monastery as it will be after the completion of the building program.

The present campus is hampered by a restrictive quadrangle, laid down in the early days of the monastery, and rigidly limiting its expansion. The new plan coordinates buildings according to related function, rather than according to a preconceived formal design.

The new monastic wing and adjoining church are seen here at lower right. These buildings will eventually connect with the school center and minor seminary by means of enclosed passages. More outlying buildings are reached by a network of footpaths.

This site plan accomplishes the difficult task of separating monastic and scholastic elements, though still permitting easy circulation between the two. The monastery, toward the southeast, and the school buildings, toward the northwest, are separated by the complex of church, library, and administration building that are

thus convenient to both groupings. Work shops are placed farther out to the west and a stadium to the north. The walled public forecourt opens toward church, stadium, and college buildings.

Breuer has worked out a schedule of construction that will allow new buildings to go up in the shadow of the old, before these are demolished. Thus the function of the monastery will at no time be interrupted.

References

Breuer, Marcel. *Sun and Shadow*. Dodd, Mead & Co. New York (1955).

Stoddard, Whitney S. *Adventure in Architecture*. Longmans, Green & Company, New York (1958).

37. PRIORY OF ST. MARY AND ST. LOUIS

For the Order of St. Benedict, Creve Coeur, Mo.
Dedicated 1962
Hellmuth, Obata & Kassabaum, architects
George F. Hellmuth (b. 1907)
Gyo Obata (b. 1923)
George E. Kassabaum (b. 1920)
Paul Weidlinger, structural engineer
Pier Luigi Nervi (b. 1891), consulting structural engineer
John P. Nix, supervising engineer
Bolt, Beranek & Newman, acoustical consultants
Hideo Sasaki & Associates, landscape architects

"Functionally, a church must be a space big enough to contain a certain number of people so that all can see the altar. But it must also, in all subtleties of size, shape, appearance, and arrangement, be a space which makes a positive contribution to the act of worship."

— GEORGE E. KASSABAUM

The delicate, flower-like Priory of St. Mary and St. Louis presents a striking contrast to the solid, bluntly honest Abbey of St. John the Baptist that precedes it, although both are designed for the Benedictine Order. St. John is adapted to the rugged northern climate of Minnesota and to a part of the country settled by Germans and Scandinavians. The Priory of St. Mary and St. Louis is located in the hot, humid, southern state of Missouri, in a region that still prides itself on its French heritage. Although this is to be a new dependent mission priory of a Benedictine abbey in Ampleforth, England, the father abbot wisely did not attempt to impose English qualities upon it, but left the prior free to choose a suitable architecture for the new environment. Dom Columba Cary-Elwes, prior of the new monastery, explains his position on the architectural problem as follows:

It might have been thought, and some people did expect, that the plans would be traditional in style, Gothic or Georgian, or what you will, more especially as this was a venture by Benedictines, whose roots are so deep in tradition. Strange as it may seem, the very fact that the Benedictine spirit is so deep in tradition made it unlikely that any of these expressions of the past would be the expression of the present-day members....

Tradition in theology is not sticking to the letter of a primitive text, but rather an intrinsic growth, a repeated restatement in new terms, intelligible to each age. So too in architecture, tradition is not static but living. To quote from the words of Cardinal Lercaro: "The artist who is creating a church must be deeply imbued with the idea of liturgical worship, and must experience and assimilate its spirit; then it will be an easy and almost spontaneous reaction for him to bring to the men of his time, in their own language, the echo of the Divine Word."

...once we had decided that we would take living architecture, that is, an architecture which used the *methods of the day, and the style of the day, and the materials of the day, inevitably we looked for an architect who used those things supremely well.... We were seeking someone with imagination, technical skill, who was receptive, perceptive, sensitive, and also for someone who knew his own mind and would not pander to our ignorance. The only way to do this, we discovered, was to see what had [been] done; deeds, not words, were the only criterion.*

The most striking building, one both simple and majestic, with both grace and power, was the airport building of St. Louis.... We decided that a firm that had the courage, insight, imagination, and technical skill to put up such a building was the one we were looking for.

We were not particularly dismayed that they had not designed a church. We thought that while the churches we had seen were skillful in their design, they lacked that character of aspiration which traditionally a church should have. Further, they suffered from the horizontal line, from the straight line. A church should soar upwards! The St. Louis Airport building was one in the technique of the day which had escaped the box look, and had elegance as well as usefulness.

In choosing the firm of Hellmuth, Obata & Kassabaum, the St. Louis priory chose a comparatively new firm of younger men, unhampered even by the traditions of modern architecture itself. They had already proved their boldness and originality in the St. Louis Airport, handling its reinforced concrete shell construction with both discipline and grace. Later, their little stone church of St. Sylvester (No. 6), revealed also an unusual ability to temper architecture to client and environment.

The priory shown on the following pages combines the most advanced shell construction with a building plan interlaced by courts and planting. The effect is of a garden, from the midst of which blossoms the flower-like priory church.

Photos: Mac Mizuki

Priory church rises in petal-like tiers from the central plaza of the monastic compound, shown here in model. It will be set on high ground at the summit of the main approach to the priory, overlooking a lake — the first building seen by the visitor, and a striking silhouette even from the far distance. Flowering trees in the monastic gardens will surround the church on three sides.

Excepting the Cathedral of Brasilia (No. 17) and the Church of La Virgen Milagrosa (No. 3), this design is structurally the most advanced of any church in the book. It exploits to the full the plastic potential of reinforced concrete, but unlike La Virgen Milagrosa, it does not compromise artistic excellence to the demands of technology. The artist's eye of the architect is here in complete command of his technical skill. As in the Cathedral of Brasilia, form, function, technique, and symbolism become truly one.

Although the design appears intricate, it is actually quite simple. Successively smaller circles of parabolic arches have been placed atop one another, building up to the climax of the central cross. Each tier defines a distinct area within the church. The lowest encloses side chapels and a continuous corridor that allows direct access to any part of the congregational seating. The middle tier defines the nave. The topmost tier is a "lantern" skylight, directly over the central altar, proclaiming its primacy even at the exterior of the church. On the interior, this device concentrates a shaft of descending sunlight upon the sacred table.

In addition to the central skylight, the open arches of the parabolas are to be enclosed throughout with stained glass, punctuating an otherwise white interior with inserts of luminous color. These will cast changing reflections upon the repetitive concrete vaulting, bringing the entire church into glowing life.

The plan enclosed by this soaring concrete and glass shell is one of the most successful expressions of the Liturgical Revival to be found in any contemporary church. The encirclement of a central altar by congregation and choir is the simplest and most logical answer to the requirement that all worshippers be brought into intimate communion, close to the celebrant. Here, no one is more than six pews removed from the sanctuary. This design, similar in arrangement to the tiny Chapel of St. James (No. 22), illustrates the practicality of circular seating in a much larger church.

Such a scheme also has other benefits. The central placement of the altar expresses its centrality to the act of worship, further emphasized by the successive rise of ceiling height to the soaring apex directly above it. In this way the focus, both inward and upward, is upon the altar. The placement of the exterior cross directly over the altar adds the final touch to a climactic symbolism.

The aptness of this design is not limited to liturgical expression, however. Its openness, delicacy, and flower-like form make this church a part of its garden setting and a part of the southern region in which it stands.

In describing this design, the architects stress that they were under no obligation to do anything startling or "different" when they designed this church. But they add that from the outset the monks made it clear that their own traditions compelled them to demand the very best in a project intended to have real religious significance. "As we studied the building and the program, the design evolved from our deepening awareness of the needs of this particular church. The church is designed as it is, not because we wished to be daring, but rather because it came to seem to us the only way for this church to be."

Church interior, as developed experimentally in the model, indicates the possibilities for decorative stained glass windows, contrasting with the unadorned sweep of parabolic arches that frame them. The bays formed by the arches will be used for 20 private chapels, separated from the main nave by the continuous corridor, which serves both outer and inner areas. A perforated metal screen may be used to partially shield the chapels from corridor traffic. This photograph also shows how a vertical divider separates two altars, set back to back, creating two chapels in each bay. This leaves 10 of the 20 bays free for other uses, including those of baptistry, confessionals, sacristy, and entrances.

The cost of this church is estimated at $500,000, or $20 per square foot. It contains a total of 22,300 sq. ft., including both first floor and basement.

View looking into the nave, toward the altar, along the major axis of the church. The focus of the entire plan and structure upon the sanctuary is here clearly visible. All aisles, from whatever direction, lead straight to the altar. The ascending curves of the parabolic arches and their tiers of stained glass windows build up to the great central skylight above the altar.

Because of the simplicity of the church structure, the architects feel that it presents an unusual opportunity for enrichment by works of art. In addition to stained glass and metallic screening — the latter to enclose the nave as well as the periphery chapels — they expect to incorporate painting, sculpture, mosaic, and tapestry in appropriate places.

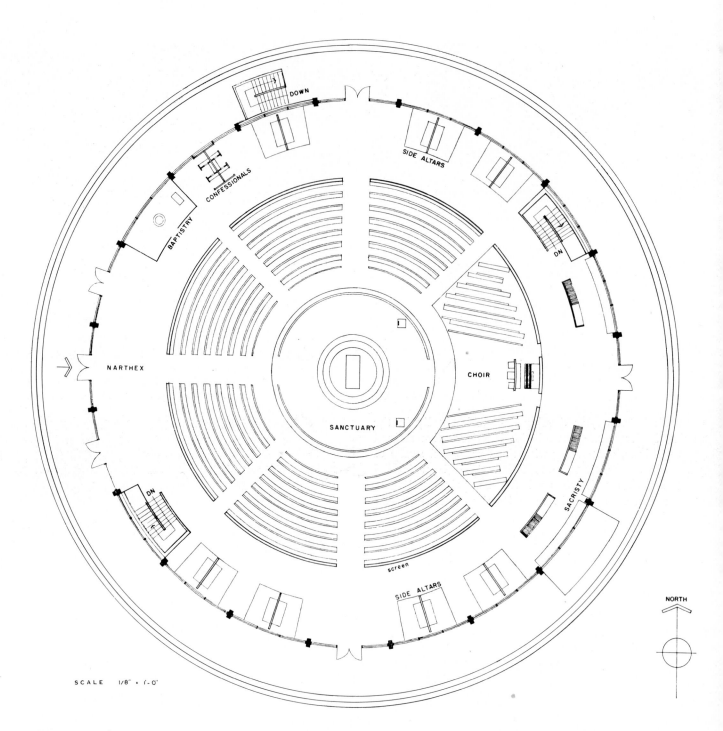

SCALE   1/8" = 1'-0"

Plan shows congregation disposed in six equal banks about the altar, with the choir in two sections facing each other. This comparatively small nave seats 600, of which 100 seats are for the monastic choristers and 500 for the congregation, composed mainly of boys from the two schools that the priory will maintain.

For convenient access to any part of this circular plan, there are three subsidiary entrances, two leading directly to side aisles in the nave, one giving access to the choir. The fourth and main entrance, leading in from the plaza approach, has been made the central axis of the plan. It consists of three portals in separate bays. The center portal opens directly toward a major aisle, facing the front of the altar and on a line with the bishop's throne. Most round churches suffer from the lack of a central axis, so fundamental to Catholic liturgy, but here this problem has been admirably resolved.

It should be emphasized that this plan is integral to the total design of the church. Although it represents the simplest and most forthright embodiment of the aims of the Liturgical Revival, these can also be expressed by other plans. A circular church of such flower-like delicacy would be inappropriate to many settings. And the finest architecture includes always the surrounding environment as governing factor in design.

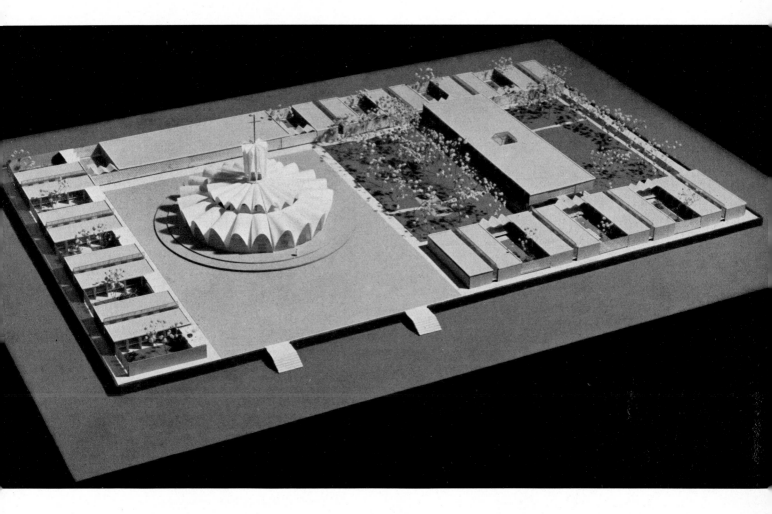

Air view of model shows the church as it is related to surrounding structures. This is the monastic enclosure, including living quarters for all members of the order, as well as library and administration buildings.

In the plan for St. John, these elements are concentrated in close relationship to the church and are connected to it by enclosed passages. That solution, at least in part, is a response to the rigors of the Minnesota climate. Here, a plan of "cottage dormitories," interlaced with courts and gardens, is a superior solution.

Note also that subsidiary buildings, as they face on private courts, are glass enclosed to take full advantage of the garden setting. All have been given flat roofs, so as not to detract from the drama of the curvilinear church.

The largest of the subsidiary structures combines library and living quarters for the teaching monks, flanked on either side by the main gardens. Living quarters for clerics, serving their novitiate, and for the lay brethren, are contained in the group of buildings at lower right. A similar grouping at upper right contains housing for retired monks, calefactory, and infirmary. At left, separated from private monastic grounds by the church, are guest houses and administrative offices. The long, one-story structure directly behind the church is the communal dining hall. A continuous, perforated fence shuts off all except the large monks' building from plaza view. In this way, the church, although conveniently near to all, stands alone and dominant within the open plaza.

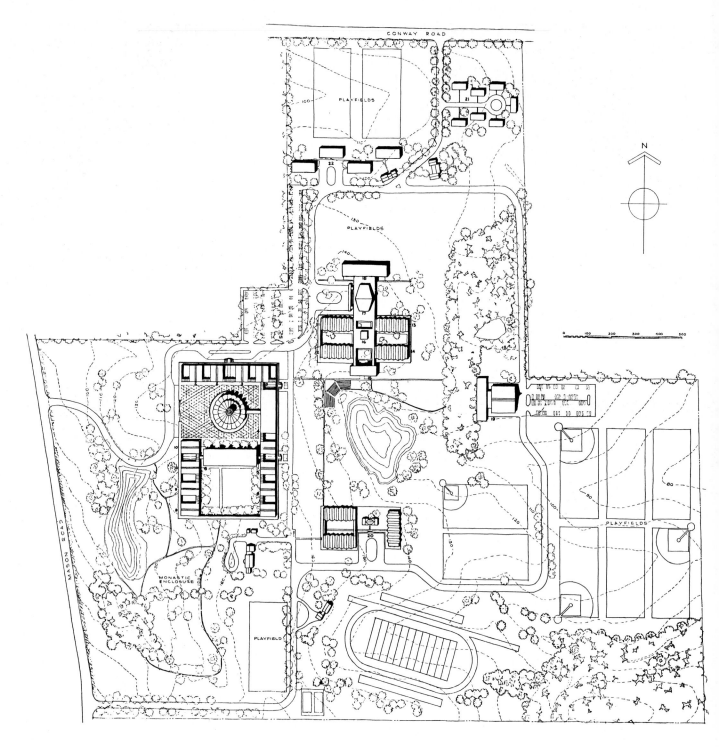

Ground plan of entire monastery shows relationship between the monastic enclosure and the two boys' schools that are to be maintained by the priory. The elementary school is to the south, the larger, preparatory school to the north, with boys' dormitories and housing for the lay faculty at the northernmost part of the plan. The two schools are located near the monastic enclosure for easy access to the church, by the students, and to classrooms, by the teaching monks. A common gymnasium is conveniently located to the east of the two schools.

This is a beautiful, rolling, wooded site, and its natural features have been skillfully exploited as part of the total design. The church occupies the highest ground and the schools are located on two other gently rising slopes, overlooking the lake. This design creates a central lakeside court, toward which all school buildings are oriented. At the northwest corner of this lake, a small open auditorium has been planned for outdoor concerts and services.

1. church
2. guests
3. administration
4. refectory
5. elder monks
6. calefactory
7. infirmary
8. library and monastery
8. novitiate
10. lay brethern
    Upper school
11. classrooms
12. classrooms
13. classrooms
14. science classrooms
15. library
16. administration and
    multipurpose rooms
17. auditorium
18. music, art, and shops
19. gymnasium
20. lower school
21. faculty housing
22. dormitories

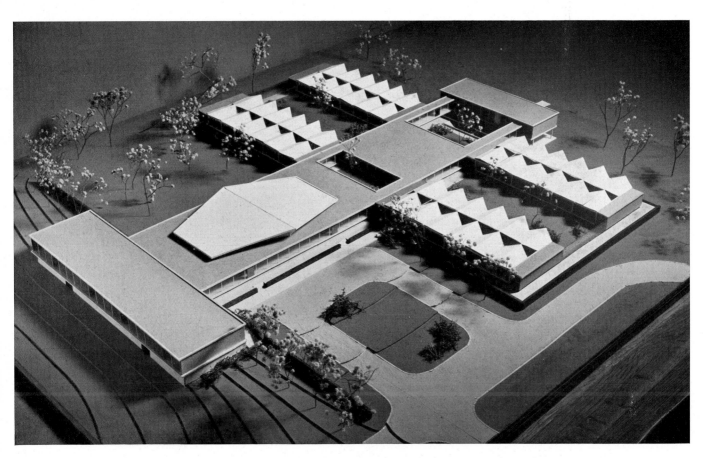

Preparatory school of St. Louis Priory is one of the finest educational designs to be found in the country. One example of its excellence is the separation of noisy and quiet areas by means of a many-winged plan. At one end of the central element, as seen in left foreground, is the music and art wing, including also workshops. Next is the hexagonal auditorium, its shape defined on the exterior by a raised roof. Administrative offices, opening on two inner courts, follow. At the far end, away from all noise, is the library, also opening upon one of the inner courts.

Classrooms extend in four wings from the central element, convenient to library, offices, and auditorium — and yet at the same time isolated from them. Each wing contains two parallel rows of rooms with a central corridor between. These are small rooms designed to accomodate no more than 10 to 15 students, seated about a table with their teacher. Such a scheme is based on a modified version of the English tutorial system that emphasizes individual instruction. Here groups of students are taught together, but classes are kept small and are organized as discussions, rather than as formal lectures.

In order to break the cell-like atmosphere of the necessarily small rooms, each has been given a pitched roof — actually two repetitive pleated shells of reinforced concrete that extend the length of the wing. In addition, each row of classrooms is glass-enclosed at its outer wall, facing planted courts. Where folded classroom roofs meet over the central corridors, they have been opened up with glass, thus providing excellent skylight illumination for otherwise windowless inner passages.

Gymnasium also separates its functions into two distinct building elements. The taller building is the sports center itself, simply one large, open room. The low building at front contains locker rooms and offices, connected to the main gymnasium by a short, enclosed passage. This is a more convenient arrangement than basement lockers and provides also pleasant above-ground space for offices without complicating the design of the sports hall. Except for small, high strip windows, the gymnasium hall is lighted entirely by a central skylight — actually a continuation of the steel truss roof construction, here sheathed in glass.

Reference

Cary-Elwes, Dom Columba. "Planning a Monastery and Monastic Schools," *Liturgical Arts*, February 1958.

38. PRIORY OF ST. GREGORY THE GREAT

For the Order of St. Benedict, Portsmouth, R.I.
Erected 1948—1961
Pietro Belluschi (b. 1899), and Anderson, Beckwith &
Haible, associated architects
Lawrence B. Anderson (b. 1906)
Herbert Lynes Beckwith (b. 1903)
William Egler Haible (b. 1914)
Severud, Elstad, Krueger, structural engineers
Bolt, Beranek & Newman, acoustical consultants
Richard Lippold, sculptor

"And now that most of the battles against dogmas have been won, I hope architects may also gain a certain amount of tolerance for all the human symbols and forms of the past, because people need them and live by them to a greater extent than is realized, because they furnish a feeling of continuity which gives them faith in their evolution." — PIETRO BELLUSCHI

In the church for the monastery and school of St. Gregory the Great, Portsmouth, R.I., Pietro Belluschi illustrates once more his rare ability to transmute the symbols of an ancient heritage into modern terms. The two monastery churches that precede it are clear statements of religious life in the twentieth century, belonging to this age alone. The Portsmouth priory spans the centuries, at once a reminder of the roots of the Benedictine Order and a proclamation that its visible flowering is in the vital present.

The precedent for the plan, its tower, and great arched ceiling, passes over the Baroque, Renaissance, Gothic, and Romanesque traditions to two octagonal churches of the early sixth century built in the cities of Ravenna and Milan. The *Portsmouth Bulletin* explained:

"Lacking the evidence, we may draw no conclusions; but had Benedict, in his younger days, visited (as is not improbable) either of these ancient Italian cities, he could have seen a church shaped fundamentally along the lines of that presently to arise in Portsmouth. It is not, then, entirely fanciful to think of the father of western monasticism — who, of course, could never have dreamt of a church in the colonial style, to whom Gothic (even the genuine Medieval, as distinct from the fake Victorian) was unknown — feeling himself architecturally, as well as (we hope) spiritually, at home at the future Portsmouth Priory."

The Benedictine community responsible for erecting this church is a comparatively small and new one, founded in 1918 as a dependency of the English congregation of Black Monks at Downside Abbey, and later taken over by a Scottish monastery. Independence was achieved only eleven years ago, in 1949. The present community is composed of 32 monks, all Americans, who conduct a preparatory school for approximately 200 boys, assisted by lay masters. In addition, the monastery operates a sheep and dairy farm.

Prior Aelred Graham, the author of several books, has been characterized by the architect as "a man of unusual intellectual powers, who carries on the Benedictine tradition with great brilliance." He is also a man who exhibits refreshing humility in matters beyond his field. Reporting on a decision to submit the plans for the new church to an outside architectural expert, Prior Graham explained in the *Portsmouth Bulletin*:

Modern Benedictines, it might well be argued, are no better equipped than their fellow clergy to pronounce on the merits of a piece of architecture. Clerical training, let it be honestly admitted, is not much concerned with cultivating a sense of the beautiful. Sound esthetic judgment, in fact, is hardly the most desirable quality to be looked for in a priest. But the limitations of ecclesiastics in this matter should be frankly acknowledged — the average member of the clergy has no more title to be listened to when he praises, than when he condemns, a work of art. His competence lies in other fields of human endeavor.... Awareness of this fact was what led to the designs for Portsmouth priory's permanent church being submitted to the appraisal of a competent lay expert.... Mr. John Walker...Director of the National Gallery of Art in Washington, D.C.

The following is an excerpt from Director Walker's reply to Prior Graham:

First let me congratulate you on the selection of Professor Belluschi for this project.... In my opinion he has provided you with the scheme for an ideal modern church.... Belluschi has retained the tradinional features of Christian churches, such as steeple, stained glass, and bell tower. These he has used in an original and perceptive manner. Like the great architects of the past,

he has derived inspiration from antecedent buildings. He has adapted, in his own way, the central type plan of church, a plan to be found in so many Medieval baptistries. The central type plan always affords a particularly close contact between altar and congregation.

In addition to its links with the past emphasized above, the new church, like all designs by Belluschi, is closely related to its region and immediate environment. The use of wood and native fieldstone links it to other monastery buildings, which are mainly modest farm structures. School buildings designed by the outstanding Boston architectural firm of Anderson, Beckwith & Haible, before Belluschi entered the picture, are simple wooden structures also conforming to the rural character of barns and workshops.

It is a commentary upon the skill of the collaborating architects that the church and monastic wing — although remaining in perfect key with the rural buildings — achieve an elegance and quiet authority unsurpassed among modern monastic designs. The church, especially, is of such height and presence that it dominates the entire monastery, asserting itself as the focal point of the community.

Main entrance to the priory church shows it set on high ground against the backdrop of connecting monastic wing and a farther hillside, topped by a distant cross. The approach is up an open, gently rising plaza, which separates church and monastic quarters from school and farm buildings on lower ground.

The church plan consists of two superimposed octagons, the lower containing nave, sanctuary, and periphery chapels, the upper forming a gallery and tower above the central parts. In this way a sense of soaring verticality is achieved over nave and sanctuary. The design is topped by a slender spire and crowned by a cross. A central lantern skylight of brilliant stained glass forms the lowest portion of the spire, directing light downward into the center of the nave.

The walls of the lower octagon are mainly of stone, set in separate, convex slabs. These stone slabs are interspersed with smaller concave panels of redwood board and battens, joined to the stone by narrow, vertical "lancet" windows of gray cathedral glass. By contrast, the tower walls consist entirely of a delicate latticework of redwood board and battens inset with colored glass. Roofs are surfaced with sheet copper.

The stone used in the lower walls of the church is a local Rhode Island fieldstone similar to slate in texture and color. Redwood in all areas is creosoted a dark brown. Thus, the subtle coloring of the church combines the deep slate-gray of stone and the rich brown of redwood with the lovely blue-green verdigris of weathered copper. The monastic wing in the background repeats the same stone and wood used in the church.

The structural system of the church is similar to that of the Lutheran and Episcopal designs by Belluschi (No. 19 and 23). The tower is supported by a rigid frame of laminated hardwood arches, fully exposed on

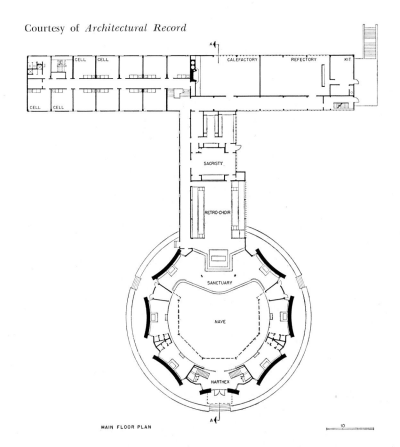

MAIN FLOOR PLAN

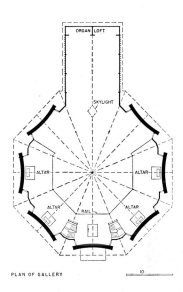

PLAN OF GALLERY

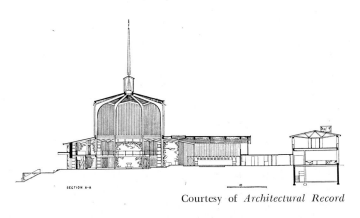

SECTION A-A

the interior, but visible here only in part as they project to frame the tower wall sections. On the interior, these arches extend outward and downward in a continuous sweep from the apex of the tower to ground level, supporting the inner edge of the gallery and defining the continuous side aisle that nearly encircles the nave.

The lower portion of the church is similarly supported by a series of rigid, laminated arches, descending outside the wall enclosure and entirely free of it, as indicated in the exterior view opposite. This system of supporting frame and curtain walls, clearly defined as separate elements, marks this church as a structure that could have been built only in the twentieth century. It is an honest expression of contemporary building techniques, which at the same time makes use of the ageless symbols of tower and arch to create a church at once traditional and modern.

The choice of the octagon as the basic figure of this church stems, in part, from the monastic need for numerous private chapels. Main and upper floor plans show how side altars are disposed around the nave and in the encircling gallery overhead, always against the great stone wall slabs. Confessionals and stairways occupy smaller bays behind the redwood partitions.

In addition, the octagon is capable of providing that closeness between all participating worshippers that is fundamental to a revitalized Catholic liturgy. The simple, circular arrangement of seating, focused upon a central altar is, however, inappropriate to this church. The St. Louis priory, which made such commendable use of the circular arrangement, was a freestanding structure, unconnected to the living quarters of the monks. Here, with the cold New England winter and the driving rains typical of this coastal region, enclosed passage between monastic wing and church is a necessity. In addition, the monks requested a certain privacy for their choir, as opposed to the St. Louis plan which makes the choir a part of the congregational circle, entirely open and exposed.

For these reasons, the congregation has been disposed throughout the octagon, with sanctuary at the wall line. Behind the altar, yet open to it, and to the nave, is the retro-choir, which extends out from the main encirclement of the octagon, in a link with the monastic wing. With this arrangement, choir and congregation are still grouped about a central altar, even though the choir occupies a physically separate, and more private space. During the daily chanting of divine offices, monks are alone in the church. Yet in the small retro-choir they are not oppressed by the unoccupied nave.

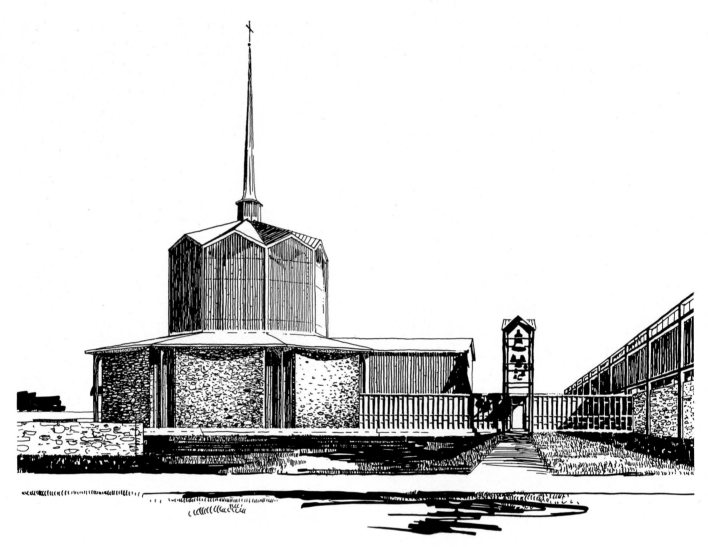

Side view of church shows it linked to rear monastic wing by means of the retro-choir. Sacristies and robing rooms are also contained in this passage. In order to bring the church up to a level with the monastic building, on slightly higher ground, it is placed upon a circular stone platform that serves also as an exterior walk.

The bell tower, which is little more than an open wooden frame, forms a portal to the side entrance of the sacristy. It is located functionally at the rear of the church, rather than symbolically at front, as its purpose is to call the monks to their canonical duties. However, it is an important element in the design, breaking its sweeping horizontals with a decorative, vertical punctuation — a smaller echo of the lines of the church tower and of its pleated copper roof.

This view reveals also the exquisite care with which the designs of church and living quarters have been integrated. Each has lower walls of the same fieldstone, upper walls of redwood. Narrow, horizontal windows in the monastic wing repeat, at large scale and in an opposing plane, the narrow, vertical windows in the lower portion of the church.

Joseph W. Molitor

Interior views, looking toward the altar, suggest the sweep of ascendant space that characterizes the new church. This sweep is powerfully defined by the great, exposed framing members that soar straight upward, commencing their inward curve only at the roof of the tower. Two strong horizontal bands — at the gallery and also at the juncture of lower church and tower — visually tie the arches into a continuous framework.

The convex curves of the stone wall slabs, enclosing the lower portion of the church, act as a counterpoint to the inward sloping curves of the arches. However, this shape was actually dictated by acoustical considerations. It prevents the usual reverberation between hard surfaces when these face each other in a flat plane.

The materials of the church are essentially the same, inside and out. Stone walls are left exposed. Tower walls are of redwood board and batten with stained glass inserts, set in redwood frames. Ceilings — above the gallery and atop the tower — are surfaced in cedar decking, with a natural wax finish. The far wall of the retro-choir, which acts as a backdrop for the altar, is covered with fabric in a texture and coloring sympathetic to adjoining areas of redwood and cedar.

Not seen is the central stained glass lantern, part of the exterior spire that together with the stained glass of the tower walls will pour a benison of colored light downward upon the nave. Another skylight is located directly over the altar. The tower skylight is the most brilliant, using nearly all available colors in purest hue; the altar skylight is a pale, muted version of the colors used in the tower. Vertical lancet windows in the walls of the nave are gray cathedral glass, providing elegant luminosity, without distracting from the more important concentrations of color. Stained glass represents the only brilliant color in the church, which otherwise offers a subtle harmony of natural grays and browns.

One of the most beautiful features of the interior is barely visible in this photograph. It is an altar "sculpture" consisting solely of taut wires of stainless steel and pure gold, and described in the *Portsmouth Bulletin* as follows:

Inspired by the symbolism of the Holy Trinity, Mr. Lippold's sculptural design is distinctive in that it is expressed through the medium of light rather than masses. A triangle of fine silver beams descends from a skylight in the roof of the sanctuary, the triangle's apex terminating at the foot of the large crucifix immediately above the altar. From the head and hands of the Corpus, beams of gold radiate back into the choir, out to the sides of the sanctuary, and high into the nave of the church itself. All this is achieved by wires...of minutely small gauge, so that the brilliance is concentrated at the crucifix and dispersed as it moves outwards and upwards from this focal point.

Belluschi had added of this design: *All of us here are very excited about the possibilities and if it turns out as well as we believe, it will be one of the outstanding modern sculptures on the American scene. It is an unusual transcendant concept, with the weightless quality of light — a web of golden light proceding from and leading to the Corpus.*

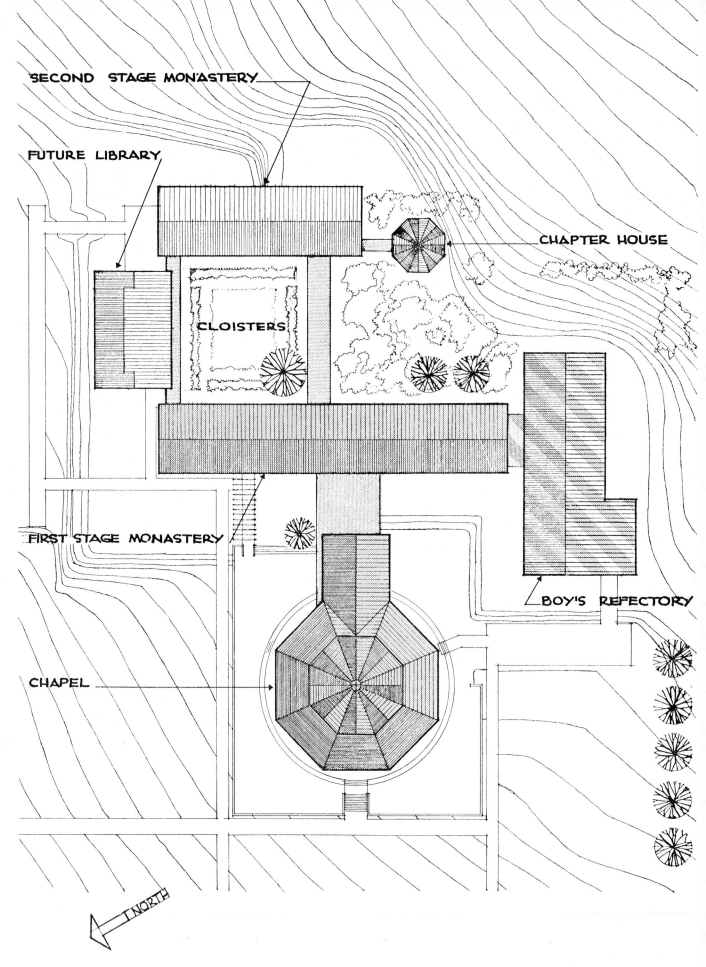

SECOND STAGE MONASTERY

FUTURE LIBRARY

CHAPTER HOUSE

CLOISTERS

FIRST STAGE MONASTERY

BOY'S REFECTORY

CHAPEL

NORTH

Ground plan of church and monastery shows its eventual development with cloisters, library, a second monastic wing, chapter house, and refectory, or communal dining hall for the schoolboys. The chapter house will repeat at small scale the octagonal shape of the church. Cloister gardens, completely enclosed, will provide an area of private meditation belonging to the monks alone. Footpaths connect the various elements and lead also to school and farm buildings on lower ground, dropping away from the front of the church.

Richard Garrison

Gymnasium, designed by Anderson, Beckwith & Haible, with Harkness & Geddes, associated architects, shows the distinguished character that can be achieved with the simplest of materials. A frame of steel I-beams, exposed on the interior, and of steel roof trusses, also exposed, allow easy spanning of the great open sports hall. Basement walls are of cinder block. Above the basement level — containing locker and shower rooms — the main hall of the gymnasium is enclosed with vertical tongue-and-groove wood siding.

An immense window extends the entire length of the hall at either side. Sun control is provided by vertical wooden louvers that create an interesting textural pattern on the exterior.

The framework of the building is exposed on the interior, except along the lower portion of the gymnasium wall, where a plywood dado functions as backboard. This also contains warm air grilles and conceals unit heaters that have been set within the wall. The connecting one-story element contains lobby, a classroom, and storage space.

This building, which has much of the character of a large barn, has been consciously designed to harmonize with existing farm structures. At the same time its masterly handling of windows and its clean, crisp detailing make it an outstanding piece of modern architecture. Erected in 1948, it is typical of subsequent school buildings designed by Anderson, Beckwith & Haible for the monastery. It cost $181,444 and contains a floor area of 14,732 sq. ft.

References

"Church and Monastery for Portsmouth Priory," *Architectural Record,* July 1959.
The Portsmouth Bulletin. Fall 1957 and Fall 1958.

39. CONCORDIA SENIOR COLLEGE

For the, Lutheran Church, Missouri Synod
Fort Wayne, Ind.; Erected 1957
Eero Saarinen (1910-1961) & Associates, architects
Dan Kiley, landscape architect

Pach Bros.

"From the beginning, our common concern was the creation of an architecture which would support and express the idea of the college." — EERO SAARINEN

The late Eero Saarinen, brilliant son of a brilliant father, was one of the most versatile architects practicing in America. Because of his overriding concern with the appropriate architecture for the job at hand, a sampling of his designs gives the impression that they were executed by a half dozen different architects, each a master of his particular technique. There is no such thing as a recognizable Saarinen style.

His daring and fluid uses of reinforced concrete in the TWA terminal building for Idlewild Airport and the skating rink for Yale University placed him at the forefront of experimental engineering, along with Pier Luigi Nervi and Felix Candela. His General Motors Technical Center, executed in the precise idiom of steel frame and glass curtain wall, rivaled the discipline of Mies van der Rohe. His Milwaukee War Memorial, with its blocky form, jutting cantilever, and bold separation of frame and enclosure, could have been designed by Marcel Breuer. In the peak-roofed buildings for Concordia Senior College, shown here, Saarinen also revealed the influence of the peasant architecture of Northern Europe, especially of Germany and Finland (the latter the country of his birth, where he lived until he was thirteen).

Like Belluschi in the Portsmouth priory, Saarinen here translated a plan and form evocative of the client's heritage into modern structure and usage. The Missouri Synod of the Lutheran Church was established by German immigrants, and it was from an old drawing of the early North German village of Aichbuehl that Saarinen took his inspiration. Its region has a counterpart in the flat lands of northeastern Indiana, the site of the new college. Because the sharply pitched roofline of the primitive Aichbuehl houses has persisted as a building shape in village architecture, not merely in Germany, but also in Scandinavia, its use here reflects several sources of the Lutheran cultural heritage.

The Concordia Senior College, an entirely new institution, was established concurrently with its building program. It has been in operation only since 1957, when the campus shown here was nearly completed. As a training ground for pretheological students, Concordia College closes the gap between the Missouri Synod's nine junior colleges and its Concordia Theological Seminary in St. Louis. The new campus consists of 25 college buildings, plus housing for 450 students and a faculty of approximately 30. Classrooms, dormitories, library, dining hall, and indeed all elements subsidiary to the church, have been housed in separate buildings, rather than concentrated in large institutional structures, creating the desired village atmosphere. Saarinen said of this design:

The strategic question was the relation of the buildings to the world. On the one hand, we all felt that they should not be inward-turning and removed like Medieval monasteries; but, on the other hand, we felt the group must — for its purpose — have a tranquil atmosphere of at least partial self-sufficiency. The solution seemed to lie in the village concept: a group of buildings that would have a quiet, unified environment into which the students could withdraw to find a complete, balanced life and yet one that is related to the outside world . . . .

The pitched roof seemed to give the right architectural expression to the whole complex . . . . By using it on all the buildings, the group was united in one spirit. By making the pitch of the roofs on the other buildings lower than on the chapel, the lesser buildings seemed to rise up toward the most significant one. Since the group of buildings will be seen not only from within, but across the fields as well, the silhouette of the whole was an important consideration . . . .

We tried to make each building fulfill its functional requirements and to express its special purpose, but also to fit gracefully into a harmonious whole by the site-planning and the consistent use of whitewashed brick walls and black-tiled pitch roofs . . . [rising] strong against the white sky.

Robert L. Bastress

Air view of Concordia Senior College shows it set down upon the flat Indiana countryside, overlooking an artificial lake. It occupies a 191-acre site that at present is almost barren of vegetation. In the future, lavish planting will soften the buildings, eliminating the barracks-like quality of the design as shown here, immediately after construction. Currently, its appearance is comparable to that of the stark, white, box-like houses of a New England village if their giant elms and other shade trees and shrubbery were suddenly removed. Trees, however, would effectively obscure an air view of the buildings, here visible in their masterly disposition.

The church faces the lake on a slight rise, giving it dominance over surrounding structures. The major college buildings are close to the church and are distinguished from dormitories and faculty housing by their black tile roofs. Most are grouped around an open, two-level plaza commanded by the church.

Immediately to the right of the church is the library, with connecting health center barely visible behind the church. Adjacent to the church at left rear is the dining hall, and to its left the smaller student commons. At the left of the entire building group, and connected to the commons by a sheltered outdoor walk, is the auditorium. Behind the walk, and set slightly apart from the main building group, is the gymnasium. A small administration building is at the front of the church, immediately adjacent to the lake. To the left,

and connected by a sheltered walkway, is the long classroom building, from which branches a wing at left containing faculty offices. Dormitories are scattered at the periphery of the plan in four main groups, two of which are visible here. Faculty housing and the president's residence are out of view in right foreground.

This view is toward the main approach to the theological village, served by Martin Luther Drive. The road turns back on itself to skirt the main campus at left and rear. Because cars are excluded from the educational part of the campus, spacious parking lots have been provided at front and rear. Pedestrian entrance to the village, at front, is beneath the roof of the walkway that connects administration and classroom buildings. With this arrangement, the visitor and prospective student can be interviewed or ask directions in the administration building before entering the campus proper. Farther on, steps lead up to the main plaza, giving access to either church or educational structures.

This site plan is in striking contrast to those of the Roman Catholic monasteries shown previously. There, church and monastic living quarters are closely associated and in turn, both are separated from school and other working structures. In those plans, also, only a portion of the grounds is open to the general public.

The cost of the entire building group as shown here was $ 7 million, a modest amount for a whole campus. The church, which seats 600, cost $ 600,800.

Alexandre Georges

View of church and bell tower reflected in the artificial lake, with administration building to the left, directly on the water. Whitewashed brick walls and black tile roofs impart an Old World peasant quality to buildings that are contemporary in structure, window treatment, and interior planning. Structures flanking the church are (right) library and (left) dining hall.

Alexandre Georges

Church as seen from the lower plaza stands starkly silhouetted against the sky. A central skylight runs the full length of the nave. Altar lighting is provided by a similar window strip set flush into the roof and running down from peak to eave. It is placed on the opposite side of the church and is not visible here.

The structure of the church amalgamates roof and walls into one element, forming the unbroken triangle of aspiration. It is composed of bricks that brace each other at top and are supported at bottom by concrete piers. This form can be executed in a variety of materials. Its economy of construction and the ease by which it creates an open interior, free of supporting columns, has made it one of the most popular of modern church designs. There is an outstanding modern church of this type in Salla, Finland, one in Cedar Hills, Ore., one in Florissant, Mo. (the latter two of wood), and other versions too numerous to mention.

However, the alluring simplicity of this form and structure can lead to inappropriate uses. Denominations other than the Lutheran should think twice before adopting this design so evocative of a specific cultural heritage. In addition, it does not fit easily into the environment of the American city. It is therefore most appropriately used in rural surroundings or with its own harmonious building group as shown here.

The nave is mysteriously illuminated by reflections of light from the skylight at top and from the lower wall apertures, obscured by piers. For night services, or overcast days, artificial illumination creates a similar effect from the same sources. This night view shows the altar spotlighted from above. During the day the chancel is flooded with a soft radiance from the great, vertical, louvered window, shown in the close view.

The side walls are surfaced with plaster. The dia-mond-shaped brick of the end walls is exposed, forming a quiet textural backdrop for the chancel. Liturgical furnishings are held to subdued simplicity: an unadorned block of marble for the altar, and communion rails of natural wood. The effect of this interior is one of utter serenity. The architect has written:

We realized that light is an effective agent in creating a spiritual atmosphere. We used very low lighting from above to get the restful, balanced quality we sought.

By placing additional windows so that they would high-light the altar, we were able to emphasize this focal point. We wanted to work with the simple chapel shape appropriate to the Lutheran Church and to create an interior in which the relationship of human beings to enclosed space would be appropriate and inspiring. The problem was also to find a shape and the materials which would allow the spoken word to be clearly heard and also one in which the organ could swell to its full-est. We believe the high interior of the chapel has an-swered these requirements.

The chapel justifies the reasoning behind the Mis-souri Synod's habitual choice of modern architecture. As stated by Martin J. Neeb, President of Concordia Senior College, modern architecture has been purposely adopted "to stimulate ministerial students to relate their work to the present, and to undertake new and daring things for God."

Alexandre Georges

Detail of lower wall of church shows supporting piers, between which glass is set, casting light upward into the nave. This view also shows clearly the unusual, freestanding bell tower, which is at once an echo and a contrast to the church itself. A white frame and dark tile enclosure repeat the materials of the larger structure. The narrow, pointed shape repeats in even sharper form the peak of the church roof. At the same time the tower stands as a vertical, swiftly ascending element, making the slope of the church appear almost gentle by contrast. Bells, not yet installed, will eventually be suspended within the tower framework, immediately below the tiled upper portion.

Beyond the church is the student dining hall, one of the several buildings in which floor-to-ceiling windows alternate with pierced concrete screens, painted white. A view of the interior of the dining hall is shown at top right, on the facing page.

Student dining hall uses its high central space under the peaked roof for balcony seating, with the serving line of the cafeteria beneath. This is one of the most refreshing designs for communal dining to be found on any college campus. The supporting frame of the building is exposed and clearly separated from enclosing walls and roof. Painted white against a ceiling of dark-stained wood, it becomes the most important decorative element in the design. White chandeliers add delicate punctuation, also an integral part of the interior effect. The natural wood used in partitions and also in tables and chairs, provides a medium contrast to the dark-stained ceiling and white structural frame. This design, executed in the simplest of materials, cost no more than the barracks-like halls usually provided for college students. It proves once more that taste and artistry in building cannot be measured by dollars expended, but rather by the talent of the superior architect, applied to any problem.

Student commons is similar, on both exterior and interior, to the adjacent dining hall. Here the decorative effect of the pierced masonry screening is seen from within the building. As in the dining hall, white walls and framing members contrast with dark-stained wood ceilings. Suspended lighting fixtures, also white, concentrate light on the seating area.

This main lounge is designed around a handsome, freestanding fireplace of steel and plaster. Part of its hood and flue are visible at left. The judicious use of modern paintings against bare, whitewashed brick walls adds small concentrations of color and pattern to the room. Its major charm, however, lies in the tracery of light and shadow etched by the diamond-shaped screens, and in its play of white against dark wood. There is a certain peasant character about these buildings, even on the interior, that makes them most appealing. But this quality has been refined into a delicacy impossible to achieve by rustic methods of construction.

Alexandre Georges

Alexandre Georges

Alexandre Georges

View looking toward the side of the chapel shows it partially obscured by the library. In the background, the small health center, and beyond it the dining hall, present the optical illusion of one building. Side walls of these buildings are solid whitewashed brick, broken only by small floor-to-ceiling windows. Contrasting end walls, at front, are pierced concrete screens, as shown in the preceding photographs.

Student dormitories are in right foreground. Their side walls are identical to those of the educational buildings, but end walls repeat the small, diamond-patterned brick used at the front of the church. These dormitories are no larger than large houses, but they are based on an unusual plan of staggered floor levels. The middle section of each building, where its height under the pitched roof is greatest, contains three stories; the outer sections, under the eaves at either side, only two stories. These are at different levels from the floors of the inner section, but are connected to them by stairways.

All stories contain student bedrooms, providing a total in each dormitory of 18 double rooms, housing 36 students. In addition, part of the lowest floor in the middle section is a lounge with a large, open fireplace. The floor above contains a soundproofed study, impervious to noise from surrounding living quarters. As in the dining hall, Saarinen utilized the pitched roof to give added usable space to the interior. It thus becomes, not an affectation of design, but a functional element.

Alexandre Georges

Main reading room of library one of the buildings seen in exterior view opposite, shows white brick
side walls and screened front wall clearly exposed on the
interior. Unlike the dining hall and student commons,
wood ceilings here are painted white in order to reflect
light downward, providing the high level of illumination
required in a library.

Again, Eero Saarinen utilized the space under the
pitched roof for a balcony. Here are placed an office
and subsidiary reading rooms, with book stacks below
opening toward the main reading room. Seminar rooms
and a work room are also on the ground floor; storage
and a third reading room are in the basement.

Alexandre Georges

The long classroom building, which runs the length of the lower mall along the approach to the church, reverses the wall treatment of other educational structures. Here a side, rather than an end wall, is screened. providing excellent lighting for side corridors that give access to all classrooms on both upper and lower floors. One end wall of the building, facing away from the campus, is of solid brick; the other, opening toward the upper plaza, is entirely of glass.

Because of the rise in ground toward this upper plaza, the two-level classroom building appears to be a one-story structure when approached from that direction. Only the upper story is entirely above grade. The building can thus be entered at its second story from the upper plaza, with first-floor entrance at the lower mall as shown here.

Alexandre Georges

Speech room in the lower story of the classroom building as it faces toward the upper plaza has only high strip windows above grade. This room is designed on two levels, with a central table for performing students and teacher, surrounded by a horseshoe counter for observers. Both the beautiful wooden table and the counter were designed by the architect. Chairs are standard school design.

References

"Search for Form," *Progressive Architecture,* December 1958.

"A 'Village' Design for a College Campus," *Progressive Architecture,* December 1958.

40. GOLDEN GATE THEOLOGICAL SEMINARY

For the Southern Baptist Convention, San Francisco, Calif.
First phase of construction completed 1959
John Carl Warnecke (b. 1919), architect
Lawrence Livingston, Jr., planning consultant
Lawrence Halprin, landscape architect
John Blume, structural engineer
G. M. Simonson, mechanical and electrical engineer

Fabian Bachrach

"Respect for the existing terrain is a basic premise of the plan." — JOHN CARL WARNECKE

John Carl Warnecke was a student at the famed Graduate School of Design at Harvard when Walter Gropius was its director. He therefore belongs to that talented group of young modernists who came under the influence of the transplanted Bauhaus, and have since carried its philosophy into many of the outstanding architectural firms throughout America. Strongly evident in his work are the industrialized techniques of building, the honest use of materials according to their nature, and the clear revelation of structure, all part of Gropius' contribution to architectural education.

But, whereas these precepts tend to become cold and austere as expressed in the designs of some of Gropius' students, Warnecke's California background has tempered them with a regional warmth. He has never subscribed to the universalization of architecture, the postulate that underlay the development of the International Style. Instead, like Pietro Belluschi, he designs for the particular client, the particular site, and the particular region for and within which the problem must be resolved. His delicate white and gold U.S. Embassy Building in Bangkok, Thailand, for example, subtly echoes the curved rooflines, deep balconies, and grillwork of the native architecture of that country.

The Golden Gate Theological Seminary is equally indigenous to California. Here, among the wooded hills of Marin County, overlooking San Francisco Bay, Warnecke has produced a campus plan that takes full advantage of an irregular, rolling terrain, magnificent views, a benign climate, and characteristic local building materials. Generous use is made of native redwood and glass, buildings are everywhere interlaced with courts, gardens, and plazas, and the various parts of the seminary are grouped in informal clusters rising up to the climax of the church, atop the highest hill.

In the church itself, Warnecke has fully expressed the theological outlook of the Southern Baptist Convention, which stresses the unity of all believers under God, with a corresponding deemphasis of sectarian ritual and dogmatic theology. This approach is in direct contrast to the Lutheran Missouri Synod, which prides itself upon theological orthodoxy and a strong, sectarian tradition. It is interesting to note, therefore, that the same steeply pitched triangle so evocative of the Lutheran cultural heritage, has here been used in a way that entirely frees it from tradition. Instead, the design of the Golden Gate Chapel suggests the openness and universality that are fundamental to the Baptist denomination.

Golden Gate Church dominates the highest and most prominent hill within a rugged terrain, commanding unparalleled views on all sides. Unlike the Concordia Lutheran chapel (No. 39), which is one triangle, entirely enclosed except for skylights, the Golden Gate design is composed of four triangles, each widely opened to surrounding nature. As they oppose each other, looking outward in the four directions, these triangular faces symbolize the worldwide commitment of the Baptist denomination, and its outward reach toward all mankind. In addition, the lack of a single, dominant orientation emphasizes the Baptist lack of a ruling hierachy or an official creed, underscoring instead the democratic nature of its organization and the personal diversity within its faith.

Each of the soaring triangular roof canopies is to be entirely infilled with panes of glass, some stained to exploit the unusual opportunity for glowing color and play of light, some clear to permit views of surrounding nature. Once again, this design represents a symbolic solution. Unlike traditional churches, the stained glass is designed to be viewed from the outside, with internal lighting, as well as from within. To worshippers inside the church, the great ascending windows will admit the external world in the full glory of sunlight and open sky, with an overtracery of manmade color. To those on the outside, the illuminated windows will act as a spiritual beacon, a symbol of the force that gave the surrounding world its existence. The location of the church allows it to be seen from many points in the nearby bay area. It will therefore doubtless become a landmark, especially at night when it is a mosaic of brilliant color against the dark sky.

The structure of the building is simply a fourfold canopy of reinforced concrete, amalgamating in one continuous envelope the functions of support and enclosure. Glass curtain walls are set in a framework of steel mullions. Together, the design of roof vaulting and windows is intended as a single statement of the purposes and aspirations of the seminary.

Interior sketch of chapel shows the intersecting planes of concrete and glass as they create a vaulted canopy over the nave. This design fulfills to a remarkable degree the one-room concept put forward by the Liturgical Revival in Protestant as well as Roman Catholic thought. Partial screens will shield the nave from exterior view at either side and at the rear, demarking also side aisles and narthex. Another screen will act as a backdrop for the chancel. However, these in no way cut off the free flow of space throughout the interior and its sweep upward into the 100-ft. high ceiling vaults.

This large, open interior will seat 1,700 at capacity, with a choir of 100 to 200 ranged within the chancel behind the minister. The pulpit has been placed squarely in the center of the chancel and brought forward into close communion with the congregation. This placement emphasizes the centrality of the Word of God in the Baptist Church, and at the same time deemphasizes the ceremonies of baptism and the Lord's Supper, which are not considered sacramental.

In addition to regular services of worship and special Christmas and Easter ceremonies, this church will be used for commencement exercises and evangelistic conferences.

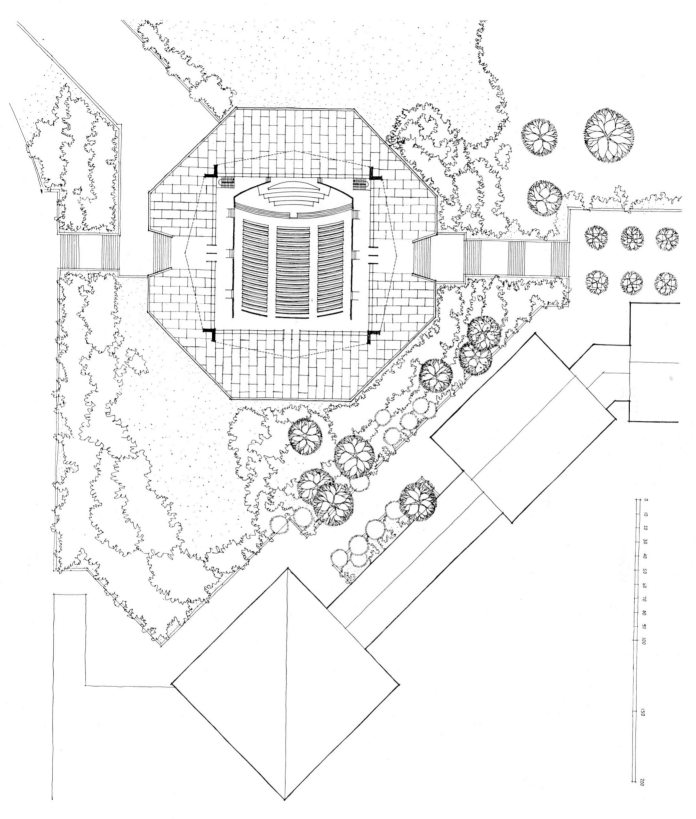

Plan shows the church placed on an elevated platform, reached by steps on opposing sides, and by a broad promenade leading off at an angle. The stairs at right connect with the central mall about which academic buildings are grouped. The two accessways at left lead to different parts of a large parking lot. Indicated in the foreground of this plan are the recital hall and the sacred music building, connected to each other by a narrow wing that contains music practice rooms.

A. Gerald Ratto

Model of the 126-acre campus shows the ridge lines of the hilly terrain, its heights, valleys, and plateaus. This is Strawberry Point, a peninsula of ancient sedimentary rock, rugged by nature, but softened by time, which juts into San Francisco Bay, commanding over-water views of both the city skyline and the nearby Marin hills. Seldom has such an inspiring setting been chosen for a theological seminary. In addition to the beauty of the hills and woods and water, the rise of the land contributes to the aspirational quality of the church that crowns its highest point. This location, near the cosmopolitan city of San Francisco and looking outward toward the Pacific Ocean, is particularly suited to the evangelical and missionary commitments that are to be a central part of the seminary curriculum.

As in the preceding Lutheran seminary, educational buildings are grouped close to the church, with housing in outlying areas, but here more distantly dispersed than in the Concordia campus. The church is close to the center of the irregularly shaped peninsula. To its right in this view is the central mall, flanked by administration and classroom buildings. Near the church and set out at an angle from the other classrooms are the school of sacred music and recital hall, joined by a narrow wing.

At the far end of the mall, facing the chapel, is the library. This building is the heart of the academic group, convenient to both teaching and living quarters, since the seminary intends to stress the research rather than the textbook method of instruction.

Immediately to the left of the library are the student union and cafeteria buildings, connecting with a pedestrian overpass that bridges a lower-level vehicular road. This overpass leads to the main residence halls for unmarried students. Other dormitories and apartment houses for both single and married students are clustered in "villages" on outlying parts of the site, some high in the hills, some directly on the bay, and all connected to the main educational group by contour-tracing roads, in-

dicated here in dark gray. This division of a large number of dwellings into several small groups produces the informal, neighborhood atmosphere requested for the campus. In this way also, each village can take advantage of a particular view or special feature of the terrain.

It is estimated that 20 per cent of the student body will be single men, 10 per cent single women, and a full 70 per cent married students. Because of the scarcity of nearby apartments at reasonable rentals, it will be necessary to house 60 per cent of the married students on the campus. Most of the housing will therefore consist of apartments and duplexes in comparatively small buildings. However, special care has been taken to diversify the size and character of housing so that each village can contain a cross section of the campus population, single as well as married. Faculty housing is in a separate village, and the president's residence occupies a site alone.

At a distance from the academic group, to the upper left of the chapel and adjoining the largest complex of residential villages, will be the main recreation area. This is situated on the largest level plot of ground within the site. Here, a gymnasium and swimming pool will be set against the hill, looking out over playfields and tennis courts. A large picnic area on the beach is also part of the campus plan.

Immediately to the left of the church in this view, and connected to it by a paved walk, is the major parking lot, terraced along the hillside and heavily screened from church view by trees. This central lot is designed primarily for those coming in from outside the seminary on business or to attend special events. It provides ready access to all major campus buildings. Student parking is provided in lots near each residential village and also near the main dormitories. In addition to automobile roads, the villages are linked to the educational buildings by footpaths and trails, because it is assumed that daily campus traffic will be mainly pedestrian.

View of chapel from the mall with classroom buildings at left, administration at right. This sketch shows the elevated position of the church, set upon a cantilevered platform atop rising ground, with a stairway leading up from the plaza. In conformity with the chapel, academic buildings will be concrete frame with light curtain walls of glass, wood, and prefabricated paneling. However, this sketch, which indicates mainly the disposition of buildings along the mall, shows little of the regional character of their architecture. All roofs will be surfaced in flat, interlocking mission tile, a terra cotta with a distinctive orange-pink cast. This is a native material with an important place in the Spanish architecture of California, and its use links the new buildings to their regional past. In combination with the deep brown of native redwood, the tile will impart a warm and informal character to the educational structures.

However, the classrooms themselves will not be small, as were those based on the tutorial system for the St. Louis Preparatory School (No. 37). This is a graduate seminary and instruction in the theological department will be mainly lecture and seminar courses with emphasis on practice preaching and research as a special training

for the pastorate. Rooms will accommodate from 50 to 200 students, the latter size being a special "activity room," modeled after a social hall in a Southern Baptist church. With a movable platform and adjacent dressing rooms, this room can be used as an assembly hall, conference, or lecture room, as well as large classroom for practice preaching.

All rooms, large or small, will contain audio-visual equipment, wall space for large maps, and generous blackboards. Even the large rooms will be so designed that all students are approximately equal distances from the teacher. Also part of the theological school will be a kitchenette, a model church office, arts and crafts room, and an audio-visual workshop.

Approximately 700 students will be enrolled in the main theological department. There will also be a department of religious education and a department of sacred music, representing facets of Baptist training for which this denomination is justly famous. An enrollment of 200 and 100 respectively is projected for these departments. Plans for the entire campus have been so executed that an initial enrollment of 1,000 can be expanded to an eventual total of 1,500.

Recital hall, across from the church, but on lower ground, repeats its triangular roofline in modified form. Here, reinforced concrete piers support the roof structure. Intervening wall areas are of glass. This hall will seat 622, with space for 75 to 100 people on the platform. It is to be equipped with a pipe organ, audio-visual equipment, and movable platform tiers for the *a capella chorus*. Adjoining it to the left is a wing containing practice rooms for music students. These are to be sound-insulated and mechanically ventilated, with large, fixed windows. In all, there are to be 23 such rooms.

The sacred music building, which is out of range at left, will contain four sound-insulated classrooms with piano, audio-visual equipment, and movable seating. It will also house a music library, listening booths, and studio offices for the staff. This large, well-planned and superbly equipped department is a testimony to the excellence of Baptist organ and choral music, which rivals the Lutheran and Episcopalian.

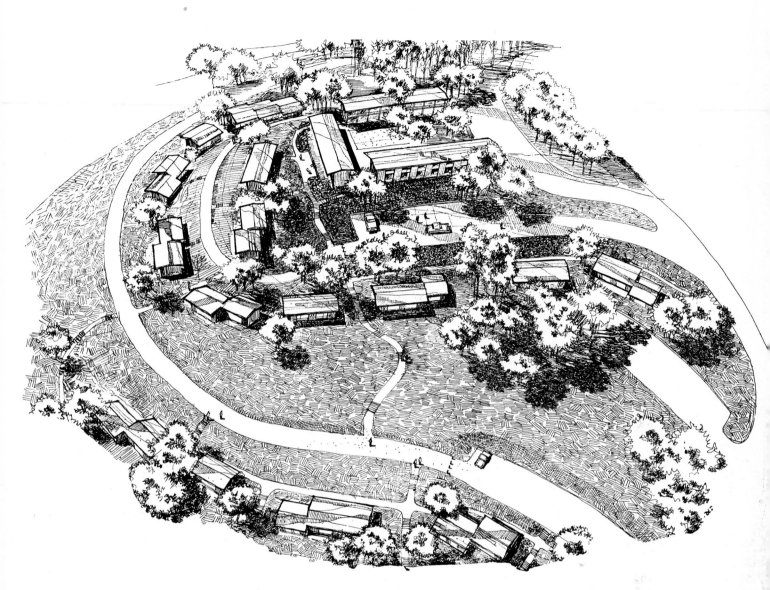

Bird's-eye sketch of one of the residential villages shows the pleasant, informal disposition of buildings, interlaced with courts, terraces, footpaths, and vehicular roads. Buildings are varied in size and interior layout, their range including single rooms for unmarried students, studio apartments for childless couples, one-bedroom apartments and duplexes for families of one or more children. The architect explains:

"As far as possible, each unit will contain a cross section of the campus population to insure a maximum variety of temperaments, backgrounds, and special interests. Such variety has a strong positive educational value, for it can enlarge viewpoints and encourage tolerance. Unmarried students learn and observe the joys and difficulties of family life. New brides can practice their cooking on unmarried colleagues. Baby-sitting services can be exchanged, and the social economy of a larger community is simulated in many details."

In addition to the social and educational advantages of small, flexible units, there is another sound reason for eliminating the large residence halls so common on other campuses. It was thought that each residence or apartment might be financed through the generosity of a single donor or group of donors.

View of one of the courts within a residential village shows how the central area has been developed as a playground. Kitchens face the court for easy supervision of children at play, but windows here are kept small to insure interior privacy. Large-windowed living rooms on the opposite side take advantage of panoramic views. Note also the ingenious balcony that joins the three separate buildings, allowing direct circulation between apartment houses at the upper level. Structure throughout is a simple wood frame enclosed by vertical siding or gypsum board.

Not shown in the preceding views of the campus is the religious education department, which will maintain a nursery and kindergarten for seminary children. These will give an added measure of freedom to student wives who could not otherwise afford to pay baby sitters. Simultaneously they will function as teaching laboratories for the religious education department which emphasizes child development as a fundamental part of training for Sunday school supervision.

The thoughtful planning for family living that dominates the entire design of this seminary has seldom, if ever, been equaled in a theological campus. It may well become the prototype plan for future graduate seminaries.

With this design, too, the evolution from the cloistered monastery is completed. The absurdity of attempting to force a modern theological school into the plan and architecture of an historic monastery here becomes clearly apparent.

Reference
Warnecke, John Carl. "Golden Gate Theological Seminary," *Architectural Record*, August 1957.

INDEX